SOCIAL BEI

WITHDRAWN

D1346868

Social Being

A THEORY FOR SOCIAL PSYCHOLOGY

Rom Harré

Basil Blackwell · Oxford

Beck
301.15
HAR

© Rom Harré 1979

First published 1979 by
Basil Blackwell Publisher
5 Alfred Street
Oxford OX1 4HB
England

All Rights Reserved. No part of this publication
may be reproduced, stored in a retrieval system,
or transmitted, in any form or by any means,
electronic, mechanical, photocopying, recording
or otherwise, without the prior permission of
Basil Blackwell Publisher Limited.

British Library Cataloguing in Publication Data

Harre, Romano
    Social being.
    1. Social psychology — Methodology
    I. Title
    301.1'01'8   HM251
    ISBN 0-631-10691-X
        0-631-12791-7 Pbk

Printed in Great Britain by
The Camelot Press, Southampton

LIVERPOOL INSTITUTE
OF HIGHER EDUCATION

THE BECK LIBRARY

Accession No.
    83284

Class No.
    301.15 HAR

Catal. CLH
        22/11/83

To Michael Argyle and the 'team',
in gratitude for ten years of
unstinted intellectual hospitality

CONTENTS

Part III *Persons*

Part IV *Diachronic Analysis*

PREFACE

This work is an attempt to develop a theory for social psychology. In consequence it draws on and criticizes the available sociological theories of man in society as much as the current methods and assumptions of psychology. Of necessity the treatment of both sociology and psychology has been schematic, and sometimes, for the purposes of developing the argument, little more than an outline form of a complex theory has been sketched.

I believe that every writer on psychological theory owes an explicit account of the political consequences of his position to his readers. Inevitably, in such a discussion, the background of existing political theory has to be represented in the most simplified form. At some later time I hope to develop the last chapter of this study into a serious and thorough examination of the philosophical psychology of politics. but I hope that the existing sketch at least fulfils the general moral obligation which all students of the human sciences should accept.

References and citations have been reduced to a minimum, so that there are many works upon which I have drawn that receive no explicit mention. I have little patience with the practice of massive citation nor the outmoded inductivist theory of science it represents

Several chapters and parts of chapters have appeared in other places in early forms. Occasionally I have borrowed a section or two from those publications. I am grateful to the Editors of *Advances in Experimental Social Psychology*, 1978, and to the Editors and Publisher of *Structure, Consciousness and History*, for permission to make use of certain passages.

I owe a considerable debt to J-P De Waele. In many conversations concerning our forthcoming joint work *The Psychology of Individuals* he has not only drawn my attention to important items in the literature, but has helped immeasurably to sharpen my perceptions of the social world.

PART I

Theory and Method

INTRODUCTION

The main burden of the argument in this part is directed to refuting the leading doctrines of various reductionist schools. By distinguishing between the analytically distinct expressive and practical orders, and by reducing the biological aspects of human life to a nest of problems calling for cultural solutions, I hope to locate the problem field proper to social psychology. The life forms we do produce are a complex series of overlays of structured complexes of meanings, the dominant motivations for the construction of which are expressive.

Traditional methods are inadequate for the study of the ways people create these forms of life. Experimental social psychology cannot be pursued without destroying the very structures within which actions are realized as socially potent acts. Macrosociology based on survey research methods is unable to penetrate beyond the expressive aspects of the research interview. But by adopting a hypothetico-deductive approach in sociology and an ethogenic approach in social psychology a powerful empirical method can be forged.

Though the expressive and practical orders are analytically distinct, social life is lived as a continuous process. Anthropological evidence is advanced to illustrate how differently the orders can be balanced in different times and places.

L. I. H. E.
THE BECK LIBRARY
WOOLTON ROAD. LIVERPOOL L16 8ND

1

SOME BASIC PRINCIPLES OF SOCIAL LIFE

ANTICIPATORY SUMMARY

Introduction: The social world as a hierarchy of innumerable structures created by active beings.

1. The biogenic and the sociogenic
   (a) The main ideas of sociobiology : that social patterns are caused by genetic inheritances, and that they are Darwinianly adaptive.
   (b) Objections to sociobiology:
      (i) the case of the 'altruism' gene: plausible only on an outmoded species selection theory of evolution;
      (ii) difficult to associate genetic causes of patterns of social action given their rapid changes and cultural diversity;
      (iii) most societies elaborate social forms beyond any plausible level of biological adaptiveness.
   (c) Biogenesis, sociogenesis and the act/action distinction: some acts of cultural or social origin utilize actions of biological origin, some biogenically derived acts use socially derived actions, and so on, showing the independence of the cultural and biological character of social activity.
   (d) Observations:
      (i) human beings are best compared to domestic animals.
      (ii) our biological nature is a source of problems, which have culturally derived social solutions, for the most part.
2. Practical and expressive aspects of social activity
   We recognize Marx as the philosopher of practical aspects of social activity and Veblen as the philosopher of the expressive aspects. In general, for most social forms and at most historical epochs the expressive is dominant over the practical.
3. The dynamics of human social action: ritual marking of respect and contempt
   (a) Most people prefer public recognition of their worth in marks of respect to private satisfactions. Societies usually include several respect/contempt hierarchies.
   (b) Respect giving is reciprocated by condescension, contempt by servility.
   (c) Expressive 'credits' accumulate in moral careers, through dealing successfully or unsuccessfully with hazards.

1

(d) Personal and social conceptions of a man's character can differ, introducing a dynamic tension.

4. Socio-materialism

(a) General definition: that social practices, person hierarchies and so on are the product of material processes of one sort or another.

(b) Examples:

(i) the socio-economics of Marx and Engels;

(ii) the socio-ecology of M. Harris and J. Goody.

(c) Objections:

(i) neither Marx and Engels nor Harris and Goody have provided even a sketch of a plausible causal mechanism by which such a production could occur;

(ii) the generality of the dominance of the expressive over the practical shows that the system of production is pressed into the service of expression, and does not function autonomously. Hence it could not be a cause of expressive social forms and practices;

(iii) speculative paleoanthropology suggests an origin for self-consciousness independent of labour.

(iv) conditions for the existence of property.

5. Summary: some general principles

(a) Social life is a cultural achievement.

(b) Social acts are achieved by doing conventionally associated actions.

(c) Individual lives are structured as moral careers.

(d) A person's character is multiple and is a property of his social collectives.

(e) There may be social patterns beyond the experience of any individual.

(f) People can and do imagine different social forms, from those currently existing.

6. Universals. Very few are plausible. I tentatively offer the following:

(a) Short-term expressive advantages are generally preferred to long-term practical gains.

(b) Social activities will be elaborated independently of instrumental and practical efficiency, under the pressure of the need to realize expressive ends.

(c) The deepest human motive is to seek the respect of others.

(d) The biological basis of life is always a source of problems, never of solutions.

INTRODUCTION

I began this work in an attempt to clear from my mind the confusion and uncertainty I experienced when trying to reconcile my experience of social life with the representations of the processes by which that life is created that are to be found in the writings of social scientists. Most social psychology seemed to me to be concerned more with the reactions of idealized automata in bland, anomic environments than with the way real human beings carry on their affairs together. The great sociologists such as Marx and Durkheim seemed to speak of times other than mine and of the preoccupations of tribes long since extinct. Weber at least offered a technique for the understanding of men's actions whatever their historical and social circumstances but it seemed too vague to use as a tool for forging a science of society. Only in the works of Erving Goffman and Thorstein Veblen did I seem to meet myself and the social worlds I knew. But Goffman has presented no general theory of human association, nor any systematically organized set of principles for understanding social change.[1]

In our critical work, *The Explanation of Social Behaviour,* Paul Secord and I demonstrated how deeply rooted in a particular philosophy are the shortcomings of the experimental approach to understanding social life. We made no attempt at a comprehensive positive theory. We tried only to lay down certain landmarks by which the path to such a theory might be recognized. In this work I am bold enough to try to remedy the deficit, but I hope modest enough to recognize the provisional and historically conditioned character of all I have to say.

I am not disposed to take an optimistic view of human life. The hopes of most young people come to nothing. The disappointments of the middle years of life are followed, for those who survive them, by the ugliness, pain and despair of old age. Most human effort, it seems to me, is ill directed or dissipated in acts of folly. The pervasive tone of life for most people is boredom, but a boredom made more acute by resentment. Our imaginations offer us visions of all kinds of possibilities of action we are usually too idle to realize. As J. S. Mill put it, '...Those who, while desiring what others possess, put no energy into striving for it, are either incessantly grumbling that fortune does not do for them what they do not attempt to do for themselves or overflowing with envy and ill-will towards those who possess what they would like to have.'.

But, at the same time, people have a deep sense of their own dignity, and a craving for recognition as beings of worth in the opinion of others of their kind. I shall be arguing that the pursuit of reputation in the eyes of others is the overriding preoccupation of human life, though the means by which reputation is to be achieved are extraordinarily various. Though men compete individually for honour, reputation is a corporate matter and its acquisition a co-operative achievement. It is the product of the recognition of one's worth by others.

The method implicit in my undertaking is primarily philosophical. I am aiming at the construction of a conceptual matrix within which fragments of knowledge can be assembled in a systematic, interlocking fashion. But the depth of analysis varies widely from section to section. I have gone into detail only where I thought it necessary to secure conviction. When I could safely appropriate an argument *en bloc* I have done so and recorded the fact in the notes. There seems no point in repeating the details of arguments which have been better expounded by others.

But though my overall picture is gloomy, the way human beings proceed to generate solutions to their problems has much that will seem to be admirable − admirable, of course, by aesthetic rather than moral standards. Morality and its ethical systems will turn out to be among the ways we present our actions to enjoy the respect of our fellow moralists − and so despite ourselves treat each other less harshly than mere calculation would advise.

I have sub-titled this work 'A Theory for Social Psychology'. This reflects the belief I share with many workers in the field that it is at the intersection of the individual and his collectives that the most interesting and significant work is to be done towards understanding the way the social order comes to be. It is a complex node, for it is also the intersection of the axes that join the personal and the social, and the private and the public. Social psychology is in need of a theory. It needs a theory in the sense that Darwinian evolutionary theory, now comfortably linked with biochemistry, is the theory of the change and development of organic forms. Darwinian theory is not so much a deductive system or a collection of axioms, as a system of concepts in terms of which explanations for a wide variety of organic phenomena can be formulated. The theory I shall be developing has the same role. It is to provide the concepts for theorizing in all manner of instances and particular cases.

At the heart of the system of concepts I will be developing is the idea that the public and collective aspects of human life are to be treated as products generated by an interplay between a practical order, concerned with the production of the means of life, and an expressive order concerned with honour and reputation. Both orders are based in but not exhausted by personal and individual competences and beliefs. The public and collective orders are created by intentional action, while the orders so created act back upon private and personal skills and beliefs.

The expressive order involves a transformation of something personal into something public. It is from the *ex*pression of oneself in public performances and the qualities of such performances that other people form an *im*pression or series of impressions through their interpretations of the action. Together, expression and impression form the expressive order. Expressive intention and action and impression interpretation and belief are not always co-ordinate.[2] Nor does the expressive order always match the practical order. In many societies economic power, generated by a person's location in the practical order may not entitle him to the highest public esteem. Sometimes the expressive order operative at a certain time and place represents a practical order that has dissolved. In all these ways tensions can appear as people come to perceive expressive incongruities and practical inconsistencies.

The most persistent theme of this work will be the thought that for most people at most times the expressive order dominates or shapes the practical order.

It follows from the thesis that social life is symbolically mediated that learning the social system is, in part, learning a symbolism. But it is also learning to use that symbolism to represent the concepts at the heart of a widely held theory. By this theory people can explain their situation and from it others can interpret their actions in such a way that they will seem to be what they wish to be taken to be.

From whence comes such a thesis and what is its justification? At the centre of any theory of a science of society is an image of man, a conception of him as a particular kind of creature, defined by his powers and liabilities. In this work I assume the Renaissance image of architectonic man,[3] according to which the unrestricted and undeformed activity of men is to conceive and try to realize a variety of structured forms, a variety controlled only by the demands of mathematical harmony and order. As Coleridge insisted, the imagination is central to human functioning, since it is there that we generate icons, sensual representations of structures which we try to realize in the public world. But, as he also pointed out, the mind soon passes to a stage of abstract or mathematical representation. Though we can conceive of abstract structures, perhaps mathematically represented, workers as diverse as poets and physicists may embody their thought in iconic representations, creating public objects such as poems and physical theories. The creation and maintenance and re-invention from time to time of the social order is, I shall be arguing, just such a process, the realization in public and collective form of privately conceived and individually registered representations of structures.

We create structures in thought, anticipating the forms we will realize in public social activity. We do not yet fully understand the principles which control our acts of creation. But we do know that our conceptions are only partly in imitation of the forms we experience in the world around us. The structures created in social life, however they are conceived, are various in their embodiment, including semantic fields, orderly sequences of action, hierarchies of reputation, networks of task and role-positions, institutions and many others.

The Renaissance conception of man saw human life as the imposition of form on a partly recalcitrant matter.[4] Machiavelli defined the most general character of human actions as the mastery of *fortuna* by *virtu*, of chance by human skill and power. According to Kepler[5] understanding was achieved by creating forms in thought that matched the structures of the world. For the purposes of social analysis I shall be taking a Machiavellian view of the genesis of social order, and a Keplerian view of what it would be to understand a world in which one kind of structured object is generated from another. But we shall need, too, something of the subtlety of Kant's critical philosophy.[6] It is only too easy to conceive of many different structures, any one of which could be the underlying icon from which the order we seem to see could be produced by some transformation or projection. To justify the choice of one rather than another as the basis for particular theories of specific social activities and institutions we must depend on some weak form of transcendental argument. That is we must try to show that the form we have chosen as the best hypothetical underlying structure is at least a necessary condition for the possibility of the order we seem to perceive. But since we have no way of telling how much of the order we perceive is the product of the schemata by means of which we experience the social world as orderly there can be no absolute resolution of the central weakness of any theorizing which depends on testing consequences to make an assessment of plausibility.

Architectonic man sets about the co-operative realization of preformed structures in public objects; in buildings, meals, works of art, schemes of protocol, rules of games and so on. I shall be assuming, with Durkheim, that some social activities are reminders or representations of the structure of other social entities. So it is no wonder that their structures are sometimes isomorphic with those of thought-forms embodied in other vehicles. Kinship systems play this kind of role in some societies. As Durkheim perceived, public events which serve as icons of other aspects of social order, events such as feasts and funerals, are endowed with a modicum of quasi-objectivity. They are not the sorts of things from which an individual can dissent. But I shall assume that they are products of thought-forms, rather than the causal agents of social order. My image of 'the' social order is of a criss-cross of isomorphisms and mutual representations, amongst which will be those discerned by Marx. But I insist upon a conception of causality tied to real productive mechanisms. And that involves a competence/performance psychology of individuals who as members create social collectives, but who are created by those collectives in a thoroughly reciprocal fashion.

To look elsewhere than to the correlations of 'social facts' for causal mechanisms and operative conditions, reference to which is needed to explain social activity, is not some form of idealism. The ethogenic way in social psychology emphasizes even more strongly than traditional sociology the existent character of social formations as public objects. But the structures of ceremonies, institutions, moral careers and so on 'fluoresce' only in the light of a rhetoric. Yet they are real. This thought would allow the student of the sociology of knowledge to turn his attention to the transformational processes by which icons in thought become realized as structures in interpersonal reality whether it is as brochures, bridges or bureaucracies. For my purpose in this work only social formations are so to be treated. When the structure of the social life within a mental hospital is made luminous by interpreting the activities therein according to the official rhetoric, it seems to be a place where there are sick people and other, healthy and competent people who are intent on effecting cures. But under the light of Goffman's dramaturgical analysis another order is revealed. The institution can now be seen as a staging for dramas of character and for the living out of moral careers. Neither picture is false, nor yet is either wholly true. Each picture is itself a resource used by members in their daily activities within the institution, for their own practical and immediate purposes. I shall be arguing for the view that the source of each structured system of activities and role-places is the transformation into action and conventions of respect and contempt, of societal icons shared among those who maintain an institution by living in accordance with its multiple rhetorics.

The ethogenic approach holds out no prospect for the possibility of bringing into being any deeply transformed kind of social life. Material abuses and miseries can be overcome but the emptiness of reputation and the shallowness of honour cannot. No doubt we will go on posturing for each other's admiration in whatever way we think suits us best. But at least by giving us some understanding of how all this is carried off, the ethogenic way will allow for the multiplication of such a plethora of hierarchies of honour that no one will be wholly precluded from a touch of minor glory. Marx said that it was in the nature of man to work. Not at least as the human race is presently constituted. It is in the nature of men to slip off to the pub to display their *machismo*, and of women to exchange anecdotes about the prowess of their children. Were the role-stereotypes of the sexes to be drastically transformed and even unified, the new androgynite would bring with him-her a new moral order and a new conception of public virtue to display. The hammer and sickle are taken up with reluctance and laid down with alacrity for the pint pot and tea cup.

What other general theories have there been as to how human beings co-operatively produce a social order? There was the natural law theory — that God's creatures, in living socially fulfilled His will. There was the political conception of society — a social contract of rational men putting themselves under the rule of law for some moral end. There was the economic analysis of social formations — human beings as puppets within a system of necessary material production of the means of life. Lately there has been the biological — social relations as resolution of internal tensions created by the bonds of organic life. We have had the theories of Aquinas, Locke, Marx and Freud.

In each phase social psychology was conceived within the dominant explanatory framework of the time. In the Middle Ages the psychological centre of social man was the concept of sin and its correlative, expiation. In the time of Hobbes, Locke and Mill how were men to be understood to have political obligations when their motivations were conceived to be deeply self-interested? In the nineteenth century Marx's idea of false consciousness provides the necessary psychological hypothesis to explain the apparent impotence of men's will within the economic order. And this century has been dominated by the psychological problem of the uneasy back and forth between the dominance of super-ego and id. So each grand theory is accompanied by its own social psychology, or at least in Marx's case by a surrogate. Each of these explantory frameworks survives within our own accounting resources as a rhetoric. Just now the biological dominates the economic, which dominates the politico-legal, which dominates the theological. I offer this breath-taking summary not as a piece of genuine history, but as a move in the evolution of my representation of the rhetoric I take to be upon us.

My pseudo-science of social behaviour is, I fondly hope, a reflection of the dominant mode of conceiving social life in my time. As such it is part of the rhetoric by which that very life is created. The fifth theory is based upon a dramaturgical conception of social action. In the interstices between the four grand theories sketched above a momentary vision of the whole appears and reappears. The Renaissance was such an interstitial time. And in the Renaissance the dramaturgical conception of social action was the commonest way of understanding. We are in a similar time.

The development of modern psycholinguistics has made a good deal clearer what is required of a psychology. There must be a theory of the standing conditions that make some activity possible, a 'competence' theory. And there must be a cluster of theories concerning the generative processes by which particular actors produce their actual activity in specific circumstances, 'performance' theories. I shall be proposing conceptual frameworks for formulating both kinds of theories for social activities. Empirical work to date, undertaken in the ethogenic way, has been almost all directed to the discovery of social competence.

But competence, in this peculiar sense, must not be thought of as exclusively an individual attribute. Some social performances may require actors to draw on a fund of knowledge and skill distributed amongst the group, so that no one person knows all that is needed. In some cases not even the group know what is required. The knowledge is stored in some public object accessible to some or all of the actors, such as a manual or a prayer book.

Nor are performance theories always exhausted by individual intentions, plans and attributions of meanings. An action which is not understood by others for what it is intended to be cannot be said to be a proper realization of the actor's intentions.

In consequence the general psychology I shall be developing in later chapters will be based upon concepts that lie along three axes: a public-private axis representing the degree to which the conditions of action are open to inspection by all, a personal-social spectrum; and an individual-collective dimension each representing in different ways the degree to which the important generative conditions of action are properties of individual human beings.

An autonomous science of human collective, public, social action, as grounded in individual competence and intentions, is threatened from two sides. On the one hand is the idea that human beings are pre-programmed social animals whose modes of behaviour have long been fixed by the reproductive success of the best adapted. On the other stands the idea that people are, as it were, post-programmed social machines. They are conceived as automata whose modes of action have been selectively reinforced by their social and material environment, and who merely reproduce the appropriate actions on stimulation. If either of these pictures were verisimilitudinous there would be no place for an independent science of social action. But that would not be the end of the matter. If the former image were to be accepted as correct, political action would be pointless, since only the recombinations brought about by the ponderous dance of the genes or the chance disturbance of heriditary patterns produced by a cosmic ray would make any substantial difference to human social behaviour. And if the latter view were allowed to dominate our practices, only technological authoritarianism, the mass reprogramming of the automata, would be likely to change their manner of collective behaviour.

Part of my aim is to defend the autonomy of men and their reflexive powers of self-intervention within the necessities imposed upon their existence by the fact that they would not be men at all unless they were creations of the collectives in which they live.

So our study begins with an examination of some of the more sweeping theories that have been offered to explain the forms that human social life has taken, theories which would effectively eliminate a psychological dimension from the genesis of social life. We shall find that no theory is acceptable which essentially simplifies that life form, or attempts to explain its character by reference to a single causal principle.

1. THE BIOGENIC AND THE SOCIOGENIC

(a) The Main Idea of Sociobiology

Recently, large claims have been made for the application of ethological principles, that is the principles which are involved in the social behaviour of animals and insects, to the understanding of the social behaviour of men.[7] Of course, this is far from being a new phenomenon in social analysis, since fables, analogies and myths have frequently drawn upon animal models. Despite the scientific garb in which sociobiology comes to us, it is, as we shall see, not much more than a new fable of the bees.[8]

Contemporary sociobiology is based on three main ideas:

(i) that patterns of social behaviour are biologically adaptive, that is that those who exemplify them in their lives have more surviving offspring than those who do not;

(ii) that such patterns derive from genetically produced pre-programming of the nervous, hormonal etc. systems.

(iii) that such programming genes could be selected by a Darwinian process, on the basis of the adaptive character of the behaviour patterns they cause.

It is clear that if these principles were unexceptionable, biological selection of gene-based patterns of social behaviour would rapidly occur. For example, in Dawkins' recent book[9] there is an elegant, though fictional, example of the way in which the genes for two different patterns of social behaviour in the mating game, namely a gene for "faithful husband" and a gene for "philanderer", could spread successively through a population, given certain plausible energy-demands, and then, finally, settle down to an equilibrium distribution.

While it would be unreasonable to dispute the success of sociobiological hypotheses in explaining the sources of the social patterns of a great many insects, fish, mammals and other creatures, as far as human life is concerned it is an essentially *a priori* theory. It will be easy to show that there are great difficulties with the attempt to take it seriously as the basic schema for explanatory theories of patterns of human social behaviour.

(b) Objections to Sociobiology

(i) The case of the altruism gene

The assumption that human beings are a species of social animal tempts one to be on the look-out for an altruism gene. That is if human beings behave altruistically on occasion could this be explicable by the hypothesis that they do so because they have inherited a gene complex, which programmes them to help each other? This hypothesis would require a very specific genetically-based programming of the nervous system so that an individual would both be able to recognize a need and then move to succour a conspecific in distress or difficulty.

Objections

(a) The form of altruistic behaviour is socially and historically conditioned (for example the Good Samaritan does not represent a universally acceptable exemplar) and situationally defined. This suggests that actual forms of altruistic behaviour are too specific to be genetically programmed, both with respect to what counts as a need and what counts as succour for that need.

(b) But even if there were only a general tendency to help built into the creature, could it be inherited as such? Helping among conspecifics seems capable of construal as selectively advantageous only on a species-selection interpretation of evolutionary theory. On a modern gene-selection interpretation males should not be unqualifiedly altruistic, except to identical twins. Helping any other male would assist a rival in the competition for the maximum number of mates and matings which are required to spread an individual gene to the greatest number of offspring. Nor should a female behave altruistically to competing females since that would detract from her ability to raise the greatest number of her own brood while enhancing that of her genetic rival. On the gene-selection theory field studies should reveal such intra-specific rivalry whenever selection pressure is high. A good popular example of such a field study is the Goodall-Van Lawick film of wild dogs. It is clear that the dominant females set about systematically destroying the litters of females of low status. In the human case, the fate of the Ik would be unintelligible if there were anything in the idea that human beings are characterized by the presence of an altruism gene in their inherited make-up.[10]

The first of the above arguments would apply to any sociobiological proposal — the second only to hypotheses which propose some form of inherited tendency to form a co-operative social order. It would not by itself refute the hypothesis of an inherited tendency to create a social group from which one could get the satisfaction of the admiration and respect of one's dominated rivals. That would be consistent with the gene-selection form of the inheritance theory of social formations. To deal with this case we must turn to another range of arguments.

(ii) The causes of patterns of social action: the problem of rapidity of variation and cultural differentiation

The most pervasive difficulty with such a theory is its assumption of a causal relation between genetic endowment and social behaviour. We know from animal ethology that there are several ways in which genetic endowment can bring about social behaviour. For example there is the complex mechanism of imprinting where the genetic endowment is expressed as a readiness to acquire, in appropriate circumstances, the neurological disposition to a certain kind of behaviour, though the physiological basis of the neurological disposition is not built in. Human social behaviour is characterized by its enormous complexity and its very wide cultural differentiation. From time to time there appear to be very rapid changes in what seems to be the essential character of social collectives. There is, then a range of problems for the sociobiologist of human life even in these very broad considerations. There does not seem to be any possibility of there existing sufficiently complex *inbuilt* neurological patterns given the kinds of structures that can be genetically inherited, nor does there seem to be time for the genetic base to change in such a way as to be responsible for wide variations in the actual forms of social life. Any causal relation from genetic endowment to social behaviour must, it seems obvious, be mediated through the culture in which an individual is born. The rapidity with which changes can occur in that culture seem to require explanation in terms of matters other than the biological.

These points have been made by a number of recent critics of sociobiology. For example, Edmund Leach has pointed out that the range of human smiles, if we think of them as distinguished by their social force, is some thirty times more differentiated than the range of inherited genetically based muscular spasms that affect the human face.[11] Dawkins, in his recent popular book, has argued for a sharp differentiation between the stately ballet of the process of genetic selection and the frenetic, and sometimes explosive, patterns of change in the human social world.

(iii) Elaboration beyond biological necessity: neurophysiological redundancy

A second difficulty, which will turn out to introduce a matter of the very greatest importance for this study, is what I might call the elaboration of human social life. The complexities of our social activities seem to go far beyond the apparent necessities of survival. Almost every human society undertakes to elaborate some of the activities in which they engage, to produce, in many cases, a florid superstructure. For example, there is intense interest in the decoration of the human body, illustrated for instance in the trouble which a New Guinea tribe will go to in preparation for some ceremonial activity. Even though the ceremonial activity can, perhaps, with a stretch of the imagination, be seen to be functional in the sociobiological sense, it is extremely difficult to conceive of any functional explanation of the enormous degree of elaboration of the decorations.[1 2] In cultures with which we are more familiar, intellectual elaboration has taken place in the absence of a connection with the functional activities of the practical world. Consider, for example, the enormous efforts in the Middle Ages to elaborate the theological theories which formed the intellectual basis of that civilization or the elaboration of music in Europe from the sixteenth century to the present day. It is clear that the theme of elaboration runs through most of human life. The attraction of elaborate forms, of complex structures and of roundabout ways of bringing about some practical end, seems widespread if not universal. The principle of elaboration seems to run counter to what I take to be the basic idea involved in the concept of adaptiveness, a basic idea which is very prominent in gene-selection theories. The advantage which a particular pattern exhibits over a possible rival is nowadays expressed in terms of expenditure of energy. In Dawkins' fictional example I referred to above, it is only in terms of energy considerations that the selection pressure, which favours one gene over another in particular circumstances, is defined.

We can bring the argument full circle by asking how it is possible for an animal species such as ourselves to be able to undertake elaborations. The answer must surely lie in the redundancy of our brain and nervous system, a redundancy with respect to the selection pressures which led to our evolution. I find it extraordinarily difficult to grasp how it could be that a semi-aquatic life along the shores of the warm lakes of the Rift Valley could have provided a selection pressure which would lead to the spread of genes which would produce in the organisms whose structure they control brains sufficiently elaborate to formulate the special Theory of Relativity, the *Summa Contra Gentiles*, symphonic music and the like. If we consider its products, the most striking thing about the human nervous system is its redundancy with respect to biological needs. Until we have had an adequate bio-logical explanation of how that enormous redundancy could be produced by the selection pressures we believe to have acted upon that sequence of primate species from which we developed in the course of the last thirteen million years or so, we must abandon sociobiological notions when we look for explanations of the specific forms of human social life.[13]

However, the argument which uses the fact of elaboration and the hypothesis of redundancy against the use of sociobiological explanations to account for the forms of human social life, can turn in one's hand. A serious problem remains. What is the elabo-ration for? There are two possible ways of dealing with this question. One might argue that the question is ill-considered. The explanation might not be functional at all. It might have been an accidental side effect of some other development that the taste for elaboration comes to be present in the human race at large. One might take the question seriously, and, perhaps in a spirit of muted functionalism, shift the problem elsewhere. Elabo-ration, it might be argued, is part, and an essential part, of the social apparatus which is required for creating a complex enough system for the forming of attitudes of respect and contempt amongst human beings and for providing the materials for the ritual marking of the judgements we make on those occasions when respect and contempt can be earned. The enormous elabora-tion of the system of social life, and its symbolic apparatus, and its supporting theories, could be understood in relation to the problem of finding a system capable of meting out and marking respect and contempt among a very wide range of highly differen-tiated human beings. On this view the most fundamental of all the structural principles around which human life is organized is that which informs the institutions of respect and contempt.

(c) Biogenesis, Sociogenesis and the Act/Action Distinction

To understand human social life we shall find ourselves forced to resort to a complex hierarchical analytical scheme for classifying the public activities of people as members of societies. For the moment we shall need only the distinction between what an activity is taken to achieve socially, the 'act' aspect of social activity, and the means by which social acts are performed, the 'action' aspect. Confirmation of a friendship is a social act, in this terminology, while entertaining one's friends to a formal meal is the social action-sequence by means of which the social act of friendship confirmation is performed, on that occasion.

The limitations along another dimension of sociobiological explanations of human social activity can be illustrated by considering the Cartesian product of the act/action distinction with the distinction between activities which have a biological origin in an inherited genetic programme selected by Darwinian processes, and those which have their origin in the creative cognitive activities of men as conscious social beings. If the biogenesis and the sociogenesis of social activities are independent, then there should be examples of the following four categories:

(i) Both act and action are of biological origin. Perhaps both the social act of demonstrating affection and the social action of kissing are genetically programmed in man.

(ii) The act is of biological origin, the action of social origin. If we allow that triumphing over a fallen rival is genetically programmed in man and other primates, we must admit that performing a triumph by putting a Spitfire into a victory roll must be a contemporary socio-cognitive creation, that is the action is a socio-cultural invention conventionally associated with the act.

(iii) The act could have a social origin, but the means of its performance could be drawn from a stock of genetically programmed interpersonal routines, ethological bricolage so to speak. The practice of making bets seems likely to have a social origin, but the handshake by which a bet is confirmed could be a genetically programmed routine for achieving solidarity or agreement.

(iv) Finally, both act and action could have originated in the social conditions of human life and in some cognitive creation, rather than be genetically programmed and selected. When a person signs a cheque to pay a debt it seems obvious that both the act of discharging a debt and the action of signing are not genetically programmed routines.

I have not suggested any theory as to how innovations are produced by individual acts of creativity in specific social conditions. At this point in the argument all I require is the intuition that such things do happen, and become part of the repertoire of social actors going about their business in specific social worlds.

(d) Observations

(i) Domestication

There can be little dispute that human beings are, for certain purposes, properly to be considered a species of animal. However, as I have pointed out, this perception, correct though it may be, is of little value in arguments for the foundation of the social sciences in this or that underlying set of principles. It is important, however, to remember just what category of animals we belong to. The observation I want to make at this point is that human beings should be considered to be a species of domestic animal. If the pursuit of the understanding of our social lives is sometimes facilitated by looking at the behaviour of other animals in similar situations, it is to analogies with domestic, not wild, animals, that we must turn. We are more like, I claim, dogs, cats, cows and so on, living contentedly in a human society, than we are like a zoo of caged wild animals. The human zoo analogy with which Desmond Morris, for example, tries to explicate the underlying principles of life in cities, seems to me radically misconceived. We domesticate ourselves to life on an animal farm. People make each other, and they can remake themselves, I shall be arguing, according to certain local conceptions of human nature and stereotypes of what it is to be a proper social person.

Indeed, we will notice that there is a strong tendency for people to think they should be what currently accepted authorities tell them they are. They strive, often contrary to many of their inclinations, to fulfil the ideals offered to them by those authorities. It is worth noticing that there is no difference in principle between the striving of a person to remake himself along the lines of the environmental automata that Skinner and his followers perceive people to be, and the desperate efforts of people in medieval times to subdue the flesh in order to fulfil an ideal conception of personhood proferred to them by their religion. These are nothing but extreme and perhaps even perverted forms of self-domestication.

(ii) 'The old Adam' : our biological nature as a nest of problems

In the course of this study I shall be deploying the consequences of the idea that some social activities can best be analysed as if they were efforts at solving problems, in a way that supports the expressive aims of the preservation of dignity and mutual respect of all those concerned. There are many sources of problems in human life. Amongst the most pervasive and perennial are the problems posed by the need to provide secure conditions for the slow maturation and long dependence of human infants, to regulate the relations between the sexes, to apportion food, and to dispose of dead bodies in a way commensurate with the dignity of these persons as they were in life; and many, many more.

The biological basis of life should be seen, I argue, rather as a source of problems for which social solutions must be invented, than a source of solutions to problems posed by the alleged social nature of human beings.

Another way of looking at the position I am developing in this study is to see it as neo-Hobbesian theory of the way social coherence is established and maintained. It seems to me incredibly naive to assert boldly that man is a social species, given the usual nucleation of his family structure, his solitary seekings for food and even for divine revelation. But he is certainly a *clever* species. Throughout this study I shall be working with the idea that men have invented rather than inherited society. We have invented a system of relationships, for both practical and expressive purposes that has turned out to be, in some respects, analogous to the inherited social structures found amongst some animals and insects. The appearance of analogies is hardly surprising since some of the same problems of relationships have to be solved. But we maintain our social relationships by a mechanism which consists of ritually created obligations and commitments, mediated by the meanings conventionally associated with certain acts and actions. In this mechanism the individual and the collective, the public and the private, the social and the personal are, as I shall show, continuously and in general successfully blended.

If all this is admitted the threatening character of sociobiology is much reduced. As we have noticed the threat from sociobiology comes from the following line of argument:

1. We are the creatures of our genes, even to the patterns of our social behaviour.
2. The only political action which would change human society would therefore be eugenic.

But the realization that social life is created and maintained by ritual, and that even its physical setting enters into social reality only in so far as it is interpreted through the attribution of meaning, allows once again for the possibility of politics. But if we follow the argument to the end, we shall come to see that it is not the politics of contemporary social reformers that we shall find legitimate.

2. PRACTICAL AND EXPRESSIVE ASPECTS OF SOCIAL ACTIVITY

The third fundamental distinction we shall need is between those aspects of social activity 'that are directed to material and biological ends, which I shall call 'practical aspects of activity'; and those directed to ends such as the presentation of the self as rational and worthy of respect, as belonging to a certain category of beings, which I shall call 'expressive aspects of activity'. [14]

This distinction cuts across that between actions directed to material and biological ends, the principles of which are the causal laws of natural science, and actions directed to social ends, in particular the creation in other members of one's collective of certain attitudes to and expectations of the actor, encapsulated in his reputation and the character attributed to him by others. But for the purpose of maintaining a contrast between the ethogenic approach and various forms of socio-materialism, it is the contrast between practical and expressive aspects of activity that is most telling. The more general contrast between material and social ends does not bring out the differences of approach sufficiently clearly.

Furthermore expressive aspects of activity are not confined to those through which we expressively represent the kind of person we wish to be seen to be. We may also express attitudes, opinions, judgements and so on, any or all of which may be taken up into the categorization others have made of us, as evidence, so to speak, for their opinions of us. The distinction here is between those aspects of social activity by which we express our opinions and those by and in which we express ourselves. In all that follows, when I speak of the contrast between practical and expressive aspects of activity, I mean that between action directed to material or biological ends and that directed to the formation of an impression of oneself in the eyes of others. The other distinctions are important and will emerge from time to time. For the most part they will be treated as subsidiary in the plans, intentions and awareness of most human beings most of the time. [15]

We should notice that expressive aspects of activity are often not strictly separable from the practical aspects. For instance, going on strike may be both a practical activity aimed at redistributing earnings in some industry or service, and an expressive activity, an illustration of the importance of this category of work. Considered thus it could be read as a demand by the workers

L. I. H. E.

THE BECK LIBRARY

WOOLTON ROAD LIVERPOOL L16 8ND

for the marks of respect they feel due to them, relative to that mode of work. Understanding the psychological sources of specific social activities even within the apparently uniform category of 'strikes' requires that we maintain the correct balance between the practical and the expressive 'motive', which may be different for each occasion.

The expressive aspects of an activity usually appear in the way the practical side of the activity is carried out; and would often be described in adverbs of action. 'She typed the letter resentfully' and the like. But the distinction between practical and expressive activity or modes and aspects of activity is not absolute. It may re-emerge at a higher order of analysis if the expressive aspect of an activity becomes the dominating instrumentality, for there may be all kinds of practical tasks that need to be performed so as to achieve the expressive presentations aimed at. One needs to have cooked an *haute cuisine* meal successfully in order to be able to serve it with the studied nonchalance that gives the impression that it is one's everyday fare.

A rough guide as to whether an activity or mode of activity is predominantly practical or expressive is to see whether the relation of means to end is causal, as for example, digging is related to cropping; or conventional, as for example wearing one's hair short in the eighteenth century advertised a radical or even a revolutionary stance to society. Even this distinction is not quite adequate since we shall see that conventions play a certain role in the causal account of action. Though it is perhaps a little early in the argument to introduce the point, it might be better to make this distinction in terms of that between physical and psychological (and social) causality; though the full explication of that distinction must await a theory of actors and of the production of their performances.

But even this more refined distinction is subject to exceptions. For example a change in material organization of the world, involving at least some principles of physical causality, such as the orientation of door to door-frame may involve a sequence in which one or more steps are mediated by convention, as for instance that the sound sequence 'Close the door' means close the door; and the conventions that orders are to be obeyed and not to be challenged, debated or used as an occasion of self-presentation by staging a public refusal. (Though all of these may be uses to which orders are put, they were not on this occasion.) More positively, if an outcome of an action sequence is taken to to be supportive of or demeaning to a reputation then the activity is to be treated as primarily expressive. This implies that the distinction practical-expressive is not given in any of the occurrent properties of the action sequence.

In the expressive aspects of social activity we make a public showing of skills, attitudes, emotions, feelings and so on, providing, sometimes consciously, the evidence upon which our friends, colleagues, neighbours, rivals and enemies are to draw conclusions as to the kind of person we are. The expressive aspect will include both natural and conventional signs. For instance, an agitated way of going about our work is a natural sign of our anxiety about its outcome, and how we will be judged by reference to it, even though we may deliberately assume an appearance of agitation for expressive purposes — while shrugging the shoulders with both palms raised is a conventional sign of our regret at the incompetence of another motorist; to be sharply distinguished from reproof. However, the distinction between natural and conventional signs is not an exhaustive and exclusive dichotomy, but a polar opposition. There are many signs that have a colour of both, and assumed agitation might be an example. While it is natural for some people it has become a convention for others.

Our general schema for the development of explanatory theories in social science can be set out as follows:

Practical aspects of activity } jointly explain social formations
Expressive aspects of activity

But the relative weight of each in an explanation will depend upon historical conditions.[16] In the nineteenth century, *for most people,* the practical aspect of an activity so absorbed the time and energy available for living that it had a dominant role in the genesis of social formations. But in the European Middle Ages or in near contemporary Melanesia the practical aspect occupies so little of the time available for social activity and its cognitive and imaginative preparation that the expressive aspect becomes the dominant influence on social formations. I take modern Western society to be more like Melanesian social formations in this regard that it is like the social world of the English midlands in the nineteenth century. Anthropologists give us a figure of between 8 to 10 per cent of living time devoted to sustenance of life in most pre-industrial societies.[17] That leaves a lot of social space and time for dressing up, gossiping and chasing other people's spouses.

We shall see Marx as the philosopher *par excellence* of the

practical aspects of social activity, and Veblen as the best guide to
its expressive aspect, in my dominant sense of that term. From
our theoretical standpoint neither will have priority in the explanation of the origin and workings of social arrangements, such as
a modern educational system. We shall see it both as a cog in the
machinery of production and a source of personal worth, dignity
and reputation, humiliation and demeaning anonymity. In short
it will appear to us as having both practical and expressive aspects.

3. THE DYNAMICS OF HUMAN SOCIAL ACTION: RITUAL MARKING OF RESPECT AND CONTEMPT

Both practical and expressive aspects of social activity should be
looked at teleologically. By this I mean that the full understanding
of an activity, or of that aspect of it to which we are attending,
could not be achieved without our viewing it as having an upshot
or outcome, as culminating or issuing in a result. This allows for
the possibility but does not enjoin the necessity of people intending those outcomes when they act.

But more importantly for present purposes it allows for the
possibility of success or failure in bringing about the outcome. For
those who share our evaluation of our goals our success would
normally lead to their respect, if perhaps only grudging, while our
failure would merit their contempt, derision, pity or sympathy.
But for those who put different evaluations upon the upshot of
our activities, our very success may merit their contempt, and
our failure at least their indifference. A keen young bank clerk
may be pitied or even despised by former school friends, bent
on different goals, on his appointment as assistant branch manager
– while the successful seduction of a child may be admired by
fellow paedophiles.

I shall be supposing that common experiences of human life
suggests that private knowledge of and satisfaction in success is
worthless to most human beings. We prefer to risk the contempt
or pity consequent upon public failure for the chance of the
respect and even admiration accorded to public success. The
concepts of respect and contempt have a useful duality. They are
the names of feelings and of the attitudes which those feelings
mark. But they are also the subject of public and ceremonial
display. 'They showed him,' we say, 'the marks of respect (or
contempt).' And of course they may have showed him those
marks not because they had the feelings or attitudes to go with

them, but because of the social demands of the occasion, the public role of the man, and so on. It is part of the point of this study to emphasize the degree to which progress in social life is forwarded by ritual and ceremonial activities, regardless of the flux of feelings and attitudes the very people who engage in them may be experiencing. It is only in very exceptional circumstances indeed that feeling will break through so to speak against the almost overwhelming power of ritual.[18] I take it as almost (but not quite) unexceptionable that any public ritual of respect is dominant over personal feeling in human social activity. So too a public ritual of respect is not to be taken to imply of necessity feelings of admiration in those who perform it — nor one of contempt or disdain that the ritual practitioners feel dislike or disgust.

I do not propose to hazard any hypothesis as to the origins of the specific respect/contempt hierarchies that are found so variously and so widely in human social affairs. I shall be building the analysis in this work on the idea that ritual marking of respect and contempt do play a large part in human life creating social relations of unique importance. But 'respecting' and 'despising' others takes very different forms in different social systems, and differs greatly in the content and complexity of local criteria by means of which the judgements upon which the giving and withholding of respect and contempt are based. There is enormous variety, too, in the symbolic apparatus by which the results of these judgements are marked.

The continuum defined by this concept pair will be used as a basic analytical tool in this work. I am claiming that in the absence of any other social universal — and we shall see that there are good reasons for being sceptical of most proposals for universal principles — a continuum between generic relations of respect and contempt will serve to bring to light similarities in a wide variety of societies and social practices.

I shall try to prove the viability of this hypothesis in the course of the work in that the illuminations, which I believe it will be seen to cast upon the enigmatic and problematic issues of the understanding of human social activity, will be enough to confirm its value if not its truth.

Like many of the concepts we need for the understanding of the psychology of social life respect and contempt refer both to publicly expressed attitudes and to private feelings one may have for another. In general we must not assume that where there is the one there will be the other. Much giving of public respect and contempt is ritualized and independent of feeling, while the demands of social propriety require the concealment or even the suppression of respectful or contemptuous feelings. We shall suppose then that real people on real occasions are seeking out occasions for acquiring respect while risking pity or disdain, and they may find these occasions in almost any social activities. But people hand out marks of respect and contempt not only for success and failure in the activities of social life, but on the basis of relatively permanent attributes and properties of other human beings. For example reasons for respecting or disdaining people may be found in their colour, stature, sex, accent, job, age, ethnicity and so on. I shall be arguing that it is impossible to predict in principle what any given society will select from the enormously complex system of properties and activities available to find occasions for dealing out marks of respect and contempt.

Respect, as I have argued above, is more than an attitude and not necessarily linked to an emotion. It is a socially marked relation, shown by deference and reciprocated by condescension. The associated presentational style of one who has respect, is dignity. In societies as we know of them, the showing of deference, the reciprocation by condescension, and the illustration of the propriety of the giving of respect in a show of dignity, have become largely ritualized. Contempt, on the other hand, is shown by disdain, and is reciprocated by grovelling. It is important to realize that both respect and contempt are reciprocal relations between people and marked in reciprocal and complementary forms of presentational style. It is not, of course, that he who shows respect is thereby brought into contempt from the other: rather, for any attribution and ritual marking of respect or contempt, two people are required who must reciprocally publicly represent their place in the relation. Respect is reciprocated by affable condescension, while contempt, which is marked by the showing of disdain must be reciprocated by the grovelling and servility of he who accepts the contempt shown to him by the other. But of course he may deal with shown contempt by resentment and even retaliation.

Respect and contempt, then, are illustrated or shown, and ritually symbolically marked in the course of particular activities of daily life. Sometimes they may be the result of specific institutions whose function in the society is the generation of respect and contempt. These I shall call 'hazards'. A simple hazard, for example, is an examination in an educational system. Associated with these momentary phenomena is a social entity which I shall follow Goffman in calling "character": that is, public social reputation. A single human individual may have more than one character, since character is what is attributed to him by a certain set of others. Human social life is sufficiently complex, at least in modern society, for a man to interact with several non-overlapping sets of others, and perhaps to acquire several characters. Public social reputation can be sought, risked, gained or lost in public, in the course of those conventional trials I have called hazards. It can be the subject of a progress, and acquired step by step in which I shall follow Goffman in calling "a moral career". But the existence of hazards and of the institutions for the giving and marking of respect and contempt allow for the possibility of a downward moral career through failure at hazard. Failure is defined reciprocally to the success from which one gains respect and dignity, and it is marked by humiliation. The experience of humiliation is the reciprocal of the maintenance of dignity.[19] Some recent studies of adolescence have shown many young people to have an almost obsessive interest and preoccupation with the maintenance of dignity and the careful scanning of the social environment for occasions and acts of possible humiliation.[20] When such acts have been identified some adolescents may undertake violent retaliation, which in their view has the aim of restoring the dignity that they have lost in the eyes of their peers before whom, and only before whom, they have been humiliated.

Finally, it is worth noticing that the conceptual system of which I have given the barest outline in this introduction allows for a disparity between a person's conception of himself and the character, or characters, which are the public representations of what sort of human being he is taken to be. This introduces a dynamical tension into social life, a tension which we shall find to be powerfully explicatory of much social activity. The resolution of this tension requires the possibility of deliberately contrived action aimed at the management of public persona, which by influencing the way others perceive us, influences their attribution of character to us. We shall be returning, from time to time, to this distinctive type of presentational activity. It is at a different order from the expressive qualification of actions in the way they are performed — since the expressive aspects become instrumental goals.

I shall not be concerned in this study with the analysis and understanding of all those practical activities which human beings undertake for the purposes of the maintenance of life and the production of goods. I shall take them to be a groundswell of activity on the surface of which, in pursuit of expressive aims, people reveal the central preoccupations of human life. I take it the extraordinary degree to which the daily activity of the industrial workers of the nineteenth century was absorbed in the mere business of staying alive was a tragic aberration of the usual conditions of human life. It is in the froth or efflorescence, as it were, of life, in presentational and expressive activities of human beings, that I propose to locate the central dynamics of society. We shall see, however, that it is possible to acknowledge the fundamental truth that Marx perceived, namely the powerful role that the system of production, in both its material and social aspects, plays in social life. But its entry into and effect upon social activity, according to this theory, will be utterly different from the way Marx is popularly supposed to have conceived it. So his intuition will be preserved at the small cost of abandoning his implausible and ill-defined causal theory as to how it might be that the system of material production and distribution generates in all its essentials the superstructure in which social lives are actually led.

4. SOCIO-MATERIALISM

Having introduced the distinction between the practical and the expressive aspects of human social activities we are now in a position to examine briefly the second important universalistic and reductionist system — socio-materialism. It is often stated in a universalistic way as a theory of all forms of human association. It is reductionist in the sense that though it admits the distinction between expressive and practical aspects of social activity nevertheless it proposes that the superstructures of societies — their systems of categorization of persons as worthy of respect or contempt, their educational practices, their laws and customs and so on — are the product of the practical activities of the people of that society as they cope with the material conditions of their life. Though there are many facets of society, on this view, there is only one kind of cause at work in producing them.

(a) Socio-economics

Marx is sometimes treated as the socio-materialist *par excellence*.

Though I have no interest in an extended criticism of his many and varied works, it seems quite clear that even in association with Engels his materialism was always heavily qualified. As Marx comments[21] ... 'the mode of production of material life dominates the development of social, political and intellectual life generally ... is very true of our time, [the nineteenth century] in which material interests preponderate, but not for the middle ages, in which Catholicism, nor for Athens and Rome, where politics reigned supreme.' I would argue that what determines which aspect of social life 'reigns supreme' is where the people of that society find the source of their expressive 'credits', and so find the basis for their moral careers. However in their joint work, *The German Ideology*, Marx and Engels do indeed seem to be proposing a theory which reduces the causes of all aspects of social life to the way material production is organized. In this theory the practical order is accorded an absolute degree of autonomy. Historical change occurs in the system of material production, powered by the appearance and reappearance of contradictions in the interests of the classes which have themselves been generated by the material necessity for a division of labour. It is these changes which produce all other changes according to the doctrine of that work. 'A certain mode of production, or industrial stage is always combined with a certain mode of cooperation, or social stage, and this mode of cooperation is itself a "productive force"' ... 'the multitude of productive forces accessible to men determines the nature of society'.[22] In schematic form the argument runs as follows: a produces b, and then a and b produce c; where a is the system of material production, b is the social organization required to achieve that mode of material production, and c is the superstructure of social institutions and the like, generated by the two taken together. The same form of dialectic causation is found in the remark concerning history. 'The form of intercourse determined by the existing productive forces at all previous historical stages, and in its turn determining these, is *civil society*.'[23] Again the productive force generates a social formation which generates productive forces which generate a civil society and so on. It is clear that the lynch pin of the causal process is taken to be the materially grounded system of material production.

(b) Socio-ecology

In recent years several anthropologists, notably Marvin Harris and

Jack Goody,[24] have proposed a distinctive new form of socio-materialism, which I shall identify as socio-ecology. The main thesis of their position is bold and very simple:

The dominant form of social organization of a people is a product of the most energy efficient means of maintaining life in their geographical environment.

Goody relates the social organization of African villages to their geographical environment, and particularly to the soils they have to contend with. Harris relates the differing social practices of a wide range of ecologically distinctive peoples, to the maintenance of optimal energy exchange relations with their environment. Perhaps his most interesting and well documented argument concerns the relation between cow-worship among orthodox Hindus and their highly efficient ecology.

(c) Difficulties with these Theories

(i) For either explanatory framework to be convincing there must be some account of how the system of production or the geographical location or the ecological demands and so on produce the social formations with which they are demonstrably associated. And that requires that some account be given of causal mechanisms by which the influence might be exerted in concrete, particular cases. But accounts of such mechanisms are conspicuously absent from all these authors. Harris locates his work in a general positivism and so runs up against the double difficulty of having to sustain the Humean theory of causation that would absolve him from the necessity of describing a plausible causal mechanism as the content of his theory of the genesis of social practices; and then, in the absence of a theory of causal connection convincing us of the plausibility of the association he notices between environmental utilization and social practices. The merits of the observations of Marx, of Harris, of Goody and others are too great to be arbitrarily dismissed. A resolution comes from finding a way of acknowledging the influence of material factors without committing oneself to implausible causal connections. As we shall see in detail in later chapters the mutation/selection framework allows just such a compromise.

I will be elaborating that explanatory framework later in great detail. For the moment it is sufficient to point out how it allows one to separate the causes of social practices from the conditions of their initiation, replication and survival as part of the cultural resources of a people. We could imagine an Indian farming community having by practical skill developed a series of practices to make the best use of their environment. They are from time to time visited by fakirs, each peddling a different kind of religion. One preaches that trees are sacred. They drive him off with curses. Another preaches that the Sun and Moon are Gods. They drive him off with stones. Another tells a tale about Krishna and the milkmaids. They applaud him. After all the story fits in very well with the practical importance the cow has in their daily lives. Encouraged by the applause the fakir embroiders some more bovine tales, and Brahminism is born. On this picture of the process of acceptance and spread of a religious system no causal connection is assumed between the thought of the fakir and the practical activities of the people — but their conditions of life favour the acceptance of one sort of tale rather than another. A good contemporary example is the Cargo cults of Melanesia where there is a demonstrable independence between the causes of the invention of the cults and the conditions which favoured their rapid spread. This is the mutation/selection process in a very Darwinian form.

(ii) As I argued in the preceding section of this chapter examination of real societies using the practical/expressive distinction to classify the direction of people's interests, shows that in all but a few rare cases the system of production is soon turned from reproducing the means of life to producing predominantly goods of symbolic value for expressive, self-presentational purposes.[25] Under these conditions the practical activities of a society are controlled by prior social demands which need these goods in order to be symbolically expressed. Consider the way in which the productive capacities of medieval society were directed towards the production of expressive goods for the marking of distinctions produced by 'Catholicism'. Catholicism and its practices and its hierarchical distinctions had a historical origin independent of the system of material production it came eventually to dominate. It became the major socio-intellectual system of Western Europe as the survivor of the socio-economic pressures of the early medieval world.

The real issue at the heart of my criticism of socio-materialism is part philosophical, part empirical. To decide what are the necessary conditions for an organism to be human some empirical assumptions about the social and individual activities and attributes of men are required. I owe to a discussion with Peter Keiler the realization that the issue can be focussed by looking at the

matter in terms of speculative philosophical anthropology. How is
man defined against the rest of the organic order? And that issue
can be considered by imagining the conditions of the emergence
of human beings as a distinct species.

Looked at this way the case for socio-economics rests on the
premise that the sufficient conditions for the emergence of man,
with the potential to create the societies we know to have been
created, was the appearance of labour. As labourers men (meaning
here 'men and women') work on the material world to transform
it into products for use, the means of life. This is offered as an
explanation of the enhancement of consciousness and more
importantly of the origins of society. The elaboration of the
labour relation involves social relations and social distinctions
and differentiations from the history of which the origins and
development of all other institutions can be explained.

Two lines of counter-argument suggest themselves; that the
introjection of labour into organic life is inadequate to account
for the most characteristic attribute of man — self-consciousness;
that the labour relation as transformation and appropriation of
the material environment is inadequate to characterize even that
feature of human society nearest to the centre of the socio-
economic case — namely property. I shall try to show that what
we need for a speculative anthropology of self-consciousness is
exactly what is required to transform products to property,
namely the existence of an expressive order and its symbolic
apparatus.

(iii) Speculative palaeoanthropology. It must be conceded at
once that working on material substances to create products
involves intensional and guided action, in short the skilled realization of plans. In so far as life support work becomes production,
and is reflected in reproductive success, the physiological basis
of the cognitive conditions for skilled work would be selected as
adaptive. The human attributes thus selected would be manifested
as consciousness, a condition for well-controlled productive
activity in the material world.

But human beings are not just conscious, they are self-conscious.
From whence would derive the selection pressures to favour the
elaboration of brain structure and nervous system to sustain
that higher order attribute?

Anthropologists tell us that in most 'primitive' communities life
support work occupies a relatively small proportion of the time
and energy expended in the daily round (see note 17). Thus while

'labour' may be a necessary condition for the survival of a human group, and highly differentiated, it is by no means the exclusive human preoccupation. What is the remainder expended on? The short answer is 'reputation'; the creating and sustaining of impressions of personality and character in terms of which personal worth is continuously evaluated in a society. Even the apparently merely pleasurable activities, such as chatting and joking, are heavily loaded with expressive significance. The chatting is largely concerned with commentary upon the chatting and doings of others.[26] Of course there is much phatic activity too, empty forms of expressive performances which are there to be filled out with real social substance as matters develop.

Impression management and other forms of expressive work involve control of personal style and monitoring of performance that calls for a higher order cognitive functioning than the consciousness required for skilled labour.It requires self-consciousness. It seems reasonable to suppose that skilled impression management is a reproductive advantage, and that selection pressure would favour the neurological basis of high orders of consciousness. One can see the sharpness of the human distinctions in forms of consciousness shadowed forth among the Pongidae. One might remember the way Jane Goodall's Mike selected empty paraffin cans rather than the traditional tree branches as the accoutrements to be carried in his challenge ritual for social supremacy in his tribe. It seems not unreasonable to suppose cognitive conditions here that at least dimly foreshadow self-awareness and self-monitoring.

The biological origins of the expressive order could be imagined in the detachment and elaboration of the kinds of ritual and expressive behaviour ethologists have emphasized in sexual selection. Roughly speaking a gene-complex will spread either through favouring longevity in its dependent organisms or through favouring attractiveness. We could tie the former to the material conditions of survival, labour and the practical order; and the latter to the dramaturgical conditions of self-presentation. Thus both the practical order and the expressive order could be speculatively grounded in the organic conditions of life, and their transformation at a certain level of intelligence. One favours the refinement of consciousness within a level, so to speak. The other favours the multiplication of levels of awareness to self-consciousness.

(iv) The conditions for the existence of property. The chain of reasoning that sustains socio-economic reductior.ism involves two interesting and disputable premises about property: that property is generated simply by the labour relation, that is that production and appropriation of the product by the producer are tightly linked so that the former is an exclusive condition for the latter; and that the institution of property and the social relations incident upon it are an adequate foundation for a theory of society and its changes. The second of these premises is disposed of in the course of this work. At this point I am concerned only with the first.

I shall try to show that the apparent plausibility of the premise under discussion derives from a confusion between a moral argument concerning the origin of rights, and an empirical hypothesis about the functioning of men in society. The moral argument, found in Locke,[27] has slipped into an empirical principle (witness its rhetorical relation to the craft of historian) when it appears in the writings of Marx.

Locke's argument runs as follows:

Premise 1: A man's body and its activities are exclusively his.

In this premise is constituted the root-idea of property, since the one material thing certainly mine is my body. I am by no means clear that this is an indisputable principle but it is not necessary to my counter argument to call it in question.

Premise 2: Whatever neutral substance I mix with what is exclusively mine is also mine.

Neutrality of substance is defined in terms of work. In conditions of common ownership (equivalent in Locke's view to no ownership) the fields, woods and mineral deposits of the world lie fallow.

Premise 2A is arrived at by instantiating Premise 2 in a context of the creation of the means of life. 'Whatever he removes out of the state Nature hath provided and left it in, he hath mixed his labour with, and joined to it something that is his own ...'

The conclusion now follows '... and thereby makes it his own property'.

As an argument for labour as the *moral* basis of property this has some merit. But as speculative palaeoanthropology it overlooks the social location of property as based upon an exclusive right to use and disposal *recognized by others*. Hobbes saw, correctly, that in the absence of civil society exclusive rights can be maintained only by force. In the language of this study, product only becomes property when the practical order based upon labour is overlaid by and integrated with an expressive order based upon conventions for the recognition of persons or collectives of persons as valued or 'sacred' objects, and a symbolic system for relating products to persons or collectives.[28] Goffman's beautiful example of the sunglasses and the suntan lotion, as symbols of a person, which mark a patch of beach, transforming it into property, shows how a symbol can create of space a territory with exclusive rights of occupation.

In the *German Ideology*[29] Marx and Engels uncritically repeat Locke's mistake.

> But life involves above all else eating and drinking, housing, clothing and various other things. The first historical act is thus the production of the means to satisfy these needs, the production of material life itself. ... Therefore in any conception of history one has first of all to observe this fundamental fact in all its significance and all its implications and to accord it its due importance. It is well known that the Germans have never done this, and they have never, therefore, had an *earthly* basis for history and consequently never a historian.

Of course life involves eating and drinking, but not 'above all else'. Above all else it involves honour and the respect of persons. One hardly needs reminding that those who conceive themselves to lack these expressive goods have sometimes refrained from eating and drinking altogether. Human beings can waste away and die from shame, humiliation and loneliness as much as they can from physical privation. Property, like much else in human life, is at the intersection of the practical and expressive orders. The moral right to the products of my own work based upon the admixture of my labour is not an adequate basis for a social psychology, let alone a speculative anthropology of property.

5. SUMMARY: SOME GENERAL PRINCIPLES

(a) Social life is a cultural achievement, an enormous elaboration on the biological activities for organic survival. The pursuit of elaboration is made possible by the redundancy of our nervous systems with respect to the machinery required for the reproduction and maintenance of the human species.

(b) Social acts are achieved by convention and ritual, socially imposed but freely entered into. Every human being can distance himself from any of the rule-systems that represent his culture, if he is prepared to pay the social and practical costs of his awkwardness.

(c) Lives are lived according to the patterns of examplary biographies, generating moral careers, rise and fall in reputation in the eyes of others and of oneself. A human life has a form, from which its components gain meaning, both by the place they have in an individual's moral career and by the alternatives that they have excluded.

(d) A person's character(s) transcend(s) his role, and is in a sense his personal achievement, but it is not a property of that individual. It is a property of one or more of his collectives. It is a cluster of theories, beliefs and expectations held about him by those who have encountered him directly or indirectly, in certain kinds of episodes.

(d) Episodes overlap and interact with one another; lives interweave, forming larger patterns which are not available to the immediate experience of any one individual.

The epistemology of act-patterns and social patterns are different. Act-patterns cannot be other than the folk, the members, say they are, since they are the patterns of folk-attributed meanings. But larger social patterns may have to be discovered by assembling a mosaic of limited views. The larger patterns that emerge may be different from what any one person thinks they are. People have representations of the macrostructure and of the larger patterns of change of society, but these representations may be inaccurate. Two dimensions of disparity between representation and reality can develop. There is that between the way people believe society to be and the way it is, and that between the way they would like it to be and the way it is. Multiplying those dimensions yields the important disparity between the way people think society is and the way they would like it to be.

This allows for the possibility of people wanting society to be the way it already is. An example of this would be a campaign by students in an Oxford graduate college for closer relationships with the dons. These disparities produce psychological tensions, dynamic elements in society.

(f) The fact of social instability, coupled with the redundancy of the human nervous system, introduces the possibility of envisaging a range of different social forms in the future of a people, some of which could be realized. Notice that two different capacities are involved: (i) that of the intellectual and imaginative act of detaching oneself from the rules, conventions and rituals of the present and (ii) the capacity to envisage a concrete possible future i.e. different rules, conventions and rituals. But envisaging a possible future is an empty exercise unless we can postulate an ability to intervene in the unfolding of social action, and perhaps in ourselves, so that in some measure the future may take a different form. This is, of course, a political dimension, since it is easy to superimpose upon this a critical activity in which, according to the criteria in vogue, the present social order and possible alternative futures can be judged against one another. We shall see, however, that the disparity between the microstructures and processes of society which are more or less under our command, and the macrostructure and processes, of which we may not even have an adequate representation, forces us to develop an actual theory of social change and political possibility that is much less deterministic with respect to the capacities and powers of human beings than these remarks would so far suggest.

6. UNIVERSALS

The ethogenic approach has remained exceedingly cautious in announcing the discovery of any universal principles of social activity or organization. But without some universal principles as a guide to our investigations, however tentatively they are proposed, it is impossible even to begin an account of a conceptual system suitable for the analysis and understanding of human social life. The following principles are ubiquitous in the arguments and analyses proposed in this work, and it is hoped that the plausibility of the *whole* analytical scheme lends some support to the assumption that they are indeed among the guiding principles of human action.

(a) In general most people prefer short-term expressive advantage to long-term practical gains. This principle is related to the assumption of the basic place of respect, contempt and associated reputation in the psychology of social action.

(b) Social activities will be elaborated independently of practical advantage. Elaboration is thus taken to be a device by which the self is illustrated as creative, competent, well-guarded and worthy of respect. Again this illustrates the priority of the expressive over the practical aspects of social life. Only in exceptional circumstances does the practical dominate social life.

(c) Respect of others will be sought and their contempt avoided. In the last resort this may be the psychological process of inversion in which a contemptuous label is reconstrued as a mark of pride.[30] If expressive aims are the relatively dominant psychological attitudes, public marks of character will be the dominating public good individuals are likely to seek.

(d) Though they may not actually be genetically sustained there may be some social strategies that are so intimately bound up with biological survival that they are ubiquitous features of human associations.[31] For instance the distinctive male and female reproductive strategies, the tight bonding of groups of young males, the strength of the relationship between mother and child, might turn out to be universal. Societies which have not subscribed to them have not survived to tell the tale.

One must acknowledge the continuous and ubiquitous presence of organic aspects of human life — the necessity for food, air and water, the need for protection for the young, the efforts at clearing away waste and rubbish and the disposal of the dead. I shall be holding firmly to the view that such necessities engender a universal substratum of problems, but there are no solutions to those problems inherited along with the rest of our biological make-up. Such problems are solved by virtue of our ingenuity, and one of the cleverest of all the deivces we have invented to deal with them was society.

2

STRUCTURE

ANTICIPATORY SUMMARY

Introduction: both institutions and episodes will be thought of as structured entities.
1. A formal definition of structure requires elements, relations and invariants under transformation. Basic distinctions are between
   (a) actual and latent structures;
   (b) external and internal relations.
2. The sources of structure
   (a) The principle of production — structured products come from structured templates.
   (b) Differential relations to time; either product or template can exist either synchronically or diachronically.
   (c) Types of generative process — replication, transformation and assemblage.
3. Continuity of structure depends on integrity of relations, not continuity of elements.

INTRODUCTION

I now begin the exposition of an increasingly more detailed analytical scheme for revealing the nature of social entities. I shall be concerned both with people-structures such as institutions, and action-structures such as episodes of social life. The main system of concepts to be developed in this section derive from progressively more specific forms of the concept of structure. Structural concepts will become both the main analytical tools, guiding the direction of the search, and at the same time the basis of the main explanatory apparatus which I shall be developing in outline form in this section.[1]

1. A FORMAL DEFINITION OF STRUCTURE

(a) I shall say that there is a structure when

(i) there is a set, or there are sets of individuals of one or several categories, for which determinate criteria of identity and individuation can be given;

(ii) there is a set, or there are sets of relations of one or more categories in which the individuals specified above can stand. The set of relations defining a structure is in principle richer than the relations actually realized at any time.

These conditions are meant to cover both those cases where the individuals can be specified as to kind, whether or not they stand in the relations which determine structure, or whether they are in part or whole constituted as members of kinds by virtue of standing in those relations.

(iii) There is at least one kind of relation in which the individuals forming a structure stand, which is invariant under transformation of some or all of the remaining kinds of relations in which they stand. Satisfaction of this principle I shall call the maintenance of the integrity of the structure.

(b) Two further distinctions are required in order to lay out the extent and range of the concept of structure as I wish to understand it and to apply it to the analysis of the kinds of social entities we are likely to come across.

(i) The distinction between actual structures and latent structures.[2] For the purposes of social analysis the institutions of society considered structurally are certainly not in actual being continuously over time. For example, when the pupils leave and the doors are shut and the teachers go home, schooling as a social activity ceases. However, to conclude that the school as a social entity has only intermittent existence would be unwarranted. So long as certain beliefs, commitments and rule systems are represented in the cognitive resources, whether conscious or not, and if all the people who are involved in that institution on the occasions when it is actual continue to exist, the school as a latent structure remains, as an institution of the society. Indeed it will emerge from our investigations that most of the social entities with which we are concerned are more latent than actual, that is exist more in the powers, capacities, knowledge, beliefs and expectations of the folk, than they do in continuously realized social practices.

(ii) The distinction between internal and external relations. I have already pointed out that the definition of, or rather the necessary conditions for, the existence of a structure set out above, include those cases where the individuals, which form the elements of the structure, could exist as such even when they are not standing in the relations which constitute the structure, as well as those cases where the disappearance of the relations eliminates the individual as a member of that category. Traditionally this distinction is marked by differentiating relations rather than kinds of individuals.[3] A relation is external when no change of category occurs when individuals come to stand in it. For example, two material things which, considered with respect to the categories of the science of mechanics, are in differing spatial relations at different times, are otherwise unchanged. Spatial relations are external since by virtue of standing in them no change of kind occurs in the bodies. However, there are many kinds of individuals and many sorts of relations which are internal in the sense that if individuals come to stand in those relations they are thereby members of a new category. Compare, for example, the distinction between the concept of "man" and its correlative "woman". They are complementary concepts which partition the human race. There are independent criteria by means of which in the absence of one category we could define the other on purely anatomical grounds. The same could not be said of the complementary categories "man" and "wife" or "guardian" and "ward". By virtue of standing in the relation of marriage a woman is constituted as a wife and in the dissolution of that partnership ceases thereby to be of that category. Similarly, in grammatical structures the relation in which a word as a lexical item stands to other words, has a determining effect upon the grammatical category to which it belongs, particularly in languages like English which have a strong positional character. For example, the intelligibility of the famous Shakespearean sentence, "But me no buts," illustrates the category-creating effect of the location of one vocable in various relation to others.

We are now in possession of a set of general concepts by means of which the analysis of an enormous variety of social entities, ranging from social institutions to ceremonies, can be undertaken.

2. THE SOURCES OF STRUCTURE

The application of the analytical scheme sketched in outline above will bring out the structural properties of social entities.[4]

In doing so it poses the central problem of explanation for the social sciences as they are conceived in this work. If social entities are conceived as essentially determined by their structural properties, what are the sources of those structures? In order to undertake detailed studies, it is advisable to begin with a general account of the main principles involved in structural explanation.

(a) The Principle of Production

In general, structured products are taken to be the result of the reproduction of the structure of a template by an active agent of some sort. The structure of the template is responsible for the structure in the product.

There are a number of different cases which fall under this general principle. The product may have a structure extended over time. For example, a musical score is the structure which generates a time-extended tune, a melodic structure through the activity of the pianist as an agent following the score. On the other hand a house-plan is responsible for the time-independent structure that is eventually realized as a house by the activities of the builder in following the plan. In both these cases the relationship between template and product is at least potentially one: many, since many different performances of the same score and many different houses based upon the same plan can be constructed.

An important application of the distinction between types and tokens can be found in the relationship between template and product. In the examples just given, where the template is a physically realized structure, it can function as the bearer of a type, each individual product generated from it being tokens of that type. Of course, the plan and the score are not themselves types, but by virtue of their re-usability, are the bearers of types.

(b) Differential Relations to Time

There are a number of different ways in which the temporal properties of templates and products may be related.

(i) The template may be structured synchronically, that is realized at a moment in time, as for example, a printed Order of Service exists as a structure enduring in time, but the product created in accordance with it may be diachronic. For example, the ceremony which is produced by participants as agents following the Order of Service, is a structure of actions sequentially ordered in time.

(ii) A template may be all in being synchronically and endure through time, as in our example of the house-plan, and the product may also be synchronically organized and enduring as well. Such, for example, is the well-built house.

It is worth noticing that in practice synchronic organization is often spatial and diachronic organization temporal, though as we shall see in the case of structural properties of society, it would be unwise to conclude that all forms of synchronic organizations are spatial.

(iii) There are cases where the template is realized diachronically, as for example the development by an Indian musician, in advance of his performance, of the conception of the melodic structure he is improvising. In this case the product, the musical performance, is also diachronic.

(iv) There are cases where the template exists as a temporal sequence laid out diachronically, but in following it through the agent produces a synchronically structured entity, for example, it may be that by following his developing conception an artist produces a product which is a synchronically structured and enduring work of art.

(c) Types of Generative Process

So far I have offered only a very general account of the way in which the activities of an agent result in the formation of a product. However, some further distinctions are necessary. We must differentiate those cases where the template survives the production of the product and can be used again — cases which I shall call 'replication' — from those where the productive process is, in one way or another, an absorption of the template into the product.[5] The latter process I shall call 'transformation'. Both are to be distinguished from another kind of structure-producing activity, which has some, but a rather small, role to play in our understanding of the processes of the production and maintenance of societies and social events: a process I shall call 'repetition'. In the case of a repetitive process of production, units are assembled according to their own individual properties, but when they are put together the overall assemblage exhibits a pattern which is not simply the replication or transformation of the structural properties of any given constituent. A very simple example is the structure of ordinary conversations between two people, A and B. They have a straightforward turn-taking pattern, A B A B ... generated by the end-properties and start-properties of each speech contribution, together with accompanying paralinguistic signs. Taken together these lead to the overall pattern of the conversation exhibiting the simple repetitive pattern. I might hint at this point that the problem of the understanding of the origins and nature of macrosocial structures will have to be solved in part by drawing upon the idea of a genesis of pattern by repetition and assemblage.

Having set out the general principles governing the explanation of structures we must notice that empirical enquiry can be directed towards two separate kinds of question.

(i) By what process is a product produced from a template by the action of an agent?

(ii) How does the template come into existence prior to the process of production? Is it, for example, generated for the occasion, and by what process? Or, is it preformed, perhaps before the individual which bears it on a particular occasion has come into being? Or does it exist in individuals prior to the occasions on which it is realized? In either case, how does it come to be represented in that individual?

These are questions which empirical investigations of the sources of structure will have to answer.

3. CONTINUITY OF A STRUCTURE

To refine this scheme for application to the analysis of social life we shall have to lay down certain conditions for the persistence of a structure over time and through different sorts of transformation, which are more precisely specified than the very general conditions set out above. The most important one for our purpose derives from the distinction between those structures which can tolerate the substitution of materially distinct individuals and preserve their identity, from those which cannot. The preservation of identity will, it is clear, have to be defined in terms of some property or properties of a structure other than the material identity of the individuals which comprise it. An obvious candidate would be the preservation of the relations, and particularly the invariant relations, which enable us to identify the structure in the first place. It is clear that this distinction between substitution-tolerant and -intolerant structures is indifferent to the distinction between internally and externally related structures, for it may be that in substitution, a materially distinct individual takes on the characteristics of the appropriate category by virtue of coming to stand in the new relation. For example, a divorced man, Mr X, acquires a second wife by entering into the relation of marriage, so that a materially distinct woman becomes 'the wife of Mr X'.

I turn now to a detailed application of structural concepts to the analysis of the two main kinds of social entity with which social science can be concerned. These are what one might call people-structures, where the products, institutions and societies are relational systems whose elements are individual human beings. Each element is partly constituted as a person by virtue of the many systems of relations, actual and latent in which he stands, and partly by his biological embodiment as an embodied actor having a location or world line in space-time. On the other hand, we will be looking at the activities of human beings, constituted as persons by the collectives to which they belong, which issue in sequential structures of actions. Action-sequences cluster into structured groups, necessary for the performance of social acts, which collectively constitute a continuing and unfolding social life. We shall call these sequences 'episodes'. Since they will be analysed both with respect to public social acts that are brought about in/by their performance, and individual contributions of actions to a co-operatively created sequence, they are to be considered as act-action sequences. We shall suppose, unless we have definite evidence to the contrary, that such sequences are orderly and so we shall approach them with the structural conception of analysis and explanation in mind.

3

THE ANALYSIS OF EPISODES: ACT/ACTION STRUCTURES

ANTICIPATORY SUMMARY

Introduction: episodes reveal different structures depending on choice of units of analysis and of time-perspectives.
1. Example of simple analysis: introduction ritual for a stranger. This analysis illustrates the distinctions
   (a) between social actions and social acts;
   (b) between social semantics and social syntax;
   (c) between performative and fact-stating uses of language.
2. The description and justification of order
   (a) Rules of sequence; accountable replies;
   (b) justification of the rules of sequence; the uses of folk sociology;
   (c) comparison between grammatical structure and the orderliness of social actions. Examples show that:
      (i) orderliness is known both in terms of instances of action and of names of types of action;
      (ii) social orderliness is not at the level of grammar but of sub-categorial structure.
3. Concatenation: the comparison between sentences and episodes as between completed thoughts and completed acts.
Appendix: Generative Transformations
The structure of meals is generatively representable but it is not related to any specific message.

INTRODUCTION

In the general theory of structure outlined in the last chapter both elements and relations figure. Choosing to pick out elements of a certain kind determines in part what relations will be looked for as structuring principles — and so too for choice of relations. So in analysing episodes the structure that can be revealed will depend upon how the elements of the structure are chosen. Scale is an important variant in this matter. Courtship — marriage —

45

divorce form an orderly structure with respect to the relation
'later than', but each unit episode, treated as a social ritual, is
itself internally complex. By choosing a scale of analysis corresponding to the simplest social actions, that is actions the components of which are not themselves actions, that internal complexity could be represented as an orderly sequential structure.
Furthermore at different degrees of refinement the principles
of order are different. In the first case, if the three rituals occur
they *must* occur in that order, since 'marriage' *is* the ritual con-
formation and transformation of a male/female bond as a socio-
legal relation, and a 'divorce' *is* the ritual dissolution of that
ritually created bond. But it is surely a convention, though a
socially significant one, that the groom has precedence over the
bride in the making of ritual affirmations.

Structure, then, will be related to the 'grain' of the analysis.
J-P. De Waele[1] has pointed out that important temporal properties of sequents, such as whether they are the only sequent
of a kind, or the first, second or third and so on, depends on
the time perspective one adopts. Since an actor is living through
an episode with continually changing time perspective some of
the sequential properties of the elements of the episode are
unstable. Until one has succeeded or failed one doesn't know
whether what one is doing is or is not an attempt, and until
one has tried a second time, that it was a first attempt, and so
on. Even when one has a stable vantage point from which to
examine the structured sequence of socially distinct elements
one has lived through, other perspectives may have the effect
of amplifying some elements and even suppressing others. This
is evident, for instance, in Schutz's idea of perspectivity. A seg-
ment of one's biography may show different structures and even
bring out different interpretations of this matter or that matter,
depending on the perspective from which one is then viewing it.
This has been nicely illustrated in Ingeborg Helling's study of life
stories told to her by the carpenters of Konstanz. In different
parts of their tales they may use the very same episode for illustrating quite different social predicaments, and so as having quite
different significance.[2]

1. EXAMPLE OF A SIMPLE ANALYSIS,
USING COMMON-SENSE SOCIAL CATEGORIES

Contemporary English stranger introduction ritual, involving
three people — the stranger, his sponsor, and the host to whom

the introduction is being made — comprises, if carried through in full, the following phases:

(a) Approach and recognition

(b) Opening formula: *Sponsor*: 'Master, I'd like you to meet my guest.'

(c) Name exchange: *Sponsor*: 'This is Dr X: Mr Y, our master.'

(d) Formula of mutual recognition as persons: *X*: 'How do you do?'
                                        Y: 'How do you do?'

(e) Physical contact or substitute; confirmation of recognition: Handshake (if 'done')
     (d and e are usually simultaneous)

(f) Determination of Identity: This is a complex phase and will be analysed below.

(g) Formula of Incorporation: *Y*: 'I'm so glad you could join us.'
                                    X1: 'It's nice to be here.'
                                    X2: 'I'm very glad to be here.'

The distribution of 'Glad' (condescending) and 'Nice' (deferential) depends upon the outcome of (f)

This is a very elaborate form of exchange, though very, very common in many different variants. Each section deserves commentary, since each section reveals something about the society in which a form of this exchange is embedded.

The first point to notice is that the stranger, as stranger, has temporarily high rank, marked in (d) by the fact that his name is mentioned first, and in (a) by his speaking his part of the formula first. But by Phase (g) this courtesy is no longer extended, and the overall status determination of order of speaking becomes paramount. There are some exceptions to this structural feature we will discuss below.

The approach and recognition phase is characterized by the use of the glance as a device to communicate intention and to hold attention. Sponsor tries to catch the eye of Y, the host, and having done so glances at the stranger, back to Y again, and so on, holding Y's attention and sweeping the stranger forward. The stranger keeps his gaze fixed on Y, until Y 'recognizes' him by looking towards him, at which the stranger, showing proper deference, glances aside. Y and the sponsor exchange glances during phases (b) and (c), after which Y and the stranger become eye-locked in ordinary Argyle-type turn taking, until Y, opening the way for the closing formula in (g), looks away markedly to sponsor.

From this example we can introduce three important distinctions, that between social acts and social actions, and that between social syntax and social semantics.

(a) Acts and Actions

In the example, a particular, non-literal social meaning is given to the utterance 'How do you do?' Grammatically the utterance is a question, but it would be a mistake to interpret it as an enquiry as to the health of the counterparticipant. Socially considered it is a ritual device for my public acknowledgment that you are to count as a person, that is a being in whose welfare I might take an interest. In the last sentence I have been trying to describe the social *act* I have performed in saying 'How do you do?' in that context. The saying of that ritual formula is the appropriate, but conventionally associated *action* with which in that context and with that kind of person I perform the act. The ceremony as performance is analysed as a sequence of action-types, the doing of tokens of which are performances of instances of act-types, whose sequential order is the ceremony as a socially potent episode.

(b) Social Syntax and Social Semantics

Any sequential structure obtaining among types or categories of things suggests an analogue with the syntactical structure of language — since syntax comprises the formal principles of sequential order of categories of lexical items. 'Horse' and 'gallop' are syntactically related in 'The horse was galloping', as instances of the categories 'noun' and 'participle'. From the syntactical point of view the same relation obtains between the relevant lexical items as tokens of types in 'The water was boiling'. This is so even though no other animal but a horse can be said to be galloping, while even pitch and lead can be said to be boiling. We shall find the social parallels to these further sub-categorial restrictions on language of the greatest importance.

Since the social force of an action seems to be only conventionally associated with the means of its performance, for the most part, and bearing in mind the fact that many linguists have insisted on the arbitrary character of the relation between a sign and what it signifies, there might be some insight to be gained by treating the relation between act and action as parallel to that between meaning and sign. This suggests the idea of a social semantics.

We shall explore both parallels in detail in the sections to come.

(c) The Concept of a Performative

A performative *use* of a sentence is a use, not primarily to convey information but (i) to carry out a social act, (ii) to bring about certain effects, via (i). (i) involves the illocutionary force of the sentence-as-used; (ii) its perlocutionary force. Bruner has pointed out that standard grammatical form is not a good guide to performative force[3] since small children grasp performative force in the course of day-to-day social practices that is non-co-ordinate with grammatical form. For instance they readily grasp parental use of the interrogative form to give orders, and distinguish it from the use of the form to ask questions. The same distinction goes through into adult life where 'I wonder if you'd mind terribly retyping this Miss Jones?' is performatively equivalent to 'Do it again you silly bitch, it's all bloody wrong!'.

2. THE DESCRIPTION AND JUSTIFICATION OF ORDER

(a) Rules of Sequence

We can begin investigation of the orderliness of act/action sequences with an exposition of some examples in which types of social items are identified and individuated with the help of common-sense social categories. The elements of such sequences can be described in everyday terms, such as 'apology', 'question', 'answer', 'request', 'refusal' and so on. In the first range of examples, the analysis of brief conversations, each speaker's turn can be treated as the performance of an instance of a type of social act. In this analysis the speech is considered for its illocutionary force alone. Each speech-act as a contribution to a conversation, however cognitively complex, would be identified as, say, *a* request, that is asking something of someone who can bestow it but 'has the right to refuse. The orderliness, if any, of act/action sequences whose elements are individuated at this level of analysis, will reflect principles of order which we might wish to compare to grammatical rules. The comparison will turn out to be somewhat problematic since the combination of the level of social analysis germane to a comparison with grammar has to be discovered in the course of making the comparison.

Pursuing the analogy uncritically for the moment suggests looking for categories and subcategories of social actions at levels of generality matching those of linguistics. Let us begin with some intuitively obvious unit actions. As a first approximation actions can be categorized with respect to the social acts they are conventionally taken to perform. For example:

Act	*Action*
Greeting	Kissing, hand-shaking, nodding, etc.
Insult	Finger-raising, tongue-poking, ignoring, etc.

Common experience is enough to provide some plausible examples of order among acts. Thus greetings occur at the beginning of interactions, farewells at the end; apologies usually follow protested insults, injuries, etc. These descriptions have the character of empirical generalizations, since they describe the order in a multiplicity of particular action sequences such as 'Hullo, how are you?', 'Fine; how are you?', 'O.K.', 'See you,' 'Yea, bye'; 'Hi', 'hi', 'you going out?', 'Later', 'O.K. Cheers', 'Caio'; 'Don't talk to me like that', 'Sorry': 'You bastard', 'What did you say?', 'Nothing' ... etc.

Rules for the simulation of socially proper episodes can be formulated for both levels.

(i) *For Acts*

Greetings shall occur only at the beginning of an interaction.

Apology should follow protested insult.

(ii) *For Actions*

'How do you do?' should accompany handshaking only.

'Sorry' should follow a failure to notice an acquaintance.

The relations between empirical generalizations derived from recorded conversations and rules formulated for the construction of conversations need to be investigated.

Consider the following conversations:

(i) *A*: 'Care for a drink?'

   B1:'Thanks.'

   B2:'Don't mind if I do.'

(ii) *A*: 'Care for a drink?'

   B1:'Thanks (but)'

   B2: 'I really mustn't have another.'

   B3: 'I'm driving.'

In (i) A is making an offer. B's subsequent contributions are 'Thanks' which acknowledges the making of the offer, while 'I don't mind if I do' accepts the offer. The sequence of acts is something like this:

A1   Offer
B1   Acknowledgment
B2   Acceptance

The three distinct social acts constitute two orderly pairs, that is A1B1, A1B2. I propose to examine only the simplest of these pairs, 'Offer'/'Acceptance'. It would be of interest to try to determine whether B1B2 was a third orderly pair. My intuition suggests that it is not, that is a conversation in which acceptance preceded acknowledgment would pass as civil.

Taking 'Offer' and 'Acceptance' as the names of species of performatives classified by reference to their illocutionary force, we can formulate a rule of sequence, the following of which would generate the pair A1B2 as a proper social episode.

Speaker 'Offer' should be followed by Addressee 'Acceptance', R1.

But sometimes offers are refused. Empirical studies have shown that in Refusal Sequences the rule is more complex than R1 but related to it. It turns out that refusals are 'accountable'. A reason or explanation must follow as a second contribution by the addressee, generating the pair B2B3 of the second conversation reported above. It could be argued that the 'Refusal'/'Reason' rule, R2, is dependent upon the 'Offers'/'Acceptance' rule, since if it is polite to accept an offer, an unqualified refusal is necessarily impolite. Its potential offensiveness must be remedied by the giving of a reason.

In general acceptances are not accountable, that is it is not mandatory to give reasons. The option of giving a reason for acceptance of course remains open, as in 'Thanks, I'd love a drink, I'm terribly thirsty', which might be called for in a special setting, say very hot weather. Accounts in such conditions seem to be socially efficacious as amplifications of 'Thanks', rather than as reasons for the acceptance.

The rules are beginning to display a satisfying systematic character consonant with the mandatory force of the modal verbs in R1 and R2, reflecting norms of politeness. That these rules be followed, or at least that that structure be created, whether the psychological mechanism by which it is generated is or is not literally following a rule, is a necessary condition for the interaction to have the social property of politeness. Taking the two rules together we get: Speaker 'Offer' should be followed by Addressee 'Acceptance', and in case it is followed by 'Refusal' that 'Refusal' must be followed by 'Reason', (if politeness is to be achieved and gracious personas presented and sustained, and this is a condition derived from the necessities of the expressive order).

If the sequence A^n:Offer; B^n:Acceptance, is too long prolonged B's $n + k$ acceptance becomes accountable, for instance, 'I really must buy a round but I've left my money in another jacket.' 'Can you lend me a quid?' and so on.

The logical relations obtaining between the locutionary aspects of the speech involved in these reported conversations is not being addressed as an issue at this level of analysis. I am concerned only with the sequencing principles among the social acts 'Offer', 'Acceptance', 'Refusal', 'Reason'. I take these to be natural kinds of the genus 'illocutionary force'. Investigation of the criteria by which illocutionary forces are actually identified as a day-to-day practice could indeed involve consideration of logical relations,   for instance whether 'Refusal' is identical with 'Non-Acceptance'. Relations of a more philosophical kind are involved in the rule that 'Offer', 'Acceptance', and 'Refusal' form a sequence only if they each have the same content or putative referent, namely a drink. And there are lots of other logical relations that could be involved too, for instance scope.

(b) Justification of the Rules

But if we were to ask, in the spirit of social science, why these sequencing principles seem to be at work, intending our query to direct attention to their social aspects, two further issues can be raised. The sequencing rule (the analogue of a syntactical rule) can be associated with:

(i) a social principle, that accepting an offer is a way of showing respect to him who offers. We can ask for a justification of the principle. This might be attempted as follows: a fundamental activity of social life is the presentation of an agreeable persona or social self and the sustaining of the persona presentations of others. To accept an offer is to acknowledge the benevolence of the putative host. It allows the other to be gracious and at the same time, by providing the opportunity for this, one presents oneself in an agreeable light.

(ii) an empirical generalization: in civil society offers are usually followed by acceptances (even when this involves considerable inconvenience for the addressee).

Either or both the associated general statements could be offered in support of the sequencing rule. But is there always a sequencing rule involved in the genesis of action by particular individuals? That is, are we to take 'syntax' as part of a performance theory? Must social knowledge and action be related in this way? In a highly formalist society it is conceivable (and I think indeed often the case) that the sequencing rules would be taught without the associated supporting or explanatory general statements in that social knowledge would be exhausted by more sequencing rules. In such a society it might not be implausible to conceive a naive rule-following model as the icon of a generative mechanism of action, a description of which would be the core of a performance theory. But in contemporary society, great efforts are made to support the sequencing rules with social generalizations of both categories. Consider the 'Please'/Response/'Thanks' sequencing rule. We try to make it intelligible by reference to principles from just the two categories of general statements I have mentioned.

(a) 'It's a way of showing that you have noticed and appreciated the trouble someone has taken on your behalf.' This is to make reference to a general principle of social order of the type of (i) above.

(b) 'That's what nice little girls say.' This is clearly offered as an empirical generalization about social behaviour of the type (ii) above. The reference to 'nice little girls' excludes too easy empirical refutation, since the cost of successfully sustaining oneself as a putative counter-instance would be *a priori* exclusion from a desirable category of persons.

This suggests that a rule-following model is not likely to prove adequate as the core of a performance theory for contemporary society. Gergen has drawn attention to the possibility that even psychological mechanisms may be historically situated, and not just the conventions they operate upon.[4] Somehow people must 'see the sense of what they are doing'. This, I believe, suggests a more cognitive, problem-solving conception of the individual genesis of co-ordinated action, such as the desire/belief/intention theory sketched in recent studies in the philosophy of action.[5]

It is worth noticing that our lay efforts to support or explain an apparently formalistic sequencing rule to our children involve rudimentary social science. We attempt the exposition of a feature of our local ethnography in terms of a cultural norm and its relation to a more general principle involved in the maintenance of social order, such as the propriety of acknowledging efforts directed towards one's wellbeing by others. It may take the form of the statement of an empirical generalization concerning the orderliness actually present in a class of social interactions. Finally, one could offer theoretical and normative principles of social order in explanation of the existence of the empirical regularity. Ethogenic social psychology depends on the systematic and rigorous pursuit of the same interests, but controlled by continuous empirical testing of hypotheses as to the degree that people actually control action by reference to norms.

The sequencing rules for the orderly structures (i) and (ii) on p. 52 and for the overall structure, could be similarly developed and the associated normative and empirical general statements proposed and supported, the one in (folk) social theory and the other in observable social practice. We should notice that the identification of a social practice as having a certain significance is not, and indeed could not be independent of the theory from which the elements of that practice get their meaning, that is in terms of which they are interpreted by the members of the culture in which it has a place.

(c) Comparison between Grammatical Structure and the Orderliness of Social Actions

David Clarke has shown[6] that people recognize social order not just in sequences of particular speech-act instances, that is real and artificial conversations, but also in sequences of common-sense terms for specific performative forces, that is in cases where a conversation is represented only in a sequence of the names for acts, for instance:

A. Greeting	B. Greeting
A. Question	B. Answer
A. Apology	etc.

The importance of Clarke's discovery can hardly be overemphasized. It demonstrates that people are able to recognize social orderliness in two wholly different modes. In the first mode order is recognized in a representation of their own and other's action-sequences, for example in a transcript of a conversation, in the second in a list of names for the elementary acts generated in action-sequences. People know both that 'Sorry' should follow treading on someone's foot *and* that an 'apology' should follow an 'offence'. It is as if the native speakers not only knew how to talk and were able to recognize proper and improper forms of speech, but were also able routinely to deploy a grammar that expresses abstract knowledge of the structure of proper grammatical forms. But 'noun', 'verb', etc., though part of the language of the educated, are grammarians' terms. They are not part of the vocabulary routinely employed in the speech of daily life. They are part of a theory of that speech. Yet 'insult', 'apology', 'plea', 'excuse', and so on are terms of native speech and are routinely employed as part of the social resources of competent social actors. This discovery highlights a profound asymmetry between social action and the linguistic (as opposed to social) properties of speech. In the realm of social action we possess an explicit 'grammar' and deploy it in our day-to-day practice.

Why this asymmetry? The answer seems to lie in the dual character of human social performance. There is both action and the speech which accounts for the action. Accounts are, in part, continuous commentary upon the social propriety of the acts and action-sequences generated by ourselves and others. We could take social propriety as the social analogue of linguistic wellformedness. Clarke's discovery suggests that people have a more explicit abstract knowledge of the principles of social orderliness than they have of the rules of grammar. Grammarians must rely on native speakers' intuitions whereas ethogenists can reasonably ask directly for at least some of the rules of social orderliness.

At least two assumptions are involved in the argument of the preceding section. (i) Though grammatical categories may reflect ultimate metaphysical categories, sequencing rules are arbitrary. (ii) Selection and sequencing rules at the level of common-sense categorizations of social acts are not arbitrary. The importance of these assumptions in judging the use of the linguistic analogy in explicating social meaning comes out when we consider the level of orderliness that can be shown to exist in social act-action sequences by comparison with the structure of linguistic performances. I consider first Austin's scheme for categorizing the social force of speech acts.[6]

Consider the following exchanges:

	Common-sense categories	Austinian categories	
'Stupid bitch!'	Insult	Verdictive	V
'Don't talk to me like that'	Protest	Exercitive	E
'Sorr-*rry*'	Apology	Behabitive	B

	Common-sense categories	*Austinian categories*	
'I won't' (as act of defiance)	Defiance	Commissive	C
'Very well, then, you're not going out tonight'.	Threat/Verdict + Sentence	Commissive (or Exercitive & Verdictive)	C
'Alright, *alright*!	Submission	Commissive	C
But it's not fair'	Protest	Verdictive	V

Could the Austinian categories form the basis of a social grammar? If every possible combination of Austinian categories is 'well-formed' then the order of sequences of social acts categorized at this level is socially without significance. In fact there seem to be neither selection nor sequencing rules at the level of Austinian categories. It seems to me that any sequence of types of elements identified at the Austinian level could be realized, for instance any of CCCV, VCCC, CVCC, etc. For example:

A_1:   You're lying   V
B_1:   I promise you I'm not   C
A_2:   I'll make you tell me the truth   C
B_2:   I swear I'm not lying   C

I hope the reader shares my intuition that the quoted conversation-fragment represents a perfectly orderly sequence of social acts.

To show conclusively that the Austinian categorial structure of a sequence is irrelevant to social meaningfulness it would suffice to find another realization of each of the Austinian categories which, at the level of common- sense categorization was disorderly. The example above realizes the structure VCCC as the sequence of common-sense categories:

A_1 accusation
B_1 assurance
A_2 threat
B_2 reassurance

If on the basis of our intuitions we judged that another realization of VCCC was disorderly, and that intuition could be sustained by reference to the sequence of acts categorized in the common-sense scheme, then we have shown that the Austinian categories are too weak to serve in the setting out of structure. Disorderly sequences are readily identified at the common-sense level of categorization. For example, VCCC realized as:

A_1 convict
B_1 appeal

A_2 allow
B_2 make restoration

strikes me as clearly disorderly. Consider, for example, the realization of the above structure in:

A_1:   *You* finished the marmalade.
B_1:   No, I didn't.
A_2:   Oh, sorry.
B_2:   I suppose *I'll* have to get you some more then.

(Just as a context *can* be found in which green ideas do sleep furiously, so B_2 can be taken to be orderly on the assumption that B proposes to punish A by 'martyrdom'.)

Failure to reveal order at the level of Austin's categories could have more than one interpretation. The argument so far could be used to suggest that treating orderliness of social acts as analogous to syntax cannot be sustained at the level at which social sequences have been shown to be orderly, namely at the level of specific illocutions, since common-sense categories of social acts do not correspond to grammatical categories.

But taking the parallel to be at the level where order first appears in each realm would involve matching common-sense categories of social acts to grammatical categories. There are some obvious disparities.

(i) There are very many more categories of social acts than there are syntactical categories. The ratio might be something of the order of four hundred to seven or eight.

(ii) The range and interrelations of syntactical categories can be grounded in a rather course-grained general metaphysics of nature. The grounding of the corresponding diversity of illocutionary categories and their permitted combinations in a theory of sociality is a much more daunting task and demands more attention to social detail, so leading towards cultural specificity and thus relativity of explanations.

(iii) The taxonomy of social acts is messy, contingent and naturalistic, while the taxonomy of syntactical categories is neat, apparently necessary and *a priori*.

Alternatively, the resolution of the apparent failure to match might be found by introducing the idea of sub-categorial rules on the linguistic side of the analogy.

The principles upon which 'Hot brown icicles trade anxiety under two' is recognized as improper are sometimes called sub-categorial rules. They seem to reflect a rather wide range of considerations. Compare:

    My dog chewed the cud
    My dog chewed the wind
    My dog chewed the North Pole

Each of these could be treated in two different ways.

(i) The sentence could be taken as well-formed, but each and every use of it would issue in a false statement (provided linguistic and empirical considerations were normal).

(ii) The sentence could be judged to be ill-formed prior to any putative use, because it violated sub-categorial rules.

But unlike the categorial rules of language which are fully arbitrary in Saussure's sense,[7] the rules according to which each of the above sentences is ill-formed could be justified by reference to contingent empirical considerations such as the masticatory habits of dogs, the lack of a firm texture in the wind as material substance, and the abstract geometrical character of the North Pole.

Since dogs never chew the cud, the wind is always without texture and the North Pole defined as a purely geometrical concept, one could as well absorb these features of the world into the rules for the formation of sentences as reserve them for the inevitable rejection of proposed statements as false.

But to treat the wrongness of the above sentences as stemming from an intuition of rule-violation rather than a judgement of falsehood in every normal putative application is to extend the notion of syntax beyond the limits laid down by Saussure, limits defined by the arbitrariness of the rules. For a number of reasons not germane to the arguments of this book I would like to follow those such as Pettit, who would extend syntax in just such a way, and treat these forms of wrongness as rule-violations.[8] The rules could be thought to represent a kind of historical sedimentation of experience into the language. This move allows a neat matching between language-using and action. As I have shown, the rules which express the intuitively felt orderliness of social life are non-arbitrary, that is capable of justification with respect to general features of social experience and social theory. In this respect they match the sub-categorial rules of language. Each embeds in its formal principles some pervasive but contingent features of the world to which it is primarily related.

3. CONCATENATION

In both language use and social life, groups of elements are concatenated into complete structures. Words form up into sentences,

actions into episodes. How does this happen? Efforts to understand the way concatenation of meaning occurs in language have
so far been unsuccessful, probably because they have been based
upon the extentionalist relations of classical formal logic, while
their problem field is that of intentionally related elements. The
principles by which social actions form episodes are much better
understood and their manner of working much more easily discovered.

The basic concept is that of social act. Episodes are identified
by reference to acts performed in them. Each type of act is
performed in the performance of a conventionally grounded
sequence of actions, which *in* being performed, perform the
action. In social episodes there is no problem of how in performing a sequence of actions an act is performed, since the
conventional reading of that action-sequence is that act. The
basic semantic entity is the act, and actions have their meanings
as the utterances and movements conventionally required to
perform that act.

The formula:

Episode : Act :: Sentence : Complete thought

leaves us with a clearly understood left-hand side and a quite
unexplicated right-hand side, since the relation of word-meaning
to sentence-meaning remains obscure, while the meaning of a
sentence is conceived as a function of the meanings of its components. Part of the problem is that while the relation

Sentences :: Facts

is one between distinct existents, that of

Action-sequence :: Acts

is one between levels of interpretation of the same existents.

In studying the problem of concatenation perhaps the act/
action theories of social science could serve as analogies for
sentence-meaning/word-meaning theories in the study of language.
But that is not my concern in this book.

The conversational examples I have analysed have been chosen
for their simplicity and brevity. More extended conversations
reveal a much more complex structure, but the principles of
analysis are the same. Brenner has shown that the analysis of a
longer conversation requires the attribution to the speakers of
a hierarchy of intentions, there being a dominant theme, the
working out of each member's global intentions or projects, and
minor themes brought about by the clash and mesh of momentary intentions.[9] These generate an act-structure which is realized

in speech, gesture, and so on through a four-fold rule system which associates actions with acts, and controls their sequencing. The act/action structure so generated consists of a halting progress through loops and nesting inserts towards the realization of the dominant theme. The orderliness of the transitions in a fifteen-minute conversation of a specific social form can be represented by a total of about ninety rules.

APPENDIX

Generative Transformations

We can hardly touch upon an analogy between social order and linguistic structure without examining the possibility of an analogue of generative transformation as a way of representing members' knowledge of correct order. A very striking example can be found in tracing the source of orderliness of meals.[10] A meal is an orderly sequence of dishes, the template for which is a menu. Cuisines are distinguishable families of menus, and dishes are orderly assemblages of comestibles, the templates for which are recipes.

A plausible case can be made for treating the working out of a menu from which a meal will be prepared and served, along the lines of the transformation of a base-structure according to cuisine-specific rewrite rules. Unlike the use of transformational grammar in linguistics, which is confined to the representation of competence, we might treat the generative 'grammar' of cooks as a quasiperformance theory. Following the Burgundian cuisine:[11]

R1 M (meal) goes into (Salt plus Sweet)

R2 Salt goes into (Beginners plus Main dish)

R3 Sweet goes into (Pudding plus Dessert)

R4 Any main dish goes into (Main element plus two subsidiary elements)

R5 Any subsidiary dish goes into (Main element plus one subsidiary element)

R6 Cheese and (or) salad can be interposed between Salt and Sweet

In current degenerate versions of the Burgundian cuisine one of the subsidiary elements of the menu generated by R4 must be potatoes.[12]

Applying these rules we write a typical Burgundian menu (garnish omitted):

Smoked salmon and brown bread
Tournedos Rossini, baked celery and scalloped potatoes
Ice pudding and sponge fingers
Fruit (grapes and apples)

One could serve a Mersault with the salmon a Macon with the steak, and then a Barsac with the pudding and dessert.

To test the analogy this apparently frivolous example is just what we need. It highlights the differences between syntax and social order. Syntax is a determinant of meaning, or to put this more precisely: order in language is message specific. 'You didn't go' (an accusation), 'Didn't you go?' (a question), differ partly and significantly in syntactical order, while the disorderly 'You go didn't' conveys no message at all.

But the message specificity of meals is coarse-grained. Mary Douglas distinguishes message specificity only at that degree of analysis which would distinguish 'drinks' from 'formal dinners' from 'family meals', the sequential partaking of which she takes to be ritual markings of passage from stranger to intimate. Why, then, all the fuss about cuisine? After all, beginning with salad and thousand island dressing, then steak and Idaho baked potato, followed by ice cream and chocolate sauce, accompanied by a King-size Coke *is* a meal.

There are, I think, two complementary influences at work, both of which detract from the literalness of the linguistic analogy, as it concerns the treating of sequential orderliness in meals as parallel to syntax. One is aesthetic. A Burgundian dinner is nicer than a drug-store supper. A gastronome like Brillat-Savarin can explain why it is nicer in a convincing way. He proceeds in much the same way as a musicologist would proceed in explaining to us why a Mahler symphony is a greater work than a symphony by Brahms, that is his 'explanation' would be in part, a pedagogical exercise.

The other influence is more diffuse, but quite as important. Goffman has pointed out the importance of securing an untroubled setting for the mutual actions of social life.[13] Mere orderliness in the *Umwelt* is sufficient to reassure against the possibility of threat. The *mere* orderliness of a meal, the standardization of its sequencing, allows the accompanying social interaction to proceed unimpeded by doubts, fears of digestive upsets, or by social uncertainty, as dish follows dish in accordance with some recognized cuisine. The identification of this influence owes nothing to the specifically linguistic source of the syntactical analogy.

4

MEANING IN SOCIAL SCIENCE:
THE EXAMINATION
OF A POLYMORPHOUS CONCEPT

ANTICIPATORY SUMMARY

1. (a) Acts, actions and movements are not existentially distinct, but arise through the location of a core existent in distinct relational networks.
   (b) Saussure's theory offers a useful linguistic analogue
      (i) action-explication;
      (ii) act-explication;
   (c) Gricean conditions on meaning.
2. Commitment as meaning
   (a) Shared expectations follow on performances of acts.
   (b) Expectations as scenarios of the future:
      (i) formally defined scenarios: marriage;
      (ii) informally known scenarios: suicide.
3. Interpretations or hermeneutic explication
As Durkheim and others have pointed out, ceremonies and other significant social practices may not only involve the acts and scenarios for which they are ostensibly performed, but may also serve to represent and so remind the performers of various features of their social lives.
4. Incomplete understanding
Members may be adequate social performers without having a complete understanding of meaning at any level.
5. Natural meanings
Even ethologically derived gestures and grimaces are subject to convention as to their meaning.

1. ACTS, ACTIONS AND MOVEMENTS

The ultimate ground of the ethogenic programme in social science is the idea that social interaction is mediated by public performances which are treated by social actors as signs. They are operative through their meanings, that is *conventional* associations and not through their causal powers as physical objects in the material world, that is, not as 'natural signs'.

63

L. I. H. E.
THE BECK LIBRARY
WOOLTON ROAD. LIVERPOOL L16 8ND

My task is to give an account of meaning adequate to this general thesis about the mediation of social performance, and at the same time consonant with the conditions for the use of an analogue of syntactical analysis to reveal the structure of social episodes. The most crucial condition in this context is that we should be able to recognize elementary social actions. To achieve this we need criteria adequate to individuate and identify the components of social episodes relevant to their being interpretable as social act performances.

Attempting to carry out this task leads directly to a problem. According to what semantic theory should one attempt to explicate what is meant by treating social actions and acts as individuated and identified as 'meanings'? Contemporary semantic theories differ radically in their conception of the elementary semantic relation. In extensional theories the elementary or primary semantic relation obtains between a sign and a referent on condition that the sign and referent are distinct existences. This theory comes in two varieties depending upon whether one regards the relation to have been established baptismally, that is from sign to referent; or causally, that is from referent to sign. In intentional theories the elementary or primary semantic relation is a complex network in which a semantic element is defined by its location with respect to other semantic elements. Elements are related to the public world as experienced only as systems, referential relations being established as a secondary property of the sign system.

Empirical work in developmental psycho-linguistics — studies of how children acquire language — favours the latter theory, that in which the primary semantic relation is internal to the semantic system. I shall call these theories respectively the Harvard or *Tractatus* theory, and the Saussurean or *Investigations* theory.[1]

(a) Acts, Actions and Meanings

To decide which theory is the appropriate model for formulating a theory of 'social' meaning the relation between elements at the several levels of social analysis must be closely investigated.

Colloquially, one might be inclined to say:

(i) Actions are the meanings of Movements and Utterances;

(ii) Acts are the meanings of Actions;

in that at each level the left-hand element involves an interpretation or 'reading' of the right-hand element.

My proposal[2] is as follows:

(i) Movements, Actions and Acts are not to be treated as distinct existences.

(ii) Their distinctness derives from the embedding of the same neutral core existent in three distinct and irreducible relational systems, RS1, RS2, and RS3.

RS1: the core existent appears as uttered social pattern, bodily movement, and so on, when taken as embedded in a network of physical and physiological relations to other elements of the same sort; for example, an elbow as a bodily joint contacting a rib of another body.

RS2: the core existent appears as an action when taken as embedded in a relational network with other actions, the relations constituting conventional sequencings, conventional relations of sameness and difference, and so on, and particularly as related to actors having intentions, for instance a dig in the ribs.

RS3: the core existent appears as an act when taken as embedded in a relational network comprising a social world, that is persons, and the collectives in which they are constituted as persons, such as families, institutions and so on, and episodes that constitute, change and sustain that world. In this network the core existent of the example is read as 'a conventional indication that an apparently insulting remark is to be interpreted as non-denigrating to a friendship'.

On this view, though the networks of relations are distinct, their common node is not existentially distinguished by virtue of its embedding in distinct relational systems. This seems to rule out immediately either version of the Harvard theory of meaning as providing a framework for understanding how a movement, or uttered sound pattern, has social meaning. For example, since a saying and a speech act are not existentially distinct, it could not explain how a saying can be the doing of a speech act. Happily there are relational theories able to offer at least the main outlines for the understanding of the three-layered structure as a generator of meanings.[3]

Choosing a certain level of description brings one or another system of relationships into consideration. Changing the descriptive level does not change the world, but brings into focus different relational systems that are in the world. It is the presence of the core-existent that makes Davidson's idea of a co-reference under different descriptions empirically viable. But as an argument it does not establish the fact of causality between conceptual preparation and action. However, it does go to show that (i) intentions and actions are distinct existences; (ii) act/ action movement descriptions are descriptions of one and the same core existent, so that as far as securing reference is concerned the descriptive systems are equivalent. Whatever it is that is the core-existent in any of the three descriptive systems would be individuated under each. In each system a causal connection would have to be established by identifying a powerful particular and a shaping template. There is no *a priori* reason why these should be the same existent in the three systems of relations, that is, be the same core-existent under the three descriptive systems.

To establish causality we must ask why the conceptually connected descriptions appeared in the first place. The answer that they do so to mark the relationship between template properties and product properties is correct, and represents a necessary condition for a causal relationship to obtain. At least some of the identifying properties of the product should be produced from some antecedent feature of the conditions of production. Identifying a relevant powerful particular or agent completes the requirements for causality.

(b) The Saussurean Theory

Though the Fregerian theory of linguistic meaning would serve as well I propose to develop the idea of a social semantics by borrowing from the relational theory of Saussure. For the purposes of this study the key Saussurean analytical concepts are *valeur* and *signifié* since it is in terms of these that Saussure gives an account of what we could loosely term 'meaning in a language' (de Saussure, 1959).

Valeur (linguistic 'value') of an item is the location it has in a network of relations to other items which have *valeur* within the language. As Saussure defines *valeur* it is a composition of

 (i) 'dissimilar things that can be *exchanged* for the thing of which the value is to be determined';

 (ii) 'similar things that can be *compared* with the thing of which the value is to be determined'.

To represent *valeur* of an item, (*i*), one could construct a grid whose horizontal dimension consists of the syntagmata, structured linear sequences of lexical items in which (*i*) occurs, and whose vertical dimension consists of sets of contrasting items, either items which are similar in the sense that their substitution in the syntagmata would leave the meaning unchanged or dissimilar items whose substitution for (*i*) would change the meaning of the syntagmata.

In this way of representing Saussurean fields the dimensions are extensionally and non-generatively defined, that is as ordered sets of actual entities. The same structure could be represented generatively in terms of two intersecting rule systems. Sequencing or combinatorial rules, provided they include sub-categorial rules, generatively define the S-dimension, that is given a specific social setting, appropriate persons present and involved, the known and accepted rules generate the forms of the syntagmata. The P-dimension could be thought of generatively as a set of selection rules categorized by reference to situations, settings and personas to be presented, which generate the appropriate determinate item in the place in the sequence whose character as a determinable has been fixed by the sequencing rules. Situations and so on could themselves be replaced by higher order selection rules which select those rules to be brought to bear on a particular social occasion.

Signifié is not clearly defined in Saussure's surviving work. For the most part he speaks of the *signifié* of a sign as the concept associated with it. But in an important diagram he juxtaposes a pictorial representation of the sign as 'sound-image' plus concept, with a similar diagram blending concept and object. Whatever its exact determination it involved an external referent.

For Saussure the establishment of an external referent for a sign was contingent and arbitrary, concerned with how the sign would be applied rather than with the establishment of that sign as meaningful within a language. It might be established in a great many different ways, for example by reference to a theory of abstract objects or by experience of real things. There is no one primitive way of achieving signification.

The Saussurean approach links syntax (structure) and semantics (meaning) in an essential way. The syntagmatic dimension is essentially an extensional representation of the rules, knowledge of which would enable us to generate a potential infinity of well-formed sentences. These rules go beyond the rules of syntax proper to include the sub-categorial rules. The paradigmatic dimension is essentially an extensional representation of a lexicon, ordered by contrastive and associative principles, such as synonymy, antonymy, and by principles of phonological likeness and difference.

(i) Action-explication

Our social semantics will be based upon the proposal that actions can be individuated and identified with an analogue of a representation of *valeur*. Let us try to represent 'Please' and 'please'-phrases as social action elements. A plausible syntagm found during, say, an English children's tea-party would be:

Sees cake/'Please may I have a cake?'/Takes cake/
'Thanks'/Eats cake

All three of 'sees cake', 'takes cake', and 'eats cake' are performed not only as ingestive but as social actions, that is performed in a style proper to polite society. The item whose social meaning as action we are intent upon representing is 'Please may I have …?' The paradigmatic dimension includes such contrastive items as 'Do you think I could have?', 'interrogative eyebrows and half-smile with head cocked on one side'. This last item is included to illustrate the fact that in social interaction gestures and phrases sometimes have an equivalent social force. The phonological dimension includes 'Jeez, may I have …' (torn forth by the sheer munificence of the gastronomical offering), a hearing of the given speech which is excluded by hearing it as 'Please etc.'.

Finally, one should notice that the collapsed syntagm

Sees cake/Grabs cake/Eats cake

is barbarous in the strict meaning of that term, that is not social within the conventions of sociality of any society properly so considered since it omits the items by which the humanity of the provider of the feast is acknowledged and his concern for the guests recognized and ritually acknowledged. Action in that syntagm illustrates the perception of the feast as treasure trove.

Syntagma are individuated by reference respectively to time, place and current personas of the actors and social acts performed. Thus signification for the whole performance is ensured via act-interpretation.

(ii) Act-explication

But questions like, 'What does "Please" mean?', are not adequately answered by displaying a Saussurean grid. To complete an account, the significance of the saying of it as a social act must be described. I should like to argue that description of actions as acts draw upon folk theories of the social world and the place and possible relations of distinctive kinds of people in it.

In the Saussurean grid physically distinct behaviours or movements are collected into sets as 'ways of doing the same action' if they lie along one of the axes in the paradigmatic dimension. But the setting up of paradigmatic axes is dependent upon prior identification of syntagma as completed action-sequences. They are recognized as belonging to this or that social category with respect to the acts their performance is conventionally supposed to achieve. The conception of a social act depends upon a theory of sociality. For example, a ceremony (syntagm type) for incorporating a new member into a social group is intelligible as the performance of that act with respect to local conceptions of membership, members' ideas as to the nature of their group and perhaps with respect to a theory about how, in general, in that social milieu, the transition from non-membership to membership occurs. Consider for example the act of confirmation into the Anglican Church and the theory as to what occurs both *in* virtue and *by* virtue of the performance of the ceremony of the laying on of hands, and compare it with the ceremonies required to become a member of a Hell's Angel Troupe, or of the local lending library. In the latter case there is nothing corresponding to the descent of the Holy Spirit by virtue of the performance of the ceremony.

As a theory a description of act-significance would serve to introduce an isolated socially significant item since it would allow us to begin the construction of a grid based upon that theory and our existing understandings of other items. This introduces the other member of the Saussurean pair, *signifié*, since 'act' seems to be exactly the *signifié* of some social performance or practice.

Suppose we explain 'Please?' by the theory that we use it to obtain legitimate possession of something belonging to somebody else, that is to obtain a transfer of ownership agreed to by the original owner. The point can be illustrated with the case of a plate of cakes. Even though the cakes are intended for general consumption the effort or expense incurred in providing them for the company (free) can be acknowledged by behaving as if the provider owned them. This can be done by going through a change of ownership ritual or some fragment of it, for the case where the change is initiated by the non-possessor. This theory might even serve to explain the difficulty children seem to have in maintaining the 'Please?' and 'Thank you' rituals for such items as food provided in the family, since to treat the obtaining of this on a par with change of ownership seems bizarre.

The effect of acknowledging the underlying principle literally rather than symbolically can be catastrophic. The German students who insisted on paying their professor's wife for the drinks at a Sunday entertainment brought the Frau Professor to nervous prostration, so it is reported.

But most people competent in the use of 'Please' and 'Thank-you', of clenched fists, stabbing fingers, administration of oaths, insults and putdowns, consolation and the ritual expression of joy in another's success, do not *deploy* theories, such as the one sketched above, in the genesis of social action. Their deployment of their social resources in the cognitive preparation of action templates ought not, I believe, to be glossed as falling under the cognitive style, 'theorizing' and their resources thought of as theories. No doubt people do, from time to time, construct theories of this sort, and that they can do so is an important fact of human social life, the basis of accounting. It is significant though that, in general, theorizing of this sort is undertaken for the benefit of children and foreigners. If what people know is represented in a set of overlapping Saussurean grids, and if what they know makes up their cognitive resources, day-to-day practice seems more naturally looked upon as generated by cognitive processes of the style of rule-following, acting out of ingrained habit, and the like, where the act seems to be demanded by the situation as interpreted by the actor and all that is at issue is how properly to carry it out, that is what actions are required.

(c) Gricean Conditions on Meaning

I have emphasized that a social episode is a mutual product to which all those who are party must make their proper contributions at the socially correct place and time. This has nothing to do with whether the episode is 'nice' or 'nasty'; 'co-operative' or 'agonistic'. Lacking the detailed records we can only speculate on these matters but I would guess that social interchanges even between torturer and victim are conducted in an orderly well-defined way, and would not turn out to be any different in principle from the ways order is achieved as a day-to-day, minute-by-minute achievement, say on an outing of an old people's social club. Improvisation is the dominant mode of social interaction only in the opening and constructive phases of a social encounter. Pattern, convention and rule emerge even in the apparently most inhumane or most casual social surroundings. The tendency to identify co-ordinated social action with co-operative, altruistic action is a sentimentality and should be avoided.

Grice has proposed certain conditions by which meaning is established and sustained in a linguistic interaction with another person.[4] As is well known, they centre on an actor's beliefs about the interpretations of his intentions available to interactor. They can be summarized:

(i) The meaning of your action for me is what I believe you intend by it.

(ii) The meaning of your action for you is not only what you intend by it but what you believe I will believe you intend by it.

These are important social principles, in that (i) allows for misunderstanding, while (ii) allows for hypocrisy, deceit and tact.

If we take this not so much as a theory of meaning but as a statement of the conditions that have to be met for a social action to have a shared meaning, and to be effective by virtue of that shared meaning, the Gricean conditions fit nicely with the Saussurean account. If intentions are prefigurements of acts, qualified by a favourable attitude, rules the templates of action, and actions are understood via the syntagma of episodes as represented in our social knowledge, the items on the syntagmatic axis of the grid are the templates of action-sequences and hence must be none other than a representation of the conventional devices by which the content of intentions, that is social acts, are achieved. In so far as our Saussurean fields match we can be cognitively co-ordinated in such a way that in the course of our interaction Gricean conditions are continuously met. We *can* create a patterned episode of social life by human action. Of course we may fail, even in these favourable conditions, since there is no condition the satisfaction of which would render misunderstanding or hypocrisy impossible.

2. COMMITMENT AS MEANING

In this section I want to take up the question of the legitimacy of certain semi-colloquial uses of the word 'meaning' used as a common-sense gloss upon some further aspects of the social effects of action-sequences. The problem can best be approached through the perception of the importance of two forms of folk understanding of acts, as essential to their being effective in creating and maintaining the social world.

(a) Shared Expectations

Folk-understanding of the action-sequences locally required for the performance of an act is a feature we have already investigated fairly thoroughly. We have seen that this knowledge (it might be expressed in a local rule) is crucial to the understanding of how the content of an intention to perform a certain act is sufficiently specified to serve as a determinant of the form the appropriate action-sequence takes.

But there must also be folk-knowledge of the constraints upon the future that are generated by the performance of the act. For example, by concluding a contract, parties to the act commit themselves to a certain form of future action and are entitled to have expectations of each other. There is a colloquial use of the word 'meaning' for the specific determinations of the future consequent upon such acts. It occurs in such phrases as 'the meaning of marriage', 'the meaning of friendship'. I shall be arguing that in these phrases it is not the act but the social relations established in the performing of the act that are implied.

A beginning can be made by noticing that understanding an act involves grasping both the way the performance of an action-sequence changes the social world *and* certain consequences of the changes wrought by the performance understood as accomplishing a specific act. At first glance one might think that a simple reciprocity of understanding between the parties was all that was required for acts to have consequences. For example, unless you recognize my gesture as a dismissal, have I finally succeeded in dismissing you? It is clear, I think, that it is no part of the necessary conditions for my act to be socially potent or legally binding for you to have grasped its import. Nevertheless, it seems improper to say I have confirmed our friendship, if you do not understand my offer of a drink as having that import. On the other hand I could, I think, be said to have inadvertently insulted you and be called upon to apologize, even if I did not intend my action as an insult.

There seem to be three classes of cases: (i) those where your understanding the meaning of my actions is a necessary condition of the accomplishment of the act, for example in my confirming our friendship, (ii) those where such understanding is not required, for instance in my dismissing you, (iii) there are some cases where my intention in acting may be out-weighed by the conventional potency of the action as act. In such a case the public reading is dominant, as in the case of an inadvertent insult. Apology must be based on admitting the insult and emphasizing the inadvertence.

In explicating these cases one might be tempted to fall back on the account of meaning proposed by Grice and attempt an explanation of act as meaning in terms of your recognition of my intentions and my beliefs about your recognition of my intentions, and so on. Clearly, something of the sort must be part of the necessary conditions for some actions to be acts, since for my offer of a drink to be effective as confirmation of our friendship, it must be understood for what it is meant to be. There could not be a class of acts never intended but always understood. But that leaves what the action-sequence is meant to be, for instance a confirmation of friendship, unexplicated. Grice offers us, then, at best a necessary condition for an action-sequence to come off as an act. In order to understand how an act can be the meaning of an action-sequence, we must turn to another aspect of acts, that they have consequences.

Austin broached this matter in his distinction between perlocutionary and illocutionary forces, but left the matter unexplored. But he did see two points of importance: not every consequence of an action-sequence is relevant to its meaning as an act; the significance of the act has less to do with the actual consequences of the performance of a particular action-sequence than with the determination or limitation of possible consequences. An act, one might say, determines in advance the shape or form of a possible course of life for the parties to the act. But in real life such a course might never be realized. Thus the meaning of the act could not be taken to be a summary prediction of certain features of the future as the product of commitments acquired by the parties consequent upon the performance of the appropriate action-sequence, whose meaning it is, since the failure of the future to have those features would not show that the act had not had that meaning.

The effects of a ceremony can be distinguished into two categories. There are the social changes brought about by the completion of the ceremony; for example, the new relationship which exists between two families when a wedding takes place between a member of each. Then there is a category of effect which derives from what the members of the wedding understand as their commitments and take as their legitimate expectations having performed the ceremony. These effects one might call the determinations of a future form of life.

That these are genuinely different categories of effects is shown by the fact that they fail in different and distinct ways. If the ceremony is not adequately or fully performed, if the roles as defined in and for the ceremony are filled by persons who are disqualified in some way or another, then the social change does not occur. For example, it is impossible in England for someone who is already married to one man or woman to be wedded to another, no matter how seriously or fully he or she has taken part in the wedding ceremony. This failure is due to the fact that a married person is disqualified as an occupant of the ceremonial role of bride or bridegroom. On the other hand, what the law now calls 'the breakdown of marriage' is a failure of another sort. It is a failure to fulfil the commitments to a form of life, knowledge of which is implicit in the undertakings of those who take part in the ceremony. I will be arguing that each of these categories of effects serve to define a different aspect of meaning with respect to the marriage ceremony.

The justification of speaking of 'getting wed', as the meaning of the marriage ceremony, that is of the seriously and completely performed action-sequence, can be found in the category of effects which I have called social changes. The meaning of the ceremony in that sense *is* the set of social changes which its completion brings about, and in this sense the wedding as a social act is the meaning of the marriage ceremony. In Saussurean terms this is part of the *signifié* of the ceremony, an aspect of the act performed.

The propriety of speaking of the meaning of marriage, of the state which is a product of wedding, that is socially joining two people, derives, I propose, from the idea that explaining or glossing the socio-psychological effects of the ceremonial action-sequences is like defining the married state, perhaps in an ideal form. Performing an act has something in common with agreeing to a plan. But, unlike agreement to a plan, what is expected of the consequential lasting stage is a standardized and usually tacit part of local social knowledge. Just in case there is any doubt about the form the future state is supposed to take, in certain important act performances, a scenario is included, explicating the requirements. This, we we shall see, is an important component in the marriage ceremony. Marrying, then, as an act, sets in train the scenario by binding the partners to it as their scenario or strategic plan for the future. This act binds the future like strategic planning binds the future. In the case of two friends having a drink, the scenario tacitly included in the concept of friendship has a much less precise form in our culture, though Aristotle thought the details worth considerable discussion.[5]

To understand how an act has meaning in this sense, we must understand the way a strategic plan or scenario can control the form of the future.

(b) Expectation as Scenarios for the Future

Marriage ceremonies, that is weddings, affirmations of friendship, and the like, I have argued, are like acts of commitment to a strategic plan. The language once allowed 'rule' to be used for the scenario to which one committed oneself. The act of joining a religious order committed one, for example, to the Rule of St. Benedict. But the Rule of St. Benedict was much more like the scenario of family life included in the marriage ceremony than it was like, say, a rule of grammar. This becomes clear if we ask how closely the future is determined by the ceremony of introduction and incorporation of a stranger, a marriage, a farewell, or a friendly drink. Acts of this sort determine the future in a much less determinate way than a rule usually does. It is for this reason that I have called the anticipatory representation of the form of the future that goes along with an act, a 'scenario'.

I shall argue that though acts are not logically related to scenarios, (i.e. act-identity could be based upon the social bond produced despite change of scenarios) commission of the act entails agreement to a scenario in such a way that we may speak of *a* scenario as part of the meaning of the act. A scenario, I would argue, is part of the associative meaning of the act, following Lyons' terminology, and thus sufficiently strongly related to it to be adduced as part of the meaning.[6] One should notice, at this point, the way a word for an institution, regularly subject to qualitative assessment, tends to take on the sense of the good or proper form of the institution, as, for instance, when we speak of 'what marriage really means'.

I have already suggested that it is the scenario as represented in the social knowledge of each person that determines the future. It could be thought of as a structured template working in each of the parties like a rule or its equivalent works as a formal cause in the production of the structural properties of an action-sequence. This is in keeping with the claim central to the argument of this book, that the preponderant kind of causality at work in social life is the kind of causality by which preformed structures generate daughter structures. Preparation for social action involves, I believe, the creation and propagation of such preformed structures.

But in order to accomplish this I must show that acts do involve
scenarios, and that scenarios are structured objects meet to determine the form of the future.

A good rule in metasociology is to examine formal episodes
where there is explicit verbal representation of matters that are
tacit in other less formal episodes of social life, and then to utilize
the insight so derived to analyse interactive action-sequences
that have no formal representation. In this spirit I shall look
first of all at marriage to investigate act and scenario, and then try
to apply the same analytical framework to the attempt to make
sense of the idea that a suicide as the act accomplished or attempted in the course of the action of killing oneself, has an associated
scenario.

(i) Formally-defined scenarios: marriage
The marriage ceremony, as printed in the Prayer Book, includes
two distinct classes of prescriptions. There are rules which, if
followed, determine the action-sequence that makes it an instance
of a marriage ceremony, as, for instance, 'the woman shall answer
"I will"'. Other sentences spell out what I have suggested is
often called colloquially, but philsophically aptly, 'the meaning
of marriage'. For example, '... duly considering the causes for
which matrimony was ordained, ... it was ordained for the procreation of children to be brought up in the fear and nurture of
the Lord and to praise of His holy name ... it was ordained for
the mutual society, help and comfort that the one ought to have
of the other, both in prosperity and adversity'. And again, in the
oath of marriage, each is required to 'love, comfort, honour in
sickness and in health', to forsake all others, and to keep only
to the person one has married. As if this were not enough, the
solemnizing Minister has the option of preaching a sermon,
'declaring the duties of man and wife', or of reading excerpts
from St. Paul and St. Peter on the duties of husbands and wives.
For example, husbands are enjoined to 'love your wives and be
not bitter against them', and wives are advised 'not to adorn
themselves with gold, but with a meek and quiet spirit'.

This material, additional to the rules for the conduct of the
ceremony, represents, I believe, an attempt to make 'the meaning
of marriage' explicit and is a scenario in my sense.

(ii) Informally-known scenarios: suicide
Can we understand a dramatic but informal fragment of social

life along similar lines? Consider the case of suicide. In suicide the scenario is implicit, just as it is in an act which cements a friendship. A person performs a suicide as a structured action-sequence, according to the fairly strict conventions of the local ethnography. This action-sequence, if 'correctly' carried out, serves as the commission of the act, that which, through an associated scenario, determines the future. Provided that the death, or more commonly near-death, is interpreted as a suicide, the action-sequence as act, has potency. The interpretative process, as a gloss on a social 'text', has been carefully explored by Douglas[7] and Atkinson[8]. The person intent upon committing a suicide, and understanding its meaning in the local culture, sees the act as having consequences via the readings he or she confidently expects others to give to the death, seen as an act of suicide. Thus the person depends upon a belief in a shared interpretation of suicide involving a scenario of the future, including the actions and feelings of others. 'When they realize it's suicide they'll be sorry they treated me so badly; by their grief I will punish them, and so on.' So, for the poor soul driven to this extremity, it is essential that the action-sequence be interpreted as suicide. If we think along these lines, the 'note' is more properly interpreted as a label than a message, ensuring that the actions are given a 'correct' interpretation, that is, the interpretation under which, via the associated scenario, the form of the future is determined. This determination occurs because the others involved, knowing the meaning of suicide, have as part of their tacit knowledge, a representation of the very same scenario, drawn upon by the person committing the act.

3. INTERPRETATION OR HERMENEUTICAL EXPLICATION

The basic formulae of the analogy of social analysis to semantics in this chapter have been
   (a) actions are the meanings of behaviours and speeches;
   (b) acts are the meanings of actions;
   (c) commitments and expectations are the meanings of acts.
At each stage of the investigation of the sub-formulae we have seen that the point of introducing the notion of meaning as an explanatory concept has been the same. In each case it directs our attention to the fact that the items we are concerned with achieve their effects not through physical consequences but through conventional and other non-physical associations. In

short, their effects are cognitively mediated and culturally differentiated.

Of the three cases I have considered so far 1 and 2 are alike in
that the semantic entity is not a separate existent but a way of
speaking of a location in a relational structure. In 3, however, the
meaning of an act is a separate existent conventionally associated
with it. But commitments and expectations are not the only
existentially distinct entities conventionally associated with acts.
There is another category which I propose to call 'hermeneutical
meanings'.

Examples of this last sense of meaning can be found in the
Anglican Prayer Book in a discussion of the relationship between
marriage and the Church, and in the works of Durkheim, in
particular his theory of the way a social institution is represented
in or by a religious principle.

According to the Anglican Prayer Book the hermeneutical
meaning of marriage is given as follows: 'Matrimony ... signifying
unto us the mystical union that is between Christ and His Church
...' and 'the state of matrimony ... in it is signified and represented the spiritual marriage and unity betwixt Christ and His Church
...' The interpretative framework is carried further into the
continuous state of being married, by St. Paul in the Epistle to
the Ephesians, "Wives, submit yourselves unto your own husbands,
as unto the Lord. For the husband is the head of the wife even
as Christ is the head of the Church: and He is the Saviour of the
body. Therefore, as the Church is subject unto Christ, so let the
wives be to the husbands in everything.' It might be remarked
that in this last quotation St. Paul is not only carrying the interpretative framework further, but using it to give a particular
interpretation of the state of marriage.

Durkheim's conception of the way in which the principles
and rites of a religion are to be interpreted as representing social
facts has been elegantly summed up by Lukes.[9]

(i) Religion represents 'society and social relationships in a
    cognitive sense, to the mind or intellect'.
(ii) Religion represents in 'the sense of expressing, symbolizing,
    or dramatizing social relationships'.

I take Lukes to be saying that Durkheim claims that the religious
stories and practices of a society are to be interpreted both as a
literal representation of social relations and as a symbolic or
expressive representation. So that a Durkheimean hermeneutical
analysis would operate at two levels, the one literal and the

other metaphorical.

Be that as it may, a general definition of hermeneutical meaning can be given in the following principle:

> If the relation which obtains between signifier and signified is representation, then the signifier has hermeneutical meaning.

But since representation is a relation based upon real likenesses and differences, it is part of the theory of natural signs and not analogous to linguistic meaning which must be arbitrary in Saussure's sense. At this point the notion of meaning has diverged so far from linguistic meaning that its investigation converges on the territory of literary criticism and its further discussion would carry me beyond the limits of this work.

4. INCOMPLETE UNDERSTANDING

At the heart of the theory of meaning I am proposing is the open character of the quasi-Saussurean grid which represents our grasp of a socially significant item as having a distinct *valeur* or value as a sign. Knowing *valeur* alone we could learn to place the sign correctly in a formalistic kind of way in stretches of social life in which we could recognize sufficiently similar structures to those which we have experienced before. But the approval or disapproval or the 'not noticing' by the others involved would enable us to amplify our knowledge at the action level, by extending the axes of our Saussurean grid in the syntagmatic and paradigmatic directions.

Equally, since our grasp of the act-significance of an action is dependent on the sophistication of our theory of our social world and what is required of those who live in it, we may have only a very simplistic or superficial idea of what is or ought to be going on. For example I may not have grasped the ritual character of much professions of friendship, and be surprised to find that the relationship had been struck up and maintained by the other for some advantage. Again, as I come to understand such matters my theoretical grasp of social practices is amplified.

Though the ideal of perfect social knowledge is unrealizable, even for an ethogenically oriented and industrious machiavellian, we can nevertheless have the idea of a disparity between what I do know and recognize as socially distinct, and what I might know in similar circumstances. On the theory expounded in this chapter we can have an idea of how individual social knowledge might grow. One might argue that Weber's idea of *verstehen*, understanding of the intentions of others, could be explained in terms of what one must know to grasp the act/action character of some performance. On this view, *verstehen* as a progressively refinable understanding of the social meanings (and thereby of the intentions and projects of the actors) would be immune to the complaint that understanding has to be a single, unitary act. On the contrary, while degrees of partial understanding could be identified in terms of Saussurean value-grids and folk-theories of the social force of actions their essential incompleteness entails the indefinite improvability of any insight into social life.

Natural Meanings

My argument so far has taken no account of the possibility of natural meanings, indeed I have gone to some trouble to emphasize that the relation between social sign and social significance is conventional. This emphasis has been a consequence of the insight that the means of social action are culturally specific, even though they may be used in the performance of social acts that are found necessary by all tribes and associations of men in the conduct of their lives.

We need to distinguish between the meaning of say, a smile, as it is an outward and public sign of an inner and personal event or state, such as being amused or glad about something, or perhaps just the mark of contentment; from its meaning as a social sign. A smile seems to be a way of approving, a frown of disapproving of something. But the formulation 'A smile is an expression of approval' is seriously misleading, I would argue, since it suggests that approval is an inner state like contentment, rather than a social act like consent. Sometimes, of course, 'approval' is used to speak of the personal state of approving, but more importantly a smile is the action for performing the public act of approval. But a smile might convey a threat, a warning, a triumph, and many, many other acts depending on its location in an action-sequence, and on whose lips it forms.

What then of the idea of the natural meaning of a smile?[10] At best perhaps we might notice a general and rather weak connection of this grimace with being pleased and amused. But just as 'Spots mean he's got measles' is an incorrigible but shallow truth if that is all one means by 'measles', so 'He's smiling so he's happy' may be equally incorrigible and similarly banal. But just as the concept of measles includes hypotheses as to the cause of the spots, so in most cases concepts such as 'happy', 'content' and so on, include the personal state of the smiler. And this allows for the possibility that the smile may be assumed, ironic, subject to an inversion of meaning, and so on. If there are natural meanings one would not be advised to rely on them. There is a parallel with the way one can be misled by grammatical form — but the literal meaning of a speech is to its social meaning, as the natural meaning of a smile is to its social significance, the action by which we perform this or that social act.

5

PEOPLE IN GROUPS

ANTICIPATORY SUMMARY

Introduction: Are institutions, societies and so on supra-individuals of novel types having novel causal powers and epiphenomenal properties and in interaction with one another; or are they secondary or dependent entities, and is causality in social matters exerted through the interactions of individuals?

1. Individuals and collectives

    (a) Macro-individual theory (Hobbes, Durkheim, etc.) based upon the model of organism and organs; that is the institution or other collective is a subject of predication of emergent properties, indeed it necessarily has macro-properties since some are required for it to be individuated as such.

    (b) Relational network theory (Marx, Bhaskar, etc.). Collectives are not individuals of novel categories:

        (i) groups do not condense into supra-individuals;

        (ii) hence contingent whether there are any macro-properties, say patterns in the flux of intended and unintended consequences through the network of personal relations.

    (c) Tolstoy's theory. Structure is an artefact imposed upon a real disorder in subsequent accounts, given for expressive purposes. If there are macro-patterns they must be exceedingly simple, e.g. migrations.

    (d) The distinctions that differentiate individual from collective properties:

        (i) from individuals to collectives;

        (ii) from collectives to individuals.

    (e) The genesis of structural properties as collective and as individual properties:

        (i) assemblage;

        (ii) transformation and replication.

2. General theory of institutions: two systems of elements, social practices and people.

    (a) With people as elements, one must distinguish:

(i) personal identity — the individuality of a single human being;

(ii) social identity — the person-type or role-place occupied as of right and constitutively by that person (cf. Hollis, *Models of Man*).

(b) Institutions can now be defined as relational structures (actual and latent) which persist through changes of elements with individual difference but social identity at the nodes, but change or perish if change of elements with social identity.

Example: continuity: the King is dead, long live the King.

discontinuity: the King is deposed, viva the President of the People's Revolutionary Council.

(c) Institutions are marked by the existence of dual rhetorics, official and unofficial, both of which are necessary to a complete description of social practices.

(d) The reality of institutions: over and above the practices of people, the relations are generated from the natures of individuals which are part produced by their relational connections in institutions. Knowledge and skills required to reproduce the relational system never perfectly replicated (cf. Silverman, *Organizational Work*).

Role-theory, as the theory of internal relations between people as embodiments of social identities cannot serve as a comprehensive theory of human behaviour in and with respect to institutions. It is continuously modified by expressive aims and activities of the individuals which occupy role-positions. E.g. Nixon wanted not just to be 'The President' but to be 'Nixon, The Great President'. This forces us to consider personal as well as social identity in social analysis.

INTRODUCTION

The longest running, and perhaps the deepest philosophical issue in the theory of the social sciences has to do with the metaphysics of the groups in which human beings associate. The many discussions and controversies can, I think, be simplified and condensed into two issues:

(a) Do groups of human beings in interaction with one another have properties which are different in any causally significant way from the aggregate of the properties of the individuals and their interactions one with another? We notice, of course, that one individual can influence all the others in his group, for instance by putting poison in their water supply, or by sending each of them a copy of a pamphlet setting out his views on some matter (which need not be of common concern). But these are mere aggregates of individual influences. The question could be answered shortly and sharply if it could be shown that the groups had no properties of any kind other than aggregates of individual properties. Some groups of things, particularly structured groups such as structures of cells as organs and structures of organs as organisms clearly do have emergent properties – a person's capacity to think is not the aggregate of the thinking capacities of each of his cells, nor indeed is his capacity to run. It is looking to this kind of analogue for the relation between men and their groups that has been one historically potent source for the idea that societies as human collectives have emergent properties.

(b) Do groups of men formed as collectives have the status of supra-individuals? Do they have some of the metaphysical properties of individuals, such as continuity and identity through time? Are there criteria by which they can be individuated one from another and so on? It seems obvious that some forms of human groupings are supra-individuals. Armies and other military formations when they are in the field, teams on tour, seem to display individualistic properties. But would it be right to attribute the same kind of supra-individuality to nations, to a work force, to a bureaucracy or to other such associations, even though grammar points directly to it?

In this chapter I shall be trying to steer a course between the extremes in the classical arguments – and to forge a plausible account of men in structured groups from a judicious blending of half-truths culled from the works of each party to the dispute.

The problem is set by the need to develop suitable notions of individual and of collective which can be fitted together into a unified conceptual system adequate to control the analysis of human groups and associations. Any discussion of this perennial problem area must take account of the existence of two extreme metaphysical positions. According to one view there are no individuals, except in a bare spatiotemporal sense. There are only intersection-points of relational properties of collectives. According to the other view there are no collectives, only aggregates, that is only unstructured accidental assemblages of men. A subtle new form of this doctrine has recently been proposed by Popper,[1] that knowledge of collectives is reduceable to knowledge of individuals and their properties. Each extreme theory will be examined and will be found wanting.

1. THE METAPHYSICS OF GROUPS

(a) Individual and Collective

The extreme collectivist position holds that each human being is wholly constituted as a social person by the collective properties he or she participates in as a member of the society. These collective properties are not themselves constituted of individual properties but rather are the very structural properties which are the basis of the properties of the collective. So, by a double transition from the claim that an individual is constituted by his relations to other members of his collective, and that those relations are the structural properties of the collective itself, the individual as a social being is reduced to an entity wholly defined in terms of the properties of the collective.

(i) The failure of collectivism
There are a variety of reasons for rejecting an extreme form of the collectivist theory of humans in association.

Such a theory effectively denies any autonomy or creativity to an individual. This denial can be taken in two quite distinct ways.

(a) It could be taken as an empirical observation. But there is an observable autonomy and creativity shown by individual human beings, so that the collectivist thesis in this form is simply wrong.

(b) However, this apparent contrary fact could be accommodated by a politico-moral reading of the collectivist theory. The phenomena I have just called 'autonomy' and 'creativity' are more properly to be called 'deviance'. In consequence an individual who has characteristics which are not reduceable to the properties which he possesses by virtue of his membership of the collective is, for that reason, a distorted or defective person. It follows, if one accepts this point of view, that remedial action, political, psychological, or otherwise, can be taken to restore the defect in the individual, making him once more a perfect member of his collective. The reasoning is fairly simple. If the collectivist theory is true, an individual who shows deviant properties is an imperfect representation of the ideal member of the collective. Hence, by the definition of a person as one fulfilling the demands of the relational intersection theory of people in collectives, such a deviant individual is not truly a person. Hence it is proper to reconstitute or even, in the extreme, to eliminate him. It is clear that arguments against extreme collectivism cannot be based simply upon the empirical fact that deviant individuals exist. An argument would have to be constructed on the basis of a valuation of autonomous and creative individuals with respect to the higher development of the collective itself in such a way as to undermine the argument that all non-standard individuals are deviant. Such an argument can, indeed, be formulated. As I shall show, the only truly radical theory of social change requires that change proceed through the differential selection of new social practices and institutions created by non-standard individuals within their collectives. Only in this way can the collective evolve to a higher form. In short, the extreme collectivist thesis is essentially conservative.

It sometimes happens that the society may be convinced of its perfection and consequently may wish to maintain itself in the state in which it presently finds itself. Such a belief in the actual perfection of an existing society is likely to be associated with an extreme collectivist theory and consequently with recognizable institutionalized practices for defining non-standard individuals as deviant, sick, mad and so on. The argument moves from a sociological to a moral plane.[2]

(ii) The failure of individualism

The extreme individualist thesis, that is the theory that each individual is wholly autonomous and could exist as a person wholly independent of the collectives to which he belongs, is a reflection of the theory that the relations which a person has to his collectives are wholly external, and consequently quite contingent. This theory too cannot be effectively sustained. Again, the reasons for repudiating an extreme individualism are partly empirical and partly moral in character.

(a) It is fairly easy to show, simply by drawing attention to uncontroversial facts available to anyone, that many properties characteristic of fully developed human beings are dependent upon that person being a member of a collective. For example, I think it would be readily conceded that for any anthropoid to be properly considered a person, he must be not only capable of the use of language but actually to use it in his day-to-day social activity and in his cognitive and reflective life. I think it is also indisputable that there could not be a language-user who was not a member of a language community.

(b) Political and moral arguments against individualism are a little more difficult to formulate than those against collectivism since they have to do with the basis of responsibility to others. I would take it to be part of the necessary conditions for an anthropoid to be a person that he recognized himself as responsible to and for others in his daily life. The second component of that condition — namely responsibility *for* others — is clearly an empirically grounded necessary condition since it is an essential feature of anthropoid parenthood that the caretaking individual should be responsible for the helpless infant. However, one could imagine an anthropoid race in which that relation did not obtain. Once again as in the critique of collectivism, one could maintain that an extreme moral individualism was in itself a self-contradictory principle since it would be impossible for an individual to attain true moral stature if it were not attained through the exercise of responsibility to and for others. According to this line of thought the very idea of a person is bound up with the possibility of that person taking moral action. This itself is bound up with the idea of action in the interests not only of oneself but of others. And this is a collectivist conception.[3]

(b) Relational Theories[4]

The distinction between internal and external relations

The distinction drawn in the last section between extreme collectivism and extreme individualism could have been based on the distinction between internal and external relations amongst individuals, introduced in a general way in the chapter on structure. In order to make the individualist-collectivist distinction clearer it will be necessary to elaborate on the theory of relations.

Two or more individuals are internally related in case they are wholly or partly constituted as beings of a type by virtue of standing in that relation. A relation is absolutely internal if the individuals are wholly constituted by virtue of standing in those relations. For example, a person is wholly constituted as a member of the type 'husband' by virtue of standing in the sociolegal relation of marriage with another person. It is not possible for a husband to be unmarried. Should a person by some misfortune lose the other member of the relation which is constituent of husbandhood, he becomes a member of a socially different type — for example 'widower'. The relation of 'being married' is absolutely internal to and thus exhausts the meaning of 'husband' together with its correlative 'wife'.

There are subtleties with respect to the level of categorial organization within which we are considering the members of a type. For example, when we are considering human beings for social or psychological purposes the spatio-temporal relations which individuate them as material objects are not amongst the category-generating relations. Nevertheless these play a role as

necessary conditions for the coming into existence of those
relations which do make human individuals persons of this sort or
that. For most social categories a person is already taken to be in
existence as a spatio-temporal enduring entity. We are considering
him or her as coming into other kinds of relations, while maintaining basic individuating relations to space-time and the material
system of which space-time is a property. However, the issue of
spatio-temporal relations is not entirely irrelevant to the constitution of a human being as a social person, in that birth and
death, which commonly result from convergence and dispersal
of material, are important markers in a social career.

A relation is external in case the individuals so related do not
change their category or type when they cease to stand in that
relation. The relation is absolutely external if the individuals
related by it are not changed at all by virtue of coming to stand
or ceasing to stand in that relation. For most purposes we can
regard persons as beings for which spatio-temporal relations are
external. Spatial and temporal propinquity and contemporanaeity
are involved in people finding themselves within the same nation-
state or living in the same epoch but clearly the spatio-temporal
relations are germane only in so far as they involve distinctive
social conditions. I shall be assuming that there are almost no
external social relations.

If we refer back now to the considerations advanced in the
previous section concerning the individualist and collectivist
points of view, it is apparent that these points of view are ultimately dependent on the distinction between internal and external relations. It follows therefore that neither of the extreme
positions are tenable. The fact that most social relations are
internal however suggests that the final position that one is led
to by reflection on the problems of balancing individual and
collectivist concepts must be more collectivist than individualist.

(c) Tolstoy's Theory of Human Collectives

Our investigation of the characteristics of human collectives can
begin with the theory proposed by Tolstoy in the sociological
parts of *War and Peace*.[5] His theory is formulated in terms of
the kind of properties that collectives might have. According to
his theory, the only orderly collective properties of a mass of
mankind are of a very large scale, temporally and spatially, and
partly as a consequence of that, very simple. His favourite example
of a genuine collective property is migration, particularly the ebb

and flow of people from west to east and east to west across the European continent.

In contrast, groups of people in social interaction on a smaller scale have no properties which are not imposed upon them by the human imagination, that is smaller groups are not collectives at all. They have no properties. Small groups of human beings engage in activities which are strictly inchoate. For example, the battles that were fought between the Russians and the French in the time of Napoleon are not structured events having collective properties, but chaotic and disorderly whirlpools in the tide of migration. However, according to Tolstoy, human beings are quite unable to accept that the events in which they feel themselves to have taken part are strictly disorderly and inchoate. In consequence they undertake an active, interpretative process in the course of which these events and the masses of men involved in them are represented as orderly and controlled. There may even come into existence a special profession, the profession of historian, whose task it is to create these orderly interpretations in which collectives are generated out of nothing but chaotic aggregates.

It is as an exemplification of this theory that the Battle of Borodino forms the centre-piece of Tolstoy's great novel, since it is both an illustration of the theory and a microcosm of human affairs. Neither Napoleon or Kutuzov were really in command of the men who took part in the battle. The fighting was joined by accident and the result was a victory for neither side if the events are viewed dispassionately. Yet, as Tolstoy shows, historians from both sides had reconstructed the 'reality' of what happened at Borodino so as to contrast the tactical genius of Napoleon with the strategic mastery of Kutuzov and to represent the happenings on the day of the battle as having properties that endowed them with an existence as a collective, an orderly assemblage of men and events.

However attractive this theory may be, it makes too extreme a case. One obvious difficulty is posed by the possibility of intermediate cases which are neither as grand as national migration nor as short-lived and small-scale as battles. For example, those organizations and social practices of men we ordinarily call institutions seem to be both orderly in fact, and created and sustained in being by human interpretative activites and normative prescriptions.

Deeply embedded in Tolstoy's theory of collectives and their properties is a theory about the causes of social events. For him large-scale human phenomena have causes, small-scale human phenomena happen by accident. Only later, as a deliberate act of interpretation are they redefined so that they can be thought of as caused. But this development of the theory opens up the possibility of the question, 'How are the large-scale collective properties of masses of men caused?' One solution might be to claim that, strictly speaking, the collective properties are not caused at all, but are the aggregate of activities of individuals as, for example, a tribe migrates to the west because each member goes to the west. And this 'because' is not the 'because' of causation. The statement becomes 'the tribe migrates to the west means "each member goes to the west"'. This solution is inadequate since it does not at all follow that if each member goes to the west the tribe goes to the west. For the tribe to go to the west its organization, its internal structure, social practices, its representations of its own history, its language, must go with it, whatever may be the account of those collective properties given by members of the tribe. It would be absurd to claim that because the slaves from the Dahomey were moved to the West Indies and the United States, so were their tribes.

(d) Individual and Collective Properties in a Relational Theory

It may be possible to make a successful distinction between individuals and collectives by attacking the problem of their differentiation indirectly. Distinctions might be able to be drawn between the kinds of properties characteristic of collectives and those characteristic of individuals. Individuals and collectives could then be distinguished through the conditions they must satisfy for each to be able to accept its appropriate range of attributes. However, it should be noticed at the outset that the distinction between collectives and individuals is a relative distinction. An individual considered with respect to one kind of collective may be able to be treated as a collective with respect to another kind of individual. Similarly entities which are to be considered collectives with respect to a certain category of individuals may themselves be individuals with respect to some category of superordinate collectives. It may be the distinction between collective and individual properties must also be relativized to the kind of entity to which they are attributed. For example, though 'tall' is a non-collective property of a person, it might arguably be treated as a collective property of an assemblage of limbs or bones. It would be analysable as a relational attribute of the collection as collective.

So it seems that a circle of differentiations links the collective/individual distinction as conceived ontologically with the empirical distinctions we might draw between properties appropriate to collectives as against those attributable to individuals, with respect to some given level of analysis. Such a circle is not vicious since it could be broken anywhere and the pragmatic advantages of the distinction—drawing at that point displayed or demonstrated: "Take 'it' to 'bits' before you fix 'it'" for example.

(i) From individuals to collectives

One way of distinguishing collective from individual properties might be to propose that collective properties are structural pro-perties — that is, they are based upon, but not reduceable to, relations between more than one individual. Not all relational properties are collective properties. For a relational property to be a collective property it must be that two or more individuals, standing in that relation or relations, constitute a superordinate individual, the collective. One way in which this more stringent condition might be achieved is to require that at least one of the relations in which the elements of the collective stand should be invariant under a wide range of transformations. For example, if the relation between two elements is a distance, then if that distance is invariant under translation and rotation of the pair of elements, we might with reason take that pair to be a simple collective; that is the pair behave in certain respects as an indivi-dual. Examples of more interesting structural properties, on the basis of which a set of elements might be thought to be a collec-tive, would be, for example, an order of battle defined in terms of spatial relations between the units of an army in which order rather than absolute distance was held invariant; or a power hierarchy, based on asymmetrical relations of obedience, decision, the giving of respect and deference, the showing of condescension, etc., among a fixed group of people. It is clear that in both these cases certain invariants have to be maintained for the collective constituted by these relational properties to be maintained. For example, certain geometrical relations must continue to obtain between the units of the army. Should they break down the army ceases to exist and a new collective, which perhaps ought more properly to be called an aggregate — in some circumstances it might be called a rabble — could come into existence, and the battle — an event collective — be transformed into a rout. Similarly, a power hierarchy constitutes an institution just so long as asymmetrical relations remain invariant over time and over the conditions of the life of the people who make up its elements.

For many collectives the internal structure — the kind of property to which I have been drawing attention so far — is not in general perceptible as such, when the collective is viewed as an individual. Many structural properties appear as simple qualities, often in a different sensory mode, when a collective is perceived as an individual. In general, secondary qualities are related to structural properties of an individual considered as a collective of elements in this way. For example, a melody is an epiphenomenal or secondary quality of the time and pitch structure of a collective of individual notes; a colour is an epiphenomenal quality of a particular orderly arrangement of the components of molecules, and so on.

There are endowments from the endo-collective, that is the internal structure of the relatively elementary parts of the individual, to that individual. For example, many of the properties we are accustomed to call 'powers' are such endowments. For example, the valency of a chemical atom is a power which it has by virtue of the structural properties of the endo-collective, that is the structured set of individual microparticles which make it up. Many human powers too we regard as endowments from structural properties of the nervous system or some other part of the anatomy.

It is worth remarking that for a structural property to be manifested as an epiphenomenal property — that is as a property of the collective considered as an individual — there must be something on which that collective has an effect. An obvious example is the effect the collective has on an observer by virtue of the possession of that structure, but we might equally well be inclined to use the concepts I have just sketched to understand the effect of a collective considered as an individual on some other collective, which is not itself sentient, as for example, the magnetic field of a bar magnet has an effect on the iron filings strewn on a piece of glass.

(ii) From collectives to individuals
Many important properties of individuals are endowments to an individual from the exo-collective — that is the external structure

within which an individual is an element. For example, according to Mach's theory, the mass of an individual material body in the material universe is an endowment from the exo-collective to that individual by virtue of the relations in which that individual stands to the collective. To take up an example I have already discussed briefly, social role as attributed to an individual member of an institution could be regarded as an endowment to that individual from the institution — that is the exo-collective — by virtue of his relations to that collective.

It is not without significance that most of the examples I have chosen to illustrate the points I want to make about the way collective properties exist have been made with examples chosen from the material world and from the physical sciences. This raises the question of whether there are any socially epiphenomenal properties, that is structural properties of collectives which are experienced as, or could be treated as, simple properties in another mode from those in which they exist as relations in the collective. I think it is not unreasonable to suggest that role is just such a property, since for many people role is experienced, not as a relational property in which the individual stands to the collectives of which he or she forms a member, but rather as a systematic set of psychological and microsocial imperatives and constraints. The relational property is experienced as an individual property, perhaps because the individual receives this endowment from the exo-collective by a long process of learning and conditioning. However, the properties of the exo-collective — for example institutions or even societies — which are not represented in individual consciousness in such a way as role might be thought to be represented, are not in general experienced at all. If we know about them at all it is only by round-about and frequently dubious macrosociological methods whose epistemology, as it is at present constituted, has been much called in question: in particular the usual methods for generating 'data' by giving standard questionnaires to each member of an exo-collective, and from some totalization of their replies hypothesizing properties of the collective.[6] Even official statistics are highly suspect, for they are often constructed for some practical purpose, quite distinct from truth.[7]

(e) The Genesis of Structural Properties

The next step in an analysis of the way in which collectives and individuals differ will be to look at the methods by which structural properties, which we have seen to be characteristic of collectives, are generated. We can now apply the distinction between the three kinds of structure genesis developed in the general theory of structure.

(i) Assemblage
An aggregate of individuals can become a collective, that is have an overall invariant structure, deriving from individual properties of the members making up the collective, which constrain their ways of fitting together. For example, the overall structure of a crystal is thought to be the result of the constraints which the structures of individual atoms exert on the assemblage of myriads of atomic units which go to make it up. Assemblage as a mode of structuring would be a natural way of looking at the genesis of some of the properties which very large-scale collectives of human beings might have. For example there are structures which are thought to form patterns of unintended consequences.

(ii) Transformation and replication
The structural properties of a collective could be produced by the coming together of material to form the collective on some pre-existing template. This can occur, in principle, in two different ways. The template may be incorporated into the product so that though it exists before the product structure is generated, after the product has formed the template is no longer an independent existent. An example of such a process might be that by which the armature of a statue is incorporated in the final product. The armature serves as a template of the final overall form but has become part of the finished statue. Alternatively, the template may continue to exist after the product has been 'peeled off' it. In die-stamping of metal, the die as template is responsible for the structure of the product but die and product remain distinct existences after the process of replication is complete.

Both transformation and replication can be found in the social world. Transformation: In some African states a single family occupies all the official positions. In some cases relationships defined in the family are transformed into relationships between the offices of state. Replication of an ironic and sometimes tragic sort sometimes happens when a radical party, in order to win a revolutionary war, has to adopt the organization of the very social order which it originally set out to combat.

Another kind of replication occurs when the structure of the collective is produced by a projection from some small-scale model, or plan, which is composed of the same kind of elements. For example, in time of war the professional army may be expanded to become a volunteer, or perhaps conscript army, many times its size and many times more complicated, but preserving the same chains of command and the same strategic organization.

In applying these ideas to the understanding of social collectives we must look for the social templates from which social structure is produced, and at the same time propose an empirically testable and plausible causal process by which that production might occur. But a residual question remains to be answered. How are the templates for replication produced, and if they are replicas of earlier templates how do templates come into existence in the first place? A template is a structured object and as such must be some kind of collective, with relational structure among its elements, incorporating one or more invariants. Either the template is produced by another template (Replication) or it is produced by some process of assemblage from elements whose individual properties limit the kind of structures they can form. As far as social explanation goes the regress of templates can be continued for some time. For example historians trace the structure of the modern European state from the structure of the medieval state by successive imperfect replications of action structures. But an historical sociology and social psychology can be called upon eventually to give some kind of account of how the first template came to be. Theoretically a chain of replication could be broken only by a first template generated by assemblage. But of course assumptions of evolutionary gradualism would count against the hypothesis of a first or primal template.

The most famous example of replication relationship between one social collective and another is Marx's theory of the social formation. He believed the apparent social order to be a structural reflection of the social order concealed in the basic economic organization. This would seem to require a hypothesis of some form of replication. But which? In the absence of any plausible causal theory, we can only speculate on what Marx himself would have offered by way of an account had he expressed his theory in these terms. However, it seems clear that the relationship is not as likely to be one of replication as projection since if a social formation is generated according to an ideology, and the ideology is itself a partly false picture of the economic base (on Marx's theory it must be an inaccurate or misleading picture), then the ideology cannot serve as a causal mediator between base and superstructure if the superstructure is supposed to accurately replicate the structural properties of the economic system which forms the base. This difficulty is not resolved by turning to the idea of replication as transformation since it seems very unlikely that Marx would have been prepared to accept the proposal that the structure of the economic system itself is taken up into and becomes the structure of the whole social formation. Indeed, he was very much concerned to distinguish both ontologically and socially between these two aspects of a modern industrial society. These difficulties are really reflections of a deeper difficulty which permeates Marx's whole social thought, namely the problems that it poses for us by the striking absence of a plausible social psychology. However, in a later chapter I shall make some suggestions as to how it might be possible to salvage Marx's insight that the methods of production, distribution and exchange play an important role in the way social formations come to be while avoiding the difficulties of supposing that there is any direct causal relation between them.

2. THE GENERAL THEORY OF INSTITUTIONS [8]

The study of institutions seems to me to have been the most satisfactory form of social investigation to have yet been undertaken if we consider only institutions of a reasonably small size. Goffman's *Asylums*[9] and Hargreave's study of the social structure of the secondary school[10] are models of good work. Studies of such larger scale matters as the alleged social class system or the gross economic organization strike me as very much less satisfactory. We shall come to see some necessity in the relation between the largeness of scale and the weakness of the method of study, as we proceed.

How then in the light of the best work are we to see an institution, such as a shop, a school, a local police force, or a football supporters' club? The first point to notice is that an institution is a double relational network of social practices and of people. A Post Office contains sellings of stamps, frankings and sortings of letters, throwings of parcels, brewings of tea; and postmen and postwomen. Each aspect can be looked at separately to observe how the action units are interrelated and how the people-units form structured groups, but must then be combined. They cannot be combined arbitrarily by mere conjunction since some activities are open only to some kinds of people. And these kinds are not usually identifiable in any other way than by convention. A sorter is 'really' no different from a loader, *sub specie humanitas*, yet the difference between them in the Post Office goes far beyond merely loading and sorting, and woe betide the office where one of either kind does the work of the other!

To keep all this clear we need a distinction between personal identity, the basis of the individuality and uniqueness of existence of a single human being, and social identity, the type, kind or category of person he appears to be, or the type of role he occupies or the kind of job he does.[11] A single individual can occupy different posts and enjoy different social identities, while the same post can be occupied by different individuals. But could we simply ignore the transposition of individuals, since after all one might argue, what counts socially is what they do as fulfilling these roles? Of course different people may perform more or less well in certain roles but that seems a trivial point. There is, however, a deep reason why we cannot ignore personal identity and difference.

Role-theory, as the theory of internal relations between people as embodiments of social identities, cannot serve as a comprehensive theory of the behaviour of people in and with respect to institutions, since it is continuously modified by the *expressive* aims and activities of the individuals which occupy role-positions.[12] Richard Nixon did not just want to be President but to be Nixon-the-Great-President; to stamp the office with the mark of the man. Since expressive aims and activities may have a profound effect on the institution, a sound social science must concern itself with personal identity – manifested in the personal stamp placed by some people in the expressive aspect of social life.

We are now in a position to deal with the problem of the criteria for the identity of institutions. These will become important in later discussion when we consider the background of stabilities against which judgements of change would have to be made. An institution was defined as an interlocking double-structure of persons-as-role-holders or office-bearers and the like, and of social practices involving both expressive and practical aims and outcomes. It is not at all easy to define the boundaries of an insttitution in any general way. In many, the roles and role-holders are limited in number, by criteria of qualification or in some other way. In most there is a subclass of social practices that purport to be the activities by which the official theory of 'the' institution is fulfilled. Thus as an institution a hospital cannot be delimited by identifying sick people and those who purport to cure them, since this would include too much. Nor can it be identified by reference to curative practices of a certain intensive, externally administered kind, since this would include too little of what goes on. Sometimes a set of buildings or physical plant can define a geographical setting within which are accom- plished the practices constitutive of the institution. But this mode of demarcation would be inappropriate to many institutions which are not located in particular places. Instead let us shift to an empirical criterion, differently specified for each institution, namely where people constitutive of the institution would draw its bounds. No doubt different categories of members would draw it differently, and locate its 'centre of gravity' in diverse places, but not so differently and not so diversely as to give the impression of total chaos.

It is worth noticing that institutional continuity does not require identity of social practices. For example the City Guilds of London have completely abandoned their practical activities as cloth workers, silver smiths and so on and retained only the expressive practices and moral careers that go with them. Continuity of office and partial but overlapping short-term continuity of practices is sufficient. Thus the continuity of the monarchy through discontinuity of the monarchs is defined in the formula 'The King is dead, long live the King'. And discontinuity could be defined in the formula 'The King is deposed, long live the Revolutionary Council'.

From Goffman's account of institutions we can draw the useful idea of a contrast between the official and the unofficial life of the people in an institution, and the official and unofficial rhetorics in terms of which the institutional activities can be described, and made to seem proper and meaningful. The first directs our attention to the very different criteria of respect and worth held by people in different positions in the institution; the second to the variety of attitudes to apparently the same activities held by differently situated people — drill as a necessary training for the preservation of a soldier's life, and drill as meaningless, and perhaps even sadistic, 'square bashing'.

The reality of an institution consists in the existence of all these facets, this complex of attitudes, forms of speech and many-sided activities, and the people who engage in them. But we have already noticed that any social entity exists not just as its daily manifestations but as the habits, prejudices, beliefs, knowledge and expectations of its constituent members, and of the general public who know of it, and of the officials and functionaries who are related to it. With respect to these matters we can see an institution as not so much ideal as latent. Because of the large degree of latency of any institution compared with any of its current activities, when it is reproduced each day from the stored knowledge and skill of its members, and the expectations of their clients, it is never perfectly replicated. Even with the help of charts and forms, manuals and standing orders, some practices are forgotten and others arise to masquerade as 'proper' features of the institution. We shall be coming back to these apparently minor perturbations in a later section of this study, for they will be found to have as profound consequences for the theory of social change as did the minute thickenings of the beaks of nestling finches in the Galapagos Islands for the theory of biological evolution.

6

THE FAILURE OF TRADITIONAL METHODS

ANTICIPATORY SUMMARY

Introduction: Having developed an analytical scheme for social activity based upon the ideas of structure and meaning, the next step is to develop empirical methods by which the scheme could be applied and tested. But, it might be argued, empirical methods already exist in experimental social psychology and in the mass methods of sociology. But these methods are defective.

1. Criticism of traditional social psychology
    (a) Dependent/independent variable method assumes that social and psychological conditions of action can be broken up into elementary units which retain their identity as types of socially and psychologically potent factors. But it is easy to show that they are altered in destructive analysis, cf. Zajoncs.
    (b) We have to acknowledge the role of actors' interpretations and beliefs over and above the treatment to which they are subjected. E.g. Mixon's reworking of Milgram etc.
    Acts which actors perform are not identifiable without reference to the social character of the episode in which they occur — and since it is acts which actors intend, the psychology of social activity must take account of actors' interpretations of episodes.
    (c) Experiments are a specific kind of social event, so doubtful if they can represent other kinds of social events:
        (i) they create simplified social environments — leading to irresolvable ambiguity of interpretation, so actors do not know which role-rule system to draw upon in acting;
        (ii) at best they are a form of interaction between strangers, which involves excessive or rudimentary, but at any rate distorted, disclosure of self.
    (d) Statistical fallacies: the confusion between distributively reliable and unreliable interpretations of population distributions.
2. Criticism of traditional sociology
    (a) The Data Problem:

101

   (i) social construction of 'data' e.g. 'ethmeth' criticism of official
        statistics, cf. Douglas on suicide;
   (ii) opacity of interviews, questionnaires etc. because of dominance
        of expressive features, cf. Brenner;
   (iii) irresolvable problem as to whether the 'data', such as opinions,
        even incomes, exist to be measured or whether they are created
        by the act of asking for them; (Thomas: no data necessarily
        exist prior to the asking.)
   (iv) even if we formulate statistical hypotheses there remains the
        problem of their interpretation.
(b) The construction problem: cf. Macintyre. Idiographic studies are
needed to interpret ambiguous mass-data to avoid Durkheimian fallacy
of attributing causal potency to correlated mass-features, cf. LA suicide
statistics, which produced florid theories of urban anomie etc., resolved
by idiographic study showing that key statistical correlate was number
of available single rooms.
(c) Distributively reliable v. distributively unreliable statistical properties.
3. Interim conclusions
   (a) The mutual inextricability of the social and the individual.
   (b) Epistemological conclusion.
   (c) Methodological conclusion.

INTRODUCTION

Having developed an analytical scheme based upon the idea of
structure, and shown how it applied in principle to the analysis
of both institutions and episodes, the next step is to develop
empirical methods in which the scheme could be applied and tested as a device for understanding real life. But it might be argued,
empirical methods already exist in experimental social psychology
and in the mass methods of sociology. However, neither methodology is acceptable, given the severe criticisms to which the
experimental method in social psychology and the statistical
sampling of data as a method in sociology, have been subjected.
I shall take the trouble to sum up the difficulties the traditional
methods have run into since they are instructive both as cautionary tales and as indirect illustrations of the general points which I
have been making in the course of this study so far.

1. CRITICISM OF TRADITIONAL METHODS IN SOCIAL PSYCHOLOGY

(a) At the heart of the idea of an experiment is the assumption
that the conditions for the production of an effect can be separated into factors which can be varied independently of one another.
If this were so it would be possible to hold all but one of the

conditions steady and vary one as an independent variable, looking amongst the products of the activity initiated by that factor for another isolatable feature which seems to vary in a lawful way with the variation of the independent variable. This is the classical methodology of much of physics. For example, it lies behind the methods used by Hooke and Boyle to discover the relationship between the pressure and volume of a confined sample of gas. For our purposes the crucial assumption is that the conditions on what one might call the causal side of a possible law can be analysed not only in theory but in practice, into separably variable conditions or factors. It is supposed that, when so isolated, they are identical with the corresponding factor when all the conditions are varying at once, as they do in reality. If the conditions of social action are a structure of internally related elements, then this condition for the application of the experimental method can never be met. The extraction of an element from the structure and its separation from the relations in which it stood to other elements would, if it were internally related to them, change the nature of the element. It would be no longer what it was in the natural condition.

It is very easy to show that many classical social-psychological experiments commit just this mistake. The most striking example, perhaps, is a series of studies by Zajoncs[1] which purported to investigate the conditions under which people come to like each other. Among the conditions favouring liking, common sense suggests frequency of meeting. Zajoncs tried to detach frequency from all other aspects of the social conditions of liking and to study it separately. He tried to treat it as an independent variable tested against 'liking' as a dependent variable. The experiment consisted simply of presenting nonsense words at different frequencies and then asking the subjects of the experiment to rate the words according to the degree to which they found them attractive. It is not surprising that Zajoncs found the more frequently the word had been presented the more most of his subjects came to like it. Of course, the frequency with which Zajoncs was concerned is only formally related to such matters as frequency of meeting, and the liking which he probed is only distantly related, if at all, to the kind of liking that comes to obtain between people. Frequency as a property detached from the rest of the causal conditions of a personal attitude or emotion is wholly ambiguous. Compare, for example, the likely effect of frequency of meeting when it is interpreted as the accidental concurrence of two people on the morning bus, or where it is brought about by the deliberate attempt to induce a relation between two people by a third person who persists in inviting them together (match-making, for example), or the kind of frequency which is brought about by the fact of marriage. Notoriously that frequency of meeting does not necessarily result in liking. In at least one out of four of these cases it seems to produce dislike. The point is a simple one. When frequency of meeting is detached from specific social *milieux* in which it has social meanings for the participants, it ceases to be a social factor at all and consequently the discovery of any effects that it might have is neither here nor there for the investigation of social life. The moral is already implicit in the discussions of structure in the last chapter, namely that the elements of an internally related structure do not survive extraction out of or abstraction from that structure.

(b) The last section suggests the thought that a socially potent condition is a product of various physical and other relations interacting with the interpretative scheme of the people involved and is influenced by their beliefs. A social investigation which concerns itself only with the external treatment of subjects and their consequent activity misses the central determining factor of action. A striking example of the difficulty which arises in the interpretation of empirical investigations, in the absence of attention to actors' interpretations and beliefs, is to be found in the Milgram experiment.[2]

This notorious experiment involved the pretence that the subject was engaged in teaching a simple skill, using progressively stronger electric shocks to promote learning of the skill by a person who was, apparently, another subject in the experiment. In fact, of course, that was a lie Milgram and his assistants told to the folk taking part. It was Milgram's intention to attempt to force the citizens who agreed to take part in this experiment to give electric shocks to the one they believed to be the learner, of such magnitude that he would have been killed if the apparatus had been real. Milgram found, not surprisingly, that about 60 per cent of a sample of the citizens of Newhaven could be persuaded, under the conditions of the experiment, to give shocks to the learner which were in the lethal range. Milgram purported to be surprised by the result. The mystery of the Milgram experiment — how it was possible for otherwise kindly citizens to perform these exceedingly dangerous and cruel actions, was resolved eventually by Mixon's classic reworking of the Milgram study.[3] Milgram supposed that he was exploring the degree to which people would be prepared to obey an order given by a constituted authority, namely his assistants in the experiment. When a subject was in doubt as to whether to go on the assistants ordered him to proceed. But that was not all that was in doubt. Close examination of Milgram's material shows that though he designed the experiment, he misunderstood its nature. It was not an experiment about obedience. It was an experiment about trust. This becomes clear when it is seen that the transcripts reveal that nearly every one of the subjects, at a point where the supposed learner was showing signs of distress, protested against the procedure they had been told to carry out. At this point they were reassured by the assistant in words which ran something as follows: "I assure you that the learner is suffering no tissue damage. You may proceed with the treatment." Under the conditions of trust that obtained between the subjects and Milgram's assistant, that lie, or rather that statement which would have been a lie had the experiment been real, was taken by the subjects to be true. Under those conditions roughly 60 per cent of them were prepared to go on giving the learner shocks. Under the condition of trust they now believed their actions were not going to affect the learner at all, other than in the beneficial way of improving his capacity to learn.

Mixon, in a brilliant exercise in the scenario method, was able to manipulate the interpretations and beliefs which the subjects brought to the experiment. Under the condition that everyone believed in and trusted the assistant's reassurance that there was absolutely no possibility of injuring the learner, 100 per cent of the subjects would go to the high voltages. In those cases where no one trusted the assistant, nobody would go beyond the mildest shock. When the conditions of ambiguity that characterized the original Milgram conditions were reproduced, the very same proportion of citizens refused to continue and the very same proportion carried on. Further illumination comes from noticing that those who refused to continue after the first protest were people who either were particularly sensitive to human suffering, such as social workers or clergymen, or had professional knowledge of electricity and knew that the assistant who gave the reassurance was either wrong or telling a lie. So the interpretation of Milgram's apparently mysterious result is unproblematic once the issue is raised of what people take the scientific establishment and technical experts to be. The innocent citizens of Newhaven illustrated, in the Milgram experiment, how much trust they were prepared to put in the word of someone who seemed to have something of the aura of scientist about him.

One of the more remarkable features of the Milgram series of studies was the behaviour of the assistants who, in carrying out the experiments, were obeying Milgram. It is apparent from the transcripts and from the later record of the anxiety suffered by some of the victims, that Milgram's assistants were quite prepared to subject the participants in the experiment to mental anguish, and in some cases considerable suffering, in obedience to Milgram. The most morally obnoxious feature of this outrageous experiment was, I believe, the failure of any of Milgram's assistants to protest against the treatment that they were meting out to the subjects. At least the citizens of Newhaven in the measure of one in three had a finer moral sensibility than any of those who assisted Milgram in this unpleasant affair.

(c) Looking again at social-psychological, or for that matter any other kind of psychological experiment, one asks oneself what sort of social event such an experiment might be. After all, an experiment consists in an interaction between a number of people in which instructions are issued, tasks are carried out, personas are presented, reputations are made or lost. An experiment is a social event. The question of what sort of event becomes pressing when one asks if it is a typical event, that is, whether it is the kind of social event which occurs frequently in the real world of social activity. If it is, then there is some justification for supposing that the things that happen in it have some bearing upon the things that happen in real life. However, in two important ways a social-psychological experiment of the classical kind is not a typical social event.

(i) Experiments take place in special places, often called social-psychological laboratories, where a simplified environment consisting of undecorated walls, plain furnishings, rarely more than two chairs, the mysterious blank face of the one-way mirror, and perhaps the intrusion of the unblinking eye of the television camera. These are the usual environmental conditions in which social-psychological experiments take place. But in real life social events occur in highly differentiated environments, rich in sights and sounds, well furnished with symbolic objects, which direct or determine the interpretative procedures and the choice of rule-systems of the actors. The simplified environment of the social-psychological experiment leads inevitably to an unresolvable ambiguity of interpretation. Actors simply do not know which rule-meaning system to draw upon in acting. Every one of their actions is fraught with a kind of uncertainty. In the end, of course, one presumes, the most generalised and unspecific kind of responses are given, as they would be in the most ambiguous conditions of real life, such as, for example, a meeting between strangers in an undifferentiated public space. Deliberately ambiguous responses are made, so they can later be reinterpreted. It seems, then, that in the absence of an interpreted environment, a social *Umwelt*, no conclusion can be drawn about which of the independent rule-meaning systems individuals have employed in the activities that occur in these undifferentiated settings. There may even be a special way of going on in social-psychological laboratories, knowledge of which may be the final residue of the extraordinary tradition of experiments as a way of investigating social activities. But, as they used to say in the Goon Show, "I don't wish to know that".

(ii) Who meets in a social-psychological experiment, in the ambiguous setting of the laboratory? Friends, business partners, officials and their clients, kings and queens, policemen and traffic violaters, or what? The literature reveals that in nearly every case those who meet are strangers. Studies of the interaction between strangers have shown striking differences from interactions between those who know each other well, or between those who, though they have never met before, are nevertheless appearing in well-differentiated roles, indicated by uniforms, modes of speech, or other social signs. In interactions between strangers the exchange involves disclosure of life-histories and plans in an exceedingly untypical way. Two patterns emerge: if the meeting is thought to be unlikely to lead to any further exchanges in the future, an excessive degree of candour and a revelation of aspects of biography that would never be undertaken between acquaintances, occurs. On the other hand, it sometimes happens that a minor misunderstanding by one interactor of a disclosure by another, may lead to an elaborate series of prevarications and downright lies to maintain the persona or associated biography which the accidental misunderstanding has led one stranger to attribute to the other. These distorted disclosures arise if the misunderstanding has been let pass by as not worth correction. The crucial issue from the point of view of the application of the study of such interactions to the social-psychological experiment as a social event is that it is quite undeterminable which of these modes will occur. The distortion of biography comes about by accident, rather than through any intrinsic rule which governs the interaction. Once the accident has occurred, the interaction is set in this other mode. It is quite impossible to tell in advance, in a social-psychological experiment, which mode is being called upon by the conditions of the interaction.

(d) Examination of a large sample of published papers in the experimental tradition reveals, distressingly frequently, an elementary, statistical fallacy. Unresolved, the fallacy leaves the results of the work in a state of ambiguity. The mistake I have in mind is the assimilation of distributively unreliable statistics to distributively reliable.[4] The idea of distributive reliability can be expressed in the following principle of inference:

> From the proportion of sub-classes in a sample, one can infer the probability that any member of the sample will exhibit the appropriate behaviour.

A simple example of this would be the reasoning that if 60 per cent of subjects give lethal electric shocks when ordered to do so then the probability that any individual will give lethal electric shocks when ordered to do so is 0.6. Notice that this inference is acceptable only under the assumption that every individual has amongst his repertoire of possible actions the action in question. The importance of this assumption comes from its effect upon the way one accounts for empirical variance. If it is assumed that the action is a possible action for any member, then the variance of response among individuals is to be explained by the differential conditions under which the members acted. However, if the statistics are distributively unreliable, that is if the move from a partition proportion to an individual probability is forbidden, then the variance may be accounted for by differences in the intrinsic natures of the populations. That is, the differential behaviour is the product of different kinds of individuals in each set, so that we could say that those who do exhibit the behaviour, do so deterministically, and those who do not, deterministically do not exhibit it. Variance is explained, then, in a quite different way under the two assumptions.

We must conclude that the statistical method in social psychology should be based upon the principles of distributive unreliability. Variance should be interpreted as a partition of the relevant population. Unless there is a well-grounded theory about the available repertoire of actions of the whole population of an experiment, its results cannot be used to sustain an inference to the probability that any member of the experimental population will exhibit the behaviour in the defined conditions. It seems likely that in many cases the statistics are distributively unreliable. For example, variance in response in the Milgram experiment should lead to a partition of the population into those who do and those who do not trust people presenting themselves as scientists. For those who know anything about electricity, the action of subjecting a learner to a shock of 400 volts is impossible, that is it is not among their repertoire of possible actions. It seems, then, that the results of the classical experiment on a population of individuals are essentially ambiguous unless supplemented by a detailed investigation of the resources and nature of the individuals who were involved. That, of course, is not the kind of investigation which can be carried out by the classical experimental method.

2. CRITICISM OF TRADITIONAL SOCIOLOGY

We have already noticed that those people-structures which we identify as institutions and societies lie beyond the experience of any single individual. How, then, is it possible for us to know them? Traditional sociology depends for its methodology upon what one might call the "jigsaw" principle. It is supposed that by assembling a sufficient number of fragmentary and partial views, created by recording individual perceptions of social matters, it is possible to create a representation of structural properties and perhaps even emergent qualities of multitudinous and complex associations of people, which are necessarily beyond the social horizon of any single human individual. The jigsaw principle can be used as the basis of an epistemology only if two conditions are satisfied:

(i) There should be a way of discovering and recording elementary fragments of the social matter under investigation, so that they are not simply products of the method of investigation.

(ii) There should be a method by which the pieces of the jigsaw can be assembled in such a way that the pattern which emerges from the construction can be reasonably thought to be independent of the method by which that construction is made.

The first of these necessary conditions raises what I shall call "the data problem", the second what I shall call "the construction problem". We shall find that there are good reasons for doubting whether traditional sociology has successfully solved either.

Preliminary: Shortcomings of a Short-cut; the Limitations of Cognitive Sociology

The difficulties that beset traditional sociological methods do not arise for all collectives of human beings. Sometimes the overall structural properties of certain collectives reveal themselves in secondary or epiphenomenal properties under certain conditions. Either we should be able to view the collective from a standpoint which enables us to see it as an individual and so literally observe its properties, or we should have reason for thinking that the elements of the collective reproduce in some way or another the structural or collective properties. That is that there is a microcosm which reflects the macrocosm.

For small collectives, which we can as it were encompass at a glance and treat as an individual, some collective properties seem to pose no epistemological problems at all, as for example the movement or the size of a crowd. However, those of more interest sociologically speaking do have their difficulties. In investigating the behaviour of football fans we may wish to refer to the mood of a soccer crowd and there is no doubt that ordinary people have no difficulty whatever in telling what the mood of a crowd might be. But this immediately raises epistemological problems since our ordinary criteria for deciding whether an entity has this or that mood are individual and refer to particular people. What are we to make of the criteria for determining whether a crowd has this or that mood when we have transferred the term from an individual to a collective application? In this case we are unable to take the easy route of treating the collective application as simply a distributive property of the collective. We could regard the movement of the crowd as distributively predicated of the movements of each individual member of it. A crowd is a material thing and the motion of collectives is definable in terms of the vector properties of the motions of their component parts, Mood is not comparably definable. The crowd is not just an aggregate of individual persons. Only by dealing with the figurative character of the application of the term to the crowd seen as some superordinate individual constituted from a structurally invariant or unified set of elements can we understand what is being said in these attributions. The criteria might be derived by some sort of metonymic transformation of individual properties into appropriately related collective properties. For example the kind of noise made by an angry individual is somewhat similar to the kind of noise that a crowd makes in certain circumstances, and under those circumstances the crowd can itself be said to be, as a super-ordinate individual, 'angry'. It would be a mistake, of course, to treat 'anger' in this application, as the name of an emotion. We do not, I think, have an appropriate category for the kind of collective properties which are picked out by figurative application of terms, the criteria for which are metonymically related to the properties of individuals. But it is clear that crowds do not have emotions in the sense that individuals do. I propose that we call such properties 'collective-moods', attitudes etc. knowing full well that there is a use of 'mood' appropriate to an individual human being.

The difficulty of observing the properties of large collectives considered as supraordinate individuals could be solved if it were the case that their properties were reflected or represented in some way in the members which make up the elements of these collectives. This idea has been developed in cognitive sociology. The methodology depends upon the principle that in order for members to reproduce the collectives of which they are members by their co-ordinated actions they must have some mental representation of the properties of each collective or at least some of its important properties in order for that reproductive process to be possible. On this view all that is required to discover the properties of a collective, at least all the properties that are relevant to the study of the understanding of human action, it has been claimed,[5] is to investigate the cognitive resources of individual members who are competent as actors in that kind of society. Somewhere in their resources the relevant properties of the collective will be reflected. This can be connected with the basic methodological innovation of the ethogenic approach. One could look for a representation of these representations in the accounts that people give of their co-ordinated actions. If the principles underlying this method are correct then it seems that an elegant solution to the problem of the study of the properties of collectives can be found.

However, some doubts must be raised about any proposal to restrict sociology to the results of the methods of cognitive sociology. It seems to be a necessary condition for the possibility for social change that there be some imperfection in the reproduction of the collectives which constitute a society generation by generation. That imperfection can be accounted for partly in terms of an active, creative autonomy in at least some individuals, and partly by an imperfection in the representation of the society and its collectives. This imperfection of representation must, according to this view, be assumed as a necessary condition for the possibility of change. It would not be susceptible of empirical investigation since, if we were confined to the method of cognitive sociology there would be no way of coming to know the original collective property, so that a comparison might be made and imperfections revealed in individual representations. The very idea of an imperfect representation presupposes that the collective property which is represented exists independently of that representation: and further, that there is some sort of relation between them.

Cognitive sociology is not to be identified with methodological individualism. In its more extreme forms, that doctrine amounts to the idea that we need study only individuals because the properties of the collective are not more than the sum of the properties of individual members. The necessity for introducing a representation of imperfection of representation distinguishes cognitive sociology, at least ontologically, since it requires the independent existence of the collective properties whose representation is imperfect. One might conclude that there is a case to be made for the use of the methods of ethogenics and ethnomethodology to discover the representation of collective properties, even though this cannot be claimed to be a complete sociology. And like the simpler versions of dialectical materialism, such a view lacks an adequate social psychology in terms of which the relation between the collective property and individual representations of it can be understood.

Traditional empirical methods in sociology, such as those in the British Empirical Ameliorative Sociology Tradition[6] (the BEAST) or American Pragmatic Empiricism (the APE)[7] are versions of the jigsaw theory.

The traditional methods for the study of large collectives are based upon the idea that one can arrive at a hypothesis as to some collective property of an institution, a nation, etc., by some kind of mass survey. A large number of limited but representative views of the society are found, and when assembled form a mosaic, from which a collective property will emerge as a kind of *Gestalt*. For example, by assembling a myriad pieces of limited information about how and why people hold each other in differential relations of respect and contempt, and relating this to their relative earnings and buying power, a mosaic representation of a society is formed from which a *Gestalt* emerges, the stratified class system. The mosaic is assumed to be an adequate representation or model of the society from which the limited views have been drawn. This is the basis of the much abused British empirical, ameliorative, sociology tradition, or BEAST.

The BEAST suffers from a large number of serious ills and weaknesses which render it almost incapable of delivering anything of much scientific value. The difficulties can be summarized in the following simplified form:

(a) The 'Data' Problem

The natural sciences use instruments to detect and measure the phenomena they study. Intelligent use of the instruments generates data. But there is an assumption in this naive story, which from time to time is called in question. It is the assumption of the 'transparency' of the instruments. This is the assumption that the phenomenon being recorded is shown more or less as it is, by the instrument. We 'see' the property we are studying 'through' the instrument. Sometimes we know instruments are not transparent in this sense and if we have reason to believe that the distortions are systematic we can use physics itself to correct its own instruments. Sometimes we have no such confidence and we have to admit a halt or check in the progress of science. Such is the trouble in sub-atomic physics which has led to the development of quantum mechanics. We do not know and have at present no way of telling whether it is the world that is indeterministic in its processes, or whether it is that our instrumentation is opaque to the hidden causes of its apparent uncertainty.

To get reliable 'data' one must have 'transparent' instruments. Unhappily the sociological instruments so far invented are almost completely opaque. A reading appears on the 'dial' (an answer is filled in on a questionnaire, but we have no way of working back to the conditions which produced it. No matter how sophisticated the techniques for processing such 'data' may be, if the 'data' are artefacts, products of the instruments used in the recording, the results will be worthless. To see that this is unfortunately only too true in empirical sociology of the old style, let us look at the 'data' problem as it presents itself there.

(i) The social construction of 'data' for expressive purposes in naturally occurring social events.

Our discussion can usefully begin from Douglas' critique of

the data upon which Durkheim based his famous study of suicide.[8] One might, unreflectingly, assume that a self-inflicted death was so unambiguous a phenomenon in most cases that official statistics of suicide rates would serve as a transparent instrument for their recording. And so Durkheim assumed. But of course 'suicide' as Douglas pointed out and Maxwell has confirmed, is not an objective quality of certain acts, but an interpretative category *to* which acts are assigned for certain practical purposes and as the upshot of a complex social event. Further the upshot is highly conditioned by the kind of people involved in the negotiation. For instance, Catholics are likely to argue for the interpretation of the death as 'accident'; Muslims and Japanese are more ready to settle for an interpretation as 'suicide'.

These obvious considerations play havoc with the idea that official statistics are a reliable reflection of the real world. The suicide statistics of a town must lump together both these counts where 'accident' is a highly favoured outcome of the negotiations and those where it is not. But if official statistics took account of this the result would be only an aggregate of idiographic data — one unique biography after another. As Douglas points out the meaning of the death-attempt can only be ascertained by locating it in a reconstruction of the victim's biography; but that reconstruction is itself a process of social negotiation between interested parties, not the construction of an objective record of the past. And since each party to the negotiation has their own reputation to take care of, the expressive implications of one upshot or another are likely to play a major role in the process.

Since suicide is seemingly only attributable on an individual basis, in a complex and idiosyncratic social process, there does not seem to be an empirical sociology of suicide. In similar ways most other officially registered data can be made to melt away. This is not to deny the importance of the rhetorical effect of official statistics, but it is clear they can form no basis for any kind of science, except that of the study of modern forms of rhetoric.

(ii) Weaknesses of interviews as data collection techniques
It is essential, as a first stage before the mosaic is assembled, to acquire a very large number of limited views of whatever aspect of the social world is under investigation. The usual method involves the presentation of questionnaires by an interviewer to an interviewee. This is a legitimate method only on the assumption

that the answers to the questionnnaire are true representations of the viewpoints of the individuals interviewed and that these answers themselves are capable of being unambiguously assembled into a mass datum. However, careful studies of interviews have shown that neither of these assumptions is justified. The interview itself is a social event, heavy with ambiguity and shot through with efforts at self-presentation by both the interviewer and the interviewee, so that it is doubtful whether, in many cases, the interviewer understands the answers of the interviewee or the interviewee understands the questions of the interviewer. Each, apparently, reconstrues the speech of the other in accordance with their own conceptual framework.[9] Furthermore, the use of questionnaires with a limited range of questions and a set of instructions for the interviewer, which effectively preclude elaborations and reinterpretations on the part of the interviewee, means that the concepts deployed, at least by the interviewer, are predetermined. The effect of this is to produce not a representation of the social world being studied, but a representation of the shadow cast on the social world by the prior conceptual apparatus deployed by the person who constructed the questionnaire. These two weaknesses taken together raise serious doubts as to the 'validity' of the data that are seemingly collected.

(iii) Existential assumptions queried
S. Thomas has pointed out[10] that we have no *general* grounds for the claim that the result of any questionnaire administration or interviewing, however carefully conducted, is data. We cannot be sure that there was anything relevant present in or to the people, such as an attitude, before the investigation took place. It could just as easily have been produced on that occasion to satisfy the questioner.[11]

(iv) Equivocal data
This point is part of a more general problem, the obverse, so to speak, of the data construction problem. Even if one has tamed the BEAST sufficiently to produce a statistical hypothesis, say the proportion of women going outside the home to work as it has changed year by year, it cannot be used until we know what it means.

Suppose it were to be argued that the changing position of women in society (and here it is assumed on intuitive grounds that we know sufficiently clearly what *this* means to agree that

there is or is not such a phenomenon) is due to their now undertaking work in a public milieu, and like other such work is shown
to be valued by its being rewarded in monetary gain. This represents a change in the valuation of women's work, it might be
argued, and so leads to a change in the valuation of women as
people — and it is this change that is marked by microsocial
changes in forms of address, choice of clothes and other symbolic
practices — a thesis argued for by Pelikan.[12] In this case loss of
prestige is marked by the disappearance of social practices which
ritually mark respect.

Logically the argument commits the fallacy of *petitio principii*,
assuming what it sets out to prove. Without an ethogenic investigation we have no idea of the symbolic value of working at home
compared with outside work. Consulting my own intuitions, in
the absence of any other touchstone, I think I hold the view that
public work is devaluing, leading to a decline in the social position
of women *vis à vis* men. I have the general impression that 'going
out to work' associated as it is either with youth or economic
necessity or both, may be actually valued as a loss of worth. But
this is not the weakest point of the argument. That lies in the
assumption that money generates social value, contrary to the
well grounded ethogenic principle that social value sometimes
generates monetary reward (sometimes it does not). Most reputation seeking, I would argue, leads to social credits, and to transform these into their current monetary value can lead (and usually
does lead) to expressive loss. From an expressive point of view
the best thing one can do with the money that comes with a
Nobel Prize is to give it away. Compare the enhancement of
Dorothy Hodgkin's reputation when she gave her prize money
away with the uneasiness felt by many people when Paulette
Corrigan decided to keep hers. She had to provide a special
accounting — 'that it would free her to devote all her time to
the Peace People movement'. As J-P De Waele has rightly com-
plained, there has been no serious systematic study of the ethogenics of money, its valuations, disposition or disposal in the
day-to-day lives of particular people. In the absence of detailed
knowledge it is impossible to remedy the ambiguities of Pelikan's
thesis. Does monetary reward generate social value or does it
mark social value, or is the question of money a red herring?
We have no way of knowing how to answer that question at
present.

(b) The Construction Problem

(i) The problems of the BEAST are exacerbated further by the weakness of the assembly operations which bring together dubious individual data into mass properties. In general the methods employed tend to be summative, that is to be an averaging or abstracting operation on individual data to generate an attribute which can be ascribed as a property to some large group of persons, taken as super-individual or collective. In the course of these averaging or extracting operations certain forms of structure are eliminated, so that, for example, we have the stringencies of the 'class' theory of society, which abstracts from and stratifies across the national population, in contrast to a mosaic representation of social differentials of a more structural kind.

(ii) But supposing we have found a Durkheimian relation between one collective property and another — what then? Durkheim, of course, recommends us to treat these as cause and effect, if they seem to show Humean regularity. But that, in itself, raises a question. Alasdair MacIntyre has pointed out[13] that close examination of actual cases shows that to decide whether there is a causal relation one must descend from the collective to the individual level to find it, thus contradicting the essence of Durkheim's Humean epistemology.

MacIntyre uses the example of the suicide statistics of Los Angeles. According to official data collecting techniques, Los Angeles has the highest suicide rate in the United States. Durkheim's principle then enjoins that we formulate a causal hypothesis linking some collective property of the city and/or its population with the suicide rate, another collective property. Individuals, of course, cannot have suicide rates. But Los Angeles city and its population is an indefinitely complex object having indefinitely many properties. We can solve the problem of the explanation of the unusual rate only by abandoning Durkheim's principle and returning to the level of individual people and their actual motivations and choices, and ask what makes this one or that one commit suicide in Los Angeles. Idiographic studies showed that nothing in Los Angeles city or its population made people commit suicide. Rather there was something there in Los Angeles that led people, who for whatever private reasons they have had were bent on suicide, to come to Los Angeles to do it. This turned out to be that the city had the largest number of vacant single room apartments available per head of population of any city in the United States. Social statistics are not often, perhaps not ever, of the stuff causal laws are made on.

However deep and serious the organic complaints of the BEAST, none of them seem to have the self-destructive character that would put them forever beyond correction. It should be possible, by abandoning the use of questionnaires, and by dropping the summative statistical methods by which data are transformed to reveal mass properties, to use the general idea of the assemblage of limited views in a more satisfactory way. It would, of course, be much harder work: it would take a great deal of time but at least it would begin to have some of the verisimilitudinous quality that one finds in the natural sciences. However, there is a further point: the BEAST, as it presently shambles through the social world, involves not only an *a prioristic* methodology, which eliminates individuals' concepts in favour of investigators' constructs; it is also politically objectionable in that by the use of an interviewing method which precludes the interviewee providing his meanings, interpretations and theories about the social world, it treats him as worthy only of contempt. He becomes an object to be probed, not a person to be co-operated with. The sooner the BEAST dies a natural death, the better.

3. INTERIM CONCLUSIONS

(a) The Mutual Inextricability of the Social and the Individual

The conclusion of the argument was that, for example, a suicide as a social object is generated out of a death, a biological object, by a complex social process, involving negotiation. 'This death is a suicide' is then, not the attribution of a simple property, but the use of an interpretative category to provide the death as a human act with a motive. Are we then in a situation where there are no objective limits to what we can and can't call 'suicide'? It would be too extreme a conclusion.[14]

The negotiation of the category rests upon a relatively (that is with respect to suicide attributions) non-negotiable category, that is death. Only deaths are or are not suicides. The more difficult problem, practically speaking, of 'attempted suicide', is discussed below.

Setting aside the fact that the concept of suicide is one of family resemblance across cultures, rather than strict synonymy, *within any interpretative frame*, there are right and wrong answers to the question, 'Is it suicide?' Notice that the law tries to redefine such categories as suicide, in terms of criteria which will enable the negotiation to terminate, though it is rarely successful in this for long.

The relativity of 'suicide' with respect to 'death' and of 'death' with respect to (a) biochemical functioning which is itself defined relative to current knowledge of chemistry, and (b) religious theories, does not mean that every element in the chain is equally negotiable. We set up such chains in each microculture as devices for dealing with questions of the truth and falsity of socially important attributions, that is we set up social institutions of truth-and-falsity-determining. But any *given* attribution of truth and falsity is relative to some agreed set of fixed categories generating, for that case, the criteria of truth and falsity. For practical purposes we set up chains such that the limits of negotiations are narrower and narrower as we proceed along them, but they never decrease to zero, that is there are no logical atoms, no basic statements which are atomic with respect to all frameworks, the criteria for the truth and falsity of which would be universally agreed.

On this view each application of a social category is a hypothesis, and relative to it are relatively 'objective' facts, further along the chain, which would refute the hypothesis. And they are hypotheses relative to further links in the chain.

(b) Epistemological Conclusion

Objectivity is a direction, not a terminus. The hermeneutical circle is broken only by another circle of greater diameter.

(c) Methodological Conclusion

The data are not only constituted by reference to an account, the agreed interpretation of the fragment of biography culminating in the death, but involve a balance between the meaning I assign to your behaviour construing it as actions in the performance of acts, and the meaning you assign to it in this extreme case, in the note you leave behind. Your meaning appears in your accounts, explicitly in their content and implicitly in their syntax.

But how does the social process of negotiating an assignment to an interpretative category work as a way of making the action intelligible? It works by embedding the relatively fixed object, the death, in a negotiable structure of events, the past biography of the person involved. (The biography is literally a product of a piece of social work in the present case.) The death then takes a certain place in a network of relations to other actions, and in this way acquires a certain meaning.

'Attempted suicide' is a very much more negotiable category, since its relatively objective core, the alleged state of desperation and the taking of the pills intentionally, are much more account dependent than is the death as the relatively objective core of the successful suicide, since the person survives to take part in the negotiation.

Both critiques, that of social psychology and that of sociology, imply a theory of social objects. Events, episodes, clothes, topographies and so on, when treated as social objects, involve the assignment of meanings by the use of interpretative categories. For example in Mixon's reworking of the Milgram experiment it turns out that a crucial feature of the set-up was the meaning assigned by the participants to the accoutrements of 'doing scientists'. For 60 per cent of the victim scientists were people you could trust — how wrong they were in this case!

In Douglas' discussion, as we have seen, everything turns on the meaning given to the relatively non-negotiable object, a death. The process of the assignment of meaning involves

(i) the location of the object in a structure or pattern of events, for instance the death in a biography, the activities of Milgram's assistants in 'science', and in particular in an incident which was falsely represented as 'helpful science';

(ii) the location of the appropriate concept, for instance 'my impending death', 'giving someone an electric shock', in a semantic field having individual existence in the social competence of the person actually involved. But having collective existence as the abstract isomorph of the individual competences of the people involved, that is in shared beliefs, and theories and so on of people of that sort, in what an anthropologist might call the local ethnography. The pattern of events in (i) may have a standard representation in (ii), but it may have to be created for dealing with an untoward occurrence, for which people are not prepared.

Part of the problems ordinary people have with traditional sociology is that it postulates and sometimes claims to identify objects in the category of beliefs and motives that are not perceptible to any individual. We have already seen that these are rhetoric relative, that is they are relative to the system of concepts we are using to try to make sense of the world.

The task of psychological sociology is to investigate the degree to which such objects are represented in the tacit or explicit social knowledge of individuals, by which they acquire such competences as the ability to show the right degree of deference, to recognize the social hierarchy at some moment on some concrete occasion, and so on. By acting ably as members they somehow reproduce societies at whose overall, emergent properties we may only be able to guess.

L. I. H. E.
THE BECK LIBRARY
WOOLTON ROAD, LIVERPOOL L16 8ND

7

THE DEVELOPMENT OF ADEQUATE METHODS

ANTICIPATORY SUMMARY

Introduction: the mutual inextricability of the social and the individual, neither of which is fully independent of the other: social events involve the meeting and matching of individual projects: individual action involves interpretative procedures of social and collective origin.

1. Acceptable methods in social psychology
   - (a) Episode analysis:
       - (i) act/action analysis based upon the dramaturgical metaphor of scene (setting and situation), action and actor, using externally attributed meanings and presently existing, consciously formulated social theories;
       - (ii) identification of practical projects, both social and material in contrast to presentational or expressive projects.
   - (b) Account analysis:
       - (i) first stage accounts which members use to provide interpretations and justifications of act/action episodes and which can figure as part of the action;
       - (ii) second stage (often negotiated accounts) in which members theorize about the action and the first stage accounts, developing hypotheses in both folk sociology and folk psychology.
   - (c) The folding back of (b) upon (a).
2. Acceptable methods in sociology
   - (a) Empirical procedures:
       - (i) the intensive v. extensive design;
       - (ii) empirical domains;
       - (iii) Emic and Etic studies
   - (b) Theoretical procedure:
       - (i) hypothetico-deductive; based upon explanatory power. Too weak if considered positivistically and statistically since indefinitely many hypotheses of equal explanatory power can meet positivist criteria;

123

(ii) Realist theory introduces double criteria
- (a) from the success or failure of predictions etc. we can guess how far the theory truly describes the macrostructure;
- (b) plausibility depends on fitting general ideas about reality — more difficult since social structures and global social patterns are no other than the actual and potential relations in which people of a culture can stand to one another, and so are not independent of interpretations.
3. The relation between psychology and sociology
   - (a) Causal and interpretative sociologies.
   - (b) Kinds of environment.

INTRODUCTION

A central preoccupation of the ethogenic approach is to establish a fruitful connection between microsociology and social psychology, and in particular to base social psychology on an adequate and explicit microsociology. Contemporary social psychology is fortunate to have to hand the microsociology developed by symbolic interactionists and ethnomethodologists.[1] Social psychology need no longer depend on amateur or intuitive conceptions of the structure and meaning of social interactions. And since the main psychological technique in ethogenics is the analysis of the speech of participants in social life, we can employ the very detailed and often extremely subtle analyses of ordinary language developed by the Oxford School of Philosophers and others in the linguistic tradition, in which social and psychological theories implicit in ordinary speech are revealed.[2] These two developments, the one in microsociology and the other in language analysis, contribute an enormous but previously untapped resource which we can put to use.

I shall try to show how the link between microsociology and linguistic analysis is actually established, and why we believe that account analysis is an enormously fruitful empirical method. Indeed, this method has already proved to be important in developing an adequate social psychology based upon an empirical technique which can escape the lethal criticisms that have been levelled against 'experimental' methods and the use of statistical procedures.

The method is based on the principle hypothesis that human social action involves two closely interwoven and interacting performances. There are the contributions one makes to the episodes that together make up social life. Personal contributions consist of actions and speeches, of various social force, in the doing and uttering of which we perform the acts expected and sometimes required of us by others, and by our own conception of how we should appear in public. Performances, actions in episodes, involve two interacting motivations. They are directed to practical-social ends, to changing or maintaining the material and social world; and they are directed to expressive presentations, to showing what sort of persons we are.

1. ACCEPTABLE METHODS IN SOCIAL PSYCHOLOGY

(a) Act-Structures

Analysis of episodes depends upon the use of microsociological concepts of the kind developed by students of close-order face-to-face interaction, of whom the most perceptive is undoubtedly Goffman. In this way we discover the act-structures of an episode. But we should notice that any episode, if identified only by its time and place of occurrence and the people involved in it, may be the joint performance of several act-sequences.

(i) Act-structures are carried by action-sequences, including the utterance of various kinds of speech, and often supported by an unattended flow of adjustments and tone-setting performances, such as mutual body posture, smiles and nods, eye-contacts and and so on. To tackle the action level of the episode we need to deploy Austin's speech act theory,[3] since the utterances through which a good many acts are performed have to be considered, not so much for their grammar and literal meaning, as for their illocutionary and perlocutionary force, that is for their social effectiveness. We may also need to call on the structuralist poetics of such analysts as Cullers[4] and Torode,[5] to identify the ironic, metaphorical and other uses of language which have powerful social effects.

Co-ordinate with action are the accounts people give of the actions of members, in explanation and justification of their doings and in gossip and scandal-mongering about the goings on of others. This kind of talk is primarily concerned to make actions intelligible, that is to define, socially speaking, what has occurred. At the same time this is to make actions and acts warrantable, that is it calls for a showing of the rightness or propriety of what was deemed to have been done, by reference to rules. That is to show that it was right for those kinds of people in those circumstances. And finally in accounting one shows oneself to be a proper sort of person, having the correct social attitudes and motivations, and the intellectual capacity and inclination to deal with them rationally. Accounting too is both social-practical and social-expressive.[6]

The analysis of an episode begins with a hypothesis as to the social scene in which it is occurring. Compare for example the social meaning of the utterance of the sentence 'How about a drink?' when spoken by a business acquaintance outside a bar, and by a nurse speaking to a rail crash victim in an ambulance. Our analyses then proceed with a tentative identification of the roles or parts in which people are speaking, and the social scene in which the action is going on. The situation is a complex and changing entity, involving the physical environment as socially interpreted — the setting — and the situation(s) — the relations and predicaments the people involved find themselves in. Situations develop and sometimes have to be resolved.

To understand the interlocking activities of the people in the scene we treat their performances on two levels, each of which has two aspects. There is the act/action sequence which is directed to several kinds of ends. There are the practical ends of achieving some instrumental outcome, which might be mediated by physical laws, such as kicking a ball between two posts. Then there are the social ends which might be mediated by social convention, such as presidential signing of a bill into law. Then there are the expressive ends of achieving some self-presentational good, such as scoring a goal effortlessly, stylishly and so on. Finally there is the talk which precedes, accompanies and follows the action — talk in which the act/action sequence becomes the subject of concern. The analysis of this kind of talk will be examined in the next section.

Analysis of an act/action sequence involves the identification of the acts performed, possible only to those who know the local conventions and the local theories as to what needs to be done in that society. Then the actions which are the public (and more rarely private) realization of the acts can be identified, and their sequential order examined. Conventions link acts with acts to generate larger acts — and actions with the acts they are locally taken to be the way of performing. Actions may have an autonomous sequencing rule-system, which may have to be explained by reference to accidents of history.

Detailed study of models for analysing act/action structures will occupy us in the second part of this study.

(b) Account Analysis

In account analysis we try to discover both the social force and explanatory content of the explanatory speech produced by social actors. This then serves as a guide to the structure of the cognitive resources required for the genesis of intelligible and warrantable social action by those actors. Intelligible action is social action in which the item in question (something let us say like a handshake), is made sense of as we view it as part of a structure of actions, a structure which we recognize as having a certain social force and in which we see the handshake as having a particular and proper place. If it is to be warranted as well it must be at the right place in that structure for an item of that kind.

Intelligibility and warrantability are two quite distinct properties of social actions and both may come under critical scrutiny. Let us first consider intelligibility. I may not know what you are doing when you take hold of my hand, not knowing in what structured sequence of actions it is occurring. It might be part of a betting ritual, or an opening move in a karate encounter, or part of various other action sequences. It is obviously of great practical importance to understand its meaning in this sense. The second property, warrantability, can also be problematic. A handshake can be in the right ceremony but in the wrong place, appearing, say, with appropriate other items but in the 'wrong' order. Any piece of social action must have both properties if it is not to generate unease, doubt and uncertainty, undesirable perlocutionary consequences. But much more seriously such an action is liable to fail as an illocutionary performance, that is as the action required to generate the socially appropriate act.

The distinction between the perlocutionary force and consequences of a social action, and its illocutionary force and consequences, is basic to sociolinguistics, but may be unfamiliar to social psychologists. The perlocutionary consequences of, say a promise, would be the changes brought about in the world by its fulfilment. The illocutionary consequences include the commitment to others to fulfill the promise which falls on the promiser. We owe the distinction to Austin (cf. note 3).

The structure responsible for the presence of the two desirable properties, intelligibility and warrantability, is discerned in action-sequences by microsociological analysis. This analysis is based on the social analogue of the linguistic studies of semantics and syntax which we have explored in detail in a previous chapter. Both social syntax and social semantics are relevant to both intelligibility and warrantability. The outcome of the analysis is a set of socio-logists' generalizations as to the structure of the sequence. On the basis of this sequence we may, as social *psychologists*, propose hypotheses as to the cognitive resources of people who work together to generate, as a mutual product, a certain pattern of action. It is by means of this action that they perform the social act which they take to be required of them in that setting.

The ethogenic method is based upon the assumption that the very same cognitive resources can be employed in another task, namely the explication and justification of the manifested patterns of action in speech. Thus the bases of successful action by socially competent people are revealed in two distinct forms and are available to two different modes of empirical studies.

In the analysis of the second mode of representation, namely explanatory speech or accounting, we must distinguish the speech we use when we are talking descriptively about the prescriptions of our own culture, contributing to our own ethnography, so to speak, from the speech we use to justify some action of ours to others within the culture, the kind of speech that has come to be called accounting. It may be that both call on the same material, but one is in the scientific mode and the other is a part of social action. It is part of an argument, the conclusion of which, however informally implied, is that what we did made sense and was right at that place and that time. The action is intelligible and warrant-able and by virtue of this we are seen as worthy and rational beings. Saying, 'I'm terribly sorry, I meant to help you up' as we knock over an old lady's tea cup, is a simple case of accounting as correction of social meaning, relocating the bump in a planned sequence, and so making it intelligible in such a way that even though it went wrong it is not offensive in that situation. We leave the field of action, embarrassed perhaps, but morally in good standing, having exhibited our rationality and shown our remorse.

In sum, speech relevant to action is geared to two different tasks. One task is a conscious bit of sociology on its own account, a contribution to the local ethnography, whereas the other is part of the local social techniques for elucidating and making meaning-ful (or meaningless) something which has appeared 'out of place' in the social order. Thus, accounting may involve justificatory reference to some rule for an action whose meaning is in doubt, or it may achieve explication merely by the elucidation of meaning.

The most fundamental methodological point which distinguishes ethogenic from traditional social psychology turns on the sort of science we take psychology to be. There are two quite different kinds of scientific investigation in the natural and social sciences: those I shall call *parametric* and those I shall term *structural.* In a parametric study it is assumed that the properties referred to by the variables which describe the system are not internally related, that is, that they can be varied separately while retaining their identity. The gas law PV = RT relating pressure, volume and temperature, is a relation between parameters such that one can hold constant any one parameter and vary the others, and the property represented by that parameter will remain unaffected by the abstraction. As far as pressure, volume and temperature are concerned, a gas is not a structure of internally related properties. In a parametric process the elements interact causally but retain their identity and do not change in type if detached from the structure. Pressure remains pressure however temperature and volume may vary. On the other hand, an element of an internally related structure ceases to be an element of that kind if detached from the structure. In a structured entity each component part derives its meaning from the other parts to which it is internally related. A handshake is not the same action when embedded in a betting routine as when part of a greeting. The frequency of meeting someone is not a social item at all if detached from a particular social milieu from which it can gain significance as a meaningful feature of interaction.

It follows that we should analyse the diachronic structure of social interaction not in parametric terms, nor yet in the manner of the crystallographer, that is as if it were a mere assemblage, but rather in the way molecular geneticists or structural linguists approach their problems. That is, we should treat social interaction as a social product, and then try to discern in the people involved in the interaction the template or representation of the structure that led to a particular product.

I want to distinguish this very sharply from another kind of process by which non-randomness is generated in social behaviour. This is the kind of order revealed in studies of the way in which people take turns in a conversation. Two people, A and B, acting in concert, are found to produce an orderly sequence of utterances having the form ABABAB ..., that is the conversation involves regular turn-taking. This is a highly structured product. Argyle and others[7] have shown that the structure of such a sequence is not the product of 'formal causality', that is template following. There is no template for the whole conversation which leads to the structure ABABAB. Rather, B's speech-turn is produced by an atomistic property of the speech unit of A, something which happened at its end, a kind of pause, eye-lock, etc., which sets B going. B as speaker in turn does the same thing which sets a speech by A going, and so on. That kind of structure is produced by successive efficient causality. Such structures are rare in speech patterning.

Much more typical is the pattern demonstrated in the work of Schegloff and Sacks.[8] A discourse analysis of a whole conversation reveals an overall structure generated we must suppose from a preformed template. For example, when two people are talking they do not end their interaction by just stopping. There is a pre-closing sequence, for example, 'O.K. well ...', which allows the warrantable introduction of the closing sequence; the first 'Goodbye' suspends the transition relevance of the second so that the first speaker does not have to follow the second 'Goodbye' with another speech, but can break off. The conversation has an overarching structure which is not generated bit by bit by successive atomistic efficient causes. The pre-closing comes when it does because the conversation is divided into topics, and the pre-closing comes at the end of a topic as part of the overall structure of a proper conversation. Once the pre-closing has occurred we can warrantably insert the pair of 'Goodbyes'. In dealing with this type of structured interaction our hypothesis will be that a conversation structure is the representation in manifest form of a preformed template represented in this case by the conventions for generating whole conversations. On the other hand, turn-taking, the ABABAB structure, is indefinitely extensible, and has no closure as an overall structure. Its form derives from properties of each component speech taken atomistically. It is more like a diamond than an anatomy.

How to tackle structural analyses scientifically? I will draw upon a version of the competence/performance distinction employed by the generative grammarians to explain the central methodological idea. Generally speaking, the competence/performance distinction argues that if anyone is to be capable of performing in a certain way he must have knowledge of how he is supposed to behave. There are well-known problems with the application of this idea in linguistics.[9]

Happily, in the field of social psychology we are in a rather better situation. We have at least the theoretical possibility of

availing ourselves of two different manifestations of the knowledge that we ascribe to a person on the basis of his demonstrated
ability (say competently to introduce somebody to somebody
else). We can propose hypotheses on the basis of his performance,
and can also analyse the kind of speech that occurs in accounting
for and justifying certain related kinds of social action. Our
studies show that account analysis yields much the same sort
of hypotheses about a person's cognitive content and organisation
as does the analysis of action sequences in microsociology. Microsociological analyses could reveal product structures from which
we would then derive hypotheses about a person's cognitive
capacity to generate the template structures which lie behind the
production of the manifest or product structure. Thus, in analyz-
ing the incorporation of strangers into a group, such as a party,
we will want to say that host, sponsor and stranger each have a
replica of the structure of the ceremony of incorporation. It is
by the transformation of that template into the medium of action
that they produce the actual action-sequence. Competent people
'contain' template structures. We will not necessarily find the
template structures explicitly represented in accounts, say as
consciously attended rules, because most people do not know
explicitly how they introduce other people. Instead, the cognitive
resources will show tacit representation of template structure,
for instance in the range of judgements about the propriety and
impropriety of a given form of conduct. Whether we find tacit
or explicit representations we will have the material for a structural explanation of the person's skill.

What sort of template structures might we find? It is important
to distinguish between those preformed notions that are employed
only on one occasion and those template structures that we can
employ over and over again. And again we must differentiate
between those templates that we have to follow exactly if we are
to achieve our intention and those which are merely strategic
guides. Finally, two different kinds of preformation of template
structures must be distinguished: those which express the local
ethnography and are a permanent part of our cognitive resources,
and those which are improvised for particular occasions. An improvisation would, of course, have to be in terms of shared cognitive resources, particularly readings of meanings, otherwise what
you did would not be intelligible and warrantable as public performance to *us*.

It seems natural to use the word 'rule' for preformed, mandatory templates of the structure of action-sequences, particularly when these can be given linguistic form as written sentences or spoken utterances. On the other hand, the word 'plan' will be kept for identifying the templates of action that are improvised within our local range of intelligibility, sometimes having mandatory force, sometimes being merely advisory. Plans may be represented in quite concrete objects, such as notes for a speech or a builder's blueprint.

So far we have identified the problems addressed by ethogenic social psychology only in a very formal way. There is the analytic problem of discovering the structure of the products of mutual social action. There is the genetic problem of discovering the corresponding template, its structure and the form of representation it has in each human being competent in that social milieu. The necessity to allow for individual representation raises the problem of idiography, that is how far our individual representations of templates are unique.

Finally, we should notice that we have not yet identified a source for the conceptual apparatus with which we will be conducting the microsociological investigation and the analysis of accounts. It will turn out that the source of the analytical scheme is, in the first instance, the accounts themselves.

2. ACCEPTABLE METHODS IN SOCIOLOGY

(a) Empirical Procedures

(i) The extensive v. the intensive design

Earlier, in criticism of the naive use of statistical methods in social science, I argued that the most important and socially relevant characterization of human beings in action are distributively unreliable, and depend upon individual representations of the properties of the collectives to which they aspire.

The general conceptual framework which emerges from these considerations is very much like that Leibniz proposed for his general metaphysics of monads, in that each monad acts co-ordinatively with all others, but it does so because it represents the properties of the whole universe from its own point of view. I would not go so far as to claim with Leibniz that there is no real interaction between monads, but would agree with him that individual representations are a key feature of the capacity of people to act co-ordinatively to create collectives.

The basis of the distinction between the intensive and extensive designs is an elementary property of classes expressed in the well-known qualitative relationship; intension varies inversely as extension. The more properties that are used in the definition of a typical member of a class, the fewer individuals are likely to be found exhibiting those properties, that is the smaller the class extension.

In the ideal form of extensive design the investigator examines all the members of a class. In practice he examines some available subset which is thought to be a representative sample, and he *derives* the type by some sort of averaging procedure on the properties of the members he has examined. In the extensive design at least some result is guaranteed, however trivial, since all the members, or some suitable sample of the members, have been investigated, and there are sure to be some properties which can be averaged, or abstracted, as a type. But there are serious risks in this method. If the individuals which constitute the extension of the class are very variable in their characteristics, the results of the investigation are likely to be trivial since there will be few properties in common to all members of the extension of the class.

The intensive design, on the other hand, involves the examination of a typical member in an endeavour to discover all, or as many as is practicable, of the properties that that typical member has. In this design the extension of the class is constituted by defining it as the set of individuals who are like that typical member in relevant respects.

The intensive design, on the other hand, involves the examination of a typical member in an endeavour to discover all, or as many as is practicable, of the properties that that typical member has. In this design the extension of the class is constituted by defining it as the set of individuals who are like that typical member in relevant respects.

Again, there are both gains and risks. The advantage of the intensive design is that a great many properties can be investigated together, their structural relations and interactions ascertained, and a detailed type-description proposed. There are corresponding risks. The results may be misleading, since the member we may have chosen as typical of the class in which we are interested may not be typical of what we took to be the likely extension. Since we have no other members under empirical scrutiny, we may generate a type which is a distortion of the typical member of the class we have in mind. However, if we endeavour to resolve this difficulty by analytically defining the class as that set of individuals who are typified by the member we have studied, then the danger is that class may turn out to be very small and our discovery trivial.

A resolution of the difficulty occasioned by the advantages and disadvantages of each method comes by the joint use of the extensive and intensive designs. The extensive design enables us to identify a typical member from a known extension. Then, that member which we take to be typical in more than just those respects can be subjected to an intensive investigation to generate a detailed knowledge of the type. This can be tested and empirically criticized with respect to our original extension by choosing *an* other member, and subjecting it to intensive investigation, the two intensive studies acting as potential falsifiers of the hypothesis that each is typical. In this way we can achieve depth and breadth together. In practice, however, the results of the application of the extensive and intensive design have favoured the intensive, in that detailed investigations of individuals, as De Waele and others have shown,[10] leads one to be very sceptical indeed about the value of the original extensive class from which, for example, a typical murderer or a typical obedient citizen were selected.

(ii) Empirical domains

The fact that in practice the intensive design seems to dominate over the extensive as a viable empirical method leads us to be doubtful of the idea that there are wide-ranging categories of human beings, at least as social actors. In the light of this the results of empirical studies should be very carefully distinguished with respect to their domain of application. The best way of making this point is with respect to Windelband's well-known distinction between idiographic and nomothetic studies, that is between detailed studies of single individuals, and summative studies of sets of individuals on the basis of which nomethetic statements, the laws of the many are to be made.

This distinction and its application to the separation of empirical domains has been worked out in detail by Du Mas.[11] He shows that an idiographic domain can be defined which is not accessible from any extensive design. The proof runs as in Fig. 1:

Domain A. This domain represents all the people and all their properties at some time. It is nomothetic domain, with respect to the universe of people.

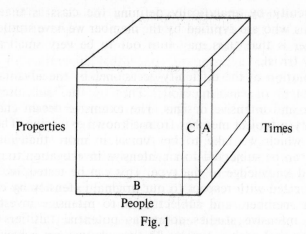

Fig. 1

Domain B. This domain represents all individuals and one property at all times. It is also a nomothetic domain with respect to the same universe.

Domain C. This domain represents all the properties at all times for one individual. This is an idiographic domain, and the exploration of it is identified with biography. For example, in Fig. 1 the Domain C is the life of the individual N and its representation is the biography (or autobiography) of Mr N. It is clear that the properties of the whole cube can be reconstituted from any of the domains by summation, so that

$$\Sigma A = \Sigma B = \Sigma C$$

But, it is not possible to recover the individual biographies of the members of the population from either of the nomethetic domains. So there is some information in the cube which can be obtained only by idiographic studies of each individual separately. It should be clear that though the exploration of the idiographic domain is empirically indistinguishable for successive investigations under the intensive design, the logical form of the investigations are quite different. The idiographic domain is not based upon any hypotheses about typicality of members. The intensive design can be derived from an idiographic investigation simply by adding the hypothesis that a member whose particular characterization is being explored is typical of some set of members and perhaps of all.[1 2]

(iii) Emic and Etic studies
The practical necessity to explore the idiographic domain by

the independent investigation of one individual after another, coupled with the criticisms that we have made of the ways in which mass investigations are currently carried out, raises the question of the appropriate conceptual apparatus for making such investigations. The question is, whose concepts are to be employed in our investigations? Those of the individuals being investigated, or those of the investigator, or both? This issue has been the subject of debate in anthropology.

Pike proposed a distinction between emic studies and etic studies[13] on the basis of an analogy with the linguistic distinction between phonemic studies in which the meaning of a lexical item in a linguistic culture is the essential identifying criterion, and phonetic studies in which the sound pattern which would in principle be investigated entirely independently of the meaning (or so it seemed). As used by Pike the distinction is supposed to identify complementary pairs of studies both of which are required to give an adequate analysis of some social group and the lives they live. Etic studies are supposedly based upon a universalistic set of empirical distinctions but they are thought to reveal a series of cultural patterns which are specific to a particular society. For example, to return to the linguistic basis of this analogue, a phonetic study uses, so it was supposed, universal criteria for the identification of sound elements, but the sound patterns so revealed are, of course, unique to each language. On the other hand, emic studies, which draw upon actors' interpretations and necessarily call upon local knowledge, though relatively idiographic from the point of view of the conceptual system employed, are nevertheless likely to reveal universal features of societies. Again, returning to the linguistic basis of the analogue, the meaning structures which are conveyed by the sound structures are likely to be the same from one language to another, in that presumably, with only minor exceptions, it is possible to represent the same proposition in a wide variety of different languages. An emic investigation, then, though local and idiographic in its conceptual system, is likely to yield universal results.

At first sight, this distinction and the analogue upon which it is based, seem extraordinarily convincing. However, difficulties abound. It is clear that the linguistic analogue is weak in that it is now widely held that there is no universal phonetics in the sense that Pike assumed. What are taken to be relevant sound patterns are not independent of the meaning structure of the discourses or sentences in which they appear. On the other hand, the suggestion that there are universal meaning structures to be revealed in emic studies, is, to say the least, an empirical hypothesis and is far from being demonstrated. It seems no more wise to assume that there is an underlying structure, or pattern, for the actions, institutions, tales, religions, and so on of many and various people as there is to suppose that human languages are based upon a universal grammar, an idea which though thrilling when it first became current, has not been able to be successfully substantiated. There have been attempts on the basis of the emic/etic complementarity as proposed by Pike, to found something called an ethno-science. But unfortunately, the way this developed was seriously distorted by an association with a positivistic conception of explanation and theory. Ironically, a recent study by Harris[14] of the ethno-science movement, a movement which grafted itself to a positivistic methodology, subjects it to a positivistic critique.

From my point of view this is irrelevant since I have no faith in positivism as a critical stance or confidence in it as an empirical method. My difficulties with the emic/etic distinction are more radical in that though it seems clear that there is no social science which does not begin from actors' interpretations and intentions, the particular analogy drawn upon by Pike and the detailed applications he makes of it seem to me to be unsatisfactory. Instead I shall develop the suggestions of the first three distinctions in more detail. That is, I would want to argue for a social science which concerns itself *in the first instance* with distributively unreliable properties, which bases itself upon an essentially intensive design, and which works from an idiographic basis. Nevertheless such a science is aimed always at a cautious climb up the ladder of generality, seeking for universal structures but reaching them only by a painful, step-by-step approach as one culture, and one way of life within a culture, and one individual's biography within a way of life make available to us detailed knowledge of the forms and conditions of human association.

(b) Theoretical Procedures

(i) The hypothetico-deductive method
The limitations inherent in the acceptable methods outlined in the last section seem to me to impose a final *impasse* on the route to an empirical macrosociology. But few sciences have ever been built on the kind of inductive methods adopted by the BEAST.

Cosmology purports to describe structures as remote from experience as those described in the conclusions of macrosociology. Some are adopted and others rejected on apparently good grounds in which observation of the heavens seems to play a part. How is this possible?

The problem is perennial. Do we abstract a pattern from experience, as Hume and Mill would have it, or do we impose patterns upon experience, as Kant and Whewell have supposed? We have seen the difficulties that surface when we are asked to develop a sociological method in the mode of Hume and Mill. But to adopt the latter programme seems to make science vulnerable to the objection that the imposed patterns may be quite fictitious. The answer seems to be that we impose those patterns which experience will bear. This thought can be sharpened into the hypothetico-deductive method.

A field of phenomena appears orderly but that orderliness is not explicable from within, so to speak. A hypothesis as to the macrostructure or as to the underlying causal mechanism, or whatever seems plausible as a source of that orderliness, is proposed. That hypothesis, if true, has consequences for the field of phenomena. If the consequences are borne out the hypothesis stands for the moment as adequate or satisfactory; if they are not borne out it must be modified, restricted or even abandoned. This is the hypothetico-deductive method.

Marx proposes a macrostructural generative process as a hypothetical real mechanism which is supposed to produce the features of society as we experience them, modified and sometimes even transformed by the theory and rhetoric we have available to express to ourselves the social order. This he calls 'ideology'. If the hypothetical mechanism is close to what really produces the social order then there should be consequences of supposing the theory to be true that are borne out in experience.[16] Marx's predictions have turned out to be wrong. This counts against the theory, though it does not falsify it strictly. The theory could be modified, its range of application restricted, its auxiliary hypotheses modified and so on. But if it continues to fail and the modifications necessary to preserve it diverge further and further from the spirit of the original theory, then in the end it would have to be abandoned. In this work I am assuming that Marx's theory in particular must be restricted in application to the practical order as it is developed in the nineteenth century.

By shifting to the hypothetico-deductive method we break

the bonds imposed on sociology by the BEAST.

(ii) Realism

But considered only with respect to explanatory power conceived in the hypothetico-deductive way the method is too weak. There are indefinitely many possible systems of hypotheses which will deductively imply descriptions of the 'known facts'. Which of them comes nearest to truly describing the processes that really occur, one might ask? What is the representational quality of this or that hypothesis?

To answer that question I shall have to consider the internal structure of theory a little more closely. A theory proposes a possible generative mechanism for an observed pattern. In sociology that may involve attributions of structure and process to society in the large. In the previous section I considered hypotheses only with respect to their consequences for what might be expected to be experienced or otherwise revealed to an observer. But hypotheses can also be considered relative to the kind of world picture they tacitly involve. Choice among the indefinite range of possible sets of hypotheses to explain the way society seems to be is usually controlled by the way the theorizer believes the world to be. A more precise explication of this point must wait upon a detailed account of the role of models in theorizing, an account which will be undertaken in Part II.

Our judgements as to the plausibility of hypotheses is based upon a balance between their power to explain those matters we do experience, while keeping within a conception of the world that reflects what we believe to be the main features of reality, and the plausibility of the kinds of mechanisms they suggest lie behind and produce the appearances.

However, the ideas of Whewell and Kant must not be forgotten. I have spoken glibly of comparing the predictions of theory with the patterns of the social world as we experience them. But as I have repeatedly emphasized, it is generally agreed that in social matters above all, the patterns that one experiences depend upon the interpretative schemata one brings to bear on a generally enigmatic scene. We enter what is plainly a theatre, but we have to guess what play is being performed. Sociology and social psychology as interpretative activities are parts of the very processes they purport to describe.

2. THE RELATION BETWEEN PSYCHOLOGY AND SOCIOLOGY

Though it is part of my purpose to dissolve traditional ways of demarcating fields of research in a scientific study of human life, nevertheless the traditional fields do exist. In some cases those who defined them had good reason to make divisions where they did. In this section I want to connect up the interests represented in traditional fields of study with more recent preoccupations.

I have already demonstrated, with success I hope, that social psychology cannot be studied successfully without drawing upon an explicit microsociology of a symbolic interactionist cast. Only thus can we find out what people can do — and only if we know what people can do can we find out how they do it. This point can be elaborated in considering the way one kind or level of study proposes problems for another kind or level.

Just as psychological studies generate problems for physiology, by raising the question as to the physiological mechanisms we use to perform certain tasks, defined in an autonomous psychology — say the question of how we distinguish meaningful patterns from meaningless jumbles — so sociological studies can pose problems it is the proper business of a psychologist to solve. Such might be the problem of what sort of skills and what range of cognitive resources must a person have to be able to make a competent contribution to the social activities in which he engages.

Part of the importance of the shift to an ethogenic approach in social psychology has been to make the sociological assumptions used in social psychology quite explicit. Much of the traditional experimental social psychology was based upon an unarticulated, common-sense sociology, often of very local provenance and application, incorporating much of the unexamined social assumptions and moral and political ideals of middle-class Americans. This set of assumptions has been clearly identified and beautifully criticized by Moscovici in what he has identified as the 'psychology' [and sociology] of the good guys.[17] The immense strength of Goffman's microsociology is its lack of sentimentality, its bending of an unwinking gaze upon the follies, foibles and sheer nastiness of much of human life.

But the relation of all this to macrosociology is not easy to sustain. The attempt to say something about the properties of societies at large does not link itself on to the rest of human science in the unproblematic way of microsociology. To get clear about these matters we need to make some further distinctions.

(a) Causal and Interpretative Sociologies

Try as one might it is impossible to consider the sciences of human life without noticing the apparently diverging paths represented by the methodologies and social theories of Durkheim and Weber. It is not part of my interest to rehearse these old issues. As Bhaskar has argued,[18] one has to concede that there are causal powers in the global network of actual and possible relations between people and their activities, different from the causal powers of any mere aggregate of individuals or activities. But it does not follow from that concession that collectives of people and the totality of their activities are supra-individuals having distinctive criteria of individuation and identity. Sometimes we can tell quite easily what the network of relations and activities is like, sometimes it has surprising effects. For instance, there was the surprised realization that introducing a comprehensive school system leads to more, not less social stratification, by encouraging internal migrations within cities so that those who can afford to move to the best suburbs get the best 'comprehensive' schools. The 'bussing' programmes in city education systems in the United States are a sharply felt acknowledgment of the correctness of this discovery.

The sociology that comes closest to human motivation, and so to psychology is, of course, interpretative (including the more down to earth forms of hermeneutic) sociology. It is the study of the giving and reading of social meanings in all kinds of items, from personal actions to geographical features, of the definitions of situations, of the variety, source, and effects of different images of the social order, and so on. Can these apparently disparate approaches be brought together?

In one way causal sociologies must be part of interpretative sociology since they can be treated as the products of certain kinds of social activity, whose meanings and symbolic role in social life will have to be investigated. For example, social theories feed into social life as accounting resources — as ways of making one's felt life situation intelligible. For instance, one's felt failure in life can be explained by the theory that life chances are determined by the income of one's parents — provided one can construe their income as 'low' — and given that the vagueness and relativity of the concept of 'income' it is clear that opportunities for a wide range of suitable interpretations are very much available.

But there might be more substantial ways of unifying causal

and interpretative sociologies. They could perhaps by unified *a priori* by some such idea as the theory of 'false consciousness'. This would give the explanatory advantage to a causal sociology. Whenever a disparity emerged between a causal theory constructed in accordance with the general causal framework and locally experienced interpretative procedure, the latter could be construed as involving illusions. For instance, it might be argued that the local interpretation is an illusion or represents an illusory view because of the necessity to mask an interest, which appears only in the 'objective' theory. Such theorizing often degenerates into conspiracy theories, but even when it is pursued seriously it runs the danger of begging the question at issue. It assumes that there must be a 'true' consciousness, a mode of awareness which reveals the causal processes as they are hypothesized in causal sociologies. As Machevski and others have pointed out, the claim by sociologists that they have an objective view of social processes must be examined sociologically, since this claim could itself be seen as a move in an attempt to seize power and become a new ruling class.[19] This is a very evident feature of the psychopolitics of B.F. Skinner, who makes the claim for a right to rule quite explicit.[20] But, as I have argued, at best causal sociologies are able to offer only hypothetico-deductively validatable theories, and in the absence of any acceptable empirical methods for the study of the collective properties of social groupings of people, no inductive validation seems possible. In consequence causal sociologies are subject to the paradox of Christopher Clavius.[21] If the only empirical link between theory and observable or ascertainable fact is deductive there are infinitely many theories which satisfy the empirical and logical conditions, so the chances of the one we may have on offer being true is really rather low.

A more plausible attempt at unification would proceed *a posteriori*. One could begin with the idea of levels of justification of action in terms of one's beliefs about the collectives one took oneself to inhabit and the proprieties of action with other members. One might claim, uncontroversially, that there is a multiplicity of accounting systems each revealing, or sometimes by the very fact of its coming to be used, creating yet another network of relations between people and amongst their activities. No one of these networks is wholly responsible for the causation in and functioning of any of the others, though there are relations between them. Some of these are causal, some interpretative. If the ultimate problem for a human being is to make his actions intelligible to others and his situation as he interprets it intelligible to himself, so as to preserve his sense of personal worth, he assembles just sufficient accounts to achieve this. His accounts may involve physics (entropy), biology (inheritance,[22] ecology), production processes of material necessities and symbolic 'luxuries' (economics), microsociology (social meanings), linguistics (modes of communication) and so on. Each could be taken diachronically and related to folk-theories of social change. Though each 'higher' level theory imposes upon or reveals in the world yet other structures the reality of all requires an ultimate realization in some material base or other.

(b) Kinds of Environment

Actions occur in socially distinguishable environments. They take their meaning partly from actors' intentions but partly from those environments, the scenes of social life. But psychologists have not been of one mind on the matter of how environments are to be construed relative to human actions within them. Rival doctrines reduce in the main to two positions, which we might distinguish as the 'Skinnerian' and the 'Kantian views.

According to the Skinnerian position an individual passing through a succession of environments is passive with respect to each. All productive processes pass from the environment to the individual. So though he changes in his life course the changes are produced successively by the environments through which he passes. He arrives at each new environment, not to act upon it, but to be acted upon. Even if he does chance to act upon the environment as a consequence of the effects of a previous environment, he can only change it so that it has different effects upon himself and others.

The Kantian position would treat the social and even the physical environment as a complex product of interaction between persons as active agents and the environment as a plastic construction that can be endowed with causal powers through the meaning-giving acts of agents. Environments do not exist in their fullness independent of the agents who enter them. They are part created by the way the individuals who enter them assign meanings to the people, activities, settings and social situations they find within them and even actively create. Then they are themselves affected by that which they have created. It is the Kantian position which I will be elaborating in the detailed discussions of situations and settings in the chapters on the dramaturgical conception of life, and the consequential conception of environment as scene.

8

OTHER FORMS OF LIFE

ANTICIPATORY SUMMARY

Introduction
1. Lives of honour: cultures in which the expressive order is absolutely dominant.
   (a) The Trobriand Islanders. Honour is engendered by munificence in a non-economic system of exchange.
      (i) The *Kula*: two kinds of valuables are passed in opposite directions around a vast cyclical array of partners, reputation deriving from the value of the object once temporarily held and then passed on: a male preserve.
      (ii) The *Dala*: disposal of the spirit value of a person involves distribution of symbolic valuables by women.
   (b) Another system of honour: Sudan. Family honour and personal worth are linked in a system independent of economic standing.
2. Mixed cultures: worth is determined by an interaction between expressive and practical or economic standing, though the orders are independent.
   (a) Maoris: honour was realized in a principle, of quasi-substantial being, *mana*, which was earned in war and debate, but had to be shown (magnified) in acts of munificence. Personal worth, however included a measure of property.
   (b) Honour in the Pueblo: in rural Spain male and female value systems depend on quasi-biological principles of maleness and femaleness. Each person has intrinsic worth shown in pride. Total personal power as illustration of total valuation however includes economic standing.
3. Indeterminacy of the practical order: Aztec inversion of status. In Mexico social standing was determined economically but represented by a cult of humility and service to others, in contrast to Veblen's conspicuous consumers.
4. The biological order apparently engenders universal structural properties of social regard, but there are notable exceptions, such as some Amerindian tribes, the medieval church, etc.

INTRODUCTION

The distinction between expressive and practical orders is not just an analytical separation but reflects a real independence. The possibility then exists of the two orders having different relations at different times and in different societies. To establish the point firmly we must find cases where the expressive is a great deal more dominant in the affairs of life than is the practical order, compared with our society in so far as we are able to perceive it.

1. LIVES OF HONOUR: CULTURES IN WHICH THE EXPRESSIVE ORDER IS ABSOLUTELY DOMINANT

(a) The Trobriand Islanders

The Trobriand Islanders have passed into anthropological folk lore as the almost mythical locus of the true origins of social anthropology. But besides their mythopoeic standing they live in ways irresistably exemplary for the theory of society, for they still live a life bounded by and founded upon honour. Their sense of honour is bound up with material things but depends upon a relation to them that is utterly unlike that which appears in the European obsessions with the gathering and the keeping of property. Trobriand honour comes from giving one's 'property' away.[1] In 1922 Malinowski discovered the Kula Ring, an astonishing institution I shall be describing below.[2] But as recently as 1971 Annette Weiner came across a system of exchanges as unconnected with the 'means of life' as the *Kula* and as central to Trobriand lives.[3] While Malinowski's discovery was made among the lives of men, Weiner's was focussed in the life-cycle rituals conducted by women.

To illustrate the separation of work between the practical and expressive orders of Trobriand society consider the cultivation of yams. Relatively small gardens will provide an adequate basic subsistence. But many more yams are grown, and in specially tended gardens. Why? The giving away (not the exchange in our sense) of large numbers of yams is the very stuff of which honour is made. The ability to engage in munificence is publicly illustrated by the size of the yam house built beside one's dwelling. Only rarely are such yams brought down into the practical order as mere food. Their distinctiveness already appears in the way they are produced. Domestic, subsistence gardens are cultivated without the aid of the magic which is reserved for the much larger gardens where prestige yams are grown.

The economy of these people is dominated then by the production of objects for the game of honour. The means of life almost take care of themselves. A very similar phenomenon occurs in Japan in the system of reciprocal gift exchange. In general one does not use the gift one obtains but carefully evaluates its price against an outstanding social obligation and passes it on.[4]

Trobriand society has evolved two fairly independent systems for the genesis of honour by munificence – the *Kula* Ring and the *Dala* ceremonials. The former is a system managed by men, the latter by women – though men are also deeply involved.

(i) The Kula

(a) *The Machinery*: there are two cycles of exchange, one in which white shell armbands are the material focus, and the other based upon red shell necklaces. These objects have no exchange value outside the ring of *Kula* objects themselves. Like authorship of a scientific paper their value is transformable only into symbolic credit in the structure of hierarchies of respect and contempt. The cycles move in opposite directions so each member of a Kula partnership exchanges a different category of object with his partner. If my obligation is to give you necklaces yours is to give me armbands. The geographical diameter of the cycles of exchange are immense, involving hundreds of islands and long sea passages.

(b) *The system*: possession, though it is a necessary condition for the creation of honour, is not ownership. Every named *Kula* object must eventually be exchanged. Honour accrues from the giving up of possession, of once having had such and such an item. One boasts not so much of what one has now, but of what one has munificently passed along. But that munificence is self-interested. It puts an obligation on the receiver to provide an object of equal reputation. When he receives this the original giver gets yet more symbolic capital since he can now pass that object along in the other direction. His fame and glory increases with each such transaction.

A lesser form of valuable is also exchanged. Minor objects are used to maintain a link when an obligation cannot be fulfilled through the lack of something of adequate reputation to pass along. Such items are constantly being appropriated for personal use, cut up or otherwise disposed of. But that could never be the fate of a genuine *Kula* object.

(c) *The exchange*: the holder of a famous item will gain glory by relinquishing it, but he illustrates the value of the item by the difficulties he raises when asked to give it up. The object itself is supposed to have preferences in these matters. It can be the victim of standard love magic. Weiner quotes a Trobriander as saying, 'Remember, a Kula shell is like a young girl; she looks over every man until she decides which one she likes best. One man is chosen and the others are sent away.'[5]

(d) *The enhancement of worth*: Malinowski describes the result of a successful Kula expedition as follows:

> The temporary ownership [Malinowski's rather misleading expression] allows him to draw a great deal of renown, to exhibit his article, to tell how he obtained it, and to plan to whom he is going to give it. And all this forms one of the favourite subjects of tribal conversation and gossip, in which the feats and the glory in Kula, of chiefs and commoners, are constantly discussed and rediscussed.[6]

(ii) The Dala

Dala is the substantial basis of cosmic continuity of local geographically based groups. At conception a spirit child derived from an ancestral being (*baloma*) enters the woman's body. The child that is eventually born thus 'has' *dala*, but this *dala* may be cultivated and augmented by certain practices. *Dala* becomes objectified in property, which, though material, is more ephemeral than *dala* spirit. Funeral ceremonies, at the other pole of the life cycle, must be complementarily concerned with the disposal of *dala*. And this is the women's ceremonial preserve.

The mortuary ceremony, in which *dala* is disposed, is like *Kula*, an occasion for acquisition of personal renown by munificent distribution of 'property', valued not for its use, nor for its exchangeability for articles of use, for it has none. It is valued only for the opportunity its temporary holding provides for divesting oneself of it. Women deal in skirts and skirt materials, but so bundled as to have no use value in the making of skirts. These are given away to specific categories of other people in ways parallel to the way men deal in necklaces, armbands and yams.

> Trobriand exchange objects, unlike Western money, cannot be detached from the human experience of regeneration and immortality. They are not alienated from the basic concerns of society, and therefore social relations are not merely relations between impersonal things in Marx's terms, but human relations that reify the cyclicity of life, death and rebirth. Thus, Trobriand women and men, exemplified in the objects they exchange, perceive the value of each other through the interface of the value of human beings and the value of regenesis.[7]

(b) Another System of Honour: Sudan

Traditionally the Sudanese live according to an expressive order as dominated by honour as that lived by the Trobrianders, but the basis of honour and the means of its preservation are very different. The dynamics of the system can be understood through the explication of four concepts: *ird, sharaf, karāma,* and *ihttiram.*

According to a detailed account by Nordenstam[8] the focus of the expressive order is the public character of the women of a family who are expected to be virtuous in all their actions, particularly with respect to sexual matters. Virtuous action leads to the having of the abstract quality of *ird*, or decency. By protecting the quality of the women of the family the male Sudanese protects his honour.

That which a man protects by the moral defence of his family is *sharaf*. It is a quality which everybody except a slave has by nature, though it is a relational attribute, devolving on to a man by virtue of the *ird* of his family. It can be the property of a collective. It does not have to be achieved like our 'character', since everyone is born with it. Though it cannot be augmented it can be lost, and once lost cannot be re-acquired. Nordenstam suggests that the nearest English equivalent is 'honour'.

But while *sharaf* is the abstract property which one has by virtue of *ird*, it is, as it were, invisible. Its expressive counterpart is *karāma*. Again it is something which is given in full and cannot be augmented. But it can be lost, either directly or by virtue of a decline in the family honour. It is realized as an expressive property both in individual and in collective form. Nordenstam suggests the former should be equated with 'personal dignity'. A family as well as an individual can possess it. The fact that it is an expressive property lays it open to two kinds of derogation. It can be lost by the improper conduct of the one who has *karāma*, or it can be lost by improper treatment meted out to one by others by humiliation or insult.[9]

Interestingly it seems that *karāma* is poised between the expressive aspect of the presentation of selves and the impressions which that presentation makes on others. For instance, the effect on *karāma* of one's own improper actions is always mediated through the attitudes of others to those actions. It has then much in common with what Goffman calls 'character', rather than the ordinary property of dignity.

But for the argumentative purposes of this chapter the most important attribute of *karāma* is its absolute independence from social or economic status. Everyone has *karāma* and has it in full unless by his own folly or by his failure to deal with humiliations heaped upon him by others, he loses it. The acquisition of wealth or property cannot augment one's *karāma*. The only differentiation between men is in the importance attached to the actions by which it might be lost. Thus the pecadilloes of very young men do not count in comparison with the shame a similar action might bring to an older man. There is a sense of 'He should have known better' that qualifies the effect on *karāma* of unbecoming behaviour.

Reciprocal behaviour from others to recognize and thus confirm one's *karāma* is collectively called *ihttiram*, roughly representable as the showing of respect. It appears in a mixture of rituals of deference, actual consideration and good manners. Upon these attributes and upon these alone the Sudanese erect an expressive order, and through them, and exclusively through them, do they value one another.

2. MIXED CULTURES

The examples so far developed are of societies whose practices are not only dominated by the expressive order and its necessities, but where the economic and practical order are not even represented in the expressive order. That degree of independence is rare. The next range of cases will illustrate progressively more intimate relations between the orders.

(a) Maoris

The practical order serves the needs of the expressive order. Munificence was amongst the virtues most highly prized by the Maoris. It formed part of a complex system of social concepts grounded in a psychological theory of the structure of human beings.

Each person was supposed to be powered by two interacting principles. One, *wairua*, animated him and was the efficient cause of his actions. The other, *hau*, controlled his moral attitudes and was a kind of repository and a source of virtue. They were each capable of a kind of disembodied but earthly existence. The one might be called the vital force, and the other the soul. Social relations both depended on and engendered accumulations of another principle, *mana*. This principle was not only the source of power in war, or debate, it was also an attribute of the things associated with people who had *mana*. It could be a collective property of families, clans and tribes.

Older commentators, particularly Elsdon Best,[10] have spoken of the Maori social order as if there were no economic differentiation within it at all. Best speaks of the Maoris as having a communistic society, as if all property were held in common. While this seems to have been true of land, it would be better to say that the very idea that the land was 'property' is misleading. It was not so much property held in common as the very being of the tribe, who were deeply associated with it in every way. Other things, such as weapons, clothes and the like were sharply individually differentiated as private property. Cutting through this was the relation of the chief to the food surplus. At first sight it might be thought that since he had disposal of that surplus within the constraints of the democratic debating that accompanied all chiefly decision-making, it ought to have been regarded as his property, at the very most something held in trust for the tribe. But this it seems would be to misrepresent the matter. Munificence enters into our analysis.

To demonstrate munificence, tribes, or sometimes lesser groupings such as the family based clan, the *hapu*, gave extravagant feasts, *hurangi*, involving not only an extraordinary distribution of food at formal dinners, but the construction of enormous wooden pyramidal structures upon which the feasting occurred. Everything was done to amplify the glory of the occasion. But though it was the chief who, as it were, executively set in motion the preparation, and under whose authority the tribal surplus was so expended, it seems that the glory accrued not only to him, but to the *iwi*, the *hapu*, or whatever social unit could readily be identified with the affair.

I remain unclear from the ethnography as to whether the *hurangis* led to increase of *mana*, or whether munificence is an outward expression, an expressive illustration of the *mana* belonging both to the tribe and to the chief. His *mana* in part glorifies the tribe, in part is created by the *mana* of that tribe itself. But much of *mana* does seem to be personal and particular. It is an attribute of places, things and people, but as they are distinct individuals.

(b) Honour in the Pueblo

In small towns in rural Spain a social order with a very high expressive content still flourishes. But unlike the Maori culture of pre-European New Zealand the expressive order and the practical order which is determined by the control of land, water and the resources flowing from them, cross cut one another in the genesis of the forms of daily life.

From the point of view of the expressive order all Spaniards of the same sex are intrinsically as equal as Arabs; but intersecting that principle is a powerful tradition of the privileges of wealth and consequent position as sharply differentiated as anything Marx describes.[11]

Here we have an expressive order based upon a conceptual relation between personal honour and maleness. All men have this attribute but they may so act as to lose it. Their failure in one way or another to maintain their standing in the table of pride is marked by a savage nicknaming system, through which the community expresses both its collective norms of proper behaviour and its judgements of how well individuals have lived up to them. But so great is the role of pride in the social psychology of rural Spaniards (and women have it too, within their own scheme of virtues) that though one knows one's nickname it is almost never used openly to one's face, since the derogatory judgement it implies would have of necessity to be resented. A detailed account of the nicknaming system can be found in Pitt-Rivers' excellent study.[12]

The idiom of moral discourse with respect to the expressive order is as Pitt-Rivers has it 'frankly physiological'. To have masculinity is to have '*cojones*' (testicles) but to act so as to lower that pride is to be *manso* (castrated). These states are, of course, figurative rather than literal. They embody a rhetoric that reminds one strongly of the chants by which doubts are cast on the masculinity of opposing groups in the aggressive rituals of British football fans. Closely connected to manliness are *amorpropio* and *honor*, which are derivative rather than substantive virtues. The relative weight of pride in the social psychology of traditional and presently rural Spain is illustrated in the predominance it plays in such a study as *The Spaniard and the Seven Deadly Sins*, where pride is linked to epigrams, proverbs, common sayings, and the many exemplary anecdotes that circulate in a society and represent its favoured stereotypes of actions and thought.[13]

The relation of this conception of manliness as the correlative virtue of pride, the defence of that pride be it personal or familial, is obvious in the interpretation of the bull fight and of the standing of the men who take part in it. What, one might wonder, is to be made of the current appearance of a female matador? What virtue does she represent?

But defence of one's own pride is possible only in a society in which one takes care to protect the pride of others.[14] Pitt-Rivers points out how necessary it is for the code of manners to enjoin respect for the pride of others, so public aggressiveness or insult is greatly deprecated. Quarrels do not issue in fights, not even in ritual fights. But just as in the culture of British football fans, the strength of the sanctions against actual bloodletting and the certainty of their realization by the most powerful members of the group ensure that a great deal of bravado can be safely shown. Actual insult or social criticism is practiced *sotto voce* or anonymously, and behind someone's back in the invention and use of a derogatory nickname. The institution of the *cencerrada*, the anonymous singing of ribald and personally insulting songs under the cover of darkness, about those who have offended against the moral code of the pueblo, takes the place of the too dangerous play with real public cricitism. In a system based on pride this would have to be recognized and retribution taken or demanded. *Cencerrada* stands in for the duels that can never be fought, not only because one risks killing one's foe, but more importantly because one chances being humiliatingly defeated oneself.

Pitt-Rivers and others have pointed out how the social order based upon the expressive virtue of pride and its defences and support works in with the practical order based upon relative control over the means of production to modify each in essential ways. The possibility of tyranny and exploitation is muted (though hardly eliminated) by the threads of influence that ramify through the society deriving from success or failure in the expressive order. And similarly, as Pitt-Rivers demonstrates in case histories of recent events in the town, the implacable power of institutions based upon public opinion like the *cencerrada* is limited by the power and protection of the rich. Neither order is dominant, and neither determines absolutely the particular social equilibrium between masculinity and femininity that prevails from time to time.

3. INDETERMINACY OF THE PRACTICAL ORDER.
AZTEC INVERSION OF STATUS, THE CULT OF THE QUIET MAN

Veblen has accustomed us to the idea that the visible representation

of power and position in the economic order is to be represented
by conspicuous consumption and flamboyant display. Not all
societies have subscribed to this relation between class position
and manners. The final step in my demonstration of the independence of the practical and the expressive orders is to show that
even where they are clearly related in such a way that the expressive order is structurally determined by the practical order (and
its offshoot, an aristocratic lineage based originally on economic
power) the determination is not strict. Inversion may occur, for
reasons that anthropologists and social psychologists have yet
to explore. Soustelle's splendid ethnography of the classical
Aztec civilization[16] includes a detailed account of Aztec manners,
a code in which display and overt manifestation of social power
and position is inverted into a muted punctiliousness, grounded
in a moral theory of service. (Again it is reminiscent of other
cultures and other practices, for it has a very similar ring to the
traditional code of manners and public morals of the English in
the high period of the British Empire.)

The code involved two kinds of conventions: those concerned
with the control of the display of feelings, and those to do with
the proper humility by which real *hauteur* might best be expressed.
Soustelle quotes a Codex to the effect that 'No vainglorious,
presumptuous or noisy man has been chosen as a dignitary.'[17]

Soustelle likens the presentational style favoured by the Aztec
upper class to the Roman *gravitas*. Again from a Codex we get
the advice that a man should present himself as 'humble and
not overweening, ... peaceable and calm.' With this demeanour
went a formal code of manners involving a particularly high
degree of politeness, both in address and in the practical business
of life. Gentlemen were enjoined neither to 'throw themselves
upon women like a dog on food', not to 'eat noisily and without
care like a glutton'. In short, public presentational style was
characterized by the display of the control of the normal appe-
tites. The humility and dignity evinced was itself continuously
providing proof of the claim to superiority of those to whom
life's accidents had given power and position. Thus Soustelle
points out that famous veterans of the wars were permitted
great licence in their talk and behaviour, and one might well
speculate how far this reflected a consciousness of the fact that
their standing had been earned by them alone, in their proper
persons so to speak, while others had inherited respect and were
called upon to show themselves worthy of it. The dominant

language of the Mexican plateau was rich in grammatical elaborations by which the tartness and brusqueness of questions, orders
and requests could be dissolved, much as the fast disappearing
subjunctive mood used to dissolve the peremptory character
of requests in Spanish, or indirect constructions ('I wonder if
you'd mind awfully ...') do in current English.

Along with the code of manners went a strong sense of the
obligation of the ruler to those he ruled. Indeed Soustelle is able
to show that the anecdotes about a particularly admired ruler
have much of the quality of those concerning Haroun al Rashid,
that is an almost obsessive care for the well-being (not to say the
dignity) of those ruled.

The image of the King or Caliph in disguise in the humble
regalia of an ordinary man is a portrayal of the central inversion.
To be truly great it is necessary to appear humble. It is another
version of the Lion and the Fox of Machiavelli's fable of political
power. One can appear to be a Lion only so far as one is known
but never seen really to be a Fox.

If we add to this catalogue of cultures nineteenth-century
industrialized Europe as the socialists saw it, and early twentieth-
century United States as Veblen saw it, we will have completed
the permutations of the possible relations of the expressive and
practical orders. There are instances of societies where the orders
seem to have been completely independent of one another. There
are societies where, though the systems are independent as orders,
nevertheless the total valuation of a person is some product of his
valuation in each order. And there are societies where the orders
interact with each other so intimately that we can say, without
distortion, that the one determines the other. Sometimes the
expressive order determines the form that subsistence work shall
take. Sometimes the social structure engendered by the productive
process influences the whole of the rest of the social relations of
a culture. But as we have seen, the Aztecs and the Vanderbilts,
archetypes of the cult of display as Veblen saw it, reflected that
order in quite opposite ways.

4. THE DENIAL OF BIOLOGICAL UNIVERSALS

Finally, one might notice that there are equally disparate relations
between the biological orders within human life and their reflection in social arrangements. The aristocratic principle maps the
reproductive chains onto the social order, and the relationship

between kinship structure and social formations has been thoroughly explored by anthropologists.[18] But Levi-Strauss has pointed out the danger of taking our own assumptions about family pride for granted as universal socio-psychological principles.[19] There are Amerindian tribes who practice abortion and infanticide, disrupting the biological chains upon which one might suppose kinship to be universally grounded. But they make up the deficit by raiding the other neighbouring tribes for older children whom they bring up to acquire a fierce family pride and so reproduce the culture.

PART II

Synchronic Analysis

INTRODUCTION

1. General theory of explanation
   Realism requires that theories describe features of the world not given in experience.
   (a) This calls for the formation of iconic models of unknown generative mechanisms, controlled by the balance of two analogy relations.
   (b) To have explanatory power a theory built on the above scheme must conform to an Aristotelian format.
2. Outline of the method
   (a) Attribution schema from social and public performance to individual competence; in analytical use of model, act/action structure is like a play.
   (b) Explanation schema from individual projects to social realization, that is collectively ratified action; in explanatory use of model act/action structure is produced like a play.
   (c) There is no adequate method for discovering the macro properties of human collectives.
Note The above schemata involve two (or more) model sources under a generally anthropomorphic base model. These form the substance of Chapters 9 and 10.
   (a) Problem solving model:
       (i) practical v. social action;
           sub-models are the ceremonial and the agonistic;
       (ii) expressive — style of action and accounting. Intelligibility and warrantability as conditions for expressive project of showing one is a rational being.
   (b) Dramaturgical model:
       (i) scene — a product of setting and situation;
       (ii) action — scenarios classified as remedies, resolutions or mono-dramas; all other scenarios are dominated by the practical;
       (iii) actor — a person psychologically distinct from but publicly immersed in a part.

159

1. GENERAL THEORY OF EXPLANATION

The troubles besetting old-style social psychology and sociology derive in part from uncritical assumptions about what is to count as an explanation.

The struggle against the simplistic attractions of logical empiricism as a theory of science has taken many forms, depending in part on which of its many weaknesses strike an opponent as a possible point of attack. Some have seen the crudeness of its empiricism as its major weakness, others its logicism. The connection between crude empiricism and logicism (the doctrine that all metascientific concepts such as 'cause', 'explanation', 'confirmation' and so on can be explicated without remainder in terms of concepts drawn from logic) has not always been seen too clearly. But an 'atomistic' impressions theory of the foundations of knowledge fits smoothly into an extensionalist, logicist conception of the nature of causal statements, of theories, of the meaning of theoretical concepts, and so on.

However, if one abandons crude empiricism there is a temptation to abandon realism as well, or at least that aspect of realism which insists upon an empirical grounding and meaning for theoretical hypotheses. Once one grasps the central role of the Verificationist Fallacy, the claim that the empirical meaning of a concept is identical with its empirical grounding, in the logical empiricist doctrine, and comes to separate the meaning of concepts from the conditions for their testing, it is easy to become relativistic about the one[1] and Kantian or even Idealist about the other.[2]

Abandoning crude empiricism frees one to entertain the possibility that scientific theories could describe features of the world not given in immediate experience. Such is the realist position. It is, I believe, the only reasonable position for an epistemologist to take. But it has to be defended and amplified since not any theory will do as a description of a candidate for reality. The problem that this thought raises is the central problem for realism: how do the concepts of a theory acquire plausible trans-experiential empirical content?

To answer this question in a way favourable to realism and likely to be convincing one must have a theory of meaning as well articulated as that of the opposition, though in the nature of the case it is likely to be more complex. Having explained how a theory gets trans-experiential content one must give an account of how, in the absence of truth-criteria as tests for acceptance or rejection of a theory we do decide on the plausibility of the 'picture' of the world it describes. Predictive success is useless for such a purpose, as we have known since Campbell's famous argument.[3] Neo-realist philosophers feel the necessity to speak of a world more complex and differently constituted from that revealed in immediate experience. They have proposed a positive account of a machinery of models and analogies which deals with both problems at once, just as the positivists' empiricism did, but in a very different way.

By consciously breaking with the logicist as well as the empiricist aspect of the old philosophy of science the question of what does constitute a theory (an explanation), if it is not logical form, can be raised. The neo-realist answer to this question is based upon an analysis of the content of real scientific theories, that are clearly taken to be explanatory by the community of scientists. There seem to be two interlocking demands placed upon them.

(a) A discourse is explanatory if it describes a plausible generative mechanism (real or hypothetical) which does (or could) produce the naturally occurring or experimentally contrived phenomenon to be explained. Usually the generative mechanism cannot be studied independently of the phenomenon it is supposed to produce, at least when it is first proposed, that is in the formative stages of theory. It is to provide surrogates for real generative mechanisms that neo-realists introduce models and metaphors into the two sides of theory construction – that is into the imagined world the theory describes, and into the vocabulary of the discourse that describes it. The realist schema for theory can be set out as in Table 1.

Table 1

	Observed Patterns OP	Generative Mechanism GM	Iconic Model of GM IM	Source of Model IM MS
World or Surrogate				
Epistemic Status	Inductive	Suspended	Hypothetical	Assumed Universal
Discourse	Empirical Generalizations	Nil	Description of hypothetical GM	Background Assumptions, Generic Laws

This is bound into a structure by transverse relations of analogy between real and imagined things in the world-aspect, and by metaphor/simile relations between concepts in the discourse-aspect. The discourse describes the world and its imaginary surrogates. The analogy relations are as follows:

(i) IM and GM must behave analogously since IM produces hypothetically and GM produces actually the phenomena OP.

'Swarms of molecules, as imagined, behave analogously to real gases.'

'Role-players, as imagined, behave analogously to people.'

(ii) IM and MS must have analogous natures since the laws of the behaviour of the components etc. of IM are analogues of the laws of behaviour of items of MS.

'Molecules are like Newtonian particles, but not exactly alike.'

'Role-players are like stage actors, but not exactly like.'

The corresponding concepts in the discourse are related as similes and metaphors to their literal counterparts, simile when they refer to possible experience, metaphor when they refer beyond all possible experience.

This structure explains how a theory can acquire trans-experiential empirical content from a source other than its observational consequences. It acquires it from its model-source. It also provides criteria for testing plausibility, namely two *testable* analogies, that of behaviour, B(IM) $\rightleftarrows$ (B(GM); and that of nature or being, IM $\rightleftarrows$ MS.

(b) A second, more stringent condition can be laid on explanatory theory, within this system as a general framework, by the imposition of a generally Aristotelian framework on the scheme outlined in (a). We reach this by asking what it is about the observed patterns that needs to be explained. If we realize that it is structure that needs to be explained, then we are already halfway to an Aristotelian restriction on the components of generative mechanisms and their surrogates, iconic models of such mechanism. For the effect of making this move is to separate two questions.

(i) Why did something, namely an OP, come into existence here and now? This calls for an efficient causality explanation, preferably non-positivistically couched in terms of an agent or agents, and the contingent removal of impediments to action.

(ii) Why does the OP here and now produced have the structure and the properties that it has?

This calls for an answer in terms of formal causes, to be found in the preformed template or structural property of the material or other structured conditions of and contributors to the causal process.

Thus generative mechanisms, GM above, can be further specified. They must include agents and templates, to account for the being and the properties of the generated product respectively. In rare cases, such as classical mechanics, most of the activity (energy) for a motion comes from outside the moving body, and shapes its motion.

If social studies are to be scientific they must conform to this account of explanation. In the chapters to come I shall be developing the outlines of an explanatory system which conforms to the demands of realism.

2. OUTLINE OF THE METHOD

(a) Attribution Schema

Human social activity consists of two main kinds of performance.

   (i) Performance 1 is the doings of actions and thus the performing of acts in socially recognized episodes.

   (ii) Performance 2 is the speaking of accounts, both to ensure that the act/action performances are given a certain meaning, and that they can be seen as the doings of rational beings.

The fundamental principle of ethogenic research is the belief that both kinds of performance stem from one and only one system of cognitively represented social knowledge and social skill, from which come our rules of action and interpretative principles. On the basis of this hypothesis one can use the results of the analysis of action and of accounting to attribute knowledge and skill to a competent actor.

To use this as a real empirical method we need analytical models for performances of kind 1 and analytical concepts for performances of kind 2. I propose two main models in this work. This does not exclude the possibility that others may be required as social studies progress.

   (i) The Problem Solving Model. This includes the treatment of act/action episodes as solving practical and social problems by the use of standard techniques, shading off into cases where the techniques are improvised. It also includes the treatment of accounts as solutions to a range of metaproblems raised by the possibility of misunderstandings of the meaning and legitimacy of actions.

   (ii) The Dramaturgical Model. This includes the analysis of

episodes according to the overall Scene, Action, Actor schema, and the treatment of accounts as presentational activities, as part of the performance by which we show what sort of person we are. In most Western and Western influenced cultures, we are required to show that we are rational beings.

(b) Explanation Schema

Having attributed knowledge and skill to a competent member of a well identified collective by the use of the methods outlined above, we have now to explain how he produces his actions in accordance with these properties on particular occasions. Generally I adopt an Aristotelian or realist theory of causal explanation as against a merely Humean one. So we must address ourselves to the question of the productive mechanisms at work, and not rest satisfied with a mere description of the conditions under which action occurs.

The outline schema for explanation runs as follows:

Social Knowledge is drawn upon by the actor to formulate intentions to perform appropriate acts. Action to realize intentions draws further on the rules and conventions as to how those acts are to be performed in cultures and within situations and settings in which the actor finds himself. Contrary to recent attempts to develop this in a Humean mode[4] I argue that the fulfilling of the conditions for action implicit in this scheme is neither sufficient nor necessary for action to occur. Empirical considerations force us to introduce the pure agent or person who acts in accordance with these conditions, but not because of them. Intentions control the content of an actor's performance as to the acts he is trying to perform and the rules and conventions of his society control the way he realizes his intentions. Neither singly nor jointly could these conditions produce action. The resolution of these matters will occupy us in Part III.

(c) The methods outlined in the above schemata do not allow us to say anything about macroproperties, structures and processes which we may want to attribute to the collectives in which action takes place. In so far as explanations developed in accordance with these schemata are felt to be incomplete, and they explain neither the presence in the culture of the practices analysed nor the knowledge of these practices which any competent individual must have, hypotheses as to macroproperties of the relational network that links people into collectives are needed. But it was established in Part I that we have no satisfactory method for empirically investigating large-scale properties of social networks. At best then we must form our ideas of them analogically and test them hypothetico-deductively. In any causal theory they must be assigned to a selectional rather than a productive role, that is of an existent but unknown environment which eliminates or encourages some microformations and individually realized practices rather than others.

But the macroproperties of social networks do not make up the whole story of the selection process, since some social and psychological innovations are non-viable by reason of conflict with psychological possibility. But since that is itself an historically conditioned matter, societies impossible today, given when and where we are in the history of mankind, may have been possible for people in the past and may again become possible for people in the future.

9

SOCIAL ACTION AS PROBLEM SOLVING

ANTICIPATORY SUMMARY

A. Act/Action sequences as ritualized solution techniques
Introduction: the basic problem for a person in society is to be recognized as of worth, and as such to be producing meaningful actions and speeches. This dominant theme is superimposed on a groundwork of co-operative solutions to practical problems.
1. Problems and Solutions
   (a) The source of problems:
      (i) contingencies in the physical environment;
      (ii) contingencies in the social environment;
      (iii) contingencies in the actors.
   (b) Types of problems:
      (i) concerning persons;
      (ii) concerning attitudes;
      (iii) concerning agreements.
   (c) Types of solutions: social v. non-social:
      (i) consequent distinctions in ontological casting;
      (ii) consequent distinctions in available effective action.
2. Standardization of solutions
   (a) Occasions for standardization.
   (b) Standardization of agonistic sequences.
3. Non-standard action sequences
   (a) Level of improvisation.
   (b) Negotiation of initial social conditions.
4. Method of study of problem solving rituals: we look for the templates of orderly action in the rules and plans established by actors prior to action.
B. Accounting as a Technique of Problem Solving
1. The nature of an account
   Accounts are public productions imposing meanings and creating a sense of understanding other people — not introspectively based descriptions

167

of mental causes usually, though they can be.
2. The dual purpose of an account
   (a) Explication: we achieve intelligibility for our actions and speeches.
   (b) Warranting: we achieve legitimacy or propriety for our actions and speeches. Taken together these ensure that we appear to each other as rational beings.
3. The content of accounts
   (a) Local v. universal accounting systems:
       (i) no grounds for universalizing any features of the content of accounts to other cultures, *a priori*;
       (ii) no grounds for universalizing any features of the contents of accounts to other times, *a priori*.
   (b) The Material revealed by account analysis:
       (i) static content: social knowledge of role-rule prescriptions relative to identifiably distinct social situations;
       (ii) dynamic content: rehearsal of action as pretesting of action projects;
       (iii) an example of organized content.
   (c) Supplementary explorations: the use of Kelly repertory grids to reveal fine-structure.
4. Accounting as part of the action
   (a) Accounting in advance of the action, to prepare a legitimated place for a performance.
   (b) Acting in advance of the accounting, to legitimize the production of an account having distinct presentational and expressive properties.
   (c) Non-verbal accounting.

A: ACT/ACTION SEQUENCES
AS RITUALIZED SOLUTION TECHNIQUES

INTRODUCTION

The great Japanese novelist Mishima once pointed out that we have to show both to ourselves and to others that we 'willed' our actions. There seem to be two aspects to such an achievement. For one, a social actor has to achieve recognition by the others around him that he is indeed a social actor. Some categories of people, for example children, can find this recognition hard to achieve. Then, too, he has also to make what he says and does intelligible, meaningful to the others present, those whom his action and speech affects and who realize that he was the author of them. Each of these aspects supports the other. To recognize him as an actor is to see his actions as informed by his intentions and he, as actor, realizing them in actions. The recognition of his speech and movements as meaningful, that is, as actions, is to see them as informed by his intentions.

In accordance with the theory of the meaning of social actions developed in earlier chapters, the problems of intelligibility are solved as a continuous day-to-day achievement by the use of two main techniques. We attain intelligibility most readily if we draw upon standardized solutions to the specific social problems our social and physical environment presents us. These solutions involve a standardized, integrated personal style appropriate to each type of problem-situation. There is a local typology of personas available to draw upon. We recognize, by reference to cues not yet fully investigated, stylistic unities of action and the appropriate heraldic regalia of such as policeman, nurse, bank clerk, leftish ecologically oriented mother of two, and so on. A detailed study of these organized styles, their aetiology and the processes by which they come to be widely enough known to be a social resource for the achievement of intelligibility would be a useful contribution. Style, and regalia associated with specific role-places in football fan groups, have been closely studied by Marsh (see note 8, Chapter 14).

The solutions to standard problem situations that are available under each persona are, it seems, learned in a standardized form in each socially distinct locality. The use of ritual and ceremonial forms for the production of an action-sequence appropriate to some recognized social task guarantees the intelligibility and effectiveness of what has been done. The ritualization of apology, for example, allows each of us to maintain our dignity as actors when one of us inadvertently bursts into the other's space or time.

Wide though the scope of these ritualized ceremonies may be in solving socially problematic situations, there is a penumbra of uncertainty remaining. Empirical studies are beginning to show that improvisation of solutions draws upon the same repertoire of actions which serve as components, that is as parts of the 'vocabulary' of standardized solutions available in a local culture.[1]

Human beings have a further resource for achieving the intelligibility required of their actions, namely accounting. Accounting is speech which precedes, accompanies and follows action. Actors give accounts to ensure the twin goals of intelligibility and warrantability, that is, the meaningfulness and propriety of their actions. Empirical studies have shown that accounts involve, among other items, statements of rules, implicit or explicit exposition of meanings, and stories and anecdotes, the social meaning of which may need some interpretation.[2] Accounts may draw on the rhetoric of causality but are not to be taken as unproblematic, introspective causal explanations. Rather, accounts reveal the sources of the structural properties of action in the resources of individuals, and allow us to develop hypotheses of ideal social competence for a given society against which the actual resources of any individual can be matched. Whatever one may think of the merits of introspective investigations of alleged cognitive causal processes is quite irrelevant to account analysis since it is not aimed at that goal. The study of the efficient causes of human action may not be possible, at least in the immediate future, because the stimulating causes of the socially identical actions of different people may be quite idiosyncratic. The common-alities of social life are structures which pre-exist action and speech and it is to the study of these that accounting theory is directed.

If we regard the day-to-day social world as a co-operative achievement, what sort of achievement is it? From the standpoint of this model we can view it as the successful and continuous attainment of solutions to a myriad of problems of action and understanding, modulating from one set of conventions to another. Clearcut gaps seldom develop in the flow of interaction. We modu-late smoothly through sequences: attending a meeting, breaking up, walking down the corridor, and having a drink in the bar. In the course of these sequences the very same topics may be under discussion but action proceeds according to distinctly different conventions of behaviour and self-presentation, but maintaining a socially coherent and continuously interacting group. To keep each stage going and to make smooth transitions from one to the next, all kinds of small problems must be solved.

Theoretically, we can draw a distinction between problems which have socially constructive solutions which bring people to-gether into a fragment of the orderly, meaningful action sequences which constitute social life, and problems which have socially maintaining solutions where threats to existing orderliness are dealt with in a ritual fashion. In detailing the importance of the socially maintaining solutions, I am not claiming that existing forms of order should be maintained; only that as a matter of fact they are preserved. Those who wish to change the social order had best know how it is achieved.

1. PROBLEMS AND SOLUTIONS

(a) The Sources of Problems

Problems arise through the interplay of the following contingencies:

(i) Contingencies in the physical environment, the social meaning of which requires interpretation. The first and most obvious contingency is the presence of human beings or other social animals, such as dogs. Though its significance may be problematic, this would pose no problem if the physical environment did not have features which force propinquity and interaction. These qualities could be spatial, such as the narrowness of a path or corridor. They might involve depletion of resources requiring the setting up of agreed practices for sharing or conservation.

(ii) Contingencies in the social environment. The appropriateness of a solution will depend upon the state of the other people, for instance their attitudes (hostile or friendly), their projects and their traditions of response to the situation, such as their formalized obligations of hospitality, politeness, and so on.

(iii) Contingencies in the actors. There are fluctuations of attitudes, projects and so on in the actor's make up which are among the conditions which create the problematic character of the situation. If the actor were not determined to ascend by the narrow path, the descending goat-herd would not constitute a problem.

(b) Types of Problems

Out of these contingencies arise three distinct types of problems:

(i) With what category of person are we dealing?

(ii) What are his current attitudes?

(iii) How am I as initiator of the action to secure agreement to the practical details of the solution I propose while remaining within the boundaries of the social?

(c) Types of Solutions

Of all the ways open to the actor at this point we must distinguish the social from the non-social as basic categories of solution. Clearly, to bash or shoot the descending goat-herd and throw him off the path is not a social solution, just as lashing out when someone bumps into one in a crowded public place is not a social solution to the problem of maintaining a social space. Compare these with greeting the goat-herd, squeezing back against the rock wall and ushering him past with a smile, or dealing with the bump by taking the blame oneself and opening with 'I'm very sorry' and getting the return, 'No, no, my fault', achieving (as Goffman calls it) the maintenance of civility. The distinction between these categories is intuitively obvious, but we must look more closely into the differentia.

(i) Each category of solution depends upon an initial onto-logical casting of the interactor by the actor. The non-social solution clearly involves treating the goat-herd as being in the same category as an awkwardly placed boulder, a thing-like impediment to be merely disposed of. To attempt the social solution involves an attribution of cognitive status and of autonomy to the interactor, that is, he is cast as a person. In that category he can now be expected to behave as such. Social psychologists have yet to address the problem of how personhood is achieved against the ever-present threat of being cast as a thing. The study of alter-casting is a beginning but so far has been sociologically naive.[3]

(ii) Further, each type of solution draws upon a technique of effective action. The non-social solution depends upon the techniques involving physical causality and requires the actor to have knowledge of elementary natural science. The social solution calls upon techniques of revealing intentions through speech and action, and the recognition of the force of speech-acts such as pleas and apologies upon which their effectiveness depends. And the actor's knowledge must include an ethnography, a represen-tation of the general form of these achievements, for instance the rule for achieving polite ushering. Much of this knowledge may be tacit or reduced to habit. It may be known explicitly only to Machiavellians.

These distinctions of ontological status and action technique are not new. They are central distinctions of Kant's theory of human interaction.[4] Moral action is identified by the degree to which we treat others as ends rather than means. And they are also implicit in everyday practice. For example, we occasionally cast a doubtful dog into the role of social actor by treating him as such, assigning him to that category by such civil attributions as, 'There's a *good dog*', 'Down *boy*', and so on.

The three problems of the social actor are solved by the tech-niques of civility. The upshot of greeting is the casting of the other into the role of a person, requiring intelligibility and warrant-ability to be sustained in *his* action sequences. The second problem is solved by the demeanour of the other person, his formalized style of self-presentation which ought to reflect and respond to the way the actor has opened the encounter with a civil greeting. How far problems of the second type can be solved independently of local cultural conventions is unknown. Finally, a solution to the technical problem is achieved by the mutual production of a standardized (or improvised) ritual action-sequence, which provides a conventional solution to the problem, preserving the dignity of each individual as a person, and characterized by a style expressive of civility.

Sometimes the local solution to the technical aspect of a social problem is itself covertly social, for example it may reflect a local social hierarchy. In some New Guinea tribes each member of the community had a right to a certain part of a kill depending upon his or her social placement. The division of the meat was regulated not by reference to the dietetic needs of various members of the community but by their social standing.[5]

2. STANDARDIZATION OF SOLUTIONS

(a) Occasions for Standardization

I have already touched on the standardization of the form of some of the action-sequences available for social problem-solving. These generally occur either when the act to be performed is socially important (consider for instance name-giving rituals such as baptisms); or when the problem situation occurs very frequently (dealing with the presence of a stranger at a social gathering). An introduction of a stranger by a sponsor to a host can be seen as a device to solve in standardized form the following problems:

(i) What is the stranger's name?
(ii) What is his relative status?
(iii) Can he be 'one of us'?

These questions are answered in one way or another in the course of our familiar introduction-rituals. Detailed studies have shown the complexity of even such commonplace action sequences as introductions (see Chapter 10). Several kinds of knowledge and several different levels of self-management are required for successful accomplishment. Analysis suggests that the linguistic distinction between semantics and syntax can be used in analysing such complex sequences. There are questions about the meaning of component elements of the ritual (semantics) as well as uncertainties about the sequential structure (syntax) of the sequence.

Both the semantics of elements of the ritual and the syntactic structure determine its overall significance. For instance, the syntactical property of relative order of speech by host, sponsor and stranger reflects and expresses the relative status each allows the other. Initially, unless the host is manifestly more socially important than the stranger, the stranger has notional high status. This is reflected in many subtle features of the interaction including the ordering of speech-turns. However, in the course of the introduction, if a microsequence occurs in which status uncertainty is resolved, there may be a formal recognition of the stranger's inferior standing, which is expressed in his losing temporal precedence in speech and action. The introduction of a stranger thus involves both the creation and the maintenance of social orderliness. It extends orderliness to include the stranger, and it serves to maintain the existing order surrounding the host by minimizing the threat the stranger, as unknown, may pose for him.

(b) Standardization of Agonistic Sequences

Action-sequences are standardized in form even when the outcome or act performed is problematic. For example, a formalized resolution of a status uncertainty involves a non-problematic and shared conception of status. But since, logically, only one of a pair of status contestants can occupy the upper position, the determination of which person achieves this status is problematic. I shall call those action-sequences, or components of action-sequences, that accomplish the resolution of such problems, *within a framework of orderliness*, agonistic sequences.

3. NON-STANDARD ACTION-SEQUENCES

(a) Level of Improvisation

The idea of a non-standard action sequence can be applied at two levels of generality. There are sequences which are non-standard relative to the social techniques generally available in a community but which are the standard sequences for some isolated group of people. The private rituals of individual families are non-standard in this sense. There are also sequences that are non-standard in that they are improvised for a particular occasion, for the solution of a problem for which a ritual solution does not exist in the local ethnography. Examples of improvisation can be seen at many semi-formal social gatherings.

It is worth noticing that the improvisations of non-standard solutions may still open out into an 'agonistic abyss' even though they are within traditions of civility. The improvisations may bring the standard components under challenge. This may even extend to pretended incomprehension of another's words. When even the intelligibility of speech is conventionally denied the possibility of improvising a civil encounter is gone. Some unfortunate people may forever feel as if they are on the edge of an agonistic abyss. There are people who, for one reason or another, find it very difficult to make themselves understood, perhaps because they do not use language or action in the standard ways. Improvisation, unless in the hands of genius, cannot extend to the basic semantic system.

(b) Negotiation of Initial Social Conditions

Finally, I would like to emphasize the role of interactive social processes as essential preliminaries in the improvisation of a solution to a socially defined problem. Standard solutions work because they are applied in recognized situations and involve recognized styles of person presentation: personas appropriate to those situations. With situation and persona settled, action can proceed smoothly to the accomplishment of the act, be it friendly or hostile. Correspondingly but problematically, a non-standard solution requires a definition of the situation within scene and relative to setting, and a negotiation of social identities or personas. These proceedings may have standard forms, but again they may be improvised for the occasion, opening up once again the possibility of an indefinitely prolonged challenge to the successful completion of the task. Some people regularly open proceedings with a stranger by adopting a probing, challenging, testing kind of stance, the effect of which is to force the other either into a display of coolness or counter-provocation or into a demeaning display of annoyance, fear, aggression and so on. These encounters are not well documented and could do with much more detailed study.

4. METHOD OF STUDY OF PROBLEM-SOLVING RITUALS

So far we have looked at action-sequences from only one point of view, that of the microsociologist, questioning neither their mode of genesis nor their relation to larger structural properties of society. Ethogenics proposes the study of the genesis of problem-solving rituals according to the structure/template methodology sketched in Part I. The schema for study of the genesis of action-sequences takes the following form:

The potent preformed templates or formal causes of the structure or pattern of standard action-sequences are to be called *rules*. They must pre-exist the action and must be known, though not necessarily explicitly, to all for whom the action-pattern is socially potent as a ceremony accomplishing an act. Our hypothesis is that in general the rules are learned, that is, pre-exist individuals.

The potent templates or formal causes of non-standard action-patterns I propose to call *plans*. They may be modulated to rules through such processes as Miller, Galanter and Pribram[6] hypothesized in their T O T E hierarchies. They must pre-exist the action but perhaps as part of the resources of only one of the interactors who has the problem of making his actions intelligible and warrantable to the others not privy to his plan. Plans are constructed; they are among the achievements of individuals.

The cognitive resources which are the basis of social competence are revealed as representations in some medium of,

    (a) knowledge of the local rule system, the immediate resource for competent social performance;

    (b) knowledge of the general principles of action, laws of nature etc., the resource for the competent formation of plans, for testing them by imaginative rehearsal, for negotiating them with others in the course of the action.

These resources can be hypothetically attributed to people on the basis of their observed success in encounters, that is, as social actors, because success constitutes an overt proof of competence. But how do we proceed to test the correctness of these hypothetical attributions? This takes us to account analysis.

B. ACCOUNTING AS A TECHNIQUE OF PROBLEM SOLVING

1. THE NATURE OF AN ACCOUNT

In accounting we produce speech to interpret and explain the action-sequences we perform and the acts we thereby accomplish. We shall have occasion to distinguish implicit interpretations and theories from explicit interpretation and explanation in the speech that deals with action. We shall credit the cognitive achievement of accounting to both implicit and explicit interpretation and explanation, provided of course that the implications are understood. Understanding may be no more explicit than the accounting, and may have to be inferred from the smooth, unbroken, unchallenged flow of action.

To forestall a common misinterpretation to which accounting theory is particularly prone, I want to emphasize again that an account is not to be interpreted as an introspective causal explanation although some accounts, *inter alia*, do have that character. Accounts are generated by ordinary people in the ordinary course of social action (and are encouraged by ethogenically oriented social psychologists) primarily to make actions intelligible and warrantable by interpreting them as proper parts of the structure of interaction sequences. Accounting could be glossed as part of the technique to achieve *verstehen*, Weberian understandings of what people are about.

2. THE DUAL PURPOSE OF ACCOUNTS

As I argued in the general introduction, accounting seems to involve the performance of two main tasks: the explication of action and the justification of action. Satisfactory performances of the tasks may be linked one with another.

(a) Explication

Explication as accounting may be explicit or implicit. A common form of explicit explication is the simple, 'Sorry, I didn't mean to ...', making available an interpretation which suspends meaning altogether and hence suspends the question of warrantability. Less common, but more committing is the formula, 'Well, what I meant was ...' It is of considerable importance to grasp the fact that the production of an account can do no more than make available a justification or explication. Mere production of the account cannot ensure that the interpretation offered will be accepted. This brings out the negotiable quality of the meanings and explanations that are going to survive in public space, so to speak, as mutual achievements.

Implicit accounting is more complex. We have already had occasion to notice the sociological distinction between *actions*, the meaningful components of action-sequences identified through their meanings, and *acts*, the social upshot of the performance of a particular pattern sequence. Cocking a snook is an action, the resulting insult is an act; saying 'Guilty' is an action, the resulting verdict is an act, and so on.

On the ethogenic view, actions are the meanings of behaviour and speeches and as such are readings of the various vehicles by which they are conveyed. As readings they are products of interpretation and can be influenced by the interpretations made available in accounting. In a certain sense, then, actions can be generated by the form a description takes.

Broadly speaking, the descriptive vocabulary available to a speaker, intent on accounting, allows three stages of description in two of which meaning is imposed.

'He bumped into her' describes mere body contact. The explanation of the contact calls upon neither private intention nor shared social convention. Another example: 'Her fourth finger went through a ring held by him'.

'He pushed her' is a redescription by which the contact becomes invested with the possibility of meaning since it is represented as an action, namely something somebody intended. The meaning is grasped when we know the place of the action in some recognized fragment of social life. The explanation of the happening as now described calls for intentions and perhaps social conventions as well. Another example: 'He put a ring on her fourth finger'.

'He tried to murder her' is a further redescription in which the action is seen as the commission of a socially defined act – attempted murder – that is, attempted unlawful killing. Another example: 'He married her'. In these examples, the act not only is a meaning, but has a meaning itself. It has its special social potency in an obvious way. For example, defining the killing as a murder rather than as an accident leads to a commitment by the state and its officers to accomplish the man's arrest, trial and conviction, all of which are themselves social acts at the second level of meaning. Clearly, the social psychological investigation of the potency of actions as acts to produce all kinds of effects in a society must take its start from the interpretation of behaviour as action. But it must also take account of the accounting, implicit in social custom or explicit in a court of law, by which an action is treated as the performance of an act.

The effect of successive reinterpretation is profound.[7] We can perhaps grasp the theoretical possibilities by supposing that even when we proceed to act-interpretations as we usually do, we have reached them by the successive interpretations I have separated above. First, there is a change in relational structures as we go from behaviour and speech to act. Behaviours are related, probably through physiological mechanisms, and these relations may be largely irrelevant to their social significance. Actions are related in semantic fields and syntactically into action patterns, but requiring knowledge of the act and its local conventions to be fully disambiguated for meaning. Acts relate to the social structure at large. Not only are the behaviours, actions and acts in non-isomorphic relational structures, but the relations of the people involved are different under each stage of the attribution of meaning. If they are merely *behaving* they are related by physical causality. When they are interacting in this way a speech made by one of them may be too piercing but it cannot be too insulting. But if people are performing the *action* of getting married, they are performing the ceremony together, are required to understand one another, and relate to each other within the terms of the role system for that ceremony. On the other hand, when they are performing the *act* of getting married they are generating a fragment of the relatively permanent social order, a fragment which involves anticipation of the future, and another ceremonial act to annul, change or undo.

(b) Justification

Transition from one descriptive system to another involves transition from one justificatory and warranting system to another. The rules specifying the variety of actions are usually person-centred and culturally specific. We would naturally treat them as social conventions. It is a social convention that defines the action of giving of a ring as part of the act of marriage. Acts on the other hand come up for judgement under moral and legal rules.

The techniques of warranting by redescription, that is of justifying actions and acts by how we categorize them, deserve careful analysis. They involve subtle relations between the presentation of the person and the presentation of his actions and acts. A person's primary move may be a recategorization of himself. He may produce an account in which he identifies himself as a mere thing, an object. The events he is accounting for are correspondingly described in the mere-happenings vocabulary, translated neither into actions nor acts. There may be explicit attention in such accounting to causality. He claims as a thing to be subject to physical causality, a form of determination which involves both efficient and material causes and by claiming which he repudiates the normal assumptions of self-management. The prime linguistic mode for achieving such recategorization separates the

speaker into an 'I' and a 'me', the former an astonished spectator
of the behaviour of the latter. This implies the breaking of control
of the 'I' over the 'me', and by categorizing the 'me' as a 'thing',
suggests either a physical cause of behaviour or, at best, an auto-
matism. The putative action is treated as a mere effect of happenings within the 'me'. Transcripts of defendants' evidence in murder
trials is a rich source of examples of the use of this technique.
'I blacked out, but when I came to I found myself with the
knife in my hand and I saw him lying on the floor'. Should the
court accept the implication, the actions of the speaker (I) as
killer could be classified not as the commission of an act of
murder, but as mere behaviour, the effects of automatic processes
within the 'me'. As behaviour they escape questions as to their
warrantability.

However, the preservation of dignity and selfhood is incompatible with the prmary mode of recategorization. It is not surprising
that this mode occurs most often in moral emergencies. More
common, and indeed an everyday technique, is the recategorization of what the actor did. The original impetus to the study of
this technique came from Austin's famous distinction between
excuses and justifications, in the context of warranting an action.[8]
Again we will see an interplay between the categorization of the
behaviour and the claim to a special status or situation for the
person. Austin proposed that we treat as excuses those speeches
in which we admit the moral quality of the act, allowing it to be
offensive, insulting, and the like, but disclaim freedom of action.
There is a corresponding technique of modest disclaimer of
virtue when we accept praise for the products of our activity
but disclaim primary responsibility as the agent of the production. 'I'm only the representative of a team, you know ...' An
excuse addresses the warrantability of what has occurred in such
formulae as 'I'm terribly sorry I'm late. I got caught in the rush-
hour traffic'. The first phase of the excuse serves the joint task
of apology and admission that lateness is an offence, while the
second phase disclaims agenthood *vis à vis* that occurrence. I
return to a more thorough study of the structure of apology-
rituals in Chapter 10.

A justification, on the other hand, denies the moral quality
of the act and claims free agenthood. This often takes the general
form, 'I did it, but it was not wrong, obscure, cruel ... etc.'
An extreme form of justification is to be found in the speech
of a participant in ethogenic studies who, when chided with

being late, turned on the critic and made a slashing attack on the institution of punctuality, arguing that it was not a matter of respect between persons but a neurotic symptom.

Austin's investigations were both incomplete and purely conceptual. Backman has recently carried out an empirical study of the speech produced by people who set out to warrant their actions. He found that justifications formed a complex category in need of subdivisions.[9] An extremely common form involves the use of the technique he calls 'conventionalization'. From the point of view of accounting, conventionalization is a redescription of the act. The action is conserved, 'Oh yes, I took the money', but the description of this action as the act of theft is rebutted, 'but I was only borrowing it ...' Utilizing the Gricean conditions for intelligibility the speaker proceeds to '... I intended to put it back next week ...' Finally, there is the technique of 'normalizing', again revealed in Backman's study. This technique may apply to action or act and involves the claim that what the actor did is normal or commonplace and hence does not in general come up for special accounting. Normalizing can be achieved either in terms of frequency ('It happens all the time') or generality 'Everybody does it'). Normalizing conserves the standing of the actor as agent and the imputed quality of the act but repudiates the demand for an account as justification.

3. THE CONTENT OF ACCOUNTS

So far we have followed Austin and Backman in examining accounts for their social function. The next step is to proceed to the analysis of the content of accounts, in search of the cognitive resources available to an individual as a member of a community. Account analysis starts always with the particular and the local. It begins idiographically and proceeds only after the comparison of the cognitive resources of a great many people of apparently similar skills and social habits to claim a limited generality for the structures it reveals. We assume there is a commonality in the use and understanding of ordinary language between analyst and accounter, but recognize this too as an assumption that may be questionable in specific cases (as an example analyst and accounter may not use the same range of grammatical forms in giving instances of the category of rule). But in general, unless some commonality is assumed as a working hypothesis analysis cannot begin.

(a) Local v. Universal Accounting Systems

The analysis of the accounts of individuals reveals the cognitive groundings of their individual social competence, and from these a hypothetical grounding for an ideal competence in that particular social milieu can be abstracted. I shall refer to the former as 'cognitive resources' and to the latter as 'the local ethnography'. The capacity for achievement, in the ethnomethodologists's sense, that is acting rightly in the appropriate situation, is rooted in the individual's cognitive resources, in so far as these are representations of the local ethnography. Looked at from the point of view of the person producing an account, it has the status of a socio-psychological theory which he makes available when required as an explanation of the actions and acts he needs to justify. But merely making the account available is no guarantee that it will be accepted by the listener. This brings up an interesting class of social events, the negotiation of accounts. Negotiations are action-sequences in the course of which accounting acts are performed, for instance acts of excuse and justification, which are themselves accountable. Our problem as social psychologists is to reveal a match between our imputations of cognitive resources to an individual on the basis of what we, by reference to *our* accounting system, take to be the structure and meaning of his performances, and those resources as indicated in his account. Difficulties abound, particularly those posed by self-deception, false consciousness and unconscious motives. We shall return to a partial resolution of these difficulties later.

The step from the local ethnography to a universal human action-centred system cannot be made at this time.

(i) The nomethetic transition from individual to local society is problematic enough and not yet clearly established. I am certainly not prepared to propose that the formal structural properties of the cognitive resources of the individuals we have studied so far should be taken as universal even within contemporary Western society. We are still smarting under the consequences of the absurd assumption that sophomore psychology students are typical human beings. The greater power of the new empirical methods in ethogenics ought not to tempt us to make the same mistake again. The empirical work reported in this chapter is to be understood as strictly of *local* significance. But we may have reason to think that though the content of accounts is strictly local, the form accounts take may have some universal properties.

(ii) Furthermore, as Gergen has pointed out in a paper of considerable significance,[10] what little evidence exists concerning the temporal stability of social formations and practices, personality-types and so on, points to their remarkably ephemeral character. We are quite unjustified in supposing that the forms of micro-social action, and even perhaps the way individuals are related to these forms, that is their social psychology, are constant over time. All the evidence we have, slender though it is, suggests that social forms and individual cognitions of these forms are highly unstable and in rapid flux. We expect stability and are alarmed and outraged by social change, but contrary to our social mythology, social forms have a very short life. I believe that this has always been true. Where detailed records exist, for example ancient Greece or pre-Columbian America, a picture of rapid change emerges. Indirect indicators point to the same conclusion; the flux and re-flux of fashion in clothes, hairstyles, furniture and so on, were apparently as rapid in Pharaonic Egypt as they have been in Western Europe.

The fact that certain artefacts, particularly tools and utensils, have a long and unbroken history in a region, shows nothing about the accompanying social forms. Few major changes in basic artefacts occurred between 1300 and 1750 in Western Europe, a period which saw enormous social and linguistic changes.

The anthropological study of 'primitive' people outside Europe reveals the forms of life current when they were examined. Linguists have long since abandoned the idea that 'primitive' societies have preserved earlier forms of language. We should abandon the corresponding assumptions for other phenomena. I propose to start with the hypothesis that human social practices are unstable. Since 'primitive' societies lack any kind of historical record, we must take their rhetoric of 'ancient ways' with considerable scepticism.

It may yet turn out that social science can present us only with a method for understanding each social formation, its practices, and the relation of competent people to it, one by one, and that no social universals may be revealed. At present, we have neither an adequate cross-cultural social psychology by which we can proceed from idiographic to nomothetic assertions, nor an adequate theory of social change. Marxist theory is too localized and Darwinian theory as yet too biological to serve as the basis for a diachronic theory of society. But perhaps some development which fuses these limited but powerful theories into some kind of synthesis will serve (see Part IV).

(b) The Material Revealed by Account Analysis

(i) Accounts reveal the social semantic system of individuals. As we have seen, that system involves social knowledge, for example the kinds of situations we encounter and the action sequences proper to each of them. But accounting is not only a method for revealing the meanings of one's actions but also for warranting or justifying what one does. The cognitive resources required for successfully warranting an action overlap the resources required for explanation of meanings, since a knowledge of the situations that are regarded as socially distinct in the culture and of the form of action sequences appropriate in those situations is required for both.

Two further items are revealed by account analysis. The public presentation of the self as a distinct persona occurs in the way the action sequences required for the performance of social acts are carried out, that is, in their style. Distinct situations call for distinct styles of performance, and hence present the self under distinct personas. Many people have explicit knowledge of the style of actions that are required in distinct situations, but though they are perfectly adequate performers at the stylistic level, they are not aware of how they appear to others. Nevertheless they do know, at the 'knowing-how' level. This knowledge can be revealed indirectly by picking up the basis of critical judgements of style in their accounts, as well as by assembling explicit fragments of tacit knowledge by forcing a participant to contemplate actions and style he previously took for granted as natural. E. Rosser and I have shown that some adolescents have very detailed and explicit knowledge of style and its relation to impression management.[11]

(ii) Account analysis reveals a further structure-linked resource. The T O T E (test unit) hierarchies, discussed by Miller, Galanter and Pribram, are run, for certain important bits of social action, in advance of the realization of the action sequences in real life. The T O T E hierarchies of social life are partly pretests run in the imagination. In some cases competence is acquired through rehearsal. Judgement of our actions by other people is replaced in these rehearsals by an imagined judgement of an imagined other, which realizes a store of intuitions of proper and improper actions, not as rules, but as the imagined approval or disapproval of some specific person. At present our knowledge of these resources grows out of studies of violent school children, murderers and rubber fetishists, a rather atypical profile of human beings. In each case, the representation by the actor of his knowledge of how his actions will be judged has been as a representation of the imagined responses of a concrete individual, his mother, the dominant member of a peer group, his wife, and so on. Which individual's reactions are imagined is highly situation specific. T. Mischel has proposed that the clash of these empirical findings with the theoretical concept of 'generalized other', proposed by G. H. Mead for a similar role, could be resolved by the hypothesis, as yet untested, that 'ordinary' people utilize a generalized arbiter of action for each and every situation in the course of imaginative rehearsal. They may not have the reactions of a specific person in mind when they consider how their actions will be viewed by others.[12]

(iii) Control and rehearsal of action in situations is represented in accounts by normative material one could summarily call 'the rules'. Again, empirical studies of accounting reveal the very situation-specific character of rule-systems. A recent study of the rules adverted to by pupils in a secondary school where traditional 'order' has broken down, revealed a twelve-fold system, based upon twelve distinguishable situations, in each of which a different rule-system operated.[13]

There is some evidence that there may be deficits in an individual's cognitive resources. It seems likely that the capacity to recognize situations as socially distinct may be well developed without a corresponding development of knowledge of the appropriate style of self-presentation or of the rules for successful action. The deficit of style may be the more damaging to competence because its implicit character makes it less readily available to contemplation and correction by self-monitoring and self-control.

The structure revealed by the analysis of accounts represents an ideal social competence for that society, that is, represents the local ethnography in ideal form. I propose that this structure also represents the ideal cognitive resources of individuals competent in that society and, coupled with known deficits, the actual resources of real individuals. The structure of social action is matched by the templates of social action, that is, the cognitive resources upon which competence is based.

(c) Supplementary Explorations

A further step, however, is required, since account analysis provides the units of cognitive resources without explicitly identifying their fine structure and interrelations. Fortunately, Kelly's techniques provide a method by which those fine structures can be revealed. Suppose that we identify 'school' as a distinct social situation in the accountings of a young person. 'School' is a complex concept and has a fine structure involving (at least) the teachers, the curriculum, the ordered time-units of the day, the socially distinct physical spaces (for example classrooms, corridors, teachers' room, boiler house, yard, gym, and so on). By building up repertory grids based upon polar 'constructs', elicited for triads in each set of elements, the fine structure of each young person's concept of 'school' can be discovered. For example, three teachers may yield the construct 'strong-weak' as a criterion by which two of the triads differ from the third. And applying this to all the teachers, we form the first row of the grid.[14]

If we imagine the material elicited in accounts as arranged in a matrix of four columns, scenes, personas, arbiters and rule-systems, each row represents the resources deployed in a given type of scene and each cell is to be elaborated by the use of a Kelly grid. T. Mischel has shown how this is to be treated as an elucidation of rules, thus subsuming Kelly's "constructs" under a generally ethogenic conceptual system.[15]

Accounting, like social action itself, is an intellectual skill that can be done well or ill, and is subject to improvement. If rough passages in social action are smoothed over by accounting, then lack of skill in accounting is sure to lead to a troubled life for the individual with that deficit. He stumbles from one minor crisis to another. Perhaps one of psychiatry's functions is to provide powerful accounting material as well as a measure of improved skill in using it. It may be that psychiatry could be a more potent technique if its practitioners made more deliberate efforts to amplify both resources for and skill at accounting.

4. ACCOUNTING AS PART OF THE ACTION

But not all accounting is offered as retrospective explanation in the attempt to make actions, which would otherwise be anomic or bizarre, intelligible and warrantable. In real life accounting becomes a social technique in its own right and not a mere ancillary of action. I would like to illustrate this with some examples taken from empirical studies of accounting speech.

(a) Accounting in Advance of the Action

Marks and Gelder have shown that fetishists may prepare for their perverse action in advance by developing an account that makes their action intelligible and warrantable under some explanatory scheme other than fetishism.[16] These people often provide in advance a context of interpretation in which the action has a pre-determined and commonplace meaning and is warrantable under the rule system for that kind of situation. For instance, a rubber fetishist, preparing to don his gear on Saturday will devote much of his talk in the preceding week to developing a definition of his dressing up as 'keeping clean while unstopping the drains'. He may even include some drain cleaning to sharpen the situational definition and ground the warranting in empirical reality.

Another form of accounting in advance of the action is pre-emptive accounting. This occurs in agonistic situations and involves B using a form of expression which traps A, the interlocutor, so that all accountings open to him are personally discreditable. An example revealed in empirical study of talk is the 'Do you mind' manoeuvre. Here is how one instance proceeds.

1. A is asked by B to do something (x) and forgets to do it.
2. B (much later) 'Do you mind doing x?'

As pre-emptive accounting this works in the following way:

Implication 1: A had an ulterior motive for not doing x, that is, he 'minded'.

Implication 2: The query offers A the mock-possibility of saying he does mind doing x, suggesting that even if A did not have a covert reason for doing x he might have. The mere con-templation of a covert reason for not doing x may be denigrating to the social relationship between A and B.

So A is trapped. If he takes the question literally and says he does (or doesn't) mind, he is discreditable, for either he has a covert reason or he did not but might have had. If he challenges the literal meaning then he is discreditable, for that challenge is itself a denigration of B. He thereby suggests that B did indeed set up a 'Do you mind?' trap for A.

(b) Acting in Advance of the Accounting

Again, there are cases where action occurs in advance of the accounting but is aimed at predetermining the form that account-ing can take. A simple example revealed in empirical study of talk is the case of a woman who repeatedly found reasons for not accompanying her husband to the theatre or restaurants. She thus accumulated evidence for an accounting of her continued remaining at home as discreditable to her husband, expressed in the accusation, 'You never take me out!' I have chosen an example of an agonistic relationship but the pre-empting of accounting also occurs in non-agonistic contexts, as when someone does something exciting or dangerous, keeping in mind the subsequent anecdote he can tell his friends. In all these cases the form either of the action or of the account is pre-empted by an initial move which constrains the possible accountings or possible actions.

(c) Non-verbal Accounting

Accountings need not necessarily be achieved by verbal means. The desirable sought-after properties of intelligibility and warrantability can also be attained in various non-verbal ways. Empirical studies reveal the following:

(i) Situational discounting: an action which would be accounted as discreditable, offensive (unwarranted) or meaningless in one kind of situation is transformed by non-verbal directing attention to the scene, with respect to which the action under enquiry acquires meaning and propriety. For instance, bodily contact which would be offensive in an open context is accounted for by the putative offender glancing about to indicate the press of the crowd, and shrugging his shoulders to indicate his helplessness in the situation. This sequence of action can be seen in underground trains (subways), football crowds and other tightly packed people-places.

(ii) Goffman has drawn attention to the phenomenon of body gloss, the using of an exaggerated form of the usual gestural accompaniment of an action to make a public action intelligible and warrantable.[17] For example, a person making a sudden turnabout in a public place accompanies the change of trajectory by an exaggerated form of the 'I've just remembered' gesture, often a finger flick followed by a sharp downward movement of the hand. Situational discounting of this sort can be seen from a vantage point in deserted plazas.

By all of these techniques we solve the problems of ordinary social life, and lay to rest some of the doubts our interactions with others can raise. At the same time we achieve the most important thing of all – the expressive advantage of showing ourselves to be reasonable and so worthy people.

10

SOCIAL ACTION AS DRAMA

ANTICIPATORY SUMMARY

Introduction: Adopting the dramaturgical model involves not only a source of concepts for analysing episodes, but induces a complex mode of consciousness in an actor, who can be both lost in and aware of the action.

A. SCENE ANALYSIS

1. Setting
   (a) Introduction: the setting as a socially defined *Umwelt*.
   (b) The structure of the *Umwelt*: boundaries and regions: how access is controlled:
      (i) time structure and its marking;
      (ii) space structure and its marking.
   (c) The social texture of space and time; the idea of locations and moments becoming threatening or reassuring.
   (d) Message specific structures:
      (i) the social meaning of furniture arrangements;
      (ii) the structure of food and drink occasions.
   (e) Interaction between *Umwelt* structures and social theories: Bourdieu's analysis of the meaning of the structure of the Berber house.
2. Situations: the dynamic tensions between people as the actors are aware of them.
   (a) People in relation to setting: tensions created by a sense of proprietorship of spaces and times, leading to a sense of intrusion as violation.
   (b) People in relation to each other:
      (i) private/personal relationships requiring public/social promulgation or ratification in the expressive order;
      (ii) an accidental concurrence of people seek a ratified relationship.

B. ACTION ANALYSIS

Introduction: practical and expressive aspects of and motivations for action distinguished.
1. Remedies: restoration of a sense of worth

189

    (a) individual: apologies and other remedies for violations.
    (b) small-scale face-to-face:
        (i) co-operative face-work: mutual sustaining of each other's preten-
            sions;
        (ii) agonistic: trouble in school.
2. Resolutions: the transformation of a relationship to remove tension.
    (a) transformation of a private into a public relationship:
        (i) *Bruderschaft* ritual: devices by which a personal relationship
            of friendship is transformed into a publicly acknowledged feature
            of the social order (cf. British custom: names first; friendship
            later);
        (ii) *Feindschaft* ritual: the complementary devices by which private
            antagonisms are transformed into public displays of enmity;
        (iii) style as public proclamation;
        (iv) resolutive acts and their social consequences.
    (b) Creation of a public relationship:
        (i) historical examples: introductions in *Everyman* and in Marlowe
            and Shakespeare;
        (ii) contemporary ritual: its phases and their social interpretation.
3. Monodrama
    (a) Ontological temptations of a form of speech.
    (b) Grammatical form as a presentational device for monodrama:
        (i) internal constitutings of voices and realms − the 'I' − 'me'
            separation;
        (ii) questions raised by the 'I' − 'me' separations
            (a) the status of the separated beings;
            (b) the relation of the 'I' and 'me' of action with the 'I' and 'me'
                of preparation;
        (iii) external constituting of voices and realms − the 'I' − 'we' separa-
            tion.

C. ACTOR ANALYSIS

1. Social identity v. personal identity
2. Techniques for the presentation of social selves:
        (i) style;
        (ii) costume.

INTRODUCTION: THE DRAMATURGICAL MODEL

This is perhaps the oldest analytical model of all. We see and hear
a simulacrum of life on the stage. Perhaps the way that simulacrum is created and the illusion sustained can be a guide to our
understanding of how real life is created. There are obvious differences between real life and stage drama, and it would be as well,
to prevent misunderstanding, to notice them now. Stage drama

selects from, simplifies and heightens the act/action sequences and personal presentations of real life. Time is foreshortened. Only a few of the many threads of everyday life are followed. Resolutions are frequently achieved in contrast to the endless postponements of the daily round. Issues are faced rather than dodged; lies are discovered and so on. Furthermore a more clearly developed and fully articulated aesthetic frame controls the presentations of the people and the unfolding of their affairs. Life, too, is partly managed in accordance with aesthetic standards, which parallel those of the stage quite closely, but they are rarely dominant.

Despite all the differences the likenesses are worth exploiting. At the very least, as Goffman has observed, the way an actor shows he is a certain kind of person must parallel the way anyone would show, in a certain social milieu, that they are that kind of person.[1] Without some such matching the actor's performance would not 'work' and the audience would not know what he was doing or what kind of person he was supposed to be. The parallel is not perfect since actors and audiences may share certain conventions about the expression of these matters that once reflected everyday life but have long since ceased to do so. For instance we have no trouble recognizing the villain in a melodrama despite the fact that no one behaves that way any longer, if indeed they ever did carry on quite like that.

What then can we draw from the model? Primarily it is an analytical scheme, coupled with a specially watchful kind of consciousness — at once the consciousness of the actor, the producer, the audience and the critic. To adopt the model is to take a certain kind of stance to the unfolding of everyday life and to the performances of the people who live it. It could be described as an ironic stance, a viewpoint from which life goes forward, becomes visible. For the means of action are not usually attended to, so much do we concentrate on the aims and outcomes of our activities.

As a source-model for developing analyses of everyday activities the dramaturgical model leads to two interlocking conceptual systems. Looking ironically at the performance we can begin to analyse it according to the scheme proposed by Burke.[2] We can look for the way the kind of scene we are to be in is indicated. Scenes are complex objects including both the setting, the physical surrounding, stage props, and so on; and the situation, the human predicament which the unfolding of the drama will, we hope, resolve. The drama unfolds through the performances of the actors, playing parts, in styles we must be able to recognize. The action of the play is usually determined by a script, though actors and producers place their own interpretations on it. In improvised and experimental theatre the script may be reduced to a bare scenario, suggesting the predicament, the persons and the resolution, but leaving the performance and sometimes even the resolution to be created in the course of the action.[3]

Interlocking with all this is the interpretative activity of the producer. He proposes a reading, though his success depends on how far the audience can be persuaded to share it. By taking something of the position of both audience and producer, critics provide informed commentary upon the action, upon the players and their performance, upon the scene and the scenario. And this too can be looked at dramaturgically. It is a performance by people playing the parts of critics in the unfolding of yet another scenario.

As people living our own lives we are among the actors performing our parts in well or ill-defined scenes, sometimes fully scripted, sometimes improvising. As producers, audience and critics, we appear as social scientists commenting upon the drama. But as people playing the parts of social scientists in appropriate scenes we are performers in yet another drama.

A. SCENE ANALYSIS

1. SETTING

(a) Introduction

All our actions are carried out against a structured background. The physical settings are not neutral. They contribute to the action. Settings broadcast messages of reasurance and threat. Until recently the messages from the background, social musak so to speak, were taken for granted as part of the common-sense world. However, the structure of settings and their manner of working on human social feelings was much discussed in the past. In the Renaissance various general theories were proposed: from Albertus Magnus to Kepler a variety of theories were broached.[4] But it is only very recently that sociologists and social psychologists have turned their attention to analysing and understanding settings. The environment of action, as meaningful to the actors, Burke called the 'scene'. It has several components. The physical scene can be considered first as to its overall spatio-temporal structure, and then as to the meaning of the various things with which it is furnished, including smells, colours, the state of the weather, and so on. In this section I shall be concerned only with the former, and shall speak of it, with a small measure of licence, as the *Umwelt*. Just as each species of animal has its own spatial environment, in every given area each category of people, professions and sexes, families and age groups, have different spaces within which they freely move, all, for example, within the one city. Each has some spaces proper to itself alone.

We must first take a stand on the central matter of the nature of the environment of social action, whether we should follow Skinner or Kant; whether we should regard the environment as external to the action, or identify at least some of the properties of the environment of action as human products. I have argued in an earlier section for a generally Kantian outlook, which seems to me so utterly indisputable that I can find little to debate about with the other side. That a traffic light is what it is as part of the environment of social action by a social endowment of 'red', 'green', etc. with meanings, and those meanings embedded and maintained within a system of rules, seems to me so obvious that the idea that it is redness as a physical stimulus that brings me to brake can scarcely be taken seriously. Furthermore, it is also clear that the Skinnerian view must be wrong if applied to the institutional environment since that is clearly a product of knowledge and understanding. I hope that as our analysis of the *Umwelt* unfolds we shall see that much the same is true of the 'physical' environment.

The socially significant environment includes many non-structural features. In countries with very variable weather the moods of the inhabitants can be much influenced by these changes. The significance of such moods may be great and read back into nature as a kind of social meteorology. I shall not be concerned with a detailed analysis of these features of the environment in this section, but only with the interrelated structures we impose on space and time, and the structures we build with things and events within space and time.

The socially meaningful physical environment within which we live seems to have two degrees of structure, two levels of granularity. The coarse-grained structure consists of distinct and separated areas in space and periods in time, distinguished as the places and times of socially distinct activities. For instance, the social activities of the street are quite distinct from those inside a bank adjoining that street, and opening off it. This is one of those obvious truths that should yet surprise us. How do I know that I am in the counting hall of a bank and that I should behave reverently therein? Part of the answers to these questions are to be found by *looking* at the décor of the banking hall. Our first task will be to examine some of the ways in which socially distinct areas and volumes of space and periods of time are demarcated and maintained. In this way the coarse-grained structure of the *Umwelt* will be revealed.

But each area and volume, and each period of time, and each thing within an area and each pattern of action within a time, has a structure which differentiates it from other things and makes it thereby a potential vehicle of significance or meaning. These are the fine-grained structures of the *Umwelt*. How are these structures socially significant? I shall try to establish, with a wide range of examples, that we create and maintain such structures and endow them with meaning as a kind of permanent or semi-permanent bill-board or hoarding upon which certain socially important messages can be 'written'. The very fact of order, when recognized by human beings, is, *in itself*, the source of a message that all is well. Orderliness of the physical environment broadcasts a kind of continuous social musak whose message is reassurance. But, as we shall see, the fine structuring of the *Umwelt* allows us to give and receive much more specific messages, public statements of how we wish to be taken as social beings. I will try to show, in broad outline, how these more specific messages are achieved.

If we define the *Umwelt* of a human being as he or she is a person of a certain social category, we could express this in a formula:

Umwelt = Physical Environment $\times$ Social meanings.

This formula could be taken literally as a Boolean product. Thus if someone were to be found to be using two interpretative schemata, A and B, then $U = P \times (A \vee B)$ leads to $U = (P \times A) \vee (P \times B)$; in short that person lives in two *Umwelten*.

(b) The Structure of an Umwelt: Boundaries in Space and Time Creating and Demarcating Socially Distinct Regions

As we pass through space and time we are continually adjusting ourselves to a complex social topography. Some regions are closed to us, some open. For some various keys or magic passwords are required, such as 'Oh yes, I'm a member here'. Looking at this ethogenically we must ask how these barriers are established and promulgated, how they are maintained, how legitimately crossed, how their accidental violation is remedied. This will reveal what the social structure of the topography thus established might be.

As an introductory illustration, consider the time barrier that separates the period before a school lesson from the lesson itself. It may be created by the ringing of a bell which separates two socially distinct regions. In the period before the lesson the social structure of the class is a complex network of microsocial groupings, one of which, usually the most socially powerful, may include the teacher. The whole interaction pattern is organized as 'chat'. After the lesson starts the social order simplifies into a one-many hierarchy, with the children oriented to the teacher, and an almost complete disappearance of the 'chatting' style of speech which characterized the previous period.

Spatial boundaries, like fences or white lines on the ground, demarcate socially distinct areas. Such social topographies may reflect the polarity between a safe and a dangerous area. But the boundaries may be invisible. Urban Americans are all too familiar with the feeling of relief and relaxation as one passes beyond Such and Such Street, into a 'safe' area.

The structures created by boundaries and associated barriers, the physical markers of boundaries, like fences in space and silences in time, can be very differently related to deliberate human effort. The English Channel is *there*, as is the moment of death, and both have to be coped with, whereas taking a stick and scratching a line on the sand, 'That's your team's home base' or beginning by 'O.K. let's get started', are more or less free creations. They can be challenged and are subject to negotiation in ways that death and geography cannot be. But some human constructions are geographical features, such as permanent architectural or agricultural arrangements. Time is structured permanently by such artefacts as clocks and calendars. Just as our only social response to such entities as the English Channel or the coming of spring can be semantic attributions of meaning, expressed in such famous aphorisms as 'Wogs start at Calais', or 'Oh to be in England now that Spring is here', so we may negotiate the meaning of an hour or of the Great Pyramid. Finally, in contrast to these permanent structurings are the wholly ephemeral, such as the lane changes in 'tidal flow' traffic schemes, and the agreement on the structure of times by which the order of speakers at a meeting is decided by the chairman. Most of the

boundaries and barriers we will be examining in detail are neither
so unresponsive to human renegotiation as the solar year or the
Atlantic Ocean, nor as ephemeral as the chalked grid for street
hop-scotch, or the intervention, 'I wish you'd shut up and let A
have a chance to say something'.

(i) Time structure and its marking
I shall call the boundaries of conventionally marked, socially
distinct time-periods, 'openings' and 'closings' following Schegloff
and Sacks.[5] A prime social differentium is whether opening and
closing is done for one or achieved by the participant himself.
We must also ask whether the openings and closings are natural
or contrived.

Close observation of the way beginnings and ends of activities
were managed in a kindergarten shows that the initial and final
moves in the sequence of an activity are separated from the rest
of the activity by being performed in a particularly flamboyant
and exaggerated way. Their natural role as beginnings and endings
is stylistically enhanced to demarcate the boundaries of distinctive
times.

Social closings are notoriously more difficult to achieve than
openings. One can, in desperation, just start. However, as a general
rule things do not just start, they are opened by the recital of a
ritual formula or the performance of a symbolic action: 'Oyez,
Oyez, Oyez, as it pleases the Queen, Her Gracious Majesty ...',
cutting the ribbon to open the road, and so on. The variety and
sources of such formulae would no doubt repay close sociological
study.

The closing of conversations as socially distinct intervals of time
has been much illuminated by the studies of Sacks and Schegloff.
The problem is created by the fact that the normal ending of an
utterance is not a sign of the ending of a conversation, rather it is
the signal for next speaker. How is this transition relevance sus-
pended?

Schegloff and Sacks found that there are two ways of generating a terminal section. A speaker can insert a preclosing phrase
such as 'Well, O.K...' to mark the end of a topic in such a way
that a terminal sequence can politely be introduced. Alternatively
one can pick up a topic at the beginning of an interaction to allow
for a warrantable lead in the closing section.

The problem of natural openings and closings arises as a separate issue. We have already noticed the technique by which natural

initial and terminal parts of a sequence can be stylistically elevated to become openings and closings. Some natural events could find no other place in the sequence than as beginnings and endings. Such for example, are spring and autumn, birth and death. They are not, therefore, available for stylistic heightening *as* openings and closings, they *are* openings and closings. But their importance is too great for them to merely pass by, unattended and unstressed. They become surrounded by ceremony. In general this network of natural openings and closings forms a closed system of metaphors, each binary opposition serving as a metaphor for the others.

(ii) Spatial structure and its marking
The boundaries of spaces may be marked by relatively insurmountable barriers, such as high walls, or wide waterways. Such barriers enter social reality only when they are given a meaning by a participant. Does the prison wall keep the prisoner in, or the unpredictable and threatening forces of society out? Is a prison a cage or a refuge? Does its wall show its sheer face inwards or outwards? Clearly the sense of the wall, its vectorial significance, is a function of the way the areas within and without are socially conceived.

Other boundaries are marked by physically surmountable barriers, visible like low walls and white lines, invisible like the high and low status areas of a schoolroom, or the volume of private space around a person. Most boundaries tend to close up on themselves, enclosing areas. Social areas have portals, visible or invisible. These portals are generally valve-like. Passage out is easier than passage in, so that while not all who aspire are admitted, all who have been admitted eventually come out. In public buildings there is often a ceremonial performance involved in achieving entry but a mere valedictory nod marks acceptable leaving of the enclosed volume or area.

Invisible boundaries must be maintained through shared knowledge. They are usually generated by some potent or sanctified dangerous object at their centre. Goffman and others have noticed that the area around a 'with', a group who are bound together by social ties and who let it be seen that they are so, moves with the 'with'. Contrary walkers skirt around it. Similarly a person may leave a potent trace such as a pair of sunglasses and a towel upon a crowded beach, creating an unencroachable boundary. A participant has reported that around the door of a school staff-room there is an arc of inviolability, beyond which the pupils will not normally go. If forced to do so they exhibit signs of considerable uneasiness and distress.

(c) The Social Texture of Space and Time

The original idea of a social texture to space and time comes from Lewin[6] who proposed a kind of vector analysis to represent the power of attributions of meaning to different features of an environment. This is particularly easy to illustrate in the behaviour of men involved in the trench warfare of the war of 1914–1918, where the terrain was textured by its potential as a source of danger and of protection from hostile action.

So far we have taken the physical topography as a datum, and seen how it can be endowed with meaning. But the microstructure of the *Umwelt* may be organized as a social topography. A concept like 'social distance' could be introduced to express the rarity and difficulty of a transition from one socially marked space to another.

Goffman's analysis of the texture of threat[7] in an urban *Umwelt* illustrates a space organized along one dimension of social meaning. In a dangerous section of a city the grid pattern of streets is replaced by a modulating structure of clear and dubious areas, areas in which someone might be lurking, the possibility constituting the threat. The boundary between the space that can be seen to be empty and the space that is obscured Goffman calls a 'lurk line'. The threat texture of a grid pattern of streets, from a momentary vantage point in the passage of O, our man on Michigan Avenue, as he passes through the street corner, would look something like Fig. 2.

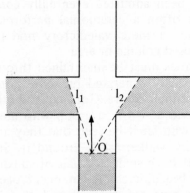

Fig. 2

L_1 and L_2 are 'lurk lines' and the shaded and unshaded areas represent the structure of the texture of threat. As O moves forward the structural properties of the space change.

A pleasanter illustration of social topography can be found in the social map of a kindergarten. The map is plotted in two dimensions, staff sanctity v. child sanctity and comfort v. threat. The geographical map of the kindergarten (including play area) looks like Fig. 3:

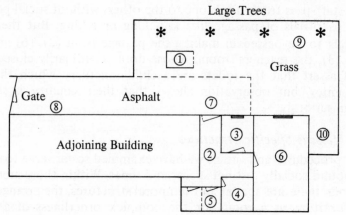

Fig. 3

Key (1) Wendy house, (2) Lobby, (3) Staffroom, (4) Kitchen,
(5) Lavatories, (6) Play room, (7) Near play area,
(8) Far play area, (9) Distant grass, (10) Unobserved areas.

Observation shows that children do not play in the areas marked (9) and (10).

Plotting these areas on the social map we get a topography such as in Fig. 4.:

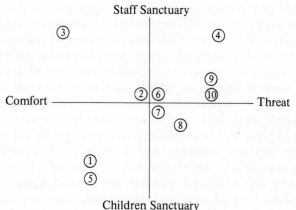

Fig. 4

(5) and (4), though geographically adjacent, and from a spatial point of view therefore easy of mutual access, are socially very

distant, and passage from one to the other is very difficult for a child. Entry to (4) is a special occasion and under close supervision, occurring only for those whose job it is to wash the cups, or for a 'cooking' group who prepare something for a playmate's birthday. (2), (6) and (7) are completely mutually open and the children and staff pass freely from one to the other, without social portals, that is rituals of passage like knocking or asking. But there are portals to be passed in making the passage from (2), (6) and (7) into (3), the teachers' room, whose door is ordinarily closed. The staff assert that the toilets are a child sanctuary which they do not enter, but observation shows that their sanctity is seldom taken seriously.[8]

(d) Message-Specific Structures

The procedures and rituals we have examined so far serve to divide or bound socially distinct spaces and times. Within those areas and periods there are spatial and temporal structures, the arrangement of furniture in a room, or the complex orderliness of a meal. Viewed dramaturgically, these entities are the props which further define the scene, and which together with the *Umwelt* make up the setting. Such structures have a social meaning. But before examining some examples in detail we must ask how a physically structured feature of an environment can have meaning. Social meanings are also given to and read off qualitative properties, such as colours, for example red flags, brown shirts, black skins and so on. These do occur in the *Umwelt*, but as separable items, so I shall not pursue the question of their semantics here, but deal only with entities differentiated by their structural properties. A semantic unit is a structure and is embedded within a structure or structures. The internal structure presents no particular problems provided we recognize that the structure of the unit may be extended in space, in which case we shall look for its synchronic form, or extended in time, in which case we shall look for its diachronic layout. Provided entities are structurally differentiated they can bear distinctive meanings. In the traffic code a triangle has one meaning and a circle another, while in dog-handling the melodic differences between one whistle and another, structurally differentiated in time, are distinct signals. In general the semantic field of an item includes relations of exclusion, such as that between a circle and a triangle, whose meanings exclude each other; and inclusive relations such as that between a triangle and its red colour, relations that range from synomyny through metaphor to metonymy. To express a meaning, then, we must lay out as much of the semantic field as is required to distinguish this entity as meaningful from other items within their possible common contexts.

(i) Furniture arrangements

If we examine a permanent arrangement of furniture in an office we are studying a structure that is physical, laid out in space. Each distinct layout can be assigned a social meaning. Studies have shown that the way furniture is arranged in an office is not just a matter of convenience but is a symbolic representation of the standing of the occupant.[9]

In general the principles seem to be the following:

(i) the desk parallel to a wall is of lower status than at an angle to a wall;

(ii) the desk against a wall is of lower status than freestanding;

(iii) sitting on the side exposed to the door is of lower status than sitting on the side away from the door.

Applying these rules together we find that the person whose desk is freestanding, at an angle to the wall, and who sits behind the desk facing the door, is of the highest category admitted by that organization, a fact expressed in his furniture for all to see. He whose desk is up against the wall, who works with his back to the door on the exposed side, is the lowest. Whatever airs he may give himself his furniture shows his position for all to see. How far this code is general among bureaucratic man is uncertain, but the study reported covered both English Civil Servants and Swedish Executives, so it has some measure of generality as a sign system. An explanation of the etymology of the semantics is readily forthcoming from Goffman's theory of front and backstage divisions of personal territory. The person of low status is totally exposed, he or she has hardly any backstage area. His whole official life is enacted frontstage. He is under perpetual threat of supervision. But a simple visualizing of the plan of the office of the highest grade shows that tucked away behind his angled desk, he has the greatest amount of private space (of backstage) of any of the possible arrangements. Equally, and probably complementarily, the topology would admit of a Durkheimian account in terms of the protection of and at the same time the exhibition of the sanctity or inviolability of the highest status person, whose body is surrounded by a large protective area, freeing him from the possibility of profanation. There must surely be an element of

truth in both accounts, and further study could probably elicit
their balance in the way the furniture arrangement is read by the
various individuals who act within it as their *Umwelt.*

(ii) The structure of food and drink episodes
A meal is a sequential eating of dishes which has a diachronic
structure, while each dish, consisting of a variety of objects,
is a synchronic structure. Dishes will be differentiated according
to the salt/sweet dichotomy, as well as more finely by their
ingredients. Along the diachronic dimension we shall ask whether
one dish is served before or after another. I will be using a
generally syntactical model for the analysis, though its applic-
ability to the analysis of meals derives from their formal properties
rather than their function as the vehicles of social meaning. As a
part of the setting a meal may be orderly or disorderly. As an
orderly event it contributes a general air of stability and rightness
to the day.

There are two sets of distinctions to elucidate, those between
cuisines and those between meals within a cuisine. Both the
rules of cuisine and the rules for meals generate menus, plans
for meals, which are concretely realized as actual structures
in time, the elements of which are dishes. The rules ensure that
despite the great variety of specific food items, repetition of
structurally isomorphic sequences occurs day after day, week
after week, at a fairly high level of perception, which are 'proper'
meals. Since structure is, by itself, a source of intelligibility,
the setting is stabilized at that point, and needs no further
referent.[10]

The high degree of structural differentiation of meals not only
serves to stabilize the setting but allows social meaning to be
given to food items and drinks, as the differentiated elements in
a simple symbolic system. A meal or meal-like social event, such
as 'drinks', can convey a message concerning the relations among
the people attending. The elements may have a more specific
semantic loading. Perhaps this is part of the explanation of the
alleged but quite mythological aphrodisiac properties of certain
foods, such as oysters and champagne. They may have come to
be sexually meaningful objects (the sea shell and the bottle with
liquid foaming out as female and male symbols respectively).
Though they have no special biochemical properties and are not
causal agents in the ordinary sense, they may nevertheless be
effective agents of sexuality through metonymy.

(e) Interaction between the Structure of the Setting and Social Theory

The structure of a setting may be an icon of the social theory, that is the physical structure of a setting may function as a meaning-bearing entity, that is as a significant icon of the content of certain propositions within the cosmology of a people. A detailed and well documented example is P. Bourdieu's analysis of the micro-cosmic organization and meaning of the Berber house.[11] One might also cite Levi-Strauss's analysis of the meaning of the siting of an Amerindian village.[12] I will not discuss those individual items which have a social or cosmological significance in themselves, but only the way messages are conveyed by various structural properties of the house. According to Bourdieu, these properties match and hence represent some central structural properties of the Berber cosmology, that is of the content of certain of their important beliefs, expressed in proverbs and sayings.

Once again we find the two dimensions of *Umwelt* analysis, the structure of the entity, in this case the house, and the structure of the larger entity into which the house fits. And, of course, certain differentiated elements within the structure of the house are themselves structurally differentiated, and some qualitatively, as, for example, light and dark, or fresh and preserved. The appearance of both structurally differentiated elements, for example forked and straight, shows that we are dealing with basic semantic units, the higher-order structure having the character of syntax.

Our problem is *how* does the house as a structure, as a social or cosmological microcosm, express the macrocosm. There seem to be two distinct ways. In one the representation is established by isomorphism of structure, in the other by conventional assignment of meaning to generate a symbol. An etymology for the symbol can be reconstructed from the folk sayings, in terms of which the particular assignment of meaning makes sense. It is as a symbol, not as structured isomorph, that the fire is conceived by the Berber as the representation of the female principle in the house.

It seems from Bourdieu's account that structural properties of the house represent at two levels of sophistication. The ridge pole rests in the fork of the central wooden pillar, and this is read as an icon of the male/female relationship. Here the structural isomorphism is exceedingly simple. A considerable amount of social meaning is taken to be vested in this conjunction, and a good many of the rituals associated with procreation are related to it. Furthermore, the ridge pole and supporting pillar are the central metaphors in a large number of sayings and expressions by which the Berber social organization of the male/female dichotomy is described (and no doubt promulgated as rules and norms).

But Bourdieu has shown that the structure of the house is a microcosm in much more subtle ways. The division of the house into a light part and a dark part matches the division of social time into night and day. The openness of the light part is in contrast to the closedness of the dark part, matching the division between public (male) life and private (female) life. But these simple homologies are only the basis for more elaborate structures. 'The opposition between the world of female life and the world of the city of man is based upon the same principles as the two systems of opposition that it opposes.' In short, private life is not just female life, but as the procreative part of life is female/male. So the fact that the light part is in some sense the preserve of the women, where cooking and weaving are done, leads to the inner homology that the light part: dark part *as* public: private *as* male; female *as* female/female; female/male. Thus in general

$$a: b \ as \ b1; b2$$

Finally, the house can be considered in its geographical isomorphisms. The door is related to the compass points of geographical space. Going out one faces the East, the direction of worship, with the warm South on one's right. But the door is also related to a kind of inner geography. Coming in one faces the wall of the loom, which being illuminated by the door is treated as bright, honourable and so on, in short as the 'East' of the inner space. On one's right on entry is the wall with the fire, the 'South' of the interior. Thus the door is the point of logical inversion through which one passes from macrocosm and back, always in the same relation to the social and cosmological significance of these structured spaces.

2. SITUATIONS

My basic thesis is that in most times and most historical conditions expressive motivations dominate practical. Practical aspects of activities will usually have some part to play, but from the dramaturgical perspective they fade into relative unimportance. Situations will arise mostly from expressive contradictions.

In a general way one can see that there can be only two kinds of situations − those in which people are related to the setting, and those in which they are related to each other. I shall try to show how each naturally provides the opportunity for expressive tensions. There are many, many ways in which expressive tension can be created, and the cases I shall describe are meant only to illustrate the kind of thing I have in mind and not to masquerade as an exhaustive catalogue.

(a) People in Relation to Setting

The simplest relation a person can have to a setting is to be occupying some part of its space and/or its time. And that occupancy seems to create in most people a sense of proprietorship. It would be very unwise, however, to follow Ardrey[13] and others in claiming a biological origin for this sense, or genetic inheritance as an explanation for its widespread appearance in the human race. But the sense of possession does seem to be close to universal. Mary Douglas has amplified our understanding of the sense of proprietorship or 'ownership' of spaces and times with the idea that we invest those for which we feel this relation with some measure of sanctity.[14] In consequence we tend to treat the intrusion of others as a profanation, a defilement of some *thing* close enough to us to be almost part of ourselves. Lyman has remarked on the way people will decorate whatever space they take to be theirs, emphasizing their proprietorship, even if the last territory for the dispossessed is their own bodies. If all this is in some measure sound, then one's dignity and worth would be seriously threatened by other people making free with those regions of space and time one felt proprietorial towards. And this provides our first source of social tension. It arises in the situation created by an actual, immanent or virtual violation of one's personal spaces and times. We shall see how this tension is dealt with in the section on action.

(b) People in Relation to One Another

Of the innumerable variety of possible cases I shall sketch only two, as illustrative of rather different forms of tension:

(i) Social tension can arise, and what I have called a situation come into being, when it is apparent to two or more people that a relationship already exists between them, but it has not been publicly proclaimed or ritually ratified. A couple may have reached the point of establishing a very formal and apparently stable relationship which has to be transformed into a socially ratified bonding, either into the informal 'They are going out together' or the formal 'They are engaged'. This is the tension of the implicit about to be transformed into the explicit, the potential about to become actual. The scenes to be discussed in detail below concern the ritual transformation of a privately or personally experienced mutual liking into a publicly acknowledged friendship.

(ii) But social tensions can also arise in cases where it is uncertain what relation is going to come to exist between people. A perennial problem is posed by the appearance of a stranger, whose place in our network of social relations and reputations has yet to be determined. We shall look at introduction ceremonials as minor dramatic resolutions of this kind of problem.

There are a huge number of such tension-situations, which life dramas resolve. There is the discovery that someone is not what they seem. There is the realization that a relation which has been certified officially has no further foundation in personal feeling — how is it to be terminated? There is the challenge to established reputation for one who aspires to the mantle. There is the sudden realization that one is getting old and the bitter discovery of the uselessness of one's life in the eyes of others, and so on, and so on. The expressive aspect of action, the dominant aspect, I claim, can be understood from the partial point of view provided by the dramaturgical model as a resolution of these and other 'dramatic' situations.

B. ACTION ANALYSIS

INTRODUCTION

Of course, a great deal of action in a great many scenes from kitchens to carpenters' shops, from space-modules to cow-byres, is practical. The actions undertaken by the folk legitimately on the scene are explicable in terms of the practical aims of the undertaking and the practically or scientifically sanctioned means of bringing these about. But it is the argument of this work that for most people, in most historical conditions, expressive motivations dominate practical aims in the energy and even in the time expended on co-ordinated social activities. In many cases too the prime motivation of the practical activities is to be found in their expressive value — space flight, scientific research and cooking are obvious examples. I shall devote no space to a discussion of the practical activities of mankind since I believe that they bear only tangentially on social life during most of human history.

With the exception of the nineteenth century in Western Europe and in certain countries whose 'nineteenth century' is still to come, practical motivations are and will be secondary. As I remarked earlier, though we must acknowledge the importance of Marx as a philosopher of the practical, for most of our own and other people's lives, Veblen and Goffman must be our guides.

Paying most attention, then, to expressive aspects of action, I propose a threefold division of dramatic scenarios – remedies, resolutions and monodramas. Each has to do with the management of a situation of tension, in such a way that the social order, though it may be changed, is maintained in some form or other. Remedies are action-sequences which serve to restore lost dignity or honour; resolutions are action-sequences which resolve a growing tension between expressive and practical activity by formally or ritually redefining relationships on another plane, for example friendship stages, marriages and so on; while monodramas are action-sequences in which an actor achieves his personal expressive projects while continuing to have the good will and respect of those who have to bend their aims and wills to his. Doubtless there are very many more kinds of scenarios played out against the background of well defined social scenes. These are offered as illustrations.

1. REMEDIES

Introduction

If the major human preoccupation in the complex interweaving of practical and expressive activities is the presentation of an acceptable persona, appropriate to the scene and the part in the action (the social collective component) associated with a sense of worth and dignity (the psychological/individual component), then since the possibility of loss of dignity, of humiliation and expressive failure exists, we would expect an elaboration of remedial activities for their restoration.

(a) Individual

The existence of boundaries creates the possibility of their violation, and violations require remedies. The general form of remedial exchanges has been analysed by Goffman, and I shall follow his treatment closely.[16] The first point to notice is that for a remedial interchange, say an apology, to be required, there must be someone who has proprietorial rights on that space or time. It must in some sense be *their* space or *their* time. For instance, a lesson is a teacher's time, and a party is the time of the hostess, just as my office is my space, and the kitchen, the cook's. If the space or time is 'owned' by no one, there can be no occasion for remedy, so if I miss the train and thus exclude myself from that period of time, that is train-journey time, I cannot apologize for my late-ness, for there is nobody whose time it is, except of course mine. It is the guard's train but not his journey-time.

Goffman's analysis depends upon an underlying distinction between virtual and actual offence. To arrive late is to commit an actual offence, and the person whose time it is must be apologized to in the proper ritual form. But the generality of Goffman's analysis is made possible by the extension of the notion of offence to virtual violations, which are remedied in advance, so to speak. In order to get the water-jug I must violate your table territory which I remedy in advance by asking politely, that is in proper ritual form: 'Would you mind passing the water-jug please?' which allows, but never admits, the response, 'Yes, I would mind'.

The general form, then, of remedial exchange is as follows:

A: Remedy: I'm terribly sorry I'm late.
B: Relief: That's O.K.

There are two further elaborations of this basic form, only one of which is noticed by Goffman. He points out that quite fre-quently the Remedy-Relief interchange, whose referent is the actual or virtual violation of someone's space or time, is supple-mented by a second interchange whose referent is the first inter-change. Thus

A1: Remedy: I'm sorry I'm late.
B1: Relief: That's O.K.

A2: Appreciation: Gee, I'm glad I didn't upset things too much.
B2: No, no, it was O.K.

where A2 in the second bracket expresses appreciation for B's granting of relief, and in B2, B minimizes the extent of his condes-cension, thus restoring to A his status as a person in equal moral standing with B.

But particularly where time is concerned there is another form of remedial interchange, the counter-apology. So far as I can see the final product, that is maintenance of the boundary and equili-bration of the moral standing of the people involved is just the same as in the Goffman ritual. Consider the following:

A1: Remedy: I'm awfully sorry I'm late.
B1: Relief: That's O.K.

B2: Counter-apology: I'm afraid we had to start without you.
A2: Counter-relief: Gosh, I should hope so.

Goffman's remedial exchanges allow for the management of the defilement of sacred or proper territory, and for the violation of spatial and temporal boundaries. But *how* is being late or early a violation of a time boundary? If early you are present in a socially distinct period which, for example, may be a preparatory period for the action to come, and a great deal of back-stage equipment may still litter the scene (the cooking utensils or the baby's toys have not yet been put away). The style of the action may be inappropriate to the presence of a stranger. Under these conditions a remedial interchange is required to maintain the social order. The equilibration of civility may even require the early arrival to join the home team, and pay the penalty by tidying up the sitting room. In short, times as well as spaces may be distinguished as front and back stage.

To be late is equally the breaching of a boundary, since you were not there for some temporal sections of the action, though expected, and you did not arrive through the time portal provided just before the beginning of the action. A remedial interchange is required. We need no special theory to account for the fact that late arrivals are very much more common than early. Of course late arrival may be part of a presentational sequence, susceptible of dramaturgical analysis, as when someone conspicuously arrives late in order to be noticed.

(b) Small-scale Face-to-Face

(i) Co-operative: face-work

Another important category of plots concerns the scenarios of the preservation or restoration of social identity and dignity in the face of actual or potential threats. I instance here, for illustrative purposes, one such plot, which may take somewhat different forms in an actual production — the plot Goffman has called 'face-work'. He defines 'face'[17] as 'the positive social value a person effectively claims for himself by the lines others assume he has taken during a particular contact', for example, he may have been supposed to have knowledge and experience of mountaineering. Since it is usually demeaning to everyone in the group if any one member, previously in good standing, loses face by some contradiction to his right to take the line emerging, it is in each person's interest to support every other person's line. By saving the face of others, each person saves his own and vice versa. Goffman calls activities directed to this end 'face-work'.

The sequence of the actions by which actual and potential loss of face can be dealt with are sufficiently standardized for them to be treated as ritual. The sequence begins with a challenge in which the actual or potential offence is 'noticed'. The offender is then given the chance to re-establish the expressive order either by redefining the action as of another social-type, 'not this act but that', or by making some form of compensation, or by punishing himself with a 'silly me!', or something of the sort. The offering is then usually accepted and the offender's gratitude made known in a terminal move. The importance of treating this scenario on the liturgical model is that we can then properly treat the personal experience and public appearance of emotions such as embarrassment or disdain as part of the ritual sequence – they are conventionally called for as expressions of ritually correct social attitudes and relations, and as such symbolically illustrate the sensibility and personhood of the actor.

(ii) Agonistic: trouble in school[18]
The point of trouble is reached by a growing feeling in some schoolchildren that the school system and the school teachers do not value them. They experience the efforts to make them study pointless subjects ('getting at me') as well as abandonment of those very efforts ('writing me off') as degrading. A gap opens up between how they would like to be evaluated, the dignity they would like to have ritually ratified, and how they interpret themselves as presently conceived by others. Children create systematic remedial exchanges in which dignity between teachers as represent-*ations* (as opposed to represent*atives*) of the educational system and pupils as persons supposedly in good standing, is equilibrated.

To understand these cycles of remedial exchange two categories of insult have to be distinguished. There are the results which preserve dignity such as a teacher swearing at a child or even hitting it. At least in principle, the child is noticed as someone of consequence as the recipient of that act. Insults of that sort are reciprocated in kind. But children distinguish another category of insults – those that demean. Demeaning insults include two main sub-categories. Failing to know a child's name or treating it like a sibling are construed as wounding to personal esteem. They

indicate both a lack of care from the teacher and a lack of reputation for the child. But worse, according to the childish interpretation, is some form of 'writing off'. This is illustrated most vividly
for them by their discovering that some of their teachers are both
weak and frightened. 'If we were being taken seriously', they
reason, 'we would not be given such feeble teachers.'

How to restore the dignity they have lost? Many such children
have devised a double cycle of retribution to balance the dignity
equation. The first cycle tests the teacher by 'playing up' or
'dossing about'. If the teacher is strong and seriously concerned
with them this will be shown in firmness and there is no dis-
equilibrium in the equation to balance. The balance is already
there. But if the teacher fails, this is read as an insult, a demeaning
not of the teacher but of the class itself, and each member of it.
An imbalance exists. The second phase of the cycle involves a
retesting of the teacher aimed at reducing him or her to a condition of indignity – breakdown or retreat. When that has been
achieved the pupils withdraw, amplifying their own dignity
by completely ignoring the impotent rage and posturing of their
official mentor. But, we have found, if the teacher tries to break
the cycle by an attempt at strength and fails a second time, the
results are likely to be violent. Physical punishment of the teacher
may be meted out, so high a state of excitement is reached.

2. RESOLUTIONS

My second category of examples of scenarios are resolutions.
Situations arise where private and personal attitudes shadow forth
or anticipate a relationship not yet publicly or socially ratified. I
take friendship and its complement as examples. (Since there is
no word for 'enemyship' in English, I shall distinguish the formally
ratified states as *Bruderschaft* and *Feindschaft*, borrowing a convenient German distinction.) I take it that the individuals who
proceed to these ritual ratifications whose scenarios I will describe
are psychologically prepared for transformation, and are aware of
each others' attitudes, though misreadings may show up in the
unfolding of the scenarios.

(a) Transformation of a Private into a Public Relationship

In accordance with the liturgical model, we could look at the action
sequences which one might have to carry out to be performing a
ritual for the creation or maintenance of a friendship or a state of
enmity.

(i) Bruderschaft *ritual*

It seems to me that there are two quite separate aspects that can be studied: (a) there are ways of speaking to friends, styles of speech manifestly regardless of content. I notice myself adopting a peculiar half-jocular style of speech with friends. I certainly use such a style for indicating and maintaining friendship. The emergence of this style could be explained by seeing it as a kind of test. If one uses language which if it were taken literally by someone would be insulting, and then make it jocular, this could be a test of friendship of the other person. As a friend he does not take offence at being called an 'old bastard' or whatever happens to be the local expression. (b) there are uses of speech and action which are strictly ceremonial in character. Alan Cook has pointed out to me, for example, the reference to fighting as a *Bruderschaft* ritual in the works of D. H. Lawrence.[19] I have outlined earlier Mary Douglas' idea that some ritual resolutions and markings of social relations can be done with food and drink. Peter Marsh has noticed that in working-class communities, except for close relatives, there is not much inviting of people to meals. Intimacy may be politely ratified by 'going out' together. We need another project, complementary to Mary Douglas's, to look at how intimacy is 'done' amongst cultures other than the British professional classes. Inversion is frequent, I believe, in anomic communities. People who are not very intimate tend to invite each other to a meal. Mary Douglas's hypothesis that passage through more structured rituals, is passing a person through degrees of greater intimacy, needs two further dimensions added (a) that when a relation goes beyond a certain degree of intimacy, then ratification rituals become less and less structured, and (b) that when one wishes to express a purely formal relation, though a close one, the rhetoric of friendship may be used metaphorically and without irony.

(ii) The maintenance of hostility among intimates involves verbal rituals I shall call 'needlings'. An apparently harmless opening pair of remarks are made by A and B. But B's remark contains two aspects: it has a literal, primary sense, but it also has a performative or secondary sense in which it could be used as a needle. If A foiled the initial needle by taking B's speech as a provocation and replying to it, then B has a further move open, namely, 'I meant it literally'. B's opening remark means q literally and r performatively. If A takes it performatively, as r, and B says 'No, I meant q', B opens up an option of condemning A for implying that B is the kind of person to needle A.' Such dialogue opens the way for B to trap A into seeming to denigrate the relationship which A and B ought to have. This structure is probably very general.

One must not suppose that *Feindschaft*-sustaining ritualized needlings are disruptive, that is necessarily lead to a break up of relationships. In marriage, where people are forced into intimacy, a complex relationship exists which involves some *Bruderschaft* and some *Feindschaft*. The relative quality of the marriage does not depend on whether *Feindschaft* is totally absent but how it is managed and how sustaining it is.

As Berne seems to imply,[20] some *Feindschaft* rituals turn out to be highly sustaining to a relationship. He has some convincing examples of action-sequences which, if taken literally, are rather vicious, but since they are played out in a ritual way, simply tend to keep the formal relationship going.

Little is known about contemporary ritual ways of transforming private feelings of enmity into a stable, hostile and publicly realized relationship. Social psychologists have tended to look at attraction and altruism rather than their opposites, and even Goffman has concentrated more on person supportive rituals such as 'face work' than the ritual maintenance of hostility. Ritualized internal family *Feindschaft* has been revealed by Berne in some of his famous 'games' which seem to express the hostile aspect of the usual inter-family ambivalences. A great deal remains to be done, both in the collection of examples and in their analysis and classification and in the investigation of how they work.

In the past there have been much more publicly visible forms of *Feindschaft* rituals. I distinguish these into two broad categories. There are negative rituals where a point of the ritual is a ceremonial and stylistic display of lack of interaction. The obsolete practice of the 'cut', the stylized refusal to acknowledge or greet someone, was an example of a negative ritual.[21] Positive rituals, on the other hand, involve hostile but stylized interaction. The hostile actions are strictly controlled by rule. A duel does not fit this pattern since it is not a sustaining of the *Feindschaft* relationship, rather it is a formalized way of resolving it. Feuds, on the other hand, are sequences of interaction by which enmity is sustained according to rule. Two avenues of historical research suggest themselves. Feuds seem to have been conducted quite non-violently at times, particularly amongst village women in rural communities. Anthropologists have studied the violent or blood feud and there should be little difficulty in abstracting their

material to reveal formal structures useful in the social psychological study of *Feindschaft*. Finally, a comparative study of
violent and non-violent forms of feuding could usefully be undertaken to try to discern any formal parallels in the initiation, maintenance and resolution of the state of enmity.

(b) Creation of a Public Relationship

Our analysis will illustrate several analytical models in use at once.
An analysis of introduction rituals will provide an example to
illustrate the theoretical points made earlier.

The arrival of a stranger in a particular social locale has, so far
as we know, always been the occasion for a flurry of ritual activity
by the local people, but there is distressingly little in ethnographic
literature on the detail of these revealing encounters. The presence
of a stranger creates a number of problems, all of which are solved,
if all goes well, by the standardized procedure of a ritual of introduction and incorporation. I shall try to elucidate the structure
and the meaning of the components of various incorporation
rituals, both exotic and local, and those in use amongst children.
I shall be on the lookout for any features, either structural or
semantic, that might be taken as possible universals.

The Rumpelstiltskin problem confronts one immediately. How
should this person be addressed, what is his name? How can we
refer to him without offence? Ignorance or forgetfulness of a person's name or title is as offensive as the degree to which his *amour
propre* is bound up in his expectations of personal recognition.

Then we need to determine his place in *our* social order. Here it
may not be simply information that we seek, since his native
order may not map readily onto ours. It may be necessary to engage him in a trial of strength of sorts.

Finally, we need to ensure his membership of our society, to
make him one of us, so that from now on he is a member of our
team whose loyalty and support we can take for granted.

I will draw upon both contemporary and historical material.
Plays, etiquette books and ethnographical reports will provide
the historical dimension, while participant observation, playing
through scenarios and covert observation will give us some information about current ceremonial.

(i) The basic elements

In plays the development of the action sometimes involves introducing a stranger. The forms employed by the playwright are

good evidence, I would argue, for hypotheses about the norms of introduction ceremonials of the time for which the play was written. Too great departure from standard ritual would surely have occasioned incomprehension, the plausibility of the play as an archetype of a slice of life depending upon the verisimilitude of these taken-for-granted aspects. When the Emperor introduces Faustus to the Court, he prefaces his utterance of Faustus' name by a status enhancing and defining description,

> *Emperor*: Wonder of men, renowned magician,
> Thrice-learned Faustus, welcome to our court.

The descriptive phrases here have reference to the fame of the learned doctor, he is *treated as* well known, though in fact known *as* himself only to the Emperor, before his name is revealed. This is a feature of introductions and their embarrassments we shall find fairly widespread, from ancient Polynesia to a modern campus.

> *A*: Professor X, I'd like you to meet Dr Y.
> *Y*: Glad to meet you, of course I know your work well.
> *X*: (*Sotto voce*, Y? Y! What the devil has he written ...?)
> Well, of course, thanks, I'm *very* glad to meet you, we know your work very well in Tierra del Fuego (England, etc.).

To which Y must *never* reply 'Oh yes, now which particular paper did you have in mind?!

The Emperor's 'gracious' formula by which he admits Faustus to his Court leads us to another feature of incorporation rituals, the performative utterance by which the ritual is rounded off and the incorporation sealed, so to speak. The forms of these closings will occupy us later. For the moment we need only notice the schema exemplified in

> 1. *Sponsor*: Mr Jackson, this is Mr Smith.
> 2. { *Jackson*: Hi
>   { *Smith*: Hi
> 3. *Smith*: Glad I could make it.

The element of personal description is fairly prominent in the simulation of introductions to be found in plays.[22] We are entitled to ask how far this element's prominence is due to the necessity for the playwright to acquaint his audience with the character of the newcomer to the scene. Participant observation shows that the person introducing the stranger, the sponsor, to a third person, is under the same necessity as the playwright, and has recourse to the same technique. Introductions in Denmark seem to involve quite a detailed descriptive phase.

> 1. *Sponsor*: I'd like you to meet Dr. Jensen* (our former

director). This is Mr B* (he's a cost accountant from Leicester, England; his company is thinking of co-operating with us). At the points marked * Sponsor turns from J to B, and B to J.

2. $\begin{cases} B: & \text{How do you do?} \\ J: & \text{How do you do?} \end{cases}$

3. $\begin{cases} B: & \text{Have you retired, or does the job rotate round the board?} \\ J: & \text{Actually, I'm semi-retired, ha! ha! (Looks at Sponsor a} \\ & \text{little sheepishly), as you say.} \end{cases}$

In Phase 3, B and J continue the information exchange process begun by Sponsor in Phase 1. It is worth noticing that as Phase 3 develops other features of the discourse than the simply descriptive begin to appear, so that B is gathering more information, should he take notice of these matters, than is present in the content of the sentences uttered.

In the examples so far examined status relations are derived, without dispute, directly from the descriptions offered by the stranger or the sponsor. But their importance to the further interaction of the parties is so great that, as might be expected, agonistic or competitive elements enter in. It is also worth remembering that Sponsor may become involved, since his prestige and standing may itself be affected by the prestige and standing of the stranger, so that he can be drawn into an agonistic encounter on the side of the stranger.

(ii) Contemporary ritual

Contemporary English stranger introduction ritual involves three people, the stranger, his sponsor representing the home social order and *the* host. They exchange speech and action in the following phrases: Approach controlled by eye-contact and glances: Name-exchange: Person recognition ('How do you do?') and Physical contact: Status determination: Ritual of incorporation. These deserve some commentary.

The meaning of the formula 'How do you do?' seems to be connected with two subtle degrees of recognition. By enquiring as to the state and condition of the other, the questioner recognizes him or her as a being with states and conditions and the capacity to communicate them, and also as a being about whose states and conditions we might be concerned. All this constitutes the mark of a civil interest in the other, an acknowledgement of personhood. Since the utterance of the formula is a formal acknowledgment of that personhood, and not an enquiry, it is not proper to reply to it as such, and the correct response is the complementary ritual recognition of the personhood of the first speaker, by repeating 'How do you do?' Sometimes a formal reply to the enquiry is inserted as an extra step, its formality shown in the fact that the person so replies as to exhibit himself sunny side up, so to speak, sparing the enquirer any real concern over his condition, however parlous it may actually be.

A: Hi, how are you?

B: (at his last gasp) Fine, how are you?

A: Fine.

It is worth noticing that this elaboration of mutual politeness does not usually occur in the incorporation rituals we have been discussing, but only in greetings, between those already well known to each other.

Physical contact is a very widespread feature of greetings and introduction rituals. But there are great variety of forms and great differences in their distribution. Generally, in England, physical contact forms no part of greeting rituals, that is rituals for remaking contact with people one already knows. But in France, and to a lesser extent in America, hand-shaking is part of greeting, though not of farewelling. Among the international community in Spain, the men do not shake hands in greeting but women greet both sexes with ritualized double cheek kissing.

But introductions are quite another matter. Even in England hand-shaking as the standard form of the third phase of the ritual is widespread.

In India the third phase includes 'doing *namastha*', joining one's own hands in a prayer-like deferential gesture. So there are some exceptions to the general rule that physical contact is made in the course of an introduction ceremonial. It is also worth remarking that though hand-clasping would seem to be the most appropriate and simplest method of achieving physical contact there are cultures where other parts of the body are used. Among the Maoris nose-rubbing was the proper form both in the introductions of strangers and in greetings for those from whom one has been some time apart. In New Guinea ethnographers report a curious introductory ritual in which, though actual physical contact is not made, certain joints are touched by the visitor and by the person to whom he is being introduced, each touching his own body, followed by a beckoning gesture from one to the other. This brings the various joint souls or *'ipus'* into some kind of contact with one another, this introducing the psychic population of each human being to that of the other. Thus it might be read, 'The soul of my shoulder greets the soul of your shoulder, the soul of my elbow greets the soul of your elbow ...' So far as I have read, the natural development in which the joints would be pressed together, in pairs, has not been reported.[2 3]

The problems solved by those aspects of the ritual of introduction we have examined have not so far included those germane to the central preoccupation of much of human life, namely relative status. They have been concerned with the establishment and recognition of the stranger as a person, that is as the kind of being who *can* be in some kind of status relation with oneself, as a member of the 'home side', so to speak. The problem of status in its most general form is this: 'In what way should respect and deference be distributed between the two people introduced?' Despite the close to universal appearance of some form of status differentials and hierarchy of persons in human life forms, there are some cultures where it seems to be absent from the preoccupations of those being introduced to one another. Among Arabs, self introduction is quite proper. In the Muslim world the fundamental religious egalitarianism is strongly reflected in the form of day-to-day personal interactions, particularly in the matter of the distribution of respect and deference, which is, to all intents and purposes, evenly distributed. Thus a person can be trusted to give his name and a great deal of personal information, and can do so trustingly, since where there is no contempt deriving from occupation or ethnicity, making personal details public can reveal nothing discreditable.

Amongst those cultures which are more than usually preoccupied with the establishment of relative status, like ancient Polynesia or modern Euro-America, the determination of the proper distribution of deference is a crucial social undertaking, and it has a conspicuous place in introductory rituals. In Denmark the sponsor describes both the person being introduced and the person to whom he is introduced in sufficient detail for the proper deference and demeanour relations to be quite clear. This occurs in Danish ritual before either of the people being introduced has spoken.

But in many introduction sequences the determination of identity is achieved by the participants rather than achieved for them by the sponsor. Status is determined in an agonistic or competitive encounter. This may go in two ways:

(i) deference and respect may be determined by reference to some standard or mutually acknowledged hierarchy,

(ii) or by 'trial of strength'.

To follow the detailed form of the ritual we must distinguish between initial and final states. In general the visitor has notional initial status advantage, shown by various marks of deference, such as his name being mentioned first. There are some exceptions to this. In Euro-American ritual women are at a notional status advantage, whether appearing as visitors or as the person to whom introduction is made. But this advantage is not absolute. A study in the Flemish community in Brussels showed that there were certain very high status men whose position demanded deference from everyone, including women.

It should be clearly understood that the rituals and the analyses offered of them are applicable only to the specific micro-societies mentioned as their source. Of course the social needs and the psychological mechanisms and linguistic devices invoked may have universality, but that remains to be shown. The dearth of ethnographic material relevant to this matter is tragic, since it is unlikely to be recoverable. If, as I have argued, introduction rituals show in a very clear way the central preoccupations of people in society, comparative data from differently founded and differently organized societies, with different conceptions of human life, would help us to uncover any social universals that might be involved in the way people come to recognize other people.

A very small amount of ethnographic material does exist for one alien society, right on our very doorstep, the autonomous social world of children. Thanks to some observations by Mixon, we can get a glimpse into rituals of introduction and incorporation in their society, the culture of childhood that is not part of the adult/child culture. Children's ritual seems to involve much the same main phases as that of adults, but differently ordered. The appearance of a new child at a school in the seven to ten-year-old age group where the autonomous society of childhood seems to be most highly developed and differentiated, leads to a performance of rituals of incorporation. The name of the child is always known in these cases since he or she first appears amongst the class as a stranger sponsored by the teacher, in a ritual drawn from the ethogenics of the adult/child social world. But at the first break the autonomous ritual takes place. The new child appears as one of a small group, who keep their eyes averted from him at this stage. They do not touch him, and speak only formally and brusquely. Some 'trial of strength' or skill is suggested, so a football played a prominent part in Mixon's observations. By coincidence the study involved only boys, but studies of girls' autonomous rituals ought to be made. The small group including the stranger went out into the playground and a sort of football game took place, clearly more to see how the stranger coped than for fun. With his skill established the group made its way back into the building, a very different mode of interaction prevailing. The 'home group' continually looked at the new boy, addressed him directly, and, milling about, tried to make as much physical contact as possible, patting, pushing and nudging him, in a kind of 'ecstasy of absorption', as it has been described.

There seem to be three distinct phases. In Phase One the new boy is treated as in some sense 'not there' socially, by a studied failure to acknowledge him as a social being. This is in sharp contrast with the adult ritual where the initial phases have precisely the effect of emphasizing and requiring the acknowledgement of his humanity and personhood. In Phase Two he is tested, and his place determined according to the criteria current in the society to which he is being introduced and in which he is being incorporated. Finally, in Phase Three, he is incorporated, and his personhood acknowledged through ritualized physical interaction and by his being accorded the ordinary marks of respect as a person, by being looked at and spoken to. A great deal more observation is required before it can be said how widespread is this kind of ritual form. Ethologists will no doubt remark how closely it resembles similar routines amongst chimpanzees and wild dogs.

3. MONODRAMA[24]

Throughout this work I have stressed the need to comprehend both action and talk about action (accounting) in our registration of social life. The distinction between practical and expressive aspects of social activity is, I claim, unevenly distributed between action and accounts, since action has both practical and expressive aspects, while accounting is primarily, though not exclusively, expressive.

(a) Retrospective Resolution of Personal/Social Tension in a Dramaturgical Mode

In this section I describe a way of resolving a kind of situation where an actor feels a disparity between how he could be taken to be and how he wants to seem to appear. The solution is to speak in a way that not only defines his part in the unfolding action of a drama, but to treat himself as a cast of characters.

One common device for the drawing of other people into playing parts is the use of syntactical forms which result in what I shall call, following Torode,[25] 'the conjuring up of Voices and Realms'. A repeated pronoun, for example, is not accepted at its face value as having identical reference, but scrutinized for its 'voice'. The structure of the discourse is revealed by linking 'voices', not instances of lexically identical pronouns. Thus,

'You never know, do you?'

addressed to another involves two voices — 'You', the voice of abstract humanity (Voice 1), and 'you' (Voice 2), that of the addressee; and via this separation of voices we can understand why the proper response is,

'No, you don't', rather than, 'No, I don't',

since the 'You' who doesn't, is Voice 1. In this way the structure of the stanza comprising the two speeches becomes clear.[26]

Realms are the characteristic territories of Voices and may be more or less well defined in the presentation of monodrama.

The retrospective reconstruction of psychological reality I want to illustrate works by a purely internal constituting of Voices and Realms. As might be expected, monodramatic presentations of social psychological matters involving the self are a prominent feature of accounts. A very common accounting technique involves the separation in speech of 'I' from 'me'. Typically, the account involves a scenario in which the 'I' is represented as losing control of the 'me', who then as an independent being, performs the action for which the account is being prepared. In some scenarios the 'I' is a helpless spectator of the unleashed 'me'; in others the 'I' fails to attend, or looses consciousness, or in some other way is prevented from knowing anything about what the 'me' has been doing. In the former scenario, the 'I' loses control and releases the 'beast within'. In the other, the 'I' in loosing consciousness reveals a mere 'automaton within'.

What are the monodramas conjured up in the use of such expressions? Their plots are based upon social vignettes, drawing upon common-sense understandings of commonplace multidrama. By virtue of their origin they have an explanatory function, for example I represent myself as using the same technique of self control as I use to control others when, for example, I say 'I made myself do something which I was reluctant to undertake': or at least, that is how I represent the matter monodramatically.

The self-justifying aspects of the resort to a monodramatic

representation of the reasons for setting about reformatory self-work appear clearly when we notice that *my* failings are transformed into personal characteristics of the characters of the monodramatic presentations conjured up in 'I talked myself into it' and so on, thus my reluctance to act or my weakness of character is masked in part by attributing it to a separated and in the plot rather feeble-willed quasi-fellow, the 'me' who can be brought round by the eloquence of 'I'. 'I' as primary self-mover, can hog all the *Herrschaft* available in the little drama.

Thus monodrama is not just presentative of the dynamics of self-management, but is also technique, a way of talking that facilitates self-mastery by separating, as into another person, situation-relative undesirable personal characteristics. Sometimes self-congratulation can also be emphatically expressed by separating off and claiming desirable characteristics for *all* the members of my self-colony of selves as in the little monodrama 'Myself, I did it!'[27]

(b) Projective Casting of Others into Roles Adumbrated in the Forms of Speech

But the same technique can be put to work in trapping others in a self-constituted monodrama. Torode has provided a beautiful example in which a Calvinistic world of exclusion and election is conjured up by a form of speech. I take this example and its general method of analysis from Torode's study of teachers' speech, though the analysis I shall propose is somewhat more elaborate than his.

'We don't have any talking when we do compositions. I hope that is clear.' The first person plural appears here in two voices. The first voice speaks from a transcendent world, the seat of authority and the source of order. The inhabitants of this realm are strict − they 'don't have any talking'. The second occurrence of the first person plural pronoun 'we' denotes a different set of voices, those of the members of the imminent world of the classroom − the subjects, those who 'do'.

Mr Crimond presents himself as a member of both realms − a status to which we shall return − and also as a separated individual able to look at them both from an external standpoint in his character or voice as 'I'. Mr Crimond is the only person in the classroom who is a member of the populations of both realms. He is benevolent towards the citizens of the imminent realm, and he hopes that the message from the transcendent world is clear.

At the same time he is the channel of mediation and interpretation between realms. His hoping is directed to the possibility of his making clear to the members of the imminent realm the authoritarian wishes of the Voices of the transcendent realm. Furthermore, as a member of the transcendent realm, he is elect, while the members of the imminent realm are mundane and unable to address the issue of order except through his mediation. However, they are shown the possibility of election. One of them, namely Mr Crimond, is a member of both realms. However, aspiration to membership of the transcendent realm is matched by the possibility of being cast out of 'Heaven' altogether into what Torode calls 'Hell', an act in the monodrama expressed by such phrases as 'you boys...' The members of the imminent realm are trapped in Mr Crimond's monodrama. In particular they are unable to address questions concerning the issue of order directly to the source of that order. If they do query these matters, Mr Crimond replies in such phrases as 'We'll have to see', conjuring up an image of lofty deliberation among the immortals and of reserved judgements which may or may not be handed down. It should surprise no one that Mr Crimond maintains a high degree of discipline without recourse to anything other than speech.

Torode also raises the question of different Voices of the 'I', particularly the 'I' of concern (that above which 'hopes') and the 'I' of action and authority, for Mr Crimond occasionally speaks in the person of that Voice, as when he says 'I will not have that sort of thing'.

C. ACTOR ANALYSIS

In this section I shall be considering a person in action strictly in accordance with the dramaturgical model, that is as analogous to an actor in a staged performance of a traditional scripted play, or an improvised happening. This consideration will throw up some very serious philosophical issues which will be treated in detail in the next part of this work.

1. SOCIAL IDENTITY v. PERSONAL IDENTITY

The most trite yet important distinction to bring to understanding life on the dramaturgical model is that between an actor and his parts. As a human being for whom acting is work or even a hobby, the person as actor in the theatre or in a film has an identity distinct from his parts. There might be problems for individual actors in keeping the distinction sharp. But clearly, ontologically, a stage or film actor is primarily himself, and his stage parts have to be adopted.

When an episode of ordinary life is looked at in accordance with the dramaturgical model, this ontological relation is reversed. Except for Machiavellian and socio-pathological individuals, people are primarily the parts they play, and the attitude of detachment that would allow them to see their actions as performances of parts is a frame of mind which has to be consciously adopted and may induce a stultifying self-consciousness inhibiting convincing performance.

The psychological distinction between personal and social identity allows for the detachment of the actor as a person from his part, that is his public self-presentations or personas in which he is usually almost wholly immersed. Detachment admits the possibility of control. As one detached from the action he can be an agent.[28] But what can the actor control?

To return to the source-model: on stage an actor must keep fairly close to the script, or in an improvised drama, the scenario, otherwise he will lose his presentation as a part. In very advanced experimental theatre that indeed may be the very effect aimed at. But usually the actor as creating his part is almost without effective agency. Only his ultimate agency remains — he could stalk off and abandon the performance altogether. But while playing the part he can put his personal stamp on it — make it his Hamlet. He does this by his control of style, of the way he performs his part. As we noticed earlier, this allows him considerable expressive power, the power he needs to illustrate the sort of person he is in the way he performs the actions required of him. He allows his personal identity to show through the social identity he is forced to adopt. In this aspect of performance the psychological condition and the ontological category of both stage actor and the performer of daily life are identical. They must both monitor and control the style of the performance without becoming wooden or self-conscious. They must both be agents with respect to these matters, that is fulfilling projects of their own devising, free of promptings and controlling influences from other people and the scenes of the action.

But adopting the stance of an actor and bringing action to explicit consciousness at certain times and moments in one's life can lead to the perception of disparities between presentations,

personas, and our conception of character. A particularly prominent example of this phenomenon is the fits of self-consiousness
that can overcome an inexperienced or uncertain social actor, so
that the reflection of himself in the eyes of others can become so
dazzling as practically to stultify action altogether. I take the
form of consciousness which children experience in what we call
'showing off' to be very similar. Struck by the disparity between
the presented self and inner being they force embarrassingly over-
presented personas on their audience. These are examples of the
condition one might describe as 'over-awareness' of the management of one's actions.

In the condition I have just described the managing self and
our conception of how we want to be, and the way we believe we
are presenting ourselves, become the focus of explicit attention.
But most people act in the social world in an unselfconscious and
often unreflective manner, lost in their activities and intent upon
their goals. This can lead to an underawareness of the actor and
personal aspects of one's life in the social world. The difficulty
of sustaining an adequate conception of the complexity of oneself
as a social person has been beautifully described by Doris Lessing:
'This is what it must feel like to be an actor, an actress – how very
taxing that must be, a sense of self kept burning behind so many
different phantoms.'

To grasp the complexity of the relationship between, and differentiation from an actor and his part, I offer as an example an
event which occurred recently in Denmark. A man went into a
chocolate shop to buy some confectionary. There was a customer
ahead of him – a lady with a little dog. The shop woman offered
the dog a chocolate. The dog refused and left shortly afterwards
with its mistress. The man turned to the shop woman and went,
'Woof, woof!' and was given a piece of chocolate by the shop
lady, who remarked, 'You ought to have begged as well'.

The first point to notice is that the legitimacy or propriety of
social acts are related to the part in which they are occurring. The
man in the social or dramaturgical part of 'Dog' could do things
he could not do in one of his other parts, for example university
professor. The shop woman was acting with perfect ethogenic
propriety in rebuking the man as 'dog' for leaving out part of the
ritual proper to that part; as 'dog' he should have begged as well.
But who was she rebuking? It seems to me clear that she was
rebuking the individual as managing or controlling self, neither
'dog' nor the 'professor'. It is the managing or controlling self

that is the proper object of rebukes of that nature, and, to put the matter more grandly, is the object of moral praise or blame. One might add that the shop woman had let down the man as managing self rather lightly since as 'dog' he should have wagged his tail after receiving the chocolate. The important point to notice is that social failures occur relative to the parts being undertaken and the personas being presented, and are part of 'drama criticism', but rebukes occur in the moral world and are directed to the man that lies behind the 'dog'.

2. TECHNIQUES FOR THE PRESENTATION OF SOCIAL SELVES

(a) Style

For the most part, the presentations of self as this or that persona proper to a certain kind of social event and amongst people of a particular sort, are achieved not so much in the instrumental activities in bringing off practical tasks such as counting money, driving cars, eating peas, making legal judgements, delivering lectures, screwing nuts on bolts, and so on, but in the style in which those activities are performed. Self-presentation is described in adverbs such as 'reluctantly', 'churlishly', 'gloomily', 'cheerfully', 'carefully', and so on, rather than in verbs of action. Impression-management, as Goffman calls it, consists largely in the control of style. Attributions of character are made to a person by others pretty much on the basis of how they see the style in which he performs the actions which are called for on particular occasions. Explicit statements or illustrations of personal qualities are usually unacceptable. They can be criticized as boasting or coming on.

(b) Costume

However, the control of style leading to the attribution of character, however effective, takes time, so that to be seen to have authority or strength of character, or to be weak and easily led, excitable or withdrawn, are reputations which may take months or even years to achieve. But the practical purposes of society require certain people to be seen to have personal characteristics such as authority, sympathy, or wisdom directly and immediately. The solution to this practical problem is found in the use of regalia, uniforms, and so on, where the regalia suggest a specific character by framing and determining the persona he can present. A glance at the uniforms of the police of various nations is enough to establish the point, but priests and professors, radicals and air line stewardesses are all dependent on the same device. In accordance with the dramaturgical framework I shall call this 'costume'.[29]

The most general form of regalia is clothes, illustrating and commenting upon the body, which they emphasize by concealing. This point has been made most elegantly in the following passage from *The Ogre of Kaltenborg*:

> I observed eagerly how their personalities altered with each [costume]. It is not that they came through the clothes as a voice does through a wall, more or less distinctly, according to the thickness. No — each time a new version of their personality is put forward, altogether new and unexpected, but as complete as the previous one, as complete as nakedness, it is like a poem translated into one language after another which never looses any of its magic but each time puts on new and surprising charms. On the most trivial level, clothes are so many keys to the human body. At that degree of indistinctness key and grid are more or less the same. Clothes are keys because they are *carried* by the body, but they are related to the grid because they cover the body, sometimes entirely like a translation *in extenso* or a long-winded commentary that takes up more room than the text, but they are merely a prosaic gloss, garulous and trivial, without emblematic significance.
>
> More even than a key or a grid, a garment is a *framing*. The face is framed and thus commented on and interpreted by the hat above and the collar below. Arms alter according to whether sleeves are long or short, close-fitting or loose, or whether there aren't any sleeves at all. A short, tight sleeve follows the shape of the arm, brings out the countours of the biceps, the soft swelling of the triceps, the plump roundness of the shoulder, but without any attempt to please, without any invitation to touch. A loose sleeve hides the roundness of the arm and makes it seem slimmer, but its welcoming ampleness invokes a caress which will take possession of the arm and go right up the shoulder if need be. Shorts and socks frame the knee and interpret it differently according to how low the first come and how high the second.

A socially symbolic object, like any other symbol, is partly defined by syntagmatic relationships with all the possible structures into which it might fit without loss of intelligibility. Sometimes these relationships may be very narrow. For example, round-lensed steel-rimmed spectacles cannot be replaced by any other form of spectacles, say *pince-nez* or horn-rims in a Sartorial Context defined by Afro-hair, Indian beads and flared jeans, without loss of intelligibility. So the paradigmatic dimension of round-lensed steel-rimmed spectacles is severely restricted. Equally we cannot insert round-lensed steel-rimmed spectacles into the context defined by low-cut shiny black shoes, white shirt, blue tie, grey suit, without loss of intelligibility. 'Just what sort of guy is that?'[30] But we can insert either *pince-nez* or horn-rims in the latter context, while horn-rims, though not *pince-nez*, can go into the context, suede desert boots, cavalry twill trousers, viyella shirts and knitted tie, and thick medium-length dark or black hair. Thus syntactically, round-lensed steel-rimmed spectacles are also very circumscribed, while horn-rims have a broader syntagmatic dimension.

Secondly, many symbolic objects do not have a meaning in isolation from their opposites. They mean only as contrasting pairs of symbols. Hair length has once again, in recent times, come into use as a social and political symbol. Historically it has not been the length as such, but the long/short contrast that has had political significance, that is the semantic unit 'long hair' is embedded in the structure 'long/short'. This explains how 'short hair' could be radical in 1640 and 1780, and reactionary in 1965. This example illustrates the way something which may appear at first sight to be a semantic unit in itself is, on more careful analysis, seen to be significant only as a member of a pair. Long hair is currently (or more accurately, was recently) used as part of a heraldic display manifesting a symbol for a radical political orientation. This went with round-lensed, steel-rimmed spectacles, flowing clothes and the like. The semantic unit comprised by the hair length is, for this total object, a diachronic entity '− as opposed to −' which is an opposition over time, that is long hair is worn, not just in opposition to the short hair of the squares, but as opposed in time to short, that is 'long, formerly short'. And of course either length can be a realization of either formula of opposition, the synchronic or the diachronic. The same explanation is available for the apparent contradiction between the role of a brassière as a radical garment in the late nineteenth century and its discarding by certain radical ladies today. It is both in synchronic relation to those who continue to wear it, and in diachronic relation to the previous state of the radical ladies. And in some lexicons it has a meaning in itself, as a way of emphasizing basic femaleness, and of course, in its absence inhibiting physical actions which are deemed proper to the male, such as running or chopping wood.

However, as a general principle the basic form 'x as opposed to y' has no particular temporal order built into it. One could choose an instantiation of the relation now, in anticipation of the appearance of its contrary later. Though peculiarly appropriate to radical heraldry the basic form 'x as opposed to y' has been a very common form for the conveying of social meaning. For example, women have used the up/down contrast in hair style for expressing socio-sexual status, for example to put up the hair showed that childhood had ended and that the woman was marriageable. In a somewhat similar way the contrast clean-shaven/ bearded expressed social distinctions amongst the Romans. In early days slaves were clean-shaven and their masters bearded, but in the reign of Hadrian a technological revolution in shaving techniques brought by Sicilian barbers to Rome made shaving much less disagreeable, with the consequence that Hadrian decreed that slaves be bearded, now that their masters were not.

However, as Cooper has pointed out, both long hair and beards have had a persistent standard meaning despite their frequent appearance as members of contrasting pairs. Long hair has generally been associated with romanticism, feminity and so on, while beards have usually been associated with intellectual and moral status as opposed to political, but *if* political, with conservatism, with the authoritarian father and the like.[31]

The design of people then forms a very striking feature of man as social actor. It is clear that such heraldic matters as hairlength and type of eye-decoration are parts of a more complex structure, the whole ensemble including clothes and shoes, and ways of walking and holding the arms, and so on. In the American West 'cowboy' is done by some cowhands even in their Sunday suits. It is predominantly marked by a way of walking.

But far the most important structural element in the design of people is clothes. There have been one or two inconclusive studies relating skirt lengths to economic factors, but they have paid little attention to the expressive features even of such correlations, if they could be established. In this chapter I can only draw attention to two features of the clothes in person design, basing my remarks on little more than impressionistic evidence.

The first point to remark about clothes as structured entities concerns their role in socially marking sexual differences, so that one can tell at a glance whether one is going to meet a member of the opposite sex, of the same sex, or a homosexual. Traditionally these have been marked by differential markers in all three possible modes, primary, secondary or tertiary differentia. By primary differentia I mean anatomical differentia based upon genitalia and mamalia; by secondary I mean anatomical differentia, such as relative hairiness, bone formation, general outline of the limbs, face and so on; and by tertiary differentia I mean markings by

different forms of clothes, or by differential regalia, such as different forms of decoration as among the Australian Aboriginals,
or by such matters as the length of hair. In societies where 'unisex'
fashions in the basic structure of clothing are predominant, such
as among Western University students, or in the Muslim world,
recourse may have to be made to secondary or primary differentia.
Muslim men and women are differentiated by subtle stylistic
differences in their *shalwa* and *kemis*, and by the use by women
of various forms of face concealment, elaborations on a tertiary
theme. Students generally have recourse to both secondary and
primary differentia, in that the current fashion of long hair in both
sexes has been accompanied by the growth of beards amongst
men, marking them off at a glance, and by the discarding of the
brassière by women, leading to a very strong visual emphasis
on the bosom, due to its mobility and prominence when lightly
covered. There are, of course, certain surviving subtle modifications of the 'unisex' style so that some tertiary differentia do
remain. But in general social marking is by secondary or primary
characteristics. The survival of these markers through the transition to different forms of clothing discloses what I should
like to identify as a 'social universal' or 'equilibrating principle'
that requires that certain differentia be preserved through whatever transformation of the form taken by the *Umwelt*. The way
such principles are recognized, learned and promulgated is a
much neglected branch of sociology. Finally one should remark
that the differentium heterosexual/homosexual, which *a fortiori*
is incapable of being marked by primary or secondary differentia,
is usually marked in both sexes by modifications of the basic
form of the biologically appropriate clothing and regalia so that
they are styled in the predominant stylistic mode of the sex
with which the homosexual is identifying. Thus women might
continue to wear jacket and skirt, but have them made in mannish
materials and styled in a mannish way. The point may be under-
lined by the choice of accessories from the repertoire of the
opposite sex, such as a handbag by a homosexual, and a collar
and tie by a lesbian. By these public displays the differentia
are the markers of the social dichotomies that go with various
biological categories.

But there are some structural differences in clothing which
are manifestly but mysteriously related to the expression of social
matters. So far as I can tell, so little is known about these phenomena that I can do little but describe them. Both men's and

women's clothing is modified diachronically along a number of dimensions, long/short, loose/tight, what I can only call 'apex up'/ 'apex down', elaborated/nonelaborated, and there are no doubt others. To illustrate, the 'zoot suit' of the nineteen forties had a very long jacket as its prime differentium, while the predominant jacket length in the fifties and early sixties was short. Trousers, which were tight in the Edwardian period, were styled in a loose manner up until the late fifties. In the forties and fifties men's clothes were designed as a triangle with the apex down, wide shoulders and narrow hips, but since then the introduction of flared jackets and trousers has created a silhouette with apex up. And of course elaboration with more buttons, waist coats with lapels, turnups and so on, has come and gone. I would like to put these changes to the social scientist as problematic, through and through, both as to their genesis and their spread through the population of clothes by natural selection, not forgetting the attempts from time to time to introduce modifications that were selected out, such as the calf-length skirt in the late nineteen sixties. I believe that in the iconography of clothing there is a ready-made model for all forms of social change, and recommend it for the closest possible study, relatively neglected as it has been hitherto.

L. I. H. E.

THE BECK LIBRARY

WOOLTON ROAD, LIVERPOOL L16 8ND

APPENDICES TO PART II

1. POWER: THE INFLUENCE OF AN ILLUSION

It might be objected that the analysis offered so far omits the most important social attribute of all — power. No doubt the concept figures very largely in sociologists' accounts. But, I shall argue, it is either irrelevant to the social psychology of the formation and maintenance of social order, or is reduceable to yet another facet of the expressive activities of individual social actors. If there are global properties, and if there are class-attributes (and there may well be) power is not among them.

I shall argue the point through three phases, in each phase dissolving any social (as opposed to personal) conception of power, demonstrating it to be an ontological illusion, real only as an accounting resource.

(a) It might be argued that there are plenty of counter-examples to the thesis that social power is an illusion. Historical studies reveal the existence of all sorts of social systems in which one race or group or profession or sex or age-grade seem to hold sway, perhaps even absolute sway over another. By this it might be meant that decisions were made by one group for the others, that projects were formulated by one group which the members of the other had to fulfil. It might even be that one group had the right to speak for another. In the second phase of my discussion I shall argue that these systems are misdescribed in this form; that we have nothing above the multiplication of personal power. In this phase I want to show how the attribution of power to this or that group is dependent on the time-span within which that society is seen. I know of hardly any human associations described by historians or anthropologists in which the time-scale is much more than a couple of decades; at most it can be measured in hundreds of years.

233

Sometimes a group presents itself with the trappings of power and its members legitimate their personal activities by reference to their membership of the group. We have overwhelming evidence for the instability of such groups. We notice how frequently they decay from within. As confidence evaporates new and usually less active generations take on the trappings of power without its substance. The Catholic Church, the Russian Communist Party, the Western European aristocracy, the Aztec nobility have one and all ceased to be absolute rulers of their domains. If social power is an attribute or disposition of the group an extraordinary state of affairs is revealed. For if social power were indeed an attribute of the group how could the decay of power be so rapid while its legitimizing theories and authenticating ceremonials are intact? Monteczuma sits calmly debating the nature and destiny of man with Pizarro and hands over his world to utter destruction. This is the phenomenon that the more romantic historians describe as the failure of will, the dissipation of energy.

(b) But the appearance of these metaphors of will, of energy and even of confidence, should alert us to the possibility that the puzzle is one of our own making. Power hierarchies have these disconcertingly ephemeral properties because, as power rankings, they do not exist. The time-scale on which we can see the exertion of power is that of a man's maturity. Everything points to the propriety of an attempt to locate power in people — and to treat the sociological theories of power as ingenious accounting procedures by which those who have personal power persuade us to accept their rule and sway; or, and it depends upon the same rhetoric, those without personal power seek to gain it.

The proof is simple: occupancy of social or role position is not a sufficient condition for acquiring power. It is not even a necessary condition.

We should notice first of all the succession of strong, weak and indifferent office holders, be it Heads of Oxford Colleges, Pharaohs or Chairmen of the Party. Office provides opportunity, but personal qualities provide power. The case of Rasputin and Czar Nicholas can represent the many. Rasputin's power and influence illustrates that office is not even a necessary condition for social power, that is for vast numbers of people to be brought to do things through influences which have their origin in the personal qualities of such a man. But that there be a state apparatus or something approximating it is necessary for his influence to ramify beyond his personal circle. To understand power we have to understand by what personal qualities and practices a smelly, disreputable monk can dominate the Russian Court. The short answer lies in the beliefs he has been able to induce in others, beliefs that represent that central social phenomenon I have called character or reputation. But it must be earned though it may seldom be consciously striven for. There must be something which can be interpreted as evidence for these beliefs. For beliefs about official office holders it is their style and accoutrements – for the unofficial, certain legendary occasions on which their power was made manifest. The former are much more easily seen to be a dramatic fiction, mere costume, hiding the ordinary man beneath.[1] We are more inclined to believe in the reality of the rumoured and even sinister practices of the unofficial power holders.[2]

(c) But, it might be argued, granted that all you say about Rasputin is true, isn't it still the case that large groups of people, identified by similarity of job, of style of life, even by choice of reading matter, have differential access to the good things of life – and particularly those that give advantage to their children. Again, one can hardly deny the half truth in this comment.[3] But set that against the evidence from historians and human biologists of the extreme rapidity with which families occupying positions of privilege and power change. I take it that Harrison and Hiorns have demonstrated that in most societies it is clogs to clogs in five to seven generations.[4] It is more often, I suspect, from an unsystematic reading of biography and autobiography, to be the traditional three. What then of the power of the group? It seems to dissolve in the harsh solvent of empirical examination. Both the social and biological descendents of the powerful ones are left muttering on the sidelines about past glories, lost in little more than a couple of generations, as the game passes them by.

It is no help to the cause of social reform to confuse the accoutrements by which the exercise of personal power is dressed up and amplified so as to encourage the beliefs of others in its social legitimacy, with the titular membership of this or that group, distinguished in some externalist way.

2. ADEQUACY CRITERIA FOR SOURCE MODELS

I began this Part of the work with a general discussion of the theory of models, and their central but unstable place in scientific method. But this Part needs rounding off with a complementary section on interpretations and the criteria for judging them adequate. Every facet of these models as applied through analytical concepts to the understanding of life requires interpretations of utterance and behaviours as actions, of actions as acts and of acts as the very stuff of social life, dominated for most societies by the expressive activities of people striving to present acceptable selves. At the same time physical arrangements of things and events in space-time are potent determinates of which fine-grain rule-system and presentational conventions are brought into operation by a performer, once he has provided them with a social interpretation.

Logically, the first step in an interpretation is a double categorization – an item is recognized as a sign, a speech, a distinct item of dress, what one might call only slightly misleadingly its 'natural' classification. Then that item must be further categorized as to its significance. This double categorization is another way of speaking of the need to see a symbolic system in terms of both *valeur* and *signifié*.

But there may be indirect interpretations brought about say by bringing something under a rule. I may conclude that what he did must have been a B-type action since it was clearly an A-type occasion, and I have reason to think that he subscribes to the rule 'When in A-type situations do B-type actions'. This is not an independent interpretation device since it works only if the occasion has been interpreted by both actor and spectators as of type A, an act involving double categorization of the first kind.

Adequacy

By what criteria do I judge that an interpretation is adequate? We cannot be concerned with truth, since the act of interpretation creates the entity as something of a certain significance, provided the interpretative principles used are in common use amongst the folk. This gives us a clue as to the most general criterion:

(i) An interpretation is adequate if it is accepted by most competent members.

This criterion alone would sanction only given interpretations. But new interpretations are being offered all the time – by ordinary people, not just by sociologists, historians or other licensed interpreters. How is their adequacy to be judged? A new interpretation is useless, even meaningless, until it is accepted by at least some of the people. This idea gives us a clue to the second criterion:

(ii) An interpretation is adequate if most competent members can be persuaded to adopt it.

By negotiating an agreement to adopt an interpretation, for most social purposes and for most social cases, we thereby enlarge the social world, since to adopt a novel interpretation is to create a new social fact. To persuade women to interpret marriage as exploitation rather than as a source of security is to alter the social reality of the institution. This can be shown in the different emotional and attitudinal consequences of the adoption of the different interpretations. Changing the causal powers of something is to change its very essence.

On the view advocated in this work the question is not 'What was marriage all along?' but 'What was it once and what can it be made to be?' Interpretations are creations, not revelations. But they are creations only if they become reality-creating interpretations, that is become the interpretations used by most people.

The two models I have offered, with their common intersection in the thesis of the dominance of the expressive over the practical in most human affairs and for most of human history are proposed rhetorically. If they make the world intelligible for you, gentle reader, as they have done for me, we have shared interpretations with which we can construct a reality. And in so far as through account analysis we can be confident that our models are also the interpretative framework of the people who live the lives we are contemplating, and that is of course ourselves, we have the only available surrogate for the unattainable and indeed in the social context, the meaningless ideal of truth.

This epistemic position should be compared with that of the natural sciences. The fact that both natural and social sciences use models in the same way may suggest misleadingly that they share a common epistemology. The differences emerge when we compare the relation of fact to theory in each kind of science. In the social sciences facts, *at the level at which we experience them*, are wholly the creation of theorizing, of interpreting. Realists in social science hold, and I would share their belief, that there are global patterns in the behaviour of men in groups, though as I have argued we have no adequate inductive method for finding them out. In the natural sciences, though interpretative schemata are intimately involved in perception and selection of what we take to be the facts and can on occasion produce illusion, nevertheless the natural world is intransigent.

By that I mean that there are limits to how far interpretation and reinterpretation can go, without distortions and inconsistencies manifesting themselves. From the simplest kind of experience we idealize a notion of truth, but it is one which we can never fully realize in practice. All our actual 'knowledge' is at best plausible. As Kepler pointed out, we judge different astronomical systems by their plausibility, the way they fit into a general physics of the universe, but one and all must have the observed relative motions of the planets as a consequence, whatever may be their claims about the real structure of the universe.

3. A THIRD MODEL: SOCIAL ACTIVITY AS WORK

A third source-model for the development of analytical and explanatory concepts for act/action episodes is work. I do not propose to deal with this source model in the same detail as the expressive models, since I believe its usefulness to be limited because of the historical rarity of societies in which work, in the sense of the production of the means of life, is the dominant activity.[5] Nevertheless even as a metaphor it throws a useful, oblique light on much that is otherwise obscure.

(a) The Abstract Form of a 'Work' Theory

To use a source model to generate concepts, that model must be carefully articulated. The 'work' model seems to me to be naturally separable into two parts, the form of the work-activity and the form of the work-organization.

(i) Work-activity
In general work-activity has to be conceived teleologically in that every form of work has a characteristic product, and the form the work takes is determined by the form of the product and the properties of the medium in which it is realized.

But work is not done with bare hands on a medium found lying about in nature. Both the tools and the work-medium ('raw' material) are already the products of the work of others. Work transforms products by using products to create products. At each stage the producer and his product must be separated for the further transformation and utilization of it by others to proceed. And here is the basic alienation of product from producer, appearing as a necessary consequence of the conditions of work.

Bhaskar has made a useful adaptation of this structure of activities to develop a theory of science as a form of work.[6]

(ii) Work-organization

In theory each phase of the process described above could be performed by the same man, and he could live off the results of exchanging his final product for the final products of others. In practice this form of production is soon superseded by that division of labour which was assumed above in defining the simplest form of alienation. Marx, as I understand him, argued that the form of work-organization derived from the form of production – but that seems to be far from universally true. I would want to form the Cartesian product of the form of production with the expressive principles currently available in a society, to define the form of work-organization in detail. For example the sense of dignity and the respect demanded by craftsmen in many industries forces on the factory a form of work-organization that is far from maximizing the efficiency of the production of the end product. One can understand the way work is organized only by looking at the interactions between the expressive and the practical systems.

It is not easily determined how far such a development runs counter to recent developments in Marxist psychology. I have in mind Garai's personality theory developed in the Budapest school.[7] According to that theory, personality is determined by an interaction between the location of the person in a social structure and the person's own need for development. Personality will change as either or both change – the former by changing the methods of production of the means of production – the latter presumably through the operation of endogenous factors. This misses the expressive dimension which in my view absolutely dominates the process of material production in modern society.

(b) Production Distinguished by Products

The products of social activity are concrete material things on the one hand and reputations, characters, socially and psychologically existing products on the other. We can generalize the production-work theory to include the necessities of the production of reputations and the symbolic devices necessary to represent them. Then this can be formally represented through the use of the idea of symbolic credit.[8] Just as a study of the way work develops requires the concepts of production, the means of production, appropriation of the products of the past, and the alienation of the producer from the product, so an analogous structure could be looked for in the production of expressive products, such as reputations. How do we produce the means for the production of reputations? How do we define the hazards necessary for moral careers (to be described in Part IV)? How do we appropriate and change the reputations and reputation creating 'tools' of the past? How far can we tolerate the detachment of our public reputations into an independent expressive order in the control of which we have little influence? The invention of an alternative expressive world by such as football fans or madmen is a possible solution.

CONCLUSION

The work model is a concrete formulation of the general teleological principle that informs the whole of this study, namely that social behaviour is to be conceived as deliberate action directed towards certain ends. By including social-expressive ends as among the main products of social activity the work model and the general ethogenic picture converge.

PART III

Persons

INTRODUCTION

What, then, must people be like to be able to do all that we have seen them able to do? I turn now to a philosophical analysis of the concept of a person in the hope that I can sustain in analysis what we have seen to be possible in real life.

Two independent conceptual schemes are required for theorizing about human action, considering people as individuals analytically independent of the social order and historical process upon which they depend ontologically.

I develop, in detail, a conceptual system for formulating explanations co-ordinate with the socially determined and determining concepts of ordinary languages. Explanations of this 'level', I argue, must follow the Aristotelian format and must make essential use of the concepts based upon the idea of an intention.

But people are embodied. A second conceptual system controls explanations referred to the material basis of individual being. In Part Four the location of that system within a socially relevant macrosystem, including material ecology is developed. I argue that the two individual centred systems can be unified only through an intermediate cybernetic representation of an abstractly defined structure commensurate with our physiological knowledge, and representative of the Aristotelian intentional explanations coordinate with folk psychology and sociology that are formulated in terms of the first system.

11

THEORIES OF THE SELF AS INDIVIDUAL AGENT

ANTICIPATORY SUMMARY

1. The conditions for agency
   (a) Representation conditions.
   (b) Realization conditions;
      (i) positive;
      (ii) negative.
2. The limits of agency
   (a) Limited reflexivity. The psychological necessity of 'Grace' since absolute self-control requires divine assistance.
   (b) Intervention can be in action or in being:
      (i) to create a new internal coherence;
      (ii) to augment self-control.
   (c) Limitless autonomy rejected.
3. Automata theories
   (a) Total external control: e.g. B. F. Skinner locates the causes of all actions and of all dispositions in the environment.
   (b) Total internal control: even rational thought is controlled by sentiment:
      (i) Hume's theory of the primary of the passions;
      (ii) Freud's theory of the power of repressed contents;
   (c) Marx's theory of socio-economic determinism.
4. An ethogenic theory of agency
   (a) Relative autonomy. Positive: an agent must be able to envisage a variety of courses of action and identify choice points, and to act independently of any particular internal or external influence.
   (b) Freedom as dissent: i.e. freedom in the context of this study requires not that an agent should be undetermined, but that a human being can shift from any specific mode or principle of determination to be guided by another.
   (c) The mode of causality mappable onto a simple linear sequence of events must be rejected:

245

(i) a randomizing link in a causal chain does not simulate the sense
of freedom from constraint we need to characterize human conditions of action;

(ii) a multi-level, multi-peak control system is an adequate preliminary model.

1. THE CONDITIONS FOR AGENCY

The most general requirement for any being whatever to count as
an agent is that it have some measure of autonomy. By that I
mean that its conduct[1] (actions and acts) is not wholly determined by the conditions of its immediate environment. In our
present state of knowledge both electrons and people fulfill this
most general criterion for agency. But for us electrons are simple
beings. They are treated as without complex inner processes
mediating their behaviour. People on the other hand are internally
complex. Their inner structures and processes endow them with
the possibility of initiating action and internally transforming
the effects of the environment and other people and things.

While people are clearly agents in the sense that their behaviour
is not determined wholly by external conditions, their autonomy
may seem to be threatened by the demonstration of determinate
inner processes issuing in action. The psychological conditions
needed to ground autonomy in the light of the possibility of internal determination are complex. I propose at least the following:

(a) Representation Condition

A person can represent to himself, internally or externally, privately or publicly, a wider range of possible futures than can be
realized.

(b) Realization Conditions

(i) Positive: a person can, after decision, realize any from among
some feasible sub-group of his conceived possible futures.

(ii) Negative: a person can abort any action-generating process
already initiated with respect to a new choice of goal. (The new
goal may be no more than the demonstration of the power to
abort any process.) This condition must include both social
trains of influence, such as that from command to obedient
performance, and physically mediated processes, for example
tiredness to yawning, being bumped to lashing out.

Together these make up the *autonomy conditions.*

For the realization conditions to be the action of a person they must exemplify reflexive action, principled action upon the self. For instance, the positive realization condition requires non-arbitrary choice of future, that is choice according to principle. And to preserve agent status at that level the principle employed in the first level must be, at least in theory, one of many possible principles from which principled choice of guiding principle was made. In practice this condition may be realized only in the possibility of a principled defence of some second order principle which could have guided choice of first order principle had deliberation actually occurred. The psychological condition of reflexivity requires an open hierarchy of possibility of higher and higher order principled choices, or the possibility of corresponding principled defences of the principles in lower levels of the hierarchy.

2. THE LIMITS OF AGENCY

To use Luke's useful term, the 'root-ideas' in the concept of human agency I take to be 'autonomy' and 'reflexivity'. Common experience suggests they are linked as I have described. That they are so elaborate suggests they are not independent of the internal complexity of human beings as organisms. Are there any limitations to the autonomy and reflexivity of which human beings are capable? We can reach a just estimation by briefly examining some extreme answers to this question.

(a) Limited Reflexivity: the Psychological Necessity of 'Grace'

In traditional Christian thought a human being is supposed to be capable of unlimited self-intervention and self-control. At first sight this appears to conflict with the absolutism of the moral theory that the Church has usually espoused. If a human being is liable for moral judgement on all his systems of action, then nothing he does, thinks or feels should be immune from the possibility of self-control. Moral failure cannot be excused as consequent upon the actual impossibility of some form of self-intervention or self-control.

Traditional Christianity resolved the difficulty by allowing that though it was in the nature of people to be incapable of unlimited self-intervention and self-control, most individuals were actually able to exercise these powers. Some individuals may lack the techniques for performing such actions, but that could be remedied by training in self-denial. This view seems to have been shared by traditional Islam in that the fasts of Id practised by members of that tradition are sometimes defended as exercises in the practice of self-control.

More importantly the gap between what human beings could really do unaided and what was normally required as possible for them was filled by Grace, a divine injection of power. If one had tried and failed to manage oneself one could call on God, through prayer, to add His power to that of the miserable but contrite sinner. In all this one remained within the moral world since one could be blamed for failing to call on God for Grace when it seemed to be required. In short, the conflict between the practical limit of reflexive control and the moral demand of absolute agency is resolved by the insistence on the autonomy a person exercises in choosing to call God to his aid. As Aquinas puts the matter:

> But it is manifest that the virtues acquired by human acts are dispositions, whereby a man is fittingly disposed with reference to the nature whereby he is a man; whereas infused virtues dispose man in a higher manner and towards a higher end, and consequently in relation to some higher nature, i.e. in relation to a participation of the Divine Nature ...[2]

The effect of living within a framework of such a complex of principles and practices would be, one suspects, to amplify the actual capacity for self-management available to individual human beings.

We too shall distinguish between psychological actuality and psychological possibility − but putting down the fallen state of man in his current dependence upon external constraints and controls to the baleful influence of behaviourism, psychodynamics and other psychologies which propose a determination of action by influences beyond the control of individual people.

(b) Intervention in Action and in Kind of Being

The empirical centre of our concept of agency is the capacity we discern in a person to act upon himself. Two kinds of self-intervention seem to be pointed to. There is that kind of self-intervention in which we pay attention to and act upon the plans, rules, impulses and sometimes even the feelings we are currently experiencing. In so doing we bring much of what we do under our control indirectly, by controlling some of the influences that in the normal course of events would shape our actions. Self-intervention, however, can also be taken to be an endeavour to alter the kind of being one takes oneself to be. Exhortations to the faithless or the unconverted often seem to suggest that what is required to bring them into the fold is some kind of self-transformation. Phrases like 'being born again', 'becoming a new person' − if only one will believe − seem to be characteristic of this way of thinking.

But can this rhetorical distinction be sustained psychologically? Is it anything other than a rhetorical device? For what more might a person be than the collective of plans, beliefs, feelings and impulses that animate his actions?

In principle it seems to me, there are two other 'things' a person might be:

(i) When 'I' am 'born again' a novel coherence and consistency gives overall structure to the psychological content of myself as person. If my rebirth takes place in a social and religious context similar to that of, say President Carter, the consistency increment might show up in my ceasing to be merely a 'Sunday Christian'.

(ii) The whole apparatus of self-intervention could be 'toned up'. In later sections we shall detach the agentive self as a simple, formal power. It might count as a change of being were I to find myself with my agentive capacities greatly enhanced. One might notice, as a pale shadow of the transformations of conversion, differences in one's capacity to get down to work when one is fresh, tired or sick.

(c) Limitless Autonomy: the Unconditioned Freedom of the Will

In traditional philosophical discussions of these matters the issue of the reality of agency is often treated as identical with the problem of the possibility of the freedom of the will. To understand agency one might then draw on philosophical analyses of the will, its freedom, its failures (*akrasia*, for instance).[4] But it is not easy to understand what is meant by *the* will. Perhaps it might be a way of speaking within a psychology of faculties of the power that is exercised in self-intervention when a person acts independently of the content of the object of reflexive action. To speak of 'the will' is just to speak of a person acting. It might be thought of as a name for a determinable power, instantiated in the genesis of each action, a power which activates every action. This would introduce a most implausible category of theoretical entities, I would hold, despite A. Kenny's ingenious defence of ubiquitous volitions, cf. note 3a. But however opaque the concept, it can be used to make some useful distinctions. The theory of the unlimited autonomy of a person is expressible in

terms of the concept of the will. It appears in the principle that
the will is absolutely unconditioned, that is that in the last resort
a human being can act independently of the influence of any
factor whatever. Philosophers have noticed that in most, if not all
human action, the will is not absolutely unconditioned. Rational
men act in accordance with principles. Irrational men act in
accordance with impulse or desire. In neither case is their action
absolutely unconditioned. Kant made the distinction between the
heteronomy of the will in practice and its autonomy in principle.[5]
That is, he accepted the thesis that in principle human beings had
unspecified and unlimited freedom of action but that action as
we knew it in our experience was always conditioned. However, he
believed that there were features of human life that required the
postulation of an unconditioned will. It was to be located in the
noumenal self, the pure agency at the core of each individual
person. But it was never manifested as itself in experience. Sartre,
too, seems to have accepted something like the distinction between the heteronomy of the will in the actual genesis of action
and the ultimate autonomy of each person. He seems to have
believed that there were absolutely unconditioned actions in the
world of experience, those by which people adopt those overall
projects or life forms which from then on condition their activity.
We shall see that in the end something of both of these theories
survives into the ethogenic theory of human action.

3. AUTOMATA THEORIES

In contrast to the idea that people are, at least in principle, free
agents, are a range of positions which take human beings to be
automata under various kinds of control.

(a) Total External Control: No Autonomy

It has been proposed that we should treat human beings as totally
under external control deriving from contingencies in the environments in which they live. The most notorious exponent of this
theory, B. F. Skinner, has argued that all human action should be
construed roughly on the model of habit.[6] Action (or behaviour)
is triggered by changes in the properties of the environment.
Environmental contingencies are said to control human action. The
relevant habits are inculcated by reinforcements of 'operants',
which are initially a field of undifferentiated, spontaneous behaviour. Reinforcement selects some from among the undifferentiated

field, encouraging those operants which are in conformity with the environment and discouraging those which are not. In the end, an adequately functioning automaton is produced which emits suitable behaviours in suitable environmental conditions, and is thus under total external control. Skinner has been quite explicit in his denial that cognitive operations or emotional states have anything whatever to do with the genesis of behaviour.[7] He takes these to be simply accompaniments thrown off by the underlying causal processes. In general he supposes the genesis of behaviour to be explicable by reference only to the physiology of human beings as organisms. This is a theory of absolute determinism of a very physicalistic sort.

Skinner's doctrine seems so extraordinarily implausible and the considerations advanced in its favour so irrational, that one is faced with some difficulty in seeing how anyone could come to hold it. There are, I think, two sources for such a theory. The traditional methods of education in use in the early Twentieth Century involved severe punishments and rigid rules, in short strong external sources of control. There is some evidence from the sociology of knowledge that the social order to which men are subject in their childhood can reappear as reflections in their mature theories. Perhaps radical behaviourism is a case in point. Secondly, the development of Skinner's psychological theories took place during and immediately after the Second World War. The wartime training of soldiers reduces the autonomy of individual people drafted into armies. Self-determination is systematically undermined by a series of practices which have been amply illustrated in Goffman's *Asylums* and in D. H. Lawrence's *The Barracks.* In place of 'thinking for oneself' the army introduces a range of simplified, rigorous routines, which are taught in such a way that they become, as one might say, significantly, 'second nature'. Then in the face of the enemy, these routines are activated and a person might, in that way, prove an effective soldier. The atmosphere of the 1940s and 1950s was not a time in which autonomy was encouraged, at least in the mass of men in national armies. Finally, it is worth noticing that the attempt to move the study of human beings from the world of field and factory, home and street, to the psychological laboratory, serves both to impoverish the environment in which social life is ordinarily lived and to undermine the autonomy of the person brought into that laboratory. In this new and unfamiliar setting he has no idea of how to comport himself and must wait upon the cues offered to him by the experimenter. He tends to exhibit simplified reactions, easily read as those of an automaton. Skinner's approach, like much in psychology, seem to be best seen, not as a putative scientific theory, but as a reflection of the social and political conditions of its time. It is a projection of the political order of a bureaucratic society.

(b) Total Internal Control

Human autonomy is not so easily rescued. There are more subtle theories to contend with, in particular those theories which postulate mental machines or total internal control.

(i) Sentiment: loss of autonomy

The sentiment theory goes back at least to David Hume, who argued for the priority of the passions in the genesis of human action.[8] He claimed to have shown '*first* that reason alone can never be a motive to any action of the will; and *secondly* that it can never oppose passion in the direction of the will'. Festinger proposes something similar, with his theory of cognitive dissonance.[9] Though not easy to formulate precisely, it amounts to the idea that inconsistencies between one's beliefs and the actions one has to perform, cause one discomfort. To dispel the feeling one adjusts belief or action or both. Control passes from the person to the sentiments or passions he is experiencing.

At the heart of these theories, whatever may be their superficial differences, are two rather simple hypotheses.

(a) In general, people have an aversion for bad feelings and a liking for good feelings.

(b) They will automatically act in such a way as to reduce the bad feelings and enhance the good feelings. In short, it is an essential feature of the theory that in the genesis of action a person is helpless with respect to the power of sentiment.

(ii) Loss of reflexiveness

In Freud's theory, human helplessness takes a special form. Certain motivations conditioned by sentiment are removed from consciousness by the defensive process of repression. As components in unconscious complexes they retain their causal powers but are removed from the possibility of self-intervention and control. They exert their baleful influence from below, so to speak. When total internal control of some important class of actions passes to hidden motivations, the condition is pathological.

Self-intervention is restored to a person only after the control of action has passed to another — the psychiatrist — who is outside the system of sentiments and beliefs in the grip of which the person has become an automaton. The psychiatrist makes the operations of the automatic mechanism controlling the action available to the consciousness of his client. The theory is not without complications since from the point of view of the self the removal of material from consciousness, and hence from the possibility of control, is a defensive manoeuvre undertaken by that very self. This difficulty has never been satisfactorily resolved, though it has recently been perceptively discussed by Fingarette.[10]

(c) Socio-economic determinism

There is a third range of theories in common circulation which derive from the works of Karl Marx, in particular from the theory outlined by Marx and Engels in their joint work, *The German Ideology*. In that work Marx's theory takes a strongly deterministic turn.[11] A person's actions, his thoughts and his theories, flow from his class position and that, in its turn, is generated by the system of material production. At least in *The German Ideology*, Marx and Engels treat the system of material production as an autonomously operating and developing system. The actions of human beings both in maintaining it and in proposing theories of the social world to make it intelligible are under the control of that very system, the social organization required by the necessities of material production.

4. AN ETHOGENIC THEORY OF AGENCY

(a) Relative Autonomy

I shall be setting out the structure of a concept of agency that is to be understood in terms of specific human powers, the objects upon which they can be exercised, and the conditions under which they can act. The theory will not propose absolutes. Every mode and sphere of human action will be treated as having only relative autonomy. Treating agency as the capacity to act independently of all principles, it will turn out to be no more than the power to shift from acting according to one principle, impulse, sentiment or whatever, to acting according to another, whatever the original principle might be. Thus, no particular principle will be binding upon an agent, but he must act according to some principle or other, to preserve his standing as a being of a certain sort. Even those who act or speak irrationally to show they are free of those old fashioned constraints, are acting in accordance with a principle. Of course in the end, despite Laing's defence, we are forced to say that some people *are* mad. An agent may, therefore, be a rational being only in a limited sense. His principles, if considered with respect to the highest standards, may be incapable of rational defence. His cognitive hierarchy may be rather short. Nevertheless, they are his principles.

(b) Freedom as Dissent

The basic conception common to the root ideas I have suggested to determine our concept of agency is the thought that as agents we can bring any specific matter to our attention. Having done so we are able to bring it under our control, but always with respect to some other matter. In principle, then, there is no particular matter to which we are always subject. But I have no wish to claim that we are not, in every one of our actions, subject to something. The point can be illustrated by looking at the way in which we make shifts of hegemony, as one might call it.

A 'sideways' shift can be made among matters of the same sort. For example, we may be accustomed to illustrate our servility by obeying the orders of a superior. As human agents we can perform an act of defiance to illustrate our pride. In both cases we are acting according to principle. We are agents because we have turned from action according to one principle to action according to another.

We can also make what one might call 'upward' shifts. We may choose to ignore a bodily prompting in order to act according to some moral or dramaturgical principle. At an interview we may resist the temptation to scratch an itch — a prompting we ordinarily scarcely attend to and simply indulge — in accordance with expressive principles that we take to govern the presentational style of candidates at interviews. And, as in the sideways shift, our move from habit to principled action may be made according to a principle or higher rule.

The way a secret ballot is organized offers an illustration of a practical solution to the problem of ensuring that the vote is the act of a human agent. The relativity of the freedom from influence which it guarantees illustrates the concept of agency I am arguing for. The arrangement of the secret ballot ensures that a vote is made independently of certain specific categories of influence such as, for example, the whispered threats of the candidates or their agents. In most countries even printed political propaganda is not permitted in the voting hall. But, of course, these arrangements do not guarantee that the vote is made by the human actor independently of all influences, particularly the voter's own prejudices, ideals, personal history, the latent effect of the persuasiveness of the candidates, the credibility of their programmes and so on.

(c) The Mode of Causality

To establish agency in what I take to be all the relevant degrees and for all the proper occasions, all that is required is to see that the concept as we use it requires the possibility of our detachment from the influences of any immediate and particular environment and from the principles according to which we have been acting until now. From a cybernetic point of view this thesis amounts to a denial that human actions are the product of processes of simple linear causality.

Determination in causal chains can break down in two ways:

(i) A spontaneous change, a random chance event, may occur at some link in a linear causal chain, leading to a divergence from what would be the usual outcome of a sequence which begins in that way. A model for this in contemporary physics is, of course, quantum mechanical transitions. It has been pointed out that this kind of breakdown does not give us the sense of agency that we want, namely the idea of a human being as a system which can control itself. I do not propose to discuss these matters in terms of freedom and determinism, the freedom of the will, and so on. It seems to me that the intransigence of the problem of giving adequate accounts of these concepts to accord both with our experience and our growing and anticipated scientific knowledge is, in part, a reflection of the slipperiness of the concept of freedom. This can be illustrated by the example I have just been considering, namely the use of quantum mechanics as a model for human freedom. I think it is arguable that random choice does reflect one of the ways in which some people wish to claim that they are free. But no adequate account of freedom as self-control can be given in terms of freedom as randomness. We shall see that the legitimate claim to freedom as randomness has a place in human life. But its force is to be located among expressive activities. Demonstrations of freedom as randomness are illustrations of the kind of person one takes oneself to be rather than amongst practical ways of acting to bring about one's plans and projects. The choice of plans and projects is not random either, since, I would argue, those choices can be referred to what sort of presentation is aimed at on the expressive plane.

(ii) A non-linear causal system can be defined in cybernetic terms as a multi-levelled, multi-peaked, control system. It is a system which can examine each causal influence to which it is subjected according to a set of principles which are built in to a higher level of that system. If the system is also multi-peak, the high level will also be complex, able to switch from one higher level sub-system to another. Such a system may have indefinitely many levels, in each of which are indefinitely many sub-systems. A system of this sort is capable of making sideways shifts, as we have described them, that is of controlling its lower level operations by moving from one sub-system to another within a level. It is also capable of upward shifts in that it may bring such sideways shifts under monitoring and control by a high-level criterial system. In such a system there is, I believe, a pale shadow of the complex shiftings and weavings of the inner activities of human agents.

The existentialists have persistently drawn our attention to the common experience of random choice. Sometimes choice lies between alternatives for which there are neither inclining reasons nor distinguishably different desires. We can neither devise a practical syllogism nor surrender ourselves to impulse. But sometimes even after deliberation the moment of choice seems isolated from the chain of prior considerations. It is clear that we sometimes experience choice in the mode of the randomly branching Markov chain. And sometimes we experience the full machinery of deliberation, willing and action, or the multi-level hierarchy of principles and rules.

But in accounting we are very much inclined to represent that which we experienced as mere randomness, as if it were principled choice. We may even go so far as to represent our actions as the ultimate product of reasoned choice of principle with which to make principled choice. To publicly represent one's actions as being generated in the linear, random mode is indeed to claim a kind of freedom, but is is the morally empty freedom of a mere patient. But to represent one's actions as issuing from the workings of complex cognitive machinery is to claim agency, not so much with respect to autonomy as reflexiveness. It is to claim that one's actions were 'principled'.

This pervasive feature of accounting is perhaps one of the things that gives Camus' story *L'Etranger* so peculiar an air. Even if Mersault experienced the shooting of the Arab in the linear-random mode, would he later so act as to favour that public impression? But if we see him as engaged in a proof of autonomy, then what seemed unprincipled on the practical plane, since Mersualt had no instrumental reason for shooting the Arab, nor was he driven by uncontrollable feelings, becomes principled action on the expressive plane. It is just the kind of action one would choose in the reflexive-rational mode of action-genesis to demonstrate autonomy.

Agency *concepts* define ideal people with fully realized positive and negative capacities. They are capable of exhibiting autonomy and reflectiveness in both positive and negative modes. Naturally enough, these ways of speaking dominate accounting in societies where ideal prescriptions for personhood reflect this sense of agency. Actual people differ in their ways of generating action. The gap is filled in various ways: in Catholic theory by Grace; in ethogenics by a philosophical psychology that emphasizes the importance of public rhetoric as well as private process as the source of action.

In summary, I propose a philosophical theory based on an account of the concept of a human agent as we use that concept in talking of men's day-to-day activities. Along with it is a sketch of a physically realizable mechanism that could produce modes of control that would properly be described as actions of an agent, the root ideas of which we have unravelled. The managing self of our tripartite concept of the person becomes our internal description of the activities of a human being in switching control from one part of the mechanism to another. Since mere switching has no content, it will always be experienced as the exercise of a pure power upon some content or other in accordance with some principle or other. Being empty it is always the same. Like any other power it cannot be observed except in so far as it is seen in action. The agentive self is an abstraction which we form for ourselves from the wide variety of activities in which we engage by controlling one part of our lives by reference to some other. But it is none the less real. In the end the referent of the personal pronoun in 'I choose...' can be none other than that in 'I run' and 'I think' – namely the whole person.

12

THE GENESIS OF ACTION

ANTICIPATORY SUMMARY

Introduction: common-sense explanatory framework
1. Trait Theory
   (a) Classical trait theory; traits are situation and interaction independent.
   (b) Empirical difficulties with trait theory:
      (i) traits appear only in lay descriptions of people;
      (ii) appear to be part of the apparatus of moral commentary upon oneself and others;
      (iii) in general lead to disapproval of others and credit for oneself;
      (iv) cross-situational consistency seems to be confined to physiologically based behaviour and to pathological personalities.
   (c) Conceptual difficulties with trait theory:
      (i) traits compare unfavourably with actions in that they are so comprehensive as to be empty;
      (ii) as behavioural dispositions traits include responses related contingently as well as those related necessarily to alleged determinants;
      (iii) many important dispositions are not attributed on the basis of observed manifestations of the behaviour in question;
      (iv) ultimately the issue between trait theories and agent-action theories turns on moral considerations concerning the nature one ascribes to man, since that serves as an exemplar for human self-construction.
2. A Performance theory for social psychology
   (a) Explanation scheme for a social psychology:
      (i) the most general principle is that both actions and accounts derive from a single system of social knowledge and skill;
      (ii) objects of explanation include choice of acts and of the actions needed to realize them;
      (iii) the content of intentions; explicit is of acts, implicit of actions;
      (iv) outline of a performance theory: there is an intention defining project and a rule guiding the naturally active agent in his behaviour;

259

INTRODUCTION

The picture that emerges from the relatively elementary considerations of the last chapter is of a great deal of automatic, habitual, customary activity, with an in-principle, all powerful agentive capacity to fall back upon when for one reason or another the action is out of joint. As we shall see, there is a whole range of social actions whose function in the expressive order is just to demonstrate that a person has pure agentive power in reserve. Such actions may appear, as they are meant to appear, random and meaningless in the practical order. No account of the underlying nature and conditions of that agentive power has yet been offered in this work.

Can we devise a unified theory of action with the possibility of accommodating both kinds of action genesis — acting in accordance with public demands and acting to realize private projects? And the many cases of compromises, balances and blendings of the two? At least we must acknowledge that a good deal of psychological processing, and even some important items of knowledge and belief exist outside individual persons in some public space.

Before setting up a theory of the genesis of action that is fully in accordance with the argument so far, it is necessary to discuss and eliminate some alternatives. Merely eliminating the extreme characterizations of human beings that appear in traditional theology and in automata theories in psychology and sociology does not yet establish the form in which human beings generate their social activities.

1. TRAIT-THEORY

According to this way of understanding the genesis of human action, a person is supposed to be endowed with a variety of simple dispositions which are taken to be permanent features of his character. In most versions of the theory traits are assumed to be stable across situations. The impetus for action is supposed to come from without, for example from some sort of stimulus which activates the disposition; for instance, a woman who has a trait of nurturance, when shown a baby will start mothering it, going 'goo goo' and so on. The explanation of her action involves a particular stimulus and the general disposition or trait of nurturance. The historical antecedents of this theory can be found in the idea of the Pavlovian reflex. Though the mother's activities are more complex, they do not differ in principle from those of a dog who salivates when shown his dinner.

Typically, traits are thought of in pairs on a bi-polar scale, so that they are differentiated from person to person by their 'strength', measured by reference to their location on the scale. For example, the pair 'extrovert: introvert' form a bi-polar scale with intermediate degrees, so people can be spoken of, for example, as 'high on introversion' or 'low on extroversion'.

(a) Classical Trait-Theory

In the classical form of the theory, proposed by Cattel,[1] and in a somewhat less sophisticated form by Eysenck,[2] traits are taken to be independent of situation and of the persons with whom the subject of the trait-attributions is interacting. I think it is correct to say that where some putative trait has been shown to be situationally differentiated, for example being manifested in one sort of situation and not in another, trait-psychologists have been inclined to rule it out as not being a genuine or source trait. By the building up of a trait profile a person gets a social psychological description which is supposed to characterize him in all his activities:

X *is* intelligent, neurotic, introverted (and is dark, thin, and bites his nails)

Y *is* stupid, extrovert, etc. (and is fair, bulky, and plays football).

It is important to notice that the collection of traits a psychologist might attribute to someone form clusters. It is very easy for us to fill in *a priori* further attributes for such an individual as I have imagined. See for example, the items in the brackets above. This suggests that there is a connection between the attributions made in trait psychology and the content of cultural stereotypes, a connection which we shall see is of considerable significance in understanding the scientific status of the trait, as an alleged personal property.

Trait theories can be distinguished by whether they treat the set of dispositions which are attributed to an individual as a mere cluster, or whether they look upon them as forming some kind of hierarchy. The most sophisticated trait theory – that of Cattel – distinguishes between traits and source-traits, treating those traits which are exhibited in day-to-day social action as deriving from more fundamental trait-characteristics of a person – source-traits. In this theory the attributes of a person form some kind of hierarchy.

(b) Empirical Difficulties with Trait-Theory

(i) Traits are easily seen to be part of the ordinary persons' common theoretical resources for describing personality. Are trait-

terms devices for speaking about people for some so far unspecified rhetorical purposes, or are traits to be found exemplified in
the activities that people actually perform? Careful studies have
shown that trait-attributions are more a product of the language
that we use in accounting than they are exhibited in objective
features of the action.

Most social psychology is conducted by the use of questionnaires, self-reports, and so on. It is often concerned with what
people would do in imagined situations, how they would describe
imaginary persons, and so on. Trait-descriptions appear very
widely in such reports. However, when people are studied in their
actual behaviour in real situations, whether natural or artificial,
and one looks at the descriptions of that behaviour and tries to
co-ordinate it across a variety of situations and through a reasonably extended time-span, then traits disappear. This has been
well established even in experimental psychology, particularly by
Argyle.[3]

(ii) The point is made sharper by some investigations of Jones
and Nisbett.[4] They showed that when people are asked to account
for their own behaviour they tend to point to some feature of
situation or setting as the responsible agent, but when they account
for the behaviour of others they make reference to traits. This
turns out to be particularly true of cases where in some way or
another the behaviour has been reprehensible in some manner,
ugly, immoral, incompetent, and so on. For example, if a person
is asked to account for stumbling, he will blame a bump in the
path, whereas he accounts for the stumblings of others in terms
of their clumsiness. But when people are claiming credit for their
own successes they put them down to personal traits. But they
are likely to explain their own failures by reference to features of
the situation, setting, or to the machinations of others. (Some
recent work by Charles Antaki casts doubt on the generality of the
phenomenon.)

(iii) However, though most of the classical traits, such as extroversion, neuroticism, and so on, seem to dissolve in the acid of
careful investigations, they remain as part of the technique of
accounting particularly, so it seems, with respect to the expressive
tasks of self-presentation.

(iv) There are some kinds of behaviour which are consistent for
a given individual across many situations and for which it seems
not implausible to use the concept of a trait. Examples of consistent behaviour can be found in such culturally differentiated

matters as eye-contact patterns, bodily attitudes in conversation, and so on. It has also been claimed that an addict will exhibit his addiction in a wide variety of settings and through long periods of time in a fairly consistent fashion. I take the addiction to tobacco to be an example. The explanation of addictive consistency can perhaps be found in Stanley Shachter's discovery that the rate at which people smoke is most nearly correlated with physiological factors such as body fluid acidity. These factors are not monitored directly by the central nervous system but are nevertheless closely related to the rate at which nicotine is consumed in the body.

But there are less obviously physiologically based consistencies exhibited by people who we would ordinarily take to be emotionally or mentally disturbed. There are those whose rigidity and dogmatism seems to verge on the pathological. Consistency — real consistency — is treated by most people as a defect in the social behaviour of another human being and is subject to all kinds of derogatory judgements. Should a trait-theorist undertake experiments with people carefully selected from the population for consistency he would find his theory amply supported. Very high consistency marks a pathological form of life. It seems to be exemplified in the kind of person to be found in extremist wings of political parties. The structure of some instances of this kind of personality has been carefully looked at in Wilson's recent work on conservatism though Wilson examined only those on the extreme right of the political spectrum.[5]

The results of careful naturalistic investigations of people's behaviour over a wide range of situations and settings can, I think, be said to have yielded quite conclusive evidence that:

(a) trait-theory is regularly and routinely used by people to describe themselves and others. It is part of lay-psychology. It is closely linked with the expression of moral attitudes in impression management;

(b) it is true only of certain elementary and unattended kinds of behaviour, and of certain extreme, and happily, rather rare, kinds of people.

(c) Conceptual Difficulties with Trait-Theory

(i) W. Mischel has objected to trait-theory on the grounds that each disposition which is offered as a trait, for example extroversion, is so broad in connotation that a very wide range of often very different kinds of human activity counts as exemplifying it.[6]

The concepts of trait-theory are introduced from the beginning in an empirically weakened form. Mischel's own proposal is to look at what people do in relation to clearly specified psychological and social conditions. What people do he argues is capable of more precise and detailed classification than the traits supposedly exhibited in their actions.

However, this move, though I shall be following it to some extent myself, does not eliminate the necessity to attribute dispositions to people and what is more, to attribute dispositions of two kinds, one of which at any rate, is rather general. We need to be able to say that people have abilities (dispositions) to learn to perform various social or cognitive routines. Having learned this we must be able to say they can do these things even when they are not currently performing. Ability to perform, for many human activities, is treated as the realization of an unspecified range of abilities to acquire or learn. Then again, the two-tier structure appears in many activities where a state of readiness must be reached before it is possible to undertake a task. An ability to make oneself ready must be attributed to anyone who, in the end, is going to be able to do whatever it is that he is required to do by acting from a state of readiness. There are various ways in which these points can be accommodated in the philosophical grammar of a descriptive language. For the former, Shotter has proposed a distinction between natural and acquired powers.[7] For the latter one might use the distinction between tendencies and abilities, though these two expressions already have a place in lay-psychology.[8]

(ii) The difficulties with the trait-theory are, in the end, difficulties with the idea of a behavioural disposition. They are as much difficulties for the theories of Cattel and Eysenck as they are for the dispositional philosophical psychology of Gilbert Ryle.[9] Traits, after all, are a psychologist's word for dispositions, or rather, perhaps, for lasting and permanent dispositions. The most general form of dispositional concepts are used to attribute dispositions to respond in certain ways in specific situations and settings. Alston's study[10] of such concepts has revealed the following problems:

(a) As psychologists, both professional and lay, have used trait-concepts, the situational or stimulus and the response categories involved in their construction turn out to be of widely different kinds. They include behavioural, interpretative, cognitive and emotional categories. On the one hand there are trait-concepts formed of such pairs as 'socially embarrassing situation' – 'blushing'; and 'presentation of a problem' – 'solution obtained rapidly and economically', and many, many others. It seems very unlikely, to say the least, that the underlying structure of a person, whether physiological or whatever, is likely to be similar for such widely differentiated kinds of situation and response.

(b) More damagingly, trait-concepts in common use include both those in which responses are conceptually related to situations and settings, as well as those where the relation seems to be contingent and perhaps learned. For instance, to take Alston's example, complying is defined as a response to requests, obedience as the carrying out of orders, and so on, whereas there are all kinds of ways of responding to social embarrassment other than blushing. In the latter there is an empirical rather than a conceptual connection. Trait concepts seem to relate to properties of individuals in very different ways.

(iii) The epistemology of trait concepts is also rather odd. Psychologists understand them in terms of situations experienced and responses emitted. One would expect the trait attributes to be ascribed on the basis of the observers having noticed that the individual to whom the trait or disposition is attributed does emit the appropriate response in a specified situation or setting. Indeed, there is no other way in which one could come to know that an individual did have such a trait. However, the most common forms of dispositional and trait concepts which we use, not only in lay psychology but in professional work as well, include such attributes as needs, abilities and attitudes. As Alston points out it is no part of the concept of a need, or an ability, or an attitude, that it should be frequently revealed or exhibited in action, or even so exhibited at all. It is perfectly proper to say that someone who never actually plays tennis has the ability to do so. The concealment of our attitudes and the redirection of our needs is a common form of human activity. 'Tendency' seems to be the most appropriate concept for the kind of attribute we may want to ascribe to an individual even though it was always aborted, frustrated, impeded and so on.

(iv) In the general discussion we noticed that alleged trait-attributes are inconsistently manifested in the full range of situations, settings and times through which a person lives. Alston makes the important point that a determined trait-theorist or dispositionalist could accommodate apparent inconsistencies by partitioning the situation element in the relevant trait-concept.

For example, take 'dominance'. If the typical response varies with the person's momentary role and situation (he may be dominant in the office and servile at home), we can partition situation and setting into two sub-concepts, S^1 in role-situation 1 and S^2 in role-situation 2. Then, since trait-concepts are contrived from a situation-response pair, we have two traits to attribute to such a person. We may then find someone else who is servile in both places, so establishing that our sub-traits are indeed independent. In this way, it is at least theoretically possible to accommodate empirical discoveries into a trait-psychology.

Two comments seem to be in order. Once this floodgate of partitioning is opened, given that the empirical evidence suggests a very wide variability in what people are likely, and even able, to do over a wide range of highly differentiated situations, trait-concepts will have to proliferate indefinitely. They would become more and more specific, culturally relative and temporally conditioned. I take this to be a serious objection to the use of such concepts if there is any alternative way of dealing with human abilities. Secondly, Alston claims that the difference between trait-theories, cognitive-theories and agent-theories of action is a philosophical issue. The trait-theory is, of course, an example of an automaton theory, in that an individual's actions are merely the manifestation of his or her traits. Mischel's shift to the idea of a person as agent who uses or fails to use the cognitive equipment, social knowledge and so on that he has to hand, is not just a philosophical advance on trait-theory. It seems to accord better with the 'facts' in so far as we know them. But more importantly, whether we choose to pursue a trait-theory, refining it and extending it in the way Alston has shown to be theoretically possible, or whether we adopt an agent-theory of some kind, is not just an empirical or even a philosophical issue. It is, above all, a moral issue. Each theory involves a particular conception of the nature of human beings. Each conception has different consequences for our policies towards others. The moral and indeed political aspects of fundamental theoretical stances in social psychology will become more and more prominent as our investigation develops.

2. TOWARDS A PERFORMANCE THEORY OF SOCIAL ACTION

In Part II I developed various analytical schemes whose application would enable attributions of social skill and knowledge to be made to individuals. These attributions correspond to the development

of a competence theory. I turn now to sketch the outline framework for formulating performance theories for social action.

(a) Explanation Schema for a Social Psychology
(i) The working proposal
Our social psychological theory in its most general act-form runs
as follows:

Characteristic features of individual contributions to act/action
sequences and of accountings related to them derive from the
same cognitive resources.

I have yet to explicate some of the senses in which a performance of either type can 'derive from' a resource. The explication
of such a metaphor is likely to involve something more than
simple associative event correlations as our concept of causality.
It is in this particular that ethogenic psychology goes beyond
psycholinguistics in proposing schemata for performance theories,
one for actions and one for accounts, in accordance with which
we will explain how agents use resources to produce actions and
accounts. But before the outline of a performance theory can be
constructed an analysis of performances is needed to identify the
several objects of explanation to which the theory must be directed.[11] According to our theory, people's actions are to be categorized with respect to the acts they are conventionally taken to
perform in determinate settings and specific situations. The style
of the action and the kind of accounts that are produced serve
the expressive task of the presentation of a person as exemplifying
an appropriate and worthy social type and creating actions and
acts by disambiguating behaviour.

An account is, among other things, a lay explanation of the
occurrence, characteristics and propriety of the actions an individual performs to accomplish the acts he intends and that are
required of him by others. For example, an account may include
not only reports of avowals of intention, that is a description of
or a reference to an act proposed by an actor, but also citation of
rules of action. A rule is one way of expressing our knowledge of
the proper form of an action or action-sequences. In this case
the resource could be the rule as explicitly verbally formulated,
and the process of production of the structured action-sequence
be conscious rule-following. By such a process the content of the
resource is replicated in the structure of the manifest act/action
sequence. A citation of the rule could function as an account
explicating and warranting the doing of that action in those social

circumstances. Thus the very same resource is the source of the socially important features of action 1, via a template in the causal mechanism of action, and of the content of an account of the action performance.

(ii) Objects of explanation
What, then, is to be explained in a theory of action-genesis? There seem to be at least the following:
- (a) the performance of some action or other by a particular person at a particular time and place and in a particular setting;
- (b) the performance of one of the kinds of action that would achieve a particular social act in those circumstances;
- (c) the choice of a particular action from among those conventionally taken to be the actions by which the required act is performed;
- (d) the medium in which the action-sequence is realized;
- (e) the giving of some account or other by a particular person at a particular time and in a particular place and setting;
- (f) the social force of the account actually given;
- (g) the content of the account actually given.

The general form of explanation will be that effects are produced by an agent following a template. The specific application of that mode of explanation in this context will be in terms of an agent's intentions and knowledge.

(iii) The content of intentions
I shall be proposing that we take the content of an intention to be determinative of certain features of the act/action structure of co-operative social activity. But intentions do not have contents of one and only one social type. In general people intend ends, outcomes, consummations, acts, rather than the actions conventionally required to perform the acts. Social rules and conventions represent knowledge of the locally recognized means for realizing this or that intention. Usually when the ceremonial or liturgical model is used to provide understanding of the action-sequences of social life the content of an intention is an act: for example 'I intend to veto this proposed legislation'. To achieve that social and legal act, namely the act of vetoing, the appropriate actions or refraining from action must be performed. Local knowledge of the rules and conventions is required to formulate a plan to carry out the required actions in a proper sequence. Frequently the

means involve secondary intentions, namely to perform the actions required. The plan can become the content of another, dependent intention, as for example 'I intend to write "Vetoed" on this document'. In this case the action that is represented in the secondary intention is that conventionally required to perform the act represented in the primary intention. In general action-intentions are usually not avowed or even entertained, since there is local knowledge shared among the participants in such a ceremony as to the action or action-sequence required to perform such a socio-legal act as that of vetoing legislative proposals.

The regress of intentions from act to action shows that the fact that intentions in social life are usually for acts rather than for actions is an empirical fact considered with respect to social psychology, since people might have been more concerned with the minutiae of social performances, taking the acts for granted. On the other hand, considered with respect to sociological analysis people must be able to intend acts since the creation and maintenance of social order is by the performance of social acts which have a wider significance than the particular actions by which they are conventionally and locally achieved.

How far can this regress go? I do not think that the question can be answered by philosophical analysis, since I take it to be determined by the empirical possibilities of bringing our bodily movements and processes of utterances and so on under conscious monitoring and control. On this view it could not be known *a priori* that the regress of intentions from ends to means and to the means to achieve these means could be terminated in any particular category of basic actions.[1 2]

(iv) Outline of a performance theory
Power to act or not to act is reserved to the person as simple agent. Using our social knowledge (resources) we proceed through the following stages:

(a) We form an intention to carry out a certain act, according to our interpretation of the situation, our beliefs about the intentions of other people involved and our theories as to what would be called for in these circumstances.

(b) We perform actions in accordance with what we take to be the local rules and conventions for carying out the acts we intend.

It is important to remember that intention is relative to attention. We intend an act, say an insult, and we carry it out unthinkingly, according to an unattended convention, say by raising two fingers. But we can attend to the means and so intend to raise two fingers, in contrast, say, to poking out the tongue, relative to which there is a further layer of unattended means. Notice further that attention is only one of the conditions under which we would properly be said to intend, the other being the sense we have of the possibility of alternative performances in the circumstances as we see them.

This outline leaves room for the elaboration of two sub-theories.

(a) To explain how intentions are formed from resources.

(b) To explain how actions are generated from rules or conventions.

By locating causal efficacy in people as agents who actively form intentions and actively follow rules, the problem of locating efficient causality is solved by *fiat*. We have already seen that the sense of agency reflected in lay psychology may have to be explicated in a scientific psychology as the phenomological reflection of an open hierarchy of causally potent principles.

But if intentions are not the causes of actions, and notoriously to intend is not to cause oneself to do, perhaps the conditions which activate or release the pre-existing activity of an agent ought to be so considered. The difficulty with this proposal is that such conditions can be specified independently of the specification of the actions in the genesis of which they are involved. The specific actions which occur are determined by the rules or templates of action, the stimulus or releasing conditions determine only that some action or other will occur.

The most striking example of this can be found in Schachter's discoveries of the role of conditions which can be specified only physiologically, in the genesis of action. For example, the pH of the body fluids is not sampled by any neural mechanism which feeds into brain, and so this condition is not representable in consciousness. Yet the overall hydrogen ion concentration is a condition for activating someone to go in search of smoking materials and to light them up. But of course the way the person deals with this burst of activity depends upon his specific project in relation to smoking, for example whether he is giving it up or not. Since the pH of body fluids is not sampled by the central nervous system it can play no part in the psychological part of an explanation of action, and serves to illustrate the mistake of taking intentions or projects as the efficient causes of action.[13]

Sub-theory I: Intentions

In the psychological aspect of a social psychology intentions are mental properties of individual actors. But in the sociological aspect intentions may be largely a matter of public expressions of commitment and determination. But since we can keep our 'real' intentions to ourselves these dual aspects are clearly distinct.

From a psychological point of view the sub-theory of intentions is very simple. To form an intention a person must

(i) form a representation of his future course of action, and/or its social, conventional or causal upshot;

(ii) have a favourable attitude to the realization of that representation in action. Colloquially we might say that he must want to do it;

(iii) he must also have a belief that he will, when ready, actually perform the appropriate actions to accomplish the act he intended.

To form an intention a person employs well-known cognitive skills and suffers much studied mental states. So the study of intentions is no unique or hazardous branch of individual psychology. The idea that intentions present some kind of difficulty for mental philosophy and science derives from muddles of various kinds. In particular confusion has arisen from the following:

(a) Some philosophers have tried to make intentions both the efficient and the formal causes of action, through an event-interpretation of 'having an intention'.[14]

(b) There has been a general failure to distinguish the expression of intention, a public act of social commitment, from the having of an intention, the existence of an individual and often private complex of mental states and conditions.

Sub-theory II: Rules as templates
Typically structured action-sequences are not the work of a single individual but a mutual product of co-ordinated contributions from several people. This is true whether the action-sequence is achieved co-operatively, for example when a family entertain their friends, or agonistically, for example when two rivals for the seat of the retiring chairman conduct an argument in the board-room. It follows that the resources of people competent in these and like activities must include more than knowledge of their own individual contribution, but some representation of the whole episode as it should develop, or at the very least some representation of the cues for making an individual contribution.

Starting then with the thought that the object of explanation is a structure, namely the orderly action-sequence which is the product of mutual co-ordinated action, what schemata are available for its explanation? Relative to the action analysed at the level of public social meaning and conventional act the person can be treated as a pure or simple agent. To produce his action he follows a rule or convention. It is the set of rules or conventions which are the source of the orderly sequential structure of the episode. According to this theory neither the rules nor conventions, nor indeed the pro-attitudes which together with representations of the future form intentions, have irresistible causal powers. To understand why someone should undertake the project of bringing about certain social acts by following the rules and conventions that specify the locally required actions we have to take another step. We have to ask how the performance of these actions falls in with a person's ultimate project of publicly illustrating in his actions that he is a rational and worthy person, that she is warm, sympathetic and briskly efficient and so on. In short to move to the final stage of social explanation we must move from the instrumental plane on which our analysis has so far been conducted to the plane of expressive activity.

But if by accounting an actor can create and recreate actions and acts by use of public, socially intelligible speech to give specific meanings to human activity, then it would be a serious error to look for the generative mechanisms of social activity only in the private and personal states and processes of individual human beings. A science of social psychology must incorporate the idea that actions are generated both from private and personal sources and by public and social influences, the illocutionary and perlocutionary effects of accounting. The understanding of the genesis of actions is made even more complicated by the interaction between personal and social matters in that private, personal beliefs about public, social demands affect modes and styles of self-presentation. All these influences flow together to create complex actions. By making a public commitment to a certain project an actor can generate actions prior to the overt behaviour that realizes them concretely, just as he can create them posterior to that behaviour by accounting. Both activities play an important part in the genesis of human social life.

Consider the 'burp' as it plays a social role amongst Arabs. It needs a chain of physical causality but it is deliberately produced at the right moment, a moment when by convention it signifies satisfaction with the quality of the meal. So produced it serves to sustain the self-presentation of the host as provider and of the guest as appreciator.

Throughout this work I have deliberately played down the role of the emotions in the genesis of action. Do fear, resentment, love, pride, contempt, anger and so on play no role in social life? That would surely be a very foolish view to hold. But it is by no means easy to say what role the emotions do play.

By concentrating one's attention on pathological conditions and on moments of breakdown in the social order, emotions and the feeling states that are their phenomenological foundation can seem to loom large among the sources of human action. But further reflection on the flurry of co-operative activity that accompanies the public appearance of personal feeling in the flow of action, suggests that face-work must be done to restore the dignity threatened by a public display of feeling.

But if emotions and feeling states are not admissible as causes of action, why do they sometimes appear without remedial work? It is I believe when they are being displayed as the proper accompaniment of actions that are called for by the liturgical and/or dramaturgical conventions for action in a defined scene. In short grief does not cause people to mourn, rather social rituals of mourning require grief to be personally felt and socially demonstrated as a proper accompaniment of the ceremonial detachment of a dead person from his social career and the proper disposal of his remains. That these social conventions still survive may of course be explained by reference to the important role the experiencing of emotions has in the personal readjustment of the bereaved.

Occasionally feelings become autonomous, losing their connections with conventions of propriety and self-presentation. It is as well to remember that there are conventions for presenting oneself to oneself as well as to others, revealed for example in the way individuals manage fear of flying. While experiencing and revealing emotion is part of the presentational scheme, while feeling and revealing 'depression' for example is part of a way of presenting oneself, all is well. In my view it is only when feelings begin to dominate or disturb the ceremonies and dramatic presentations of everyday life, that a private and personal, and even sometimes a public and social pathological condition has developed.

(v) Philosophical commentary on the proposed explanation-schema
In the ethogenic approach performance theories purport to be

non-Humean causal theories and thereby genuinely explanatory. Indeed they claim to involve the same sort of content as do non-Humean theories in chemistry or physics, geology or genetics; namely powerful particulars or agents whose activity in the world is shaped by pre-existing templates. Ironically folk psychology is more nearly an exemplification of the form of explanatory theories in natural science than much of what passes for professional psychology in the experimental tradition. So a psychologist is in good scientific company in basing his explanations on the common sense concept of actors acting in accordance with local conventions to realize their intentions within a collective. Thus the coming to be of a product is explained by reference to an agent just as the presence of a gravitational field explains the acceleration of a test particle or the presence of an acid the change of colour of an indicator. The properties of a product of the activity of such an agent are explained by reference to a template; in other words, some features of the conditions of production will account for the specific properties of the product of the activity of the agent. In the same way the structure of the gravitational field explains the direction and magnitude of the acceleration of the particle, and the chemical composition of the acid explains the particular hue to which the indicator turns. The final consideration of the analogy will be taken up in the last section of this chapter.

The logical properties of the discourse with which a theory is formulated derive from these desiderata. For example the appearance of dispositional predicates in description of individuals as members of kinds reflects the desideratum than an explanatory theory refer to an agent or agents.

Despite an avalanche of criticism the main rival to a realist theory of causality remains the positivist regularity theory of Hume. Since, according to this view, it can never be known whether there is a real connection or productive relation between causal conditions and causal products only a regular concomitance remains of the relation between causes and effects. It follows that causes and effects must be logically independent or capable of independent description. But intentions and actions come, in some measure, under the same descriptions. The Humean premises clearly imply that if intentions are to be causes of actions they must be capable of identity preserving redescription until the conceptual link is broken.

The ethogenic theory is compatible with neither feature of the

Humean theory. It depends upon a conception of causality which is based not upon external correlations and laws, but real relations between causal conditions and products based upon particular and specific existents, namely templates.

But more importantly for the issues addressed in this chapter the ethogenic theory is not compatible with the principle that causal conditions and causal products should be capable of conceptually independent description. On the contrary it is a feature of the ethogenic theory that in so far as the causal template is among the causal conditions and that template is replicated in the product, template and product must come under the same description. This feature has been dealt with differently by different philosophers. Before considering these treatments it will be as well to illustrate the important fact that this form of explanation is not unique to the social and psychological sciences.

A parallel case in the bio-physical sciences was pointed out to me by A. Grunbaum. Just because the description of the genetic code of parental DNA and a description of the genetic code inherited by their offspring must be conceptually related, it does not follow that the one may not be in a causal relation with the other since they are distinct existences. Of course the former may exist without the latter, though if the latter comes into existence by whatever contingency it must reflect the structure of the former, *ceteris paribus*. The natural necessity of the reflection of the structure of DNA as template in the properties of the mature organism as product is illustrated by the use of blood type matching as a criterion of parenthood in paternity suits.

The necessitarian character of the relation between template properties and product properties in general is illustrated by the fact that failure to replicate according to type requires special explanations. For example if the cookie cut with a star-shaped cookie cutter is not star-shaped (with apologies to C. G. Hempel), as it should be (and note the modality of that last verb), considerations concerning the texture of the dough are advanced. The appearance of *ceteris paribus* clauses in the statement of causal relations and influences is an example of the technique by which natural necessity is preserved by requiring that the natures of substances involved in causal production do not deviate radically from the set of properties which fulfil current criteria of their identity and individuation. Cookie cutting I take to be within the province of physics, where, as in other natural sciences, *ceteris paribus* clauses refer to substances and their integrity. In the case of the theory of social action, the failure of an agent to realize in public action the intention or plan he entertained, *ceteris paribus* clauses would deal with failures of various kinds in the person as agent, for instance weakness of will, fear of consequences, low vitality, and so on.[15] The frustration of action from extrinsic and/or external factors is a very commonplace occurrence but since these factors are almost bewilderingly various there seems to be no point to studying and classifying them in search for supplementary laws.

(b) A Defence of Intentional Explanations as Scientific Theories

(i) A classical objection to the ethogenic programme

The usual attack on the programme of basing a causal theory of the genesis of actions on the elaboration and refinement of common-sense and folk theories of the genesis of actions, in particular the idea of an agent realizing its intentions, freely formed but intelligently chosen, runs as follows:

An intention is individuated and identified by its being an intention to perform an action (some action or other) in the performing of which a social act is brought about, to the performance of which it is purportedly causally related. Any purported causal relation between an intention and an act/action would have to be expressed in some such proposition as:

The intention to do something of type A, led to the performance of something of type A, where the 'something' could be act or action.

One might easily be persuaded that this is a specific form of the general formula:

The cause of A caused A

whose unsatisfactory character as a proposition of science is apparent at a glance. A cause 'event' which is not describable in terms conceptually independent of the description of the 'event' it is thought to bring about, it is argued, is no cause at all, violating one of the conditions Hume laid down for causality.

Philosophers have taken different attitudes to this supposed impasse.

(a) Social studies necessarily involve propositions of the above form, hence such studies cannot be science in the proper sense. This is the way of Winch.[16]

(b) The 'event' or antecedent condition is describable in terms conceptually independent of its alleged effect. Between such events Humean regularities could obtain and spawn laws of nature, and hence a psychological science of social action is possible. This is the way of Pears.[17]

Davidson's proposal has been discussed in Part I with respect to the independence of act/action descriptions as analytical tools for social performances. Suffice it to remark that it depends upon the claim that the same items are referred to through successive redescriptions in the course of which identifying descriptions become unlocked conceptually.

(ii) A realist reply
Neither Winch's nor Pears' response to the difficulty will do. Winch's response is based upon a mistaken philosophy of science, indeed the very same Humean extentionalism that animates Pears' attempt to deal with the difficulty. I will pursue that point no further here save to point out that the argument for the agent/ template explanatory theory as a proper theory for the explanation of human action is an argument for the possibility of a science of social action, given that the natural sciences too make indispensable use of that form of explanation.

An attempt to transcend those difficulties by D. Davidson (see note 14) is more interesting since it does propose a sketch of a schema for performance theories in the following way:

The 'event', which is the having of the intention to do A can be redescribed preserving, it is supposed, the identity of the reference of the original description to that very event, in such a way that the predicate 'A' no longer figures in it. Then if a regular concomitance can be empirically sustained between intentions and actions, it will be sustained between the common referents of the independent descriptions, which can then be cited as Humean causes and effects.

There are a number of defects in this proposal:

(a) It is not clear that the redescribed events is the same event as the intention to do A.

(b) The causality turns out to be merely Humean, and the empirical basis for the claim of a real connection, necessary to sustain the hypothesis that there is a causal relation, is lost.

(c) The role of the person as agent is obscured in this account since there is no naturally given point of application for his power of action. Alternatively causal efficacy is given to the intention, contrary to the principle that intentions can be entertained without actions occurring.

The ethogenic theory resolves these difficulties by taking a different tack. There is one kind of causal condition which is distinguished by the very fact that it comes under the same description as a property of the causal product, or at least a conceptually related description. That is a formal cause or template. The defective theory above fails through overlooking the way intentions are concerned with the determination of the properties of the act/action performances an agent causes to come to be.

(iii) Philosophical problems with the concept of an intention

Taking intentions seriously as part of the generative mechanism of actions is to locate them on the practical or instrumental plane, as important components in the means by which people bring about their projects. As I have so far expressed the matter, intentions have been taken as individual representations of favoured acts and sometimes of favoured courses of action. They have been offered as part of the framework of a non-Humean causal theory of action. But intentions have another important role to play in the processes by which social life is generated, a public role. By the avowal of intentions with respect to our acts and actions (however they are produced) we claim the status of persons by speaking of our relation to our actions, that is that we intended them, that is that we produced them as agents following templates we chose for ourselves. Acting in this way illustrates our personhood. Intentions as public commitments are functioning not only on the practical plane but by creating expectations in others on the expressive plane. This can be seen most clearly by returning to our base in lay psychology and ordinary uses of psychological language in everyday life, in particular the uses of verbs of intention, want, desire and so on.

The less specific of these verbs and verb phrases are perhaps the more illuminating. Consider the expression 'I am going to...' It is exactly paralleled in Spanish in the phrase 'Voy...' as for instance in 'Voy llamar el gerente', 'I am going to call the manager'. Sentences of this sort are clearly part of the action, making public commitments to courses of action. I propose to argue that it is just this category of expression that binds together psychological and social factors in everyday life. The argument consists of a defence of the inference of personal states and conditions corresponding to the public acts of commitment, and sometimes generated by those public acts. The argument turns on the exegesis of first person past and third person present tense examples.

A statement such as 'I was going to call the manager' seems to me clearly to imply that 'I' was in a certain mental state, characterized by the content of the statement, the project of calling the manager, and its affective structure and quality, namely that I had a pro-attitude to that project. Had I, as agent, taken that course, the content of my state of mind would have structured my action into a calling of the manager.

Third person cases exhibit this basic socio-psychology even more clearly. If I report of him that he says he intends, I take folk psychology to licence two inferences, one social and one psychological. We can infer that he committed himself and, under natural assumption of sincerity and virtue, we can infer that he is in the appropriate state of mind, that is, he is entertaining the project required of him to fulfil his commitments, and has a proper attitude to it. I notice, in passing, Austin's important point that should the psychological inference be wrong, the actor remains committed, that is the social act of commitment depends only upon the saying of the appropriate sentence, not upon the having of the appropriate project and attitude. This further illustrates the underlying point that the relation between public acts and private states of mind is an empirical interest, not a philosophical problem. It is the field of social psychology.

Since I am the other to the person who interacts with me, I argue that my declarations of intentions allow attributions to me by others of the appropriate states of mind, and it is just the propriety of those attributions that allow me to use my public declarations as illustrations of my personhood. Being a person is operative on the practical plane in the carrying out of projects, but it is illustrated on the expressive plane by, amongst other things, showing my personhood by announcing my plans in advance or by other forms of public commitment.

This crucial point allows us to avoid the problem of the truth of inferences from public acts of commitment to private or personal states. It must be avoided since there is no special category of experiences that justifies my saying of myself, in the psychological mode, that I intend, want, am going to, and so on. These verbs have an epistemology quite different from verbs of remembering for instance. The expression 'I've got it!' in the context of remembering is justified if, and only if, I have got it, that is that I am experiencing the remembering of that which I wanted to remember. Nor, indeed, need I be in a continuous state of intending in order for projects as avowed to be shaping my actions, since I may be kept up to the mark by the reminders of others, the notes in my diary and so on. In short, the representation of the act/action structure to which my avowal commits me may be as public an object as my act of avowal itself. The sociology of action in the world by intelligent agents does not need a psychology of intentions and projects. It is contingently the case that that is how many projects are carried forward.

3. THE REFLEXIVE CAPABILITIES OF A PERSON

I have argued that agency involves both autonomy and reflexiveness. It will be characteristic of a person to have a range of powers of self-understanding, self-investigation and self-intervention. In studying these powers we shall have to be particularly careful not to be misled into mistaken theories of the self. The terms by which we refer to these capabilities − self-intervention and the like − seem to suggest that the self is multiple, since they seem to imply that there must be some second self which intervenes upon the first. I hope to identify the pressures to interpret the doubling of the self literally as the misunderstanding of metaphor. We will thereby be freed from the temptation to conclude that a being which has reflexive capacities must be multiple.

(a) Self-Knowledge

What is it that I might be expected to achieve when I am advised to know myself? This exhortation seems to refer to two different kinds of matters.

In speaking of self-knowledge we mostly seem to refer to a person's strengths and weaknesses, both in practical activities and in the expressive and moral sphere. Knowing oneself seems to involve knowing one's strengths and limitations. This suggests that self-knowledge is concerned with one's abilities. It can include attitudes and beliefs. It may extend to temperamental matters. But coming to know myself, that is to know these things about myself, I can plot a careful path around dangerous occasions. It might seem at first sight as if self-knowledge was an empirically based, inductively confirmed set of generalizations, largely concerned with dispositions or abilities. The matter is more complicated since it is now widely agreed that dispositions and abilities are not so much permanent traits of a consistent, unified person, as occasional attributes whose coming into being is highly dependent upon the kind of situation a person takes himself to be acting in. Knowing myself, then, involves not only knowing my dispositions and abilities but the situations and conditions in which I may be able (or liable) to have them.

(b) Self-monitoring

In the discussion in the last section I took for granted that it is possible for a person to become aware of the exercise of his abilities, of his efforts to recall his memories, and so on. Becoming aware of some matter in such a way that one can reflect upon that awareness, can come to know one remembers for instance, I shall call monitoring that matter. Monitoring, like many other human activities, can occur at more than one level. Monitoring my actions consists in being aware of them in such a way that I can recall them. But as a human being I am able also to monitor the monitorings of those actions. Furthermore, monitoring is linked to control. If action does depend upon attention then only if I am able to monitor my actions am I able to control them according to rule and in general to act in the world as an agent following templates. Only if I am able to monitor my monitorings and to monitor my acts of control, am I able to bring those acts under the control of higher order principles and rules – and so on.

Monitoring, like every other perceptual and observational activity, is at the same time an interpretative activity, so that in order to understand the products of monitoring it is necessary to identify the interpretative schemata which the monitoring agent employed in identifying and making sense of the elements and structures which were monitored. But in order to do that one must be able to call upon the second-order monitoring of interpretative schemata and identificatory criteria which were at work on the first level. But that is itself a kind of monitoring and will be carried out in accordance with interpretative schemata and identificatory criteria appropriate to the subject matter at that level of monitoring. An indefinite regress has begun.

(c) Self-Intervention

I have already claimed that it is characteristic of human beings to have second-order capacities; to have knowledge of knowledge and to take action on action. I have drawn heavily on the idea that we are able to bring the very way we perform actions under our control. We can intervene, not only in the way actions are performed, but in the way we prepare for action. We are able to intervene in the templates we have pre-constructed, our plans, or have had prepared for us in the larger networks of our social collectives, according to which we, as human agents, are going to act. In short, we can reflect upon, and take steps to alter the rules and plans, the habits, and conventions, according to which we live our social lives.

(i) The most interesting theory of self-intervention with which I am acquainted is that proposed in rather different forms by Alston and by Taylor.[18] Alston calls it a desire-belief theory. Though it was proposed as a theory of self-intervention it is, of course, also a theory of action in general. It depends upon a basic schema for the explanation of action, namely that in the genesis of action there must be a desire whose content reflects or represents an outcome, not necessarily in the world, but perhaps in the agent himself, and a belief, or set of beliefs, which represent the agent's conception of how that outcome might be brought about. Beliefs then are concerned with means, desires with ends.

According to Alston and Taylor the structure of the genesis of action is the same whether it is action in the world or action upon oneself. Acting in the world and action upon oneself require different principles, however, but different only in content. For example, for action in the world I have effective anticipations, such as wanting some pie, and practical beliefs such as 'Pies are in the cupboard'. Action, namely the taking of pie from the cupboard, is explained in terms of the conjunction of desire and belief. But in self-intervention, principles of acceptance are required which can be particularistic, such as that I want to be thin; or general, such as the duty I feel to promote the welfare of an institution. In either case the transition from an acceptance principle to action requires a belief, for example, from the principle that I want to be thin, and the belief that I am actually fat, and that pies made me so, I may abort the action which would normally follow from the existence of a desire for some pie, and the belief expressed in 'There is a pie in the cupboard'. Taylor's more elaborate theory involves the same structure. In his version effective anticipations have to do with doings, and acceptance principles with modes of being, but I believe the central structure of both versions to be the same.

Several objections can be raised to this theory as a general theory of action. The most serious is the way the theory detaches the power of action from the person and then donates it to that person's components, namely one or more desires, wants and so on. It seems to involve the transition from 'I want some pie' to 'There is a want in me for some pie', the want being a powerful particular which, in the context of my knowledge and beliefs, leads to the action. It is important to notice that the force of this powerful particular can be over-ridden by another, namely the second-order desire to be thin, so that the explanation seems to involve some kind of vector product, where desires, of different relative strengths, are able to overcome or deflect one another. However, the difficulty with this theory is that it is only too easy to ask the question 'Why do you want to be thin?' and to call for a third-order desire about, let us say, public image, and so on, to each of which the power to generate the action must be donated. None of this regress need be considered if we are willing to treat the desires and their associated beliefs according to the schema of act/action intentions and our attitudes towards them. According to that schema, at either level, either that of action or that of self-intervention, the only active particular in the story is the self, the person, the Strawsonian individual. The reconciliation of both ways of explaining action must await the final section of this chapter.

(ii) A second difficulty is to be found in Taylor's conception of doing and being. The difficulty I have in mind concerns the relationship between what it is to *be* a certain kind of person and what kind of practical projects one must have on the plane of practical action. It seems clear that at least for many modes of being there are necessarily associated forms of action, in the absence of which a person could not legitimately claim to be a person of that kind. So, for example, an inability to do can be offered as the ground for a claim that it is impossible to be. For instance, someone who on the second-order plane of self-intervention wants to be a Trappist monk, may have to be warned that in his case it is impossible, since he cannot keep quiet for five minutes. I believe a similar case could be made even for role-related positions, like that of being a judge. Being a certain kind of person is not ontologically distinct from covert, overt and potential doings. It is not clear, then, how in Taylor's way of setting out his theory, the distinctness of the levels can be maintained since there does not seem to be a distinct category of forms of want and belief which are located firmly on the second-order plane. However, Taylor's position could be defended by the claim that all the wants and beliefs he is talking of are in the field of action, but that our way of speaking of some of them as if they concerned an ontologically distinct mode, is simply a device for representing the groupings of actions which are necessary to the representation in public of the kind of person I take myself to be. That is how that society, given my location in the system, requires that I am. It seems more correct, then, to treat the Taylor-Alston theory as another version of the formal cause or template theory and to attribute the ultimate power of action in normal people, in most circumstances calling for reflexive control, to the person himself and to interpret the desire-belief structures as those cognitive entities which guide his action so that it has the appropriate social form for the projects he has conceived. And on the expressive plane he can legitimately cite these projects as evidence for his claim to be this or that sort of person.

4. PERSONAL PROPERTIES

(a) Public-Private Dualities

(i) Each personal-private property has its public-social dual

In the light of the analysis so far, how are we to specify the personal properties of individuals the study of which would be a psychology of social action? The competence theories of Parts I and II allow us to represent personal standing conditions of competent action in a matrix of cells representing at least a taxonomy of socially relevant beliefs and skills. Individual cognitive matrices have a social dimension by virtue of their likenesses to one another. But the items that would seem necessary for performance theories of social action have quite a different standing. Using the double distinction between personal-social and private-public processes, states and events instead of the old subjective-objective dichotomy, it seems that characteristic categories of items relevant to performance have an essential duality. I have already demonstrated this duality for the case of intentions − as private-personal conditions and as public-social commitments. The fact that the rule-systems controlling the form of many collective activities and even of some individual processes are sometimes represented only in public form in etiquette books, manuals and so on, is a commonplace.

I believe private-public duality can be demonstrated for most 'psychological' attributes. For example it seems clear that rationality is as much a public attribute of the systematic relations of speech and action determined by social convention as it is a property of mind or of mental processes and constructions. Logical form is socially imposed upon accounts as part of the locally defined presentational scheme. It could be looked upon as part of the display of personal worth. Philosophers have often missed this important point. For example in Aune's otherwise excellent account of rationality he assumes that it is an attribute of inner processes only. The duality of rationality admits of the possibility that there could be societies in which public presentations of consistency or the logical framing of complexes of speech and action are not valued or admired.[19]

The essential duality of rationality as an attribute of people and processes initiated by people is reflected, I think, in two well-known distinctions. The distinction between *a* reason and *the* reason for an action, now a commonplace in the philosophy of action, could be looked upon as exactly the distinction between the content of a plausible account of conduct for public consumption and that given privately. Such accounts are produced under the control of public demands that one expresses oneself in such a way as to create an impression of rationality. This can be achieved by suggesting that the actual template or actual representation of end that functioned as formal and final cause respectively of the act/action structure produced are all co-ordinate, and that both 'reasons' coincide.

Sociologists have proposed a distinction between instrumental rationality, exemplified in the efficient production of artefacts (social, material etc.) by the scientifically sanctioned best means, and rationality as an attribute of the ends of social life, partly realized through the production of those artefacts.[20] Social pessimists have been inclined to conclude that modern society has substituted the former for the latter. For some cases this distinction clearly coincides with that between rationality as a property of the personal antecedents of intentional action, and some (other) property of public demands on expressive qualities of the self.

Many other 'psychological' properties, processes and states can be shown to have this essential private/public, individual/collective duality. Coulter, echoing and extending much that is in the psychologies of Ryle and Wittgenstein, has argued for a systematic reinterpretation of all psychological attributes into the public-collective sphere.[21] Less spectacularly, but more importantly for the foundations of social psychology, the duality of motivation has been amply demonstrated by Blum and McHugh.[22] And in a recent paper of considerable power and ingenuity Silver and Sabini have shown the essential personal/

public duality of such an apparently individual attribute as envy.[23]

A profoundly important conclusion follows for the domain of psychology: for those personal properties which are publicly constituted as duals of private properties, such as rationality, motivation, intention etc., psychology and the study of rhetoric must become one. Psychology thus necessarily includes the study of accounts as part of the activity of generating certain psychological states, namely the public-collective duals of the private-individual conditions. Sometimes, as we have noticed, there may be no private dual to a public psychological condition, and the process generating action may involve attention to templates (formal causes) that are socially constituted and publicly represented, powered by intentions that have their being only in the expectations of others, expectations that have arisen consequent on public avowals of projects and plans by an actor.

(ii) Attribution: the actor-spectator paradox

Throughout this work I have argued for a method that combines the analysis of public-social aspects of action and the conditions of its genesis with the analysis of private-personal matters. Social psychologists are to make their attributions to actors and to the *Umwelten* of different categories of person and domestic animals from both vantage points. But standing in the way of using these methods to put together a unified theory of human social action is the actor-spectator paradox.[24] Characteristically actors explain descreditable events as due to contingencies external to them and not under their control, while spectators attribute the happening to dispositions and other personal properties of the actor, such as inattention, malice and so on. There is some evidence that this tendency is reversed when creditable actions and events are being explained.

It is not difficult to see how these practices could have grown up in societies dominated by expressive orders in which there was rivalry for limited amounts of public esteem. Attributions, according to the principles sketched out above, could be seen as ploys in a Goffmanian exchange. But there may be more to it. Fowler has argued that there is an element of illusion in the readings of the actions of others not unlike the illusion that hampers our reading of the comparative lengths of lines in the Muller-Lyer diagram.[25] However something deeper still may underlie this curious asymmetry. Langford has recently put forward a

persuasive case for assuming a systematic asymmetry in the way
people perceive each other as persons, deriving from the very
structure of persons themselves.[26]

In essence his argument shows that there is a hierarchy of
'person' concepts, such that each individual must treat all the
others with whom he comes in contact as persons one order
simpler than they really are, if he is to perceive them as persons
at all.

Langford's analysis shows that there is a hierarchy of possible
categories of persons, P1... Pn... such that persons actually on
level Pk assign themselves and others to level Pk-1. Human beings
are at least third-level persons, capable of seeing others as persons
too, and having the concept of both themselves and others as
persons capable of perceiving other beings as persons. According
to Langford 'Two P3's ((a) and (b))... will see themselves and
each other as P2's, and, since P2's possess only the concepts of
a P1 and of a physical object, P3(a) will see P3(b) as seeing him
(P3(a)) as a P1, that is as a being who has nothing but the concept of a physical object.' P3(a), therefore, expecting P3(b) to see
him as capable only of deploying the concept of a physical object
will produce a public account of his misfortunes, *for P3(b)*, in
terms of external, physical causality. But P3(b), actually seeing
P3(a) as a P2 will attribute manageable dispositions to P3(a),
because as a P2, P3(a) can have a concept of himself.

On this analysis the Jones and Nisbett asymmetry is a mere
reflection in accounting of a necessary asymmetry in the way
people must conceive other people as conceiving them – and
adjusting their accounts accordingly. (In the anomic conditions
of experimental psychology all one could do would be to reflect
the structure of concepts, in this case that of the person.)

(iii) Empirical work on personal performance processes

The social reality of human agency is scarcely in need of demonstration. Even B. F. Skinner tacitly concedes its reality in the fer-
vour of his denunciation of the uses of human freedom. Detailed
studies of innovation, creativity, madness and so on should lead
to further understanding of the forms and degrees of autonomous
action.

The form of action, I have proposed, derives from certain antecedent conditions distributed in various degrees between persons
and their *Umwelten*. Psychological studies are naturally distinguished as the investigation of the personal properties necessary to

competent action. From a performance point of view these are intentions to perform acts and knowledge of the rules and conventions for realizing the content of such intentions in locally recognizable actions.

There are two conditions in which the personal-private antecedents of action are represented in consciousness. Both are conditions of uncertainty. A stranger, required to act in a well-ordered community, has to formulate his social and practical intentions in such a way that he can consider their propriety before he realizes them in action. And since similar acts are realized very differently in different communities the rules and conventions linking actions to acts may also come to be formulated consciously.

Hesitations in speech and action have been shown to mark moments of conscious awareness of both the means and the ends of action. Actors can be reminded of these moments simply by playing back the recordings of the events in question.

In these ways an investigator can obtain empirical entry into some of the conditions of action. But to transform this into a method of study of performance processes in general a philosophical issue must be faced. Do these moments of awareness represent the 'surfacing' of the very template actually determining the properties of action, in its proper form? Or are they occasions for the representation in consciousness of processes of other kinds, by some unknown principle of projection. The processes might, for instance, be physiological.

There seems to be no way to resolve the issue by further studies of this sort. The same problem infects interpretations of Freudian explanations – namely what is the ontological status of the entities which cause neurotic behaviour and which 'surface' in dreams under some symbolic transformation? Though issues such as these seem irresolvable my own preference would be to argue for the necessity of a terminology of mentalistic metaphors to describe such hidden processes and conditions, while holding the mode of existence of the beings so described to be physiological. Though this eliminates the unconscious as a problem, it has the effect of bequeathing the nature and status of consciousness to later generations of philosophical psychologists to worry over.

(b) Properties Unique to Individuals

(i) Agency

A distinction between the fact of agency and the sense of agency should be consistently maintained as a guide to preparing an analytical scheme. A person's agency, his agentive capacities as I have described them in general in the last chapter, is demonstrated in two main contexts, related to the root ideas of autonomy and reflexivity, set out in Chapter 11.

(a) The act of principled choice is not reducible to being caused to opt for one of a set of contemplated alternatives by the principle one has adopted for choosing (and for justifying one's choice) if it can be argued that that principle is itself a product of a higher order principled act of choice, and the principle of that choice, the product of principled choice and so on. The sense of agency in choice then could be thought to derive from the felt openness of the regress. At any level another level could be referred to. The fact of agency, in this context, could be reduced to the cybernetic properties of the human organism as an information processing system. It would be empirically demonstrable in a person's capacity to rationalize his choices, since in the context of a demonstration of agency the distinction between *the* reason for a choice and *a* reason for a choice is empty.

(b) An Aristotelian style of performance theory, as I have argued earlier in this chapter, attributes intentions and knowledge of rules and conventions to an actor, but these represent only some of the necessary conditions for action. A full explanation will require reference to an efficient cause. While this may sometimes be an external influence there do seem to be plenty of cases where no such influence can plausibly be assumed.

Folk psychology, even in those societies that lay great emphasis on the possibility of external influences, *uniformly* admits a residual agentive power to people — the real foundation of autonomy. Philosophers have varied greatly in their treatment of this feature of persons. It has been treated as a faculty (conation), as an attribute (volition) and as a transcendental condition comparable to a field potential (noumenon).

The argument of this study has been based upon the assumption of a generally Kantian treatment of this aspect of agency, namely that it should be treated as an unanalysable, simple causal power, when we are considering it in a psychological context; but that it can also be treated as a grounded disposition when we are considering the phenomenon of acting in an organic or psychophysiological context. In such a context it is a disposition grounded in a physiologically realized cybernetic property of the brain and nervous system.

From the standpoint of social psychology one would look for some form of public demonstration of the possibility of pure (unconditioned) action as a proof of the psychological reality of the pure, agentive power. There are such public demonstrations. They depend upon an analytical separation of the 'plane' of practical action from the 'plane' of expressive action. Thus an action that is seeable on the practical plane as irrational, random, quirkish, perverse and bloody-minded can be seen as the action of a pure agent unconditioned by any practical principle. But on the expressive plane it can be seen as indeed an action of a rational being, since it is the very action such a being would choose to perform to illustrate his agency. It is at once principled and unprincipled.

(ii) Consciousness

Our brief excursion into speculative paleoanthropology in Chapter 1 brought out the importance of distinguishing consciousness as having to do with the representation of things other than the being which is conscious, from self-consciousness, a condition having to do with the representation of that being as representing its own states and conditions, and perhaps even the fact of its having those states and conditions to itself. The former seemed to be an attribute of animals in general, and only the latter defensible as a distinguishing property of human beings. Care must be exercised in analysing the nature of self-consciousness since the self as a pure centre of consciousness cannot be the intensional object of any kind of consciousness. When I think of myself as that which is conscious that mode of thinking cannot be rendered as 'aware of ...' or 'attending to ...' the centre of that very consciousness. The point has been made variously and vigorously by Hume, Kant, Husserl, Wittgenstein and many other philosophers.

The concepts appropriate to consciousness can be sharpened still further by confining their use to ascribing a condition or state to a person. Thus persons will be said to be conscious, unconscious, self-conscious and so on. The expression 'conscious states' and others like it will be taken to be perspicuously rendered as 'states of which a being is conscious'. Consciousness ought to be considered as having degrees. I propose to express that aspect by systematic elimination of terms such as 'conscious of ...', in favour of 'aware of ...' and 'attending to ...' The former is to be understood as rendering the most general sense of 'conscious of ...' while the latter refers to a focus of consciousness on specific and circumscribed items.

Awareness of and attention to various items plays a crucial role in the social psychology advocated in this study. The construction of theories of social performance depends upon taking the mode of controlling action used by participants in formal ceremonies, as a source-model for other modes of action. Formal ceremonies are created by people actively following rules or exemplars of which they are then and there aware, and of attending to the actions they perform to ensure conformity with those rules or exemplars.

Furthermore the emphasis I have placed on the interest people have in the expressive order presumes their paying attention, from time to time, to the impressions they take themselves to be creating, and not least to the means by which correlative expression of self is being conducted. And this requires awareness of and attention to personal performances, an attention which could be summed up as self-consciousness. But it is no part of my argument to suggest that these levels of consciousness are consistently or even often maintained.

(iii) Empirical methods for the study of agency and consciousness
Very few attempts have been made to study empirically the role of conscious awareness in the genesis of social action.[27] One could ask whether being conscious of social ends and environmental means made any difference to the way one acted, by comparison with habitual responses. Scott and Lyman have argued for the ubiquitousness of the threat posed by the possibility of stage-fright − the appearance of a paralyzing self-attention.[28] This sort of study could reveal little more than the formal properties of conscious awareness as a possible necessary condition for certain modes of action.

The exploitation of hesitation phenomena, advocated as a useful method in the last section, could be extended to develop a method based on the recording of simultaneous commentary on the contents of consciousness, when an agent had become aware of at least some aspects of the way he was generating his actions. And using the Aristotelian framework as a guide for formulating hypotheses some progress in these matters might be made.

5. IDENTITY OF PERSONS

Introduction

Following the analytical strategy established for this Part I propose to distinguish between the philosophical and socio-psychological aspects of the fact of personal identity on the one hand, and those of the sense of personal identity on the other.

(a) The Fact of Personal Identity

(i) Dual criteria

Personal identity, the given permanence and discernible uniqueness of human individuals, is as indisputable as any feature of the world. But the precise differentiation of necessary and sufficient conditions for the ascription of identity to persons has been the focus of longstanding discussion. The problematic character of personal identity derives from the appearance of two clusters of criteria — bodily and mental. Plausible cases can be described in which consideration of bodily criteria seem adequate to determine an individual's uniqueness and continuing identity. But equally plausible cases can be thought of which seem to need tests of some form of mental continuity to determine the self-identity and individual uniqueness of a person. For example there seem to be some cases where memories serve as definitive tests for 'same person'.

In these circumstances a resolution may be found by a philosophical analysis of the concept of a person, in the hope of being able to rank criteria in order of relative importance in central cases. In an ideal analysis, marginal cases which suggest contrary orderings of criteria would be set aside as cases for which our conceptual system is not prepared. We would then be free to resolve them in any convenient way.

In my view Williams has provided the most measured range of arguments along these lines.[29] The upshot of his analysis is to give final priority to the bodily criteria. They serve as back-stop determinants of questions of identity in hard cases. In short we recognize each other as distinct persons primarily through our seeing each other as individual and continuously animated bodies.

(ii) Personal identity as an achievement

But one ought not to conclude that personal identity is something given. Many close students of social life have emphasized how personal identity has often to be worked for, even undertaken as a project. Social life based upon role-rule structures of a dramaturgy generates categories to which people must conform and be seen to conform for the proper realization of scenarios in action. The problem is to establish personal identity within given social identities. Sometimes the qualities that seem most naturally to place one in a certain social identity are those which define a stigmatized kind of person. Such qualities must be hidden by those 'passing' in the society. In those conditions people become anxious and thoughtful about their categorization by others. For instance the cognitive operations Tajfel has called 'social comparison processes'[30] seem to come into operation when the given social identity becomes problematic. All this conspires to emphasize social identity at the expense of perceived individuality.

In these circumstances we should expect to find people setting about constructing evidence for others to judge them to be distinct and worthy individuals. And the best way to construct such evidence is to publicly take on the appearance of individuality and worth. There seem to be three components to take care of.

(a) Bodily distinctiveness: even in modern China individual ways of dressing the hair, and even individual restyling of standard clothing are used to accentuate numerical distinctiveness of persons as physical objects within a given social identity.

(b) Standardized action in fulfilment of role requirements can create the impression of personal distinctiveness, just as an actor can impose his own interpretation on the most well scripted parts.

(c) The development of a personal history and a reputation in the impressions received by others, reading the expressive aspects of one's actions, is an inevitable product of life with others. In Part IV I shall be emphasizing the importance of the construction of a personal history in understanding the form of a personal life course.

(b) The Sense of Personal Identity

One might have the idea that an individual's sense of personal identity could be exhaustively analysed in the same terms as the fact of his identity is determined among others. If this were so the criteria by which an individual is recognized by others ought to yield the components of his experience of himself as a unique being, and so predetermine the analysis of the sense of personal identity. Bearing in mind the personal and private character of a sense of identity one might be inclined to make a first attempt at analysis by turning to the socially secondary criteria of avowed memories, stable dispositions and so on, in short to the cognitive aspects of a person.

(i) Having memories of a continuous personal past will not do as an account of the sense of personal identity. In the first place MacIntyre has given a convincing argument to show that a sense of personal identity could be sustained with only short term linkages of successive memories.[31] In this condition memories of one's early life would not be available to one in old age, but one would nevertheless be the same person. One would have sustained a sense of self throughout the life course by remembering the immediate past of each new stage, and then forgetting that memory as one passed to yet another experience.

Further, to adapt an argument of Shoemaker's,[32] the very question as to whether some feature of memories constituted the sense of personal identity is somehow misplaced. That a memory, or any other psychic content is a thought of mine (as opposed to a thought of someone else's) can hardly be called in question. Only the verisimilitude of the thought can be at issue. Personal identity seems then to be presupposed rather than explicated by turning to some feature of psychic contents.

(ii) Bodily identity remains the only resource. It seems clear that a sense of bodily identity cannot be identical to the sense of personal identity. However there do seem to be convincing arguments that it is an indirect source. Strawson has argued that one acquires the concept of a person by being treated as a person by others.[33] His theory can be given a philosophical interpretation as an account of what is presupposed in the concept of a person. It could be used as a theory of personal pronouns. Someone can only acquire the use of 'I' by being treated as a 'You' by another being who is already competent in the use of 'I' and 'You'.

For my purposes the theory could be given a psychological interpretation as the principle that one acquires a notion of personal identity by being treated as a person by others. They appear to one as individuals through the use of the dual criteria which determine the fact of identity. They are treating the nascent person as an individual according to the same criteria. No further criteria are needed since he comes to see himself as unique via the reflection of his dual criteria for recognizing them in their treatment of him. There is no need to suppose that he is somehow applying these criteria to himself. Once he has the idea of himself as a person, continuity and coherence of point of view and of locus of actions initiated by himself, sustains his sense of unique personhood.

13

THE EMBODIED ACTOR

ANTICIPATORY SUMMARY

Introduction. I assume that the identity of an actor is partly grounded in his embodiment as a kind of thing having spatio-temporal identity. How are his other attributes related to the properties of this thing? I argue that there must be different modes of embodiment for different kinds of human attributes.

1. Mode I: close-coupling
   (a) Both instances and types of mind-states and body-states are given in 1-1 correspondence.
   (b) The philosophical theory of this mode is the Contingent Identity Thesis.
2. Mode II: loose-coupling
   (a) Instances and types of mind-states and brain-states are not given in 1-1 correspondence, but correspondence can be established.
   (b) The philosophical theory of this mode is the Taxonomic Priority Thesis, which defines a general procedure for defining kinds of brain-states to complete the 1-1 correspondence incompletely given in experience.
3. Mode III: mapping of cybernetic functional nets
   (a) Conceptual structure and processes are systems, not always fully actualized.
   (b) A heroic generalization of TPT is inadequate.
   (c) The philosophical theory of this mode is functional homomorphism — that an abstract cybernetic representation of 'mind' processes must be constructed as the intermediate object to be mapped onto the physiological processes of the brain, which also have this character.

INTRODUCTION

I have assumed throughout this work that the powers of human beings are ultimately grounded in their physiological constitution and neural structure but in order to make that idea plausible I

297

shall consider in some detail the problems, both philosophical and technical, of embodiment.

I shall take for granted that the argument of Strawson[1] and Hampshire,[2] which relates the identity of an actor, both socially and psychologically, to his embodiment, is well-founded. But there are residual difficulties with embodiment-theses; these do not arise at the level of generality at which the arguments of Strawson and Hampshire operate, but more particularly in the ways in which any embodiment thesis is to be understood as implying an account of the 'interface' between mental and physiological processes, states, dispositions and so on. I have placed considerable emphasis in this work on the idea that the mental or psychological realm is not to be identified with the contents of private, subjective, experience. But the embodiment arguments have to do more with the relationship between private or personal states and their physical foundation than that between public acts and their physical medium. I take it that it is uncontroversial that public activity of a symbolic kind must be physically grounded so that there is an uncontroversial embodiment thesis for the public forms of psychological activity, a thesis I defended in the chapter on social semantics (Chapter 4). I shall be concerned, then, with the problem of establishing a way or ways of considering the possibility that the more private activities of human beings, and states which are normally known directly only to themselves, are to be considered as embodied.

The literature on this issue is vast. I shall be drawing upon fragments of it to construct my argument. However, I shall be breaking with an assumption which seems to run through almost all of it, namely the assumption that the problem of embodiment, or if you like the relation between mind and brain, or between psychology and physiology, or however it may be put, can be understood in terms of a single model of embodiment and a single associated theory. I shall be arguing that so diverse are the entities whose embodiment we must consider, we shall need not one but three models. Many arguments making out an exclusive claim for one of the modes of embodiment are no more, I believe, than an empty clash between exemplars, and a mock battle between two modes, neither of which will generalize to all cases, but both of which can be defended in some.

1. MODE 1: CLOSE-COUPLING

I shall be arguing in favour of each mode by trying to show the relationship between that mode of embodiment, a particular range of exemplars of it, and an associated philosophical theory as to the appropriate concepts for expressing that mode, and the logical properties of theses associated with it. The first mode I take to be concerned with what I shall call close-coupled state. States are close-coupled when:

(a) the taxonomies of mental and of physiological states and conditions identify an individual element or psychic atom in association with an individual physiological state, and

(b) as a matter of fact the psychic state and the physiological unitary state are found at the same place, at the same time and are associated in intensity;

(c) and that the origin and extinction of the psychic state can be associated precisely with a threshold in the physiological state.

There are many examples of close-coupled psychic and physiological states; for example, anxiety, 'that sinking feeling', sensations of heat and cold, many pains, muscular tiredness, sexual ecstasy and so on. In a phrase, the principle of close-coupledness could be put something like this: States are close-coupled when there is a leakage of physiology through to consciousness.

The associated theory for close-coupled states, which aptly deals with these and similar exemplars is, I believe, the contingent identity-thesis associated with the Australian school of materialism.[3] I take the contingent identity-thesis (CIT) to be expressible in three principles. In order to facilitate the setting out of CIT and the other theses of embodiment, I propose to use the phrase 'M-state' for states of consciousness and/or states revealed in consciousness, and 'B-state' for physiological states. For purposes of CIT, M-states and B-states will be supposed atomistic individuals according to the appropriate taxonomy. This presupposes the possibility of an artificial decomposition of structures which cannot in fact be achieved — but with respect to the exemplary case of close-coupling that difficulty does not affect the argument.

(i) It is impossible to infer the description of an M-state from the description of a correlated B-state, or the description of a B-state from the description of a correlated M-state.

(ii) It is impossible to infer the existence of an M-state from the existence of a B-state and impossible to infer the existence of a B-state from the existence of an M-state.

(iii) As a matter of fact, psychological M-state descriptions and physiological B-state descriptions describe the same entity.

If the three sub-theses of the contingent identity-thesis are correct, then we have a theoretical framework in which to understand close-coupling. It is to be emphasized that the contingency of the identity expressed in sub-thesis (iii) involves the independence of the taxonomies, according to which the M-states and B-states which are to be related are identified as members of kinds, so that in CIT there is necessarily no melding of the taxonomies of mental and physiological entities.

There are considerable difficulties in generalizing CIT as the theory of a universal mode of embodiment in terms of which the various relations between M-states, processes and structures can be related to B-state processes and structures. CIT is an adequate theory of embodiment only for states which are atomic, each according to its appropriate taxonomy. Furthermore, psychological studies have shown that the kind of M-state which a participant reports as correlated with a B-state is highly dependent upon interpretative procedures and social factors, so that there are many cases in which for a given kind of B-state there are many varieties of M-state in good correlations. I conclude, then, that the contingent identity thesis and the close-coupled mode of embodiment are adequate for only a narrow range of cases.

2. MODE II: LOOSE-COUPLING

Counter examples to the first mode of embodiment are exemplified in S. Schachter's studies of the relationship between gross physiological states and the emotions, moods and so on, and modes of behaviour which are reported by conscious participants. Schachter has shown in a wide-ranging series of investigations that the gross physiological basis is insufficient to provide criteria to identify the variety of M-states associated with physiologically identified particulars. The existence of a particular physiological condition is only a necessary condition for experiencing an identifiable emotion, and so on. In his well-known studies of the emotions associated with an excess of adrenalin Schachter established that the emotions reported by participants in the experiment depended for their particular identifiable character on factors other than the level of adrenalin in the blood.[4] In particular, identification of an emotion depended on the social meaning given to the situation in which the generalized feeling of arousal, produced in a close-coupled fashion by the adrenalin, was experienced. Becker has shown that the same sort of considerations apply to the effects of hallucinogenic drugs.[5]

A more homely example of loose-coupling is to be found in

the way in which people may search for an appropriate meaning for some generalized physiological state. For example, it may be obvious to an outsider that someone is seeking a quarrel, mostly to be able to give a proper meaning to a generalized feeling of being out-of-sorts. In the light of these examples it seems that we will need a more elaborate theory than CIT to cope with the coupling of mind and brain.

The principle that lies behind the theory I shall be arguing for in this mode is the hypothesis that in the end all states, processes and structures which are represented in consciousness will be found to have a physiological basis. However, in order to maintain that thesis, such phenomena as the loose-coupling of M-states and B-states have to be resolved in such a way as to preserve the underlying principle of embodiment.

The Associated Theory

To deal with loose-coupled states I shall take the Taxonomic Priority Thesis (TPT).

The discovery by Schachter that an interpretative component is required in order to understand how a close-coupled M-state is understood as an emotion, requires the hypothesis that the interpretative procedure is also, in the very generalized sense I am using in this argument, an M-state. According to TPT it should have an associated B-state, though we do not yet know what it is. TPT is a principle which enables us to add taxa to the physiological taxonomy on the basis of the identification of uncoupled mind-states such as interpretative procedures. In this way TPT generates empirical problems of existential identification for the physiological sciences of the brain.

The Taxonomic Priority Thesis can be expressed in a general principle of correlation.

For every type of M-state there is a type of B-state. It is worth noticing that the principle that for every type of B-state there is a type of M-state is obviously false. There are states of the physiology of a human being which are associated with no M-state at all, such as, for example, the physiological state which is associated with unconsciousness, or that complex of changing physiological states associated with death. In order to sustain the central thesis of TPT as a necessary truth in terms of which new taxa are to be imposed on the physiological classification of states of the body, we must examine the ways in which TPT deals with apparent counter-instances to its central principle.

Counter-instances are likely to be one of two kinds:

(a) Should we find a kind of physiological state which in many cases is associated with an M-state of kind M1 but on some occasions with an M-state of kind M2,

(b) Should we find an instance of a kind of M-state which is frequently found with a kind of physiological state B1, but on occasion is found with an instance of kind B2.

TPT can be preserved by treating these counter-instances as the occasion for setting up disjunctive taxa. With respect to the first counter-example, we institute an M-taxon, M3, which is equivalent to 'M1 or M2'. In the case of the second counter-example we institute a B-taxon, B3, which is formed as a disjunction of 'B1 or B2'.

The final step in the preservation of TPT is to rationalize these disjunctions, taking them to be the occasions for the introduction of hypothetical, physiological states. In the first case the new M-state type, M3, in accordance with the general principle, is taken as the occasion for the postulation of two hypothetical physiological states B' and B'' which account for the differentiation of B, our original physiological state, into a mind-state of type M1 on one occasion, and M2 on another. To cope with the other kind of example, one can postulate of a further physiological state – kind B'''. By using TPT it can be associated with the original physiological state of type B1. Reference to B'''-states explains how both B1 states and B2 states are represented in consciousness as states of type M. On such occasions each is associated with an instance of the hidden physiological parameter B'''. In this way TPT maintains a type-correlation between the mind-state taxonomy and the brain-state taxonomy, by identifying the occasions when it is appropriate to add physiological hypotheses to the system.

However, there are limitations to TPT. It should be clear that if either kind of counter-example proliferated so that the disjunctive taxa became rather long, the plausibility of the move which uses TPT to introduce new physiological state kinds, would become doubtful. In the end a correlation which had many of the marks of necessity might have to be abandoned in the face of the empirical facts which forced the disjunctive taxa to grow beyond reason. Secondly, the procedure of TPT depends upon the possibility of individuating the correlated states and processes in an atomistic way, so that the correlations which are established *a priori* by TPT are of a one-to-one kind. The empirical pay-off of establishing a relation between kinds of M-states and kinds of B-states comes in the discovery of particular correlations between instances of these states. It is by no means clear that instantiation is a general property of either the mental or physiological structures and systems we are concerned with.[6] But since I am convinced that 'the mind' is a complex of activities and self-representations of the brain, there must be yet another mode.

3. MODE III: MAPPING OF CYBERNETIC NETS

The plausibility of Modes I and II depends on the existence of good empirical evidence for at least a partial one-to-one correlation of an instance of an M-state kind and an instance of a B-state kind. TPT justifies the theoretical introduction of further B-state kinds to maintain an overall correlation. But there are many cases of activities which are represented in consciousness, or structures which are available to consciousness, where there is no link of the appropriate correlative sort to form the foundation of a taxonomically creative move such as TPT will license, nor is the associated atomistic assumption at all plausible for many cases. A typical example of such a matter is the sort of mind-state kind to which we might wish to assign the meaning of a sign. The most satisfactory theory, as we have already shown in an earlier section, involves a structural isomorphism between a system of signs and a set of experiences. On both sides of the isomorphism much of the structure is latent, the whole structure being rarely, if ever, fully realized. For example, if we argue, following Wittgenstein, that the semantics of colour terms can only be understood by considering the meaning of each term to be given in the relations of that term to the others, then it is rare that experience presents us with all the colours in a suitably ordered spectrum. Indeed, the classical spectrum is far from sufficient as the empirical correlate of the colour vocabulary. There are many other examples of structures, mostly having to do with cognitive operations or knowledge systems, for which no consistent *point* of attachment could be found upon which TPT could force a growth of physiological hypotheses.

I conclude that a third mode of embodiment, the mode which I shall call homomorphism, will be required.

In order to clear the ground for the third mode, it will be necessary to examine what I shall call a heroic version of TPT in which a one-to-one correspondence is sustained without the founding of each application in a given empirical correlation. U. J. Jensen has argued that the correct interpretation of psychological vocabularies and the use of those vocabularies to identify kinds of conscious representations is not to be understood in terms of two independent taxonomies, which are linked together on occasion as in the Mode II application of TPT. According to Jensen there is only one taxonomy.[7] In short, he argues that psychological talk involves a further branch of a physiological taxonomy. There are no entities of a psychic kind being classified in the course of that talk; rather that talk involved ways of classifying physiological entities all along.

Jensen's argument runs as follows: those speech acts which at first sight seem to be descriptions of mental particulars can be interpreted without loss as acts of classification according to an extended taxonomy of non-mental particulars – namely material particulars of the nervous system. Thus 'a pricking pain' is not a specification of a mental particular (pain), but brings something under a type. But what does it bring under a type? Jensen argues that 'mental phenomena statements are never *specifications* of particulars as kinds of mental particular, they are *classifications* of something *as* mental phenomena'. Mental phenomena are ways of bringing physiological phenomena together into new taxa so that mental discourse 'is an ontologically empty way of conceptualizing particulars in the world'. Those particulars are material constituents of the nervous system.

Jensen's argument is clearly a version of TPT but it is stated in a very much stronger fashion. It does not admit of the possibility of there being an uncoupled state where the issue of whether a classification according to an M-state taxonomy is or is not a way of classifying B-state particulars is an open empirical question. TPT, it should be noted, allows for the possibility of an indefinite empirical failure to establish the existence of the hypothetical physiological state kinds which TPT enables us to propose.

I conclude that the cautionary footnote to TPT, which allows for the possibility of an implausibly extended disjunction of counter-examples, must also be entered as an objection to the heroic form of taxonomic priority proposed by Jensen. In the absence of an independent argument to show that such disjunctive taxa are impossible, the Jensen argument, attractive though it is in general, is not strong enough to sustain the universal application which he proposes.

Homomorphism offers a more modest form of relationship in

which structural mapping is substituted for atomistic correlation. It allows for the possibility that the same structure is being realized at different times in the same individual in quite different material. It seems to me at least physiologically possible that the physical network which corresponds to a Saussurian meaning-field, for example, might be realized from time to time in quite different molecules, provided only that the relational structure is preserved. Recent physiology suggests that cognitive processes may be plausibly treated along similar lines. As I have argued,[8] the transition from a psychological theory to a physiological hypothesis as to the machinery in which that theory is realized, ought to be achieved through an intermediate representation. On the one hand we can represent cognitive functioning in a cybernetic model, while the physiological processes of the brain can also be looked at in a cybernetic way. We can then consider the possibility of various mappings between the two networks. It seems to me implausible, given the possibility of the breakdown of TPT, to attempt to map cognitive and other psychological functioning directly on to physiology since that would require the correlation or identity of particulars. All that we need to establish to maintain functional identity, as proposed for example by Boden[9] and Fodor,[10] is that there should be matching networks. That is what I mean by homomorphism as a mode of embodiment. If homomorphism can be sustained then the third mode of embodiment can be defined colloquially somewhat as follows: that the processes which are represented in consciousness as thinking, contemplating, imagining and so on, are the activities of physiological systems which operate in ways which are rich enough for at least part of their operation to be mapped in an orderly fashion in conscious representation.

However, the very idea that homomorphism is possible depends upon the success of prior applications of TPT. In the absence of a defensible correlation between states represented in consciousness and the elements of the physiology of the nervous system, homomorphic hypotheses could not even be entertained. TPT provides the initial and coarse-grained identificatory clues as to the relevant physiological mechanism. For example, TPT seems to me to have been the mode of argument used to identify the brain as the organ of thought and to sustain the empirical investigation of that organ for clues as to its cybernetic character. As it was applied in the sixteenth and seventeenth centuries in the arguments which led to the identification of the brain as the seat of thought and emotion, TPT depended upon quite crude correlations such as loss of cognitive function due to massive brain damage, and the like.[11]

Once TPT has been used to bring about a coarse-grained correlation, then systematic empirical study of the mind-brain identity is possible emerging finally, as I have argued, in a kind of matching where the assumption of a correlation of atomistically identified instances of kinds can be avoided.

Like many arguments in philosophical psychology, the argument I have proposed, which suggests that mind-brain identity is to be considered in terms of a progression of successively more elaborate hypotheses, does not establish *a priori* whether in the long run we must settle for ontological identity or ontological diversity in the understanding of the way human beings function. The argument for the three modes steers a middle course between Jensen's heroic version of TPT and a strict Cartesianism. In my terms the Cartesian argument bases ontological diversity upon taxonomic differentiation. This will not do as basic principle since it is possible to turn taxonomic diversity into a powerful argument for ontological unity, at least for the first two modes. It seems to me that there is no good reason for accepting either heroic thesis and that the progression of modes has the merit of continuously sustaining the unity of a person as an embodied actor at the same time as it identifies fairly precisely the points at which empirical considerations are brought to bear.

PART IV

Diachronic Analysis

INTRODUCTION

The conceptual systems that have been developed in the first three parts of this study have been designed for the analysis and explanation of short-term activities of people in society. Studied in a restricted time-scale it is possible to assume without too much distortion that the knowledge and skill of the individual actors and the structure of the society they mutually create, are relatively stable. I have been arguing that whenever we set about the analysis of the activities of people in society at whatever epoch, we ought to employ the very same analytical system. It is also part of my contention that the specific psychological processes, the particular forms of knowledge and skill that emerge in the course of our studies, are unlikely to be stable over time. The next step in the investigation is to develop conceptual systems for diachronic analysis, that is for the study of changes in people, their social practices and the social formations they create.

I shall consider first the development of a conceptual system for the analysis of individual lives assumed to be led against a relatively, but only relatively, stable ground. Then I shall turn to examine the changes in that social background and the consequential changes that occur in the people by virtue of those changes. We shall finally emerge with a conceptual system for formulating theories of the origin, development and extinction of societies. No one way of explaining change will emerge. The influences on human social practices and psychological functioning are so diverse that we shall be forced to acknowledge not only that the sources of change are various but that at least two major mechanisms of change are at work. Sometimes the expressive order is dominant and sometimes the practical order. Sometimes change is produced by the tension between these orders in a dialectic resolution. At other times and with respect to other matters change is consequent on the spread of innovations in somewhat the manner of organic evolution. It is an important part of my purpose to identify principles for the appropriateness of selecting one explanatory mode rather than another, but in almost every real case both dialectic and evolutionary models will be required.

14

INDIVIDUAL LIVES

ANTICIPATORY SUMMARY

1. The study of life forms: sociological analysis
   (a) The concept of moral career: the history of a person with respect to the opinions others have of his qualities and worth.
   (b) The places of moral careers: these histories are usually formed in institutional settings:
       (i) entry is marked by divesting an individual of the marks of previous moral careers;
       (ii) the institution includes hazards and a career structure.
   (c) The problem of similarities in moral careers.
       (i) Case 1: ordained careers. A stable and structured institution through which people pass, e.g. the Turkish Ulema.
       (ii) Case 2: the cult of heroic failure. A shared theory of moral and aesthetic qualities of the ideal life form shapes careers independently of institutions, as e.g. the Japanese conception of the heroic.
   (d) The free construction of institutions for unofficial moral careers:
       (i) Simmel's 'adventure';
       (ii) football hooliganism.
2. The study of life forms: psychological analysis
   (a) The autonomy of the idiographic domain.
   (b) Methods of systematic study: the De Waele system:
       (i) the biography and autobiography: interpreted accounts of life events;
       (ii) methods of biography construction: time slices, theme slices and problem-and-conflict situations;
       (iii) philosophical issues: the historical accuracy of a construction.
3. The beginnings and ends of social careers.
   (a) The birth of an actor:
       (i) infants as whole social and psychological beings completed by their mothers;
       (ii) the autonomous social world of play: verbal and symbolic control.

311

(b) The death of an actor:

    (i) the closing of a physical career: philosophical problems of death;

    (ii) the termination of agency: Pascal's Wager yet again;

    (iii) the completion of the moral career: 'good' deaths and funeral orations, obituaries, etc.

1. THE STUDY OF LIFE FORMS: SOCIOLOGICAL ANALYSIS

Our problem is to devise a conceptual system for analysing and understanding the diachronic structure of a human life as it develops in the eyes of other people and to test it against examples. It will be a system of concepts for analysing the social trajectory of a human life.

(a) The Concept of a Moral Career[1]

Our analysis will be based upon Goffman's idea of a moral career. It is the social history of a person with respect to the attitudes of respect and contempt that others have to him and of his understandings of these attitudes. The attitudes are realized and represented in the institutionalized and ritualized forms in which respect and contempt are tested for and meted out, in particular societies.

A moral career is generated in the first instance by the opinions that other people form of someone from their experience of his success and failure in coping with occasions of hazard. An occasion of hazard is a social event in which a person can gain respect by risking contempt. For example, in the moral career that accompanies education an examination is a hazard. It can be treated as a social event, the results of which are publicly promulgated and which a candidate could fail. He gains respect by passing and he risks contempt in failing.

In this context respect and contempt are not just the private, unexpressed opinions of others about the person, since a moral career is a life trajectory defined in terms of public esteem. The results of hazard will be publicly recognized in social rituals and conventional acts espousing respect or contempt. In reciprocal acknowledgment the moral careerist makes the appropriate response in his demeanour to others. By showing condescension, modesty, or whatever may be the appropriate response to the ritual recognition of his success, and chagrin, apologetic humility, or whatever is called for in the face of ritualized contempt, a person shows that though he may have failed a particular test he is still a worthy human being. Noble endurance of failure may actually lead to more social credit than arrogant exploitation of success.

However, as I have emphasized in earlier sections, an essential element in the understanding of the social activities of human beings derives from their attributions to each other of permanent moral qualities. I have called this attribution 'character'. It is made up of the attributes that a particular group of people ascribe to an individual on the basis of the impressions they have formed of him on the basis of his expressive activities. These attributes, or rather the beliefs that people have as to these attributes determine the expectations that a group form of a person. They are the foundations, as individual beliefs of the willingness of others to defer to and praise an individual or to denigrate him, or simply to ignore him. They are the ultimate basis of his moral career. Correlatively, an individual social actor forms beliefs about himself, concerning his standing in the tables of respect and contempt, that is his beliefs about how he is viewed by others. Social psychologists have shown that there is a sustained difference between an individual's opinions about himself and the views others have of him. In that difference lies part of the dynamics of social life. A moral career, then, is a history of an individual person with respect to the attitudes and beliefs that others have of him, and the attitudes to and beliefs about himself that he forms on the basis of his readings of the attitudes and beliefs of others.

(b) The Places of Moral Career

Very few people live their moral careers in public space, as it were, gaining and loosing character as their reputations wax and wane in the beliefs and expectations of the public at large. Most people live out their moral careers in very limited regions, socially speaking, with respect to a very limited range of other people, and involving a limited number of hazards. In general, then, moral careers are to be understood as relative to institutions, which provide the occasions for hazard. The education system can be looked on as a confederation of institutions in which the sequence of examinations and the public promulgation of their results constitutes a system of hazards sufficient to generate the possibility of moral careers.

Goffman has pointed out the equivocal character of many institutions which at first sight we would describe in an instrumental or practical rhetoric, that is we would describe activities that occur in them as means towards practical ends.[2] For example, a hospital would be unthinkingly described as an institution in which the activities undertaken by the staff and inmates are directed towards the instrumental end of the cure of sickness. But a close examination of such institutions suggests that this rhetoric would be quite insufficient to provide a conceptual system for understanding everything which goes on, particularly those activities which have to do with reputation. In his famous study, *Asylums*, Goffman points out that closed institutions which provide for many moral careers have certain very characteristic common features.

(i) Entry into such an institution is marked by rituals of depersonalization in which in the extreme all traces of the previous moral career of an individual are wiped away. A person may even be given a new name in the course of the incorporation ritual as happens in the entry to monastic orders. A new career with new possibilities for the earning of respect and contempt then begins. In most such entry rituals there is a phase in limbo in which the individual bent on entering is reduced socially to nothing. For example, most armies subject every entrant to a medical examination in the course of which he is required to appear naked before those who are fully dressed. Looked at sociologically, this nakedness is not just a medical convenience but a stripping off of the conventional marks of prior identity. Similar limbos occur in the examination of potential immigrants to the United States in the Consular Offices of that nation.

(ii) In order for there to be the possibility of a moral career within an asylum there must be two complementary arrangements. There must be a system of hazards in the course of which reputation can be gained or lost, and a sequential system of social places in occupying which an individual receives the marks of deference due to him for successful passage through the hazards. Goffman has pointed out that the organization of wards in mental hospitals is best understood by bringing together two conceptions, that of the course of cure and that of the moral career. The passage from one ward to another is read according to the official rhetoric in terms of mental health, but it may be read according to the unofficial rhetoric of perceived moral careers as a rise or fall in prestige, as a matter of punishment or privilege, and so on. Goffman's sociological account has been beautifully amplified in Kesey's semi-fictional novel, *One Flew over the Cuckoo's Nest*, the tale of the epic conflict between Big Nurse and Mac.[3] The story turns on Mac's attempts to gain the moral advantage of Big Nurse and her ultimately successful efforts to destroy him by causing him to fail at hazard.

The necessity to consider the career of an individual within an institution in accordance with both an instrumental and an expressive or moral rhetoric raises the general question of the degree to which an institution is balanced between those activities. There must be some way of maintaining a sequence of real actions as means to its official ends, against a growing tendency to perform sequences of metonymic actions, only symbolic of real activities. The latter, as we have seen, are functionally related to hazards and their outcomes, and the rituals by which consequential respect and contempt are expressed. For example, an institution may so evolve that none of its activities, even though described in terms of its official rhetoric, are actual performances of what would count as real actions in accordance with that rhetoric. The City companies of London, descendants of the medieval Guilds, call themselves Dyers, Clothworkers, Fishmongers, and so on, but their members have not dyed cloth nor mongered fish in hundreds of years. This example will serve as the occasion for the introduction of a principle which will prove to be of importance in looking at the dynamics of institutions in a later section. All other things being equal, an institution will develop in such a way that its expressive aspect − that is the apparatus for the development of moral careers − will become more and more dominant in the determination of individual action in that institution.

So far we have discussed the concept of moral career in terms of the positive engagement of the social actor in the construction of his career by actively engaging in hazards. By risking failure, he or she is able to enhance reputation. But we owe to Goffman another important concept, namely the idea of fatefulness and the correlative conception of stigmata.[4]

A fateful action brings about a state of affairs which, if disclosed, would lead to a decline in reputation. It is a threat to moral career. For example, a graduate student who steals a book from Blackwell's Bookshop is undertaking a fateful hazard, for should it become public knowledge his reputation is seriously damaged and his moral career substantially set back.

Stigmata are fateful attributes of individuals, which they can do nothing to remove and which they cannot help but acquire. A graduate student need not steal a book, but someone born into a despised ethnic group cannot by his own actions slough off that ethnicity. Some stigmata, then, have to be managed in the interests of a moral career. The management of stigmata has been admirably described in Goffman's *Stigma*. For the purpose of this work, it is sufficient to draw the reader's attention to the cases described in that book, and the details of self-management there set out.

(c) The Problem of Similarities in Moral Careers

An examination of the structure of moral careers suggests that, in many societies, life trajectories considered with respect to the growth and decline of an individual reputation take very similar forms. What sort of explanation can be given for this fact? I shall consider two examples to illustrate two different ways in which life conformities can come to exist. In the first case there is a synchronic structure of institutions and associated hazards which can serve as a template for a diachronic structure of moments of test, in which respect or contempt can be gained. In such a case there is a way of recording the outcome of these moments in public acts and signs. Under these circumstances a moral career takes a standard form. In the other case the members of a society share a theory in accordance with which they each aim at the construction of a life form which exemplifies the most favoured life-trajectory of their society. The question as to why in a particular society there exist shared theories as to the best life trajectory, and why in others life-forms are the products of institutional structures, is susceptible only of a historical explanation.

Case 1. Ordained career

In these cases the *cursus honorum*, the diachronic life-form conceived as a career of respect, derives from a stable and structured social institution. For example, the Ottoman Turkish teaching profession, the *Ulema*, had just such a form.[5]

Its basic structure consisted of a graded sequence of *medreses*, universities which were attached to Mosques. In the Turkish Empire the Mosques were sharply differentiated and ordered in relative prestige. This ordering was transferred to the attached *medreses*. The teaching profession was organized around the sequential occupancy of a post in each grade of *medrese* so that an aspirant rose in the learned hierarchy by moving from post to post in successive universities. The criterion for advancement was reputation – that is appointments to higher graded *medreses* were made on the basis of recommendations to the Sultan from members of the learned hierarchy. And here we see the operation of one aspect of the notion of character, as the public reputation that a scholar has with those who are high in the hierarchy of his profession. In order to understand the system, however, it is necessary to notice that it depended upon an expressive and evaluational structure which involved matters other than reputation as a learned man. To each post there was attached a fixed salary. The numerical order of salaries matched the prestige order of the *medreses.* The cash differentials were enormous, of about the order 1:25. Thus, success in passing up the learned hierarchy provided the occasion for the expressive representation of that success according to more general criteria, namely the possibilities for display opened to a person by virtue of his relative wealth.

The system did not, of course, remain entirely unchanged, but it was remarkably stable. It was formalized in the *Kanunname* of Mehmed II about the year 1470.

Our analysis, then identifies an instrumental hierarchy, depending upon ability in learning and teaching, and an expressive hierarchy of public reputation and social power, depending upon financial reward. In the early days of the *Ulema*, the expressive hierarchy was in one to one correspondence with the instrumental hierarchy. Jobs and salaries matched ability, and ability was reflected in reputation. However, as Repp, the authority on the system points out, the *Ulema* fulfilled the general principle of the evolution of institutions which was proposed earlier in this chapter, namely that in the course of time activities became more expressive and progressively less instrumental. The corruption seems to have been very largely the effect of nepotism. Members high in the learned hierarchy recommended to the Sultan the promotion of relatives independently of their effectiveness as scholars and teachers. The result was a transformation of the *Ulema* from a teaching institution to an expressive institution, in which the salaries were used for the purchase of mere icons for public display. The respect/contempt criteria were transformed. They lost their connection with the official task of the *Ulema* – the activities proper to learned professions – and became associated with public display of outward marks of learning and wisdom, robes of office, portentous speech, and so on.

Case 2. The cult of heroic failure

Similarity of the lives of learned Turks is to be explained by reference to the structure of the institutions in which their careers were made. However, there are other life trajectories which fall into sets of similar form and for which there exists no such institution. The most striking example I know of is the Japanese cult of heroic failure. Each life is constructed by the hero who lives it in a similar fashion to the lives of other heroes, and yet it is a personal creation. I shall be proposing that we understand this in terms of the sharing of a number of interconnected theories about the ideal life form.

To understand the cult we must compare two main conceptions of the heroic.

(i) In the Western conception the heroic life culminates in success. The correlative emotions are pride and contentment, or satisfaction.

(ii) The Japanese conception of the heroic life culminates in failure after a high peak of initial success, and the correlative emotions are sadness and regret.

Of course, each culture contains in minor form the heroic life form of the other. In Western literature the tragic hero bears some similarity to the most popular form of Japanese heroic life, while the Japanese themselves recognize, though do not greatly admire, the heroic life in the Western mould. According to Ivan Morris, whose study *The Nobility of Failure*, examines the Japanese conception of the heroic in detail,[6] the admiration which the Japanese give to the life of heroic failure is to be explained by the imposition of characteristic aesthetic categories on the life trajectory. According to Morris, a central aesthetic principle realized in Japanese art forms is that beauty is to be seen in decay, in the falling of the cherry blossom, in autumn, and so on. 'Yet in the very impermanence and poignancy of the human condition, the Japanese have discovered a positive quality, their recognition of a special beauty inherent in evanescence, worldly misfortune and "the pathos of things".' A tragic life form, the moral career of the failed hero, could be seen as yet another symbol realizing this conception. As Morris puts it, 'his [the hero's] fall represents in human form the quintessential Japanese image, the scattering of the fragile cherry blossoms'. Morris produces a great deal of evidence for the claim that for millenia the Japanese have chosen to admire and sometimes to construct lives which fulfil this aesthetic design. He claims, for example, that the phenomenon of the Kamikaze pilots is to be understood in terms of this aesthetic principle. The kamikaze phenomenon, so he argues, depended heavily on the perception that Japan had already lost all hope of winning the war. The young men who piloted the suicide planes were not seeking immortality like heroes in the Valhalla tradition, but rather in making a useless sacrifice on the declining stage of the war they were fulfilling their traditional conception of the heroic life form.

The explanation, then, for the similarity of many Japanese moral careers, including the recent suicide of Mishima, the Nobel prize-winning novelist, is to be sought in aesthetic theory and a shared conception of the heroic. There are no Japanese institutions which impose this form upon life. Indeed, rather the contrary. One can compare the careers of the brothers Yoretomo and Yoshitsune. The former was the founder of the traditional Japanese state. His influence persisted for six or seven hundred years and, in consequence, he holds a place of muted respect in the Japanese hierarchy of great men. But as a hero he is overshadowed by Yoshitsune, his younger brother, who, after a spectacular beginning as a revolutionary leader, failed completely in his campaign. He eventually committed suicide in the traditional Japanese fashion, almost alone, under a pine tree beside a lake.

This example draws our attention to a further and very striking feature of this cult, namely the role of time in the consciousness of the individual who is constructing his own life form. It is very different from the role it plays in the heroic life of Western tradition. For the Japanese adventurer, intent upon the heroic, the culmination of his moral career and the reputation he acquires in the eyes of others may be postponed until long after his death. He is seeking respect from succeeding generations, and he buys this at the cost of being seen as a failure by his contemporaries. Such a conception requires a further shared idea, namely a belief in the persistence of the essential forms of Japanese culture. Amongst a people who have no sense of the longevity of their national culture, the Japanese cult of the heroic would make no sense.

In Morris's classical study of this cult there is a notable weakness, a weakness which I am in no position to resolve. He has no well-worked-out theory to account for the preservation and continuous sharing of a conception of the heroic over so long a period. Morris offers two rather lame explanations. He suggests without much conviction that the persistence of Mahayana Buddhism may have been a contributory factor to the stability of the aesthetic conceptions upon which the Japanese heroic life form is based. But one might equally argue that it was the persistence of the aesthetic ideals that sustained the Mahayana form of Buddhism. The geographical features of the Archipelago, for example its earthquakes, he proposed, might have led to the ideas of evanescence, of impermanence, becoming implanted as permanent features of Japanese conceptions of the beautiful and the good. But the Greeks, the Italians and the Icelanders are equally plagued by earth tremors and consequent disasters, and have developed no such aethetico-social theory. Indeed, the Icelanders, I suppose above all, have been proponents of the Western cult of heroic success.

(d) The Free Construction of Institutions for Unofficial Moral Careers

The cases I have just been considering are embedded in coherent and well-formed societies where institutions and shared theories are strong. The construction of moral careers in more open societies, and particularly societies where the conceptions of a well-ordered life are very diverse, is a much more difficult and uncertain matter. Indeed, for many people moral careers are lived wholly within institutions. However, it has been pointed out by Goffman[7] and others, that in industrialized society many people undertake a secondary career in the pursuit of respect which lies outside the main institutional structures of the society and is catered for by special arrangements in special places.

(i) Simmel proposed the term 'adventure' for the social activities which take place in Time-off, so to speak, and which can be seen as engagements in a series of hazards. Only a limited reputation can be gained in these activities since they must either be secret or occur in places far from the location of the normal occupations of the individuals involved. Goffman has drawn attention to the possibility of treating gambling as a form of 'adventure'. In Nevada the adventure has degenerated into a form in which the display of the expressive attributes of character occurs merely in the sight of machines.

(ii) The kind of activities that Goffman and Simmel have in mind are generally developed by someone other than the adventurer they are provided for. I want to consider briefly an example of the construction of alternative moral careers where the institution is created and sustained even against the hostility of the surrounding societies by the adventurers themselves. A recent phenomenon in British society has been the elaboration of formalized rituals by football fans. Our studies have shown that the lads taking part in these events are generally devalued in the official careers that the society at large provides for them. They are those whose life in school has been a progression of humiliations and ritual affirmations of their valuelessness to society. It becomes apparent to them that in the official world there is no possibility whatever of their obtaining respect. But on the terraces of football grounds on Saturday afternoons they bring into existence a highly structured and hierarchical society in which a moral career, the growth of a public reputation through a series of hazards successfully overcome, can be attempted. In brief, a lad may begin such a career sitting on the concrete wall separating the spectators from the field of play watching and learning from the actions of the competent members of the group arrayed before him on the terraces. Slowly he acquires the 'gear', the regalia symbolic of his position in the hierarchy. Eventually, after a year or two's apprenticeship, he takes his place on the highest tier of seats. As the years go by and he comports himself successfully in the 'fights' in which his fellow-fans engage, he moves down, each descent marking social advancement. At first he acquires the uniform in all its splendour and then, as his reputation becomes established, sheds it bit by bit. Enough successful actions and his reputation as a 'hard' man is established. Finally he reaches the full glory of 'town-boy' whose personal fame is sufficient to allow him to dispense with any symbols of glory such as scarves, rosettes and so on.

The occasions of hazard are represented by the fans as 'fights'. Close empirical study of these encounters has shown that they are to be treated as events of much the same kind as aggressive threats and ritualized territorial defences seen amongst many animals. They are more matters of the display of the signs, marks and instruments of aggression than they are of actual bodily encounters. In fact, bodily encounters are very rare. The result of a successful 'fight' is the retreat of the enemy and the enhancement of the reputation of the protagonist of the side who has forced the other to back down. The well-ordered hierarchical microsociety provides a clear *cursus honorum*. It is an institution, stable over time but created by the very people who use it to develop their moral careers. It has the form of a Turkish *Ulema* but it is a creation independent of the over-arching society. Nor is there any constitutional device such as the edicts of the Turkish Sultan which publicly represent and hence serve to determine the form of the hierarchy. It is an institution constituted by custom and preserved by tradition.

The conceptual system I have developed in outline and illustrated by application to several cases is, of course, a scheme for sociological analysis. It says nothing whatever about the mode of representation of the knowledge of the hierarchies, rituals and judgemental criteria and so on which individual people must have to undertake the activities constitutive of moral careers. Nothing whatever has been implied about the mode of individual psychological attachment to moral career activities either. Is it through attitudes, knowledge, emotions or beliefs or through the activation of genetic imperatives based in biological adaptations, or both or neither? For the next stage of our investigations we must turn to the examination of ways in which we might come to know the psychological aspects of a life considered as extended in time.

2. THE STUDY OF LIFE FORMS: PSYCHOLOGICAL ANALYSIS

The problem of developing a conceptual system and an associated methodology for the study of the psychological aspects of a human life centres on the perennial problem of empirical psychology, namely whether an extensive method aimed at investigating the common properties of a large class of individuals is to be preferred to an intensive method in which individuals are examined, one by one, with no prior assumptions about the similarities or differences that may emerge among them. Traditional life-course psychology has been based on the extensive method. Large numbers of individuals at different ages have been investigated and the common properties of each age-set determined. The results have been as disappointing in fact as they might have been expected to be in theory. Almost all that has emerged from this kind of analysis is a re-affirmation of the known biological differences between one age cohort and another. The arguments in the critical chapters of this book concerning the traditional methods of psychology have pointed to the necessity to employ an idiographic method as part of an intensive design, that is to study individuals one by one, without any prior assumptions as to the generality of the psychological processes revealed.[9] The point can be put quite sharply in terms of the concept of ergodicity. It cannot be assumed that if we study life forms by looking at different individuals, one for each time-slice, we will find a profile of change that is identical to, or sufficiently similar to, the profile of change that we would find by allowing one individual to evolve his own life form over time. In short, life-course properties are very unlikely to be ergodic.

(a) The Autonomy of the Idiographic Domain

In discussing the development of an adequate sociological methodology I introduced Du Mas' theory of the idiographic domain (Chapter 4). May I remind the reader that Du Mas proposed three empirical domains: (i) D1: The distribution of properties over individuals at a time; (ii) D2: The distribution of individuals with respect to a given property at different times; (iii) D3; The idiographic domain, the distribution of properties of a given individual over times. Since the domains are orthogonal, it is obvious that the structure of the idiographic domain cannot be deduced from knowledge of the structures of D1 and D2 unless the study has already incorporated D3 by exhausting D1 and D2. It follows from this that there is at least the possibility that the psychological histories of each individual may turn out to be unique. The principles of sequence and order in each member of the idiographic domain may turn out to be unlike the principles of sequence and order of any other members of that domain. The way one individual's life evolves may show certain longitudinal, structural properties, to be called themes, which may, in principle, be different from those of any other individual.

(b) Methods of Systematic Study: The De Waele System

Methods for the study of the psychology of individual lives must then realize Du Mas' idiographic domain. The De Waele method, the only systematic life-course psychology so far developed, consists in the construction of documents which represent an agreed account of the distribution of an individual's psychological attributes at different times, including such matters as emotions, beliefs, accepted rules, experiences of the self and others, and so on.[10]

Broadly speaking, there are two kinds of life-course documents, the biography and the diary. These documents are generated after the events they describe, but they are built on the basis of those events. The diary is a contemporaneous record of the psychological life-course, whereas the biography must be constructed from a past which must be revived before it can be described. In consequence biography and autobiography are epistemologically distinct from diary.

(i) The biography, including the autobiography

A biography is characterized by the relative conceptual sophistication of the analysis and interpretation which it contains. It involves events from the past as they are interpreted in the light of the knowledge and experience which a person has at the time the biography is constructed, which may be much later than the events described. Of course, correspondingly, a biography is historically problematic. The method of biographical construction that I shall describe has been developed for the study of the lives of murderers but it can be generalized to any human life. The construction of a biography can be conceived within the ethogenic approach as a process by which very large-scale accounts are successively negotiated with an individual encouraged to show his actions to have been reasonable at the time of their performance.

(ii) Methods of biography construction

There are two main methods for the construction of a biography, methods which interact with one another.

1. The participant prepares an autobiography which is partitioned into time slices, each representing a distinct phase in his life. The phases are identified from the autobiography. They are not defined with respect to any *a priori* scheme for the analysis of lives. The team of investigators — let us suppose that there are six — is each offered a slice and has the task of reconstructing the rest of the biography, using common-sense social and psychological knowledge. The reconstructions are then negotiated with other members of the team and then with the participant himself. In the final phase, the products of these negotiations are brought together into an agreed version.

2. The second stage of the investigation involves a different set of investigators and a different partition of the autobiography, this time into theme slices, such as work, education, relations with the opposite sex, and so on. A similar process of reconstruction and negotiation is undertaken, the final stage of which is the construction of another agreed biography.

In the last phase of this part of the investigation, the time reconstruction and the theme reconstruction are finally brought together.

And there are, of course, difficulties with the very idea of 'the way things were then'. There is no solution to the ultimate problem of historical accuracy. In the Brussels method historicity is abandoned as a criterion in favour of authenticity; that is, do the recollected features of the events of the life course form a co-herent thematic order? This is not to be confused with a criterion of consistency, since it is not suggested that the various themes of an individual's life should be expected to fit together into a consistent whole.

I have made use several times of the idea of a theme. A life may show a number of themes both in its public actions and private interpretations. A theme can be thought of as a distinctive style of action. For instance, in one of the Brussels biographies, the dominating theme of the life of one individual was 'simplifica-tion'. Any form of complexity, moral, physical, practical or theo-retical, is routinely denied or avoided. The approach of that individual to the successive problems posed to him by life has always been "Simplify".

What of the status of the knowledge that has been generated in the person under study as his biography has become known to him? And how do the changes in the participant during the biographical reconstruction relate to the historicity or authen-ticity of the final document? It follows from the above consi-derations, that it is impossible to say whether we have discovered the truth about an individual life course, or whether we have created in a participant a current conception of his life relative to the point of view he has now reached. Psychologically, the effect of a Brussels investigation on a participant is to enlarge his knowledge of his own life-form. This knowledge now becomes part of his resources for generating action and action-plans. In rare cases it can be reduced to 'That's the sort of person I am', in which his whole life-form is condensed into a pre-given instance of a typology. But in most cases such a condensation is impossible, and indeed the participant is very unlikely to undertake it. The status of a biography, then, is not that of a simple historical document.

However, this is insufficient to complete the study and a further set of investigations are now undertaken. The final agreed biography can be seen to contain a whole range of situations which are felt by the participant to be problematic or to have involved some sort of conflict. Once these situations are identified their formal structure can be discovered, for example, did the problem emerge from a sequence of similar, but solvable situa-tions, and so on. In the next stage of the investigation the partici-pant is expected to relive episodes which are formally isomorphic

with those which he represented in his agreed biography as problematic and agonistic. The participant is not told which of the
events in his past the artificial problem and conflict situations are
supposed to replicate. Indeed, in an ideal application of the
method he is brought to experience a wide range of possible forms
of such situations. In the course of this experience of artificially
constructed problems and conflicts, he is asked to remember those
situations in his past life of which he is reminded as he experiences
the emotions, the frustrations, the methods, by means of which he
deals with those which he is presently undergoing. The structure
of the situations of the past can be inferred from the predetermined structure of the situations which he is currently experiencing. Predetermination affords some leverage against the besetting
epistemological problem of all life-course studies, namely how far
do recollections of the past accurately represent the events as they
occurred. The results of this phase of the investigation are then
combined with the agreed biography to produce the final document which is now organized for themes — that is for longitudinal
lines of similar occurrences according to criteria provided by the
participant himself.

(iii) Philosophical issues

The De Waele method, which I have outlined above, is an exceedingly powerful empirical method, generating a well-ordered and
very rich psychological biography of an individual. However, there
are philosophical problems of an epistemological character at
which I have already hinted.

The idiographic method reveals in a very detailed way, the
conception of himself that an individual has developed in the
course of his life, and which has been amplified and modified in
untestable ways in the course of the experience of constructing
the biography. The biography, then, is partly a representation
of the individual's current psychological structure.

The first level of philosophical inquiry relative to the implications of the method can be reached by assuming what will later
be questioned, namely the continuous identity of the individual
participant, P, whose autobiography we are assisting, together with
the idea of there being some sequence of events el, ... en, which
we take to be P's life course, as it happened. Against this background the first problem emerges:

Since there seem to be no sharp criteria for deciding deter-
minatively whether the (auto)biography considered as a collection

of hypotheses about the life course events el ... en are true, what is the status of the (auto) biography under these conditions?

This question is readily answered if we distinguish the cognitive state of P, the participant, at the time of the beginning of the De Waele experience from his condition at the end. As an active participant in every phase of the (auto)biographical construction P has become knowledgeablè about his past life to the extent that the content of the (auto)biography at the end of the experience is almost identical with his conception of his life course as he now believes it to have been. As explicit knowledge it is available to him as part of his resources for action at times running even some distance into the future. But if a man's cognitive resources are the bases of his action-planning and so on, then our knowledge of them enables us to predict his acts and actions in parallel to the way they enable him to form intentions to perform acts and actions.

This accounts for the success of De Waele and his team in predicting the future life course of a prisoner in their parole reports. It is not as if they had succeeded in showing the prisoner to be an instantiation of some ideal type, nor his actions to be predictable from a covering law, unless it is the banality that people often do what they intend.

But the assumptions upon which this discussion was based are themselves questionable. Whose (auto)biography have we constructed? The question arises in this dramatic form against the background thought that the state of the participant after a year's investigations may be so different from his state at the beginning of the De Waele experience that we need to register an ontological change. He is no longer, we may feel inclined to say, the *same person* as he was. This remark makes sense only if the conceptual system within which the concept of a person is embedded admits dual criteria for continuous personal identity. As philosophers have shown[11] neither the spatio-temporal continuity of world line of the person as embodied agent, nor qualitative identity of cognitive contents is sufficient alone to control our uses of the person concept.

It seems clear that it is always an empirical question whether, relative to the conceptual system deployed in the culture, the second identity criterion has been met. We might, in certain cases where there has been profound change in knowledge, attitude and so on, be ready to say that though it was P1, who entered the experience at the beginning, and who lived the history el ... en, it is P2 who has come into being in the course of constructing the (auto)biography. Only P knows that he lived it. The paradoxical status of the 'he' in the last sentence cannot be wholly resolved since at least P2 must be able to remember that 'he' was once P1. We owe to Proust the literary exploration of the paradox. But there can be no philosophical solution, since in these cases P2 has access to some of the features of P1 that figure in judgements of personal identity.

But this question and its philosophically indeterminate answer is itself embedded in a nest of further assumptions concerning the description of a life course. It is assumed that the episodes we have crudely represented by e1 ... en are able to be given a univocal description, as if finally there was only one perspective on a life course. And behind that lies the assumption that there is indeed a singular sequence, *the* life course, as one and only one thing. This assumption has been called in question by Schutz.[12] As a person shifts from one 'perspective' to another in the interpretation of his life, he transforms the events under each interpretation. Though they may have spatio-temporal identity, they are not socially singular. The life course must be treated as indefinitely multiple while no criterion for limiting perspectives is to hand.

The shift of significance of 'an' event with shift in perspective has been nicely illustrated by Helling[13] in the case of the life story of a man working as a carpenter. An incident in which he was asked to do some work in the boss's house is referred to twice in a fragment of autobiography. In one instance it is embedded within a perspective which is used to illustrate the man's position in society as a fall from previous heights. He is now the sort of man who can be ordered around by the boss. In the other perspective he is to be seen as rising to a position of trust, the kind of man who can be relied upon to do a good job even when not under supervision. Was *the* incident an occasion for feelings of pride or of humiliation? The question can now be seen to be ill posed. Spatio-temporal identity does not entail social uniqueness. One event occurred, but contemporaneous with it were two 'incidents'. They were both real in their effects upon the sense of personal worth experienced by the carpenter and illustrated in the perspectival duality of his account.

3. THE BEGINNINGS AND ENDS OF SOCIAL CAREERS:
THE BIRTH AND DEATH OF ACTORS

I turn now to consider the ways in which we can see a social actor coming into existence and ceasing to exist. We must sharply distinguish social careers from biological careers since it is by no means clear that the beginning and end of a social career is identical with the birth and death of an organism.[14]

(a) The Birth of an Actor

(i) It has sometimes been assumed that an infant is born into the world as an empty vessel or *tabula rasa* and becomes a social actor by a process of learning, of socialization. This has sometimes been called 'internalizing the norms'. An infant is supposed to acquire, bit by bit, skill by skill, and even, according to Piaget, in a necessary sequential order that reproduces the phylogeny of civilization, the knowledge and abilities which eventually emerge in adulthood as the competence of a social actor. Recently both these ideas, the *tabula rasa* and progressive staging,[15] have been challenged.

Richards, Shotter, Newson and others[16] have criticized the traditional view of the infant as an empty vessel into whom first his mother and then the other adults and children who form his social milieu pour an increasing amount of social competence. They have proposed that a child should be imagined as a component of a synthetic but complete social individual — the mother-child dyad. The mother, as an independent social being, interacts with this dyad, as if it were another social entity. Careful studies of the way mothers speak to infants, suggest that much of the mother's speech serves to complete the infant by attributing intentions, wants and plans to him. She does for him what he cannot presently do for himself, so that he is always part of a fully competent, social individual. For example, she systematically and routinely attributes cognitive states and operations to the infant on the basis of faint, and sometimes false cues, in his movements and expressions.

The birth of an actor could be said then to occur at the moment at which the mother-child dyad is formed — that is when she takes on the completion of a social individual of which the infant is, for the first part of his life, merely a component. The Shotter-Richards-Newson picture of social maturation is of the transfer of responsibility for certain functions from one component of a complete being to another. There never is a *tabula rasa* out in the social world. As Trevarthen has demonstrated the mother, as herself, interacts with the mother-child as a pseudo-self, in many conventions and games.[17]

(ii) There are good empirical reasons for seeing this symbiosis continuing until a child is about four years of age, at which point most of the transference from the mother component to the infant part of the dyadic but socially unitary being has been achieved. In the next phase of life, adult skills and methods of social action are rapidly developed in social activities fairly well isolated from adult influence. Social apprenticeship begins in the underlife of school, in the playground, and the unattended parts of home. Here, the children create an autonomous precursor world. They engage in symbolic activity such as the exchange of tokens as a binding of friendship; they arrange the creation and maintenance of aspects of social order, such as turn-taking, by the use of rituals. They control their interactions by means of systems of rules; and they defend their persons by a whole series of equilibrating procedures ranging from protests against failures of distributive justice to insulting rhymes by means of which a person can restore the dignity he has lost when brought low by the actions of adults. Detailed studies of both the infant period and the autonomous precursor world presents a very different picture of development from that of the sequentialists, Piaget and Kohlberg.[18] Studies of the lives of children when they are not in interaction with adults suggest a very high level of social competence, but exercised upon a material content which is quite alien to the adult world. For example, there is a strong verbal contractual basis to orderly and rule-governed activity in the playing of marbles. Furthermore, Kitwood's extremely detailed studies have shown that the idea of stages in the moral competence of a child can not be sustained empirically. It seems that most children are in command of most moral theories most of the time, but apply them in a highly situation-specific manner, so that they are sometimes intuitionists, sometimes utilitarians, and sometimes even depend upon the categorical imperative.

I shall assume without further argument that the Carey-Block/Bryant explanation of the stages which Piaget seemed to see, is an adequate one (cf. note 15). So once socio-psychological symbiosis has been dissolved and the child separates from the mother as a competent individual, he is in possession of most of the skills that he needs to manage an adult life. His problem is to bring these skills together in situations where one or more seem to be called for at the same time. As Susan Carey-Block and Bryant have shown, Piaget's settings for his investigation have characteristically led to an uncertainty as to which of a pair of principles a child should use in solving a problem. The confusion is resolved as one principle comes to mask others which might be applicable in these situations. Later, the principles separate. The unmasking of an old skill has been taken by Piaget to be the staged, sequential appearance of a new skill. The Piagetian and Kohlberg picture of stages seems to be quite unsustainable empirically with respect to social activity. A seven-year-old co-operatively creating and sustaining a complex social world in the playground of a school is already operating with a very full bouquet of the skills required of an adult. The situations in which he uses them, however, are neatly separated for him, and perhaps by him, so that conflicts that acquire multiple operations are very rarely encountered.

The idea of a socio-psychological symbiosis and the infant as one component of a composite being, can be related to a long-running and very deep philosophical argument. How is inter-subjectivity possible? The Cartesian separation of mind from body not only individuates consciousnesses as non-intersecting spheres of awareness, but also involves the separation of the private from the public domain. Cartesian scepticism with respect to individual knowledge of those domains, based on the confinement of know-ledge to the subjective deliverances of consciousness, throws into doubt the very possibility of common experiences, of any con-scious and joint appropriation of the public domain by a multi-tude of people. Husserl ran aground on the problem, working his way forever inwards towards solipsism. Each epoché distanced the public domain still further from experience. (See his Medi-tation V.)[19] Schutz adopted a heroic solution. Intersubjectivity must be taken as primitive and given. What is problematic is the possibility of an individual consciousness, a private domain. Almost all the currently accepted empirical evidence supports the Schutzian alternative.

(b) The Death of an Actor

An actor, as conceived in this study, is a social being, though he is necessarily embodied. The ending of his life trajectory involves a complex interaction of processes closing off different aspects of his career. In particular, his life must be rounded off as an agent, as a bearer of character, and as an embodied being. Death may not be simultaneous in each mode and indeed, there seems to be very good reason for thinking that it is not.

(i) The closing of the physical career

In general in contemporary thinking, the dissolution of embodiment is treated as a progressive phase-by-phase process. There are serious philosophico-legal problems about the precise point in this process at which a human life should be thought to be terminated. These concern, it seems, the physical signs of person-termination, and of course depend upon specific embodiment theses as well as particular philosophical doctrines as to the nature of persons. There is a complex interaction between the concept of agency, consciousness and physical death, which it is not part of my purpose here to analyse. All that we need to notice is that with respect to the biological progress, an arbitrary point of closure is defined which is closely related to legal and other considerations. However, for ceremonial purposes a simulacrum of embodiment may be produced. For example, the body of a person may be embalmed and so decorated as to seem to be alive, that is to seem to be still a member of a social world. Leave-takings may occur in which one of the participants is a corpse.

(ii) The termination of agency

The argument that was developed earlier, concerning the nature of the self as agent, suggested that our conceptual apparatus called for persons to be attributed an abstract, contentless agency capable of being exercised on any concrete matter whatever. It is logically possible for agency in this sense to survive the abstraction of any particular content entailed by the organic death of a person. If the agency is pure, it could be transferable in principle to any content whatever. However, in a further stage of the argument, when we analysed the conditions for the existence of selves, human persons, abstract agency turned out to be a metaphysical representation of a process feature of the physiological system, which forms the material basis of human individuals. It represents the indefinitely multipliable possibility of one part of the system being able to represent and control another part. This abstract agentive capacity is materially grounded. So the logical possibility of the survival of agency beyond organic death will never actually be empirically realized. But this is a contingency, and whether we hold it true or false is very closely related to the kind of embodiment mode which we take to be associated with human agency. For example, if it were possible to sustain the Cartesian mode as an empirically possible form of embodiment, then the history of the self with respect to the history of its physical bearer, its point of application under the Cartesian mode, would be quite different.

From the actor's point of view, the concept of the self as agent that is relevant to the closures of death is the capacity of the self to reflect upon its own contents. The capacity of the self to act in the world is a relevant property only as far as determination of agency as a social or public matter is concerned. We have already seen the close connection between criteria for deciding the point of physical death and the ending of action in the world as it is experienced by other people. But, as far as the actor is concerned, it is rather the possibility of reflection upon any of his own contents than the possibility of action that is the crucial issue. Action in the world and reflection can be radically distinguished. They are aspects of the distinction between and joint necessity of both autonomy and reflexivity, the distinction we found to be central to the concept of a person-in-society. From this point of view, the actor's appropriate stance in the face of organic death is a form of Pascal's wager.

(a) If the self as reflexive agent survives the end of the physical career it will have some content to reflect upon.[20]

(b) But if the self in this sense does not survive, then there is no standpoint from which its failure to survive might be regretted.

(iii) The completion of the moral career
From the actor's point of view, death is a presentational moment which can be managed in the interests of completing a moral career, that is, it is a very important testing point for persona management and the completion of character. The contemporary custom of removing the moment of death from a public or social milieu is, from the actor's point of view, disastrous, in that he has no chance of completing his character, or even revising it, by making a good death. 'Nothing in his life so became him as his leaving of it.' According to the theory advocated in this work, the management of death in other epochs was socially very much more satisfactory. Opportunities were provided for deathbed repentance, for speeches at the foot of the scaffold, and so on. The management of death as a presentational moment was placed firmly in the hands of the actor, and he was surrounded by a

supporting cast who enabled him to carry out his last dramaturgical activity in the best interests of the character he would
leave behind him.[21]

Organic death, however, even on the scaffold, is not the end of
moral career, for that is completed, at least in Western societies,
by the funeral. This is the occasion for a rite of passage involving
the ritual disposal of the persona, and the generation of a document to represent the character, the public repute, of the individual whose moral career is being closed. This takes the form of
funeral oration, or an obituary, in which an attempt is made to
sum up the reputation of the individual actor. It rounds off the
moral career.[22] This is in sharp contrast to the moral careers
of Japanese heroes, as I described them in a previous section, in
that they look to a reputation which has to be achieved in the
eyes of others long after the moment at which, in Western societies, an obituary would have been published and a funeral oration
would have been given. There are, of course, in the Western world,
such activities as the re-consideration of the reputation of an
important person, the waxing and waning of public esteem for
musicians, artists, novelists and the like. So, character, even in
the Western world, is for certain people at least, a long-term
property. However, I take these to be exceptional. For most
people moral career ends in a funeral oration.

15

SOCIAL CHANGE:
THEORIES AND ASSUMPTIONS

ANTICIPATORY SUMMARY

Introduction: change can occur in people-structures (institutions) and act/
action structures (social practices). In most cases this is an analytical rather
than a material distinction. Change must be defined by contrast to whatever
does not change. Invariance is the best test for universality.
1. The search for invariants
   (a) Biologically-based invariants:
       (i) drives: unsatisfactory because either trivial or tautological;
       (ii) ethological analogy: analogous patterns of social activity does
            not prove analogous origins.
   (b) Cognitive preformation theories:
       (i) the preformed structures of the human mind predetermine the
           basic structures of all human products (Levi-Strauss), but the
           empirical evidence for the theory is weak;
       (ii) human beings are genetically determined to select only some of
            the possible regularities in social practices, upon which they
            develop their own practice: not well supported empirically.
   (c) Ethogenic universals
   Some acts seem to be widespread in human societies, as do some rather
   general expressive categories; but the evidence does not support a claim
   for the universality of behavioural invariants; the case for some structural invariants is stronger.
   (d) Compensating changes as signs of an invariant:
       (i) male/female revealed as an invariant in recent fashion changes;
       (ii) compensations usually occur through complementary changes
            in expressive practices and accounting rhetorics.
2. The location of social change
   (a) Practices; changes in acts and the actions conventionally required to
   realize them.

335

(b) Institutions: interactions between expressive and practical orders lead to tensions and resolutions of tensions.

(c) Societies: all kinds of changes, some of which we can detect only in their effects, are to be supposed to be occurring.

3. Theoretical standpoints

(a) The material-dialectic: lacks an adequate account of causal mechanisms.

(b) Dialectical cum evolutionary processes:

(i) populational theories explain adaptiveness without teleology;

(ii) and require no explicit knowledge of the properties of large collectives.

INTRODUCTION

The problems of social change cannot be identified without some careful prior distinction drawing. We must distinguish first of all between the changes that might take place in institutions and societies considered as people-structures, for instance redistribution of respect-relations in contrast to changes that come about in social practices, for example the revision of ritual forms in act/action structures. In both cases there are complexities. People-structures may change in such a way that the 'essential' nature of the people remains the same and only external relations among them undergo a differentiation over time. However, since most social relations are internally related to the natures of the members, institutional and societal changes will usually involve changes in the people as well as in relational structures. There are several ways that social practices can change. While the acts to be performed remain the same, they come to be realized in different action-structures. But it may be that through a series of imperceptible changes different acts come to be performed by means of given action-structures. For example, a ceremony which was once taken to be the performance of one act may become emptied of that content, and though retaining its action-structure, become the performance of some other act. I shall be concerned to develop concepts for formulating theories of change of social practices and for devising theories of the change of institutions and societies, so that the social psychological processes involved can be clearly identified.

However, change of practices and of institutions are not independent of one another. Social practices in institutions or societies are linked in an essential way. People-structures are realized in day-to-day living in act/action structures. For example, a hierarchical people-structure is realized in everyday practice in the act/action structures by which deference and condescension are ritually represented. In many cases the relation between change in social practices and change in institutions and other people-structures is so close that the distinction is analytic rather than material, that is one sort of change should not be seen as the cause of the other. Nevertheless, change in act/action structures must be considered independently of change in people-structures, even though they are intimately linked.

To understand change both the sources of stability and the sources of modification must be identified.

(a) Change can be discerned only against a background of stability. So it is necessary to identify some invariant properties in the institution or practice we are investigating. The first task will be to examine various possibilities for the location of universals or invariants in social life, in people-structures and in act/action structures.

(b) Having adequately identified what it is that is changing against what it is that is stable, a social analyst is in a position to begin to look for the sources of influence that bring about the changes he has identified.

1. THE SEARCH FOR INVARIANTS

In the course of the early chapters of this study detailed analysis of various reductive theories of social life were undertaken and their limitations exposed. However, they must be considered again in that such theories do offer some hints of possible invariants. I propose to recapitulate briefly the arguments against reductive theories but with the emphasis on possible sources of hypotheses as to social invariants.

(a) Biologically-based Invariants

The biological basis of life has, as we noticed in earlier chapters, been taken by some theorists as the source of a universal theory of social activity, and consequently of social invariants and change.

(i) The simplest such theory holds that there are, built in as it were to human beings, a set of fixed drives, the realization of which is triggered by contact with environmental stimuli. On this view the existence of drives is all that is required to explain the fundamental activities of social life.[1] If there are such drives, they would be invariants. And if they were conserved through all changes one would expect to find them in every society.

Differences in institutions and practices could arise only in the means by which the goals set by drives were realized. But this theory is either trivial or tautological. It is indisputable that every human being from time to time feels thirsty. But the drive to satisfy that bodily need, when it appears as a felt want, comes under the control of a meaning system and thus enters social life only through the meaning it has for members of a particular social group. For example, according to those who adopt a form of social life in which mortification of the flesh is a dominant social good, thirst will be only barely satisfied and on special occasions not satisfied at all. The same is true to an even greater extent of other postulated drives, such as that for dominance, for mating and the like. The drive theory, with respect to the problem of social invariants, is trivial. Alternatively, if every kind of differentiated behaviour is taken as the ground for the postulation of a drive, the drive theory is tautological in the absence of any independent evidence for the existence of such drives. The theory need not detain us.

(ii) Much more important in contemporary social theory is the ethological analogy. It has been argued by many biologists, and even some social theorists, that there are invariant routines in human life in just the way that there are invariant routines in animal life. Human social practices have a biological utility, it is argued, sufficient to justify the claim that the source of these routines is genetically determined. If so they will be invariant through all changes and universal in the species. I shall concern myself now only with the logic of the analogical reasoning which identifies certain forms of human action with the routines of animal life. Cultural elaboration suggests that the likenesses and differences between act/action sequences and animal routines are not alone sufficient to ground an ethological theory. To test the idea the negative and neutral aspects of the analogy must be explored by an independent examination of the human case.[2] It is not a sufficient ground for the claim that, say, the human propensity to defend territory is genetically grounded, that we can demonstrate an analogous pattern of social activity in the life of the robin. It would have to be established that the ordinary processes of social learning of a culturally devised solution to the problem of space-aportionment and the like were *not* operating in the human case, before the ubiquity of the practice of defending the home ground could be arguably grounded in genetics. Secondly, even if it were possible to establish that there were genetic sources for certain human social routines, for example male and female reproductive strategies, the differences in their meaning in different societies raises the problem of the origin of culturally specific social meaning attached to these strategies. Clearly these are unlikely to be explicable in ethological, that is genetic, terms.

But a more fatal objection can be raised to the whole etho-logical analogy programme. Writers on this topic ranging from Lorentz to Morris and Ardrey,[3] have taken for granted that the appropriate analogies are to be sought in the activities of wild animals.[4] Territoriality, ritualization, displacement, agression and so on, have been studied in feral conditions and treated as analogous to human institutions like war, property, defence, urban living and so on. But of course, human beings are not wild animals. They are domesticated by the work of mothers, psychia-trists, priests, policemen, teachers and so on. The appropriate analogies, to my knowledge, have never been explored. No one has asked how closely are those human life practices similar to the life forms of pussy cats, pet dogs, pigs, cows, horses, gerbils, budgerigars and the like. It is to the social psychology of farm animals and pets that we should be looking for useful analogies to sources of the patterns of lives of human kind. And by parity of reasoning these considerations suggest that the forms of life of domesticated animals are much more dependent on those of their human masters than they are on genetic endowment.

The alleged biologically grounded universals I have just con-sidered are all supposedly to be found in social action of various kinds, in the defence of territories, in attacks on the other animals and so on. There is another category of genetically determined features of the social life of animals which might more plausibly be ascribed to the activities of humans. These are the structural invariants ethologists call 'bonds'. As Tiger and Fox have argued[5] there could be genetic programming for various kinds of bonding. There could be a tendency to form male-male bonds, realized for instance in football fan groups. Nor does it seem implausible to assume that the male-female relations of mating and the adult-infant relations of child rearing are genetically grounded. However the evidence for such a claim is at best indirect. Discounting the enormous cultural differentiation and local elaboration of these relations in actual institutions, it could be argued that the ubiquity of the relational structure so revealed is explicable only through the hypothesis of a common genetic endowment. Tiger and Fox use the slow rate of genetic bio-evolution to argue that modern humans have the genetic endowment of their hunter-gatherer ancestors (if indeed such there were). If we suppose that that form of social organization was the last pre-civilized 'natural' life form, and that the bonding relations claimed to be discernible in the social lives of all modern men were adaptive in a biological sense in the hunter-gatherer conditions, there is at least the sketch of an argument.

But however plausible such an argument might be it is not conclusive. Similar patterns and similar relations and structures may be homologous, that is identical both in function and origin. But they may be no more than analogous, similar solutions to similar problems but arrived at and maintained by some quite different mechanism. It is a clever move to promote institutions that affirm the solidarity of any kind of social formation that strengthens the reproductive success of the members of a culture. And male bonding might well be adaptive for hunter-gathers. But as I pointed out in Chapter 1, though men may appear to be both clever and social, it may be that, by nature, they are just clever. They could have invented sociality as the best solution to the problems of living, and as part of sociality the institutions that illustrate and reinforce (in a non-behavioural sense) useful bonds.

In general, then, human biology enters social reality only as it is embedded in a culture. On this view biological phenomena are given specific meanings by members. Perhaps the clearest example of the dominance of culture over biology is the varying interpretations of sickness. Illness is explained on the one hand as a result of an organic defect or infestation and on the other as punishment meted out for some sin. Interestingly, contemporary Western medicine has begun to interpret many forms of sickness as psychosomatic, a theory which is much closer to the idea of illness as punishment for sin than it is to that of organic infestation.[6]

(b) Cognitive Preformation Theory

It seems that the idea of taking the biological basis of life as the source of universal and invariant properties of human social routines and social structures cannot be plausibly sustained. However, recently two theories have been proposed which skirt the issue of biological origins, while at the same time making strong claims for the existence of universal and invariant properties of social forms and social practices. In these theories it is claimed that analyses of certain human activities reveal universal structures which can be explained only by the hypothesis that they reflect fundamental features of the human mind. There are, it is supposed, cognitive preformations which have been realized in the activities identified as structurally alike by the theorists.

(i) Levi-Strauss's theory of the structural basis of human society in a system of binary oppositions in the thinking of all men is a theory of this sort. He argued that certain invariant properties of social practices and the mythological stories associated with them are the surface features which reflect deep binary oppositions in the way the human mind operates. Cultural and tribal differences are to be explained by the idea of cultural *bricolage*. The way a society represents to itself the underlying structure of the human mind which determines its forms, is differentiated by what it has available through historical accident as the material in which to realize these forms.[7] Totemism, for example, is the realization of the logical properties of sets with respect to social groupings in a rhetoric which is derived from the taxonomies of animals, plants and minerals which such societies find essential to their survival. These taxonomies are what a tribe has to hand; they are their bricolage. Though it seems to me that such a theory is philosophically impeccable, I understand that its empirical grounding is now regarded as weak. I shall assume that it would not generally be regarded as an adequate theory of social universals.

(ii) Linguistic studies have recently been the focus of a theory of deep structure which proposes universal and invariant forms underlying the grammar of all human languages. The Chomskean theory of deep structure is not, of course, a theory of the social practice of speaking, but rather of certain invariants which are supposed to be present in the forms that knowledge of language takes in every human being.[8] According to the Chomskean theory, each human being is born with a physiologically grounded apparatus which enables him to selectively receive and learn certain, and only certain, properties of the sound sequences uttered by others. Thus, generation by generation the learning of language appears to repeat certain fundamental forms. The assessment of this theory is really extremely difficult, since it is protected from empirical investigation by a number of subsidiary hypotheses and more particularly by the distinction which locates these universals in knowledge of language rather than in linguistic practice.

However, I take it that the theory is not now widely accepted, either by linguists or by developmental psychologists and we can safely shelve it along with the invariants of Levi-Straussian structural anthropology in the category of 'not proven'.

(c) Ethogenic Universals

Ethogenic theory recognizes three different rule systems and interpretative procedures at work in generating the forms of social life; etiquettes, game-ritual principles or rules, and dramaturgical maxims. No claim is made for the universality of etiquettes since there is every reason for believing that the action sequences which realize social acts in different societies are very different from one another. However, it remains a possibility that there is a range of social acts required to maintain *any* mode of social life as, for example, the acts of binding and loosing people to various kinds of social commitment, the ritual disposal of the dead, the incorporation of strangers and so on. It may be that these acts and others like them are universals. However, such a theory is empirical and it would need to be shown that every society depended for its creation and maintenance upon just such social acts. It is by no means certain that that has been established. At best, it remains as a possibility. The third kind of regularity, the dramaturgical, the compendium of social roles or ways of presenting oneself as a certain social persona, seems rather unlikely to be universal. Some widespread categorial differentiations have been identified by Argyle and Little[9] in their study of the personas displayed by middle-class people in different situations. There seem to be corresponding differentiations recognized among the Japanese. There seem to be four or five well-differentiated and socially distinct modes of presentation of a person, depending upon whether a person is acting among close family or distant family, strangers or intimates, officials or friends. Again, though these are possible universals, it is by no means clear that a sufficient empirical grounding has been provided for them.

The upshot, then, is a cautious rejection of all the *a priori* theories of invariants that have so far been proposed, since they are either manifestly defective, for logical and conceptual reasons, as we have seen with the drives theory, or they lack empirical support, as seems to be the case with cognitive preformation theories. Or the empirical support available is suggestive, but by no means conclusive, as in ethogenic theories. We must turn now to a more promising line of investigation, namely the attempt to show what sort of conditions would lead to the postulation of some form of social universal.

(d) Compensating Changes as Signs of an Invariant

Instead of arguing *a priori* for certain kinds of social universals or invariants, and then examining social institutions and practices to try to find them, an alternative strategy is to look at changing practices and changing institutions to see if in the transformations that actually occur, social universals can be discerned. If one kind of change is generally associated with another kind of change and the former can be seen to be compensated for by the latter, then it may be plausible to propose as an invariant the relation and practice or attitude or whatever which has been preserved by means of the compensating changes.

(i) Male/female as an invariant in recent fashion changes

The example I shall consider is the contemporary women's movement. I understand this as a parallel and linked series of changes in social practices and social theories which has been marked by a sharp alteration in the way in which certain spokeswomen have accounted for the form of social practices and social institutions involving women. This can be seen particularly in the transformation of female accounting by the introduction of a political rhetoric. Women have come to speak of their sex as a social class, and of their relationship to men as class-exploitation. This change in accounting techniques and resources has been paralleled by a rapid change in fashion, that is in the clothes, hairstyles and other accoutrements by which men and women are symbolically differentiated as male and female. As I shall argue we are dealing here with two distinct but related processes. The change in fashion has, at first sight, a paradoxical air, in that while there has been a shift to 'unisex' clothing in which men and women dress in very similar garments, there have been other changes which amplify sexual differences.

These changes can be understood as compensatory movements around a social invariant, the male/female difference. Before the current fashion changes began the differences between men and women were visibly marked by differences in tertiary properties, such as distinctive clothing, and distinctive ways of dressing the hair. The association of particular tertiary properties with this or that sex is clearly arbitrary. But since these associations are matters of historical origin it perhaps would be misleading to speak of them as conventions.

The obliteration of tertiary distinctions in the new fashions has come about through the adoption of men's clothing by women and women's hair styles by men. The traditional sign system for marking the sexes as distinct has become much diminished. If the male/female distinction was functioning as a social invariant we would expect compensating changes to occur in other presentational possibilities to restore the representation of the difference. This is indeed just what we find. As hair styles become more and more similar so beards and moustaches become more and more prominent. Secondary differentia take over the role of social markers from tertiary. Unisex clothing becomes tighter to allow basic anatomical differences to show through. And the abandonment of the brassière by certain women served to amplify the noticeability of the female bosom. In these latter ways primary differentia were emphasized as markers. The nett effect of the changes has been to preserve the capability for immediate recognition of the sex of most other human beings. The presentational ambiguities of tertiary marking, exploited by transvestites and homosexuals, have been reconstituted in secondary and even in pseudo-primary differentia.

At the same time the revival of traditional women's clothing, particularly long skirts and Victorian styles, serves to re-emphasize the traditional female role and to illustrate as sharply as possible the social differentiation of men from women. The value of the traditional role is illustrated, for those who hold to it, by an exaggeration of traditional tertiary markers.

How is this to be understood? We are concerned in this example with two universals: the universal differential male/female which is a purely biological invariant and the social invariant, namely the differentiation man/woman as social identities. The shift in rhetoric which tends to blunt the distinctions between men and women is compensated by a change in fashion which, by emphasizing the male/female difference restores the man/woman universal.

(ii) Expressive practices and accounting rhetorics

It is possible to state a general principle which lies behind the analysis I have just proposed. Compensating changes will occur on two planes, that is a change in accounting resources and modes will be compensated for by a change in expressive modes so as to preserve a social universal.

The most important man/woman institution is that of marriage or some informal equivalent, having similar stability. It is possible to trace distinct differences in the theory of marriage simply by examining the image of marriage in popular songs. In the 1940s, in what one might call the Sinatra era, marriage is represented in popular music as a trap set by women for men, so that they will be supported in idleness by men's work. In contemporary accounting, in what one might describe as the Greer era, popular music hardly mentions marriage at all and the relationships between men and women are differently identified. But the women's liberation rhetoric treats marriage in the Greer era as a trap set for women by men so that they will get sexual mates, domestic help and so on at the cheapest possible rates.

It is also important to notice that in some cases the compensating changes occur in different institutions. The institution that seems to have brought about the change in rhetoric and accounting modes is what one might call the intellectual-journalistic establishment, since those changes occurred by means of the publication of books, the writing of articles and so on. The compensating change in fashion, which preserves the man/woman universal as an invariant, is brought about by the inventions and reactions to demand of the artistic-fashion establishment. Though distinct, these institutions are linked, particularly through journalism. One could identify here an interesting sociological problem, which it would not be too difficult to solve, namely how are these compensating changes brought about? How does the link operate?

2. THE LOCATION OF CHANGE

(a) Practices

Theoretically there are a limited range of categories of possible social change. Broadly speaking social interactions can be divided into the instrumental, co-ordinated activities bringing social and material products into existence; and the self-presentational where the outcome is a step up or down in public reputation and moral career. Leaving aside material production and concentrating only on social activities which have social ends, the core of social episodes can be found in sequences of public actions in the course of which social acts are performed. Readers may like to be reminded that by 'acts' I mean events which have distinctive social

L. I. H. E.
THE BECK LIBRARY
WOOLTON ROAD, LIVERPOOL L16 8ND

meanings, such as insults, marriages, convictions, cementations of friendships and so on, and by 'actions' the locally accepted conventionally associated ways by which acts such as the above are performed. We can now lay out the range of changes that could occur in small-scale social interactions.

(i) A new convention might appear associating a different action with the same act: for instance, there has been a systematic change in the titles of respect used to perform acts of social deference; while arguably the acts have remained stable.

(ii) Sometimes the same action is performed as heretofore, but it is now understood as the performance of a rather different act. For instance a modern industrial strike can no longer be regarded as a protest against economic exploitation, but seems to be the performance of a self-presentational drama publicly emphasizing workers' power and dignity.

(iii) A more complex kind of change can occur when a novel act/action structure appears but the social microstructure that it generates seems to be much the same as that generated by the old act/action sequence which has been superseded. A contemporary example seems to be the spread of common law marriage, where the institution that is created is much like the old, but the ritual steps leading to its establishment are different.

Similar kinds of change can occur in presentational activities. Changes occur in the acceptable range of personas and characters admitted as legitimate and proper presentations in a society. These are often accompanied by changes in the stylistic and symbolic devices by which they are publicly displayed. So we find the same persona/character presented in different ways at different times. Sometimes different personas are presented with what seem to be traditional devices, while there may be changes in both.

And of course, along with these go changes in the accounting resources and the conventions that govern the selection of material that can be brought forward for use on accounting occasions. A splendid example of this kind of change is the growth of the use of Freudian and pseudo-Freudian concepts in accounting, the spread of which has been studied by Moscovici.

We must take account too of changes in the practical order. These could be called changes in techniques.

(b) Changes in Institutions

Institutions, considered as complexes of people-structures and admissible social practices, characteristically exhibit two life forms.

There is an overlife, the realization in those structures and practices of the official theory of the institution. That theory appears in a rhetoric for speaking of the activities of the overlife. But the human demands of the expressive order, originally nicely linked to the practical order as set forth in the official rhetoric, soon lead to the appearance of an underlife. Within this alternative social order there are moral careers for those for whom the overlife provides little opportunity for advancement. I take this duality to be the normal condition of institutions.

We can look for change in two dimensions. There may be changes in the practical order as improvements (or indeed mere changes) are made in the techniques by which the tasks of the practical order are accomplished. These may infect the expressive order by bringing about changes in the official moral career structure, by leading to the introduction of new role positions and so on. This kind of thing can be sensed in the turmoil produced by the mere proposal to appoint worker-directors to the boards of management of companies. But more inexorable by far are the changes that occur as the demands of the expressive orders of both overlife and underlife come to be felt more and more strongly. Soon they begin to dominate the motivations of members of the institution. This too will, in its turn, be reflected in the practical order, leading to routinization and formalization of the tasks which it demands. And sometimes the point may be reached when there is no more than an empty simulacrum of a real task performance.

(c) Social Change in Collectives

After the searching criticisms of sociological method, particularly concerning the social construction of 'data', by Douglas, Brenner and others, it has become clear that no method is available for the empirical study of the properties of very large aggregates of people in interaction. It seems unlikely that in the foreseeable future any such studies could be made. If we cannot have knowledge of global properties, then it follows that we have no direct knowledge of any changes that may occur in those properties. At most we can infer that some change in the background of human social action has occurred from the kind of evidence which is available, namely observable social behaviour and decipherable social interpretation and theorizing. This suggests that:

(i) We should regard statements about large-scale phenomena, particularly statements about alleged systems such as the economic organization of a culture, and about structures, such as the alleged structure of 'classes', as hypotheses which can be tested only indirectly by testing for the truth of their consequences.

(ii) In the absence of any theory as to how such properties and processes and structures could affect day-to-day practices and the workings of man-sized institutions, these features of social life, if indeed they exist at all, must be treated as an environment which acts as a selection condition for those social activities which we do manage for ourselves. This immediately suggests an evolutionary perspective to the understanding of social change, somewhat in the Darwinian style.

(iii) But, as Bhaskar has argued, the macroproperties of large social groups of men in interaction should be regarded not as the properties of some mysterious supra-individual but as the properties of a network of interpersonal relations. It follows that the properties of such networks are some function of the properties of the interpersonal relations. It does not follow from this observation that the networks can have no emergent properties. It is very likely that they do. Nevertheless there is likely to be some kind of causal influence running from changes in the properties of small-scale interactions and man-sized institutions to the network. It also seems obvious, though I know of no serious empirical study of the matter, that some small-scale changes will have no effect on the network. For instance, provided the external relations of nuclear families are conserved or stabilized, the macrostructure could tolerate great internal changes in family organization.

The focus of empirical studies of change must then be on the changes in small-scale interactions that can be studied by adequate empirical methods. This is not to advocate methodological individualism. The institutional structures and small-scale practices of men in association are through and through social, as I have argued throughout this work.

3. THEORETICAL STANDPOINTS

Several different kinds of mechanisms of social change have been proposed. There are at least the historicist, the dialectic and the evolutionary. Each has different consequences for social psychology, since each supposes different relations of the individual and private aspects of human functioning to the public and social co-ordinative products of human action. I shall be arguing that so diverse are the various components of the mechanisms of social change that an adequate theory must draw upon both dialectical and evolutionary schemata.

I shall use the term 'historicist' rather more restrictedly than most commentators, confining it to the description of those theories that postulate mechanisms by which the future state of an institution or practice is causally generated by some linear sequence of events deriving from a past condition of the society within which the institution or practice occurs. The difficulties with historicist theories are not only to be found in failure to turn up any convincing cases of linear social causality, but in the philosophical assumptions involved in the very conception of such kinds of explanation. I shall not take the matter any further here.[10]

The theoretical scheme I shall be building up in the following chapters depends on a judicious blending of the remaining general theories of social change, the dialectic and the evolutionary. As I shall understand them, dialectical processes have a preliminary stage with the building up of some kind of tension, while the overall structure remains stable. Change occurs through processes which release or resolve the tension to reach a new state of stability. Contrary to the grand theorists of the German tradition I shall be finding the proper place for dialectical explanations in the understanding of change in rather small-scale social formations and practices, where individual members can have some hazy recognition of the tension. After all, in this work I am trying to locate the social psychological processes and not to solve the great traditional problems of sociology! But dialectic resolution of tensions is not enough to explain social change. An evolutionary, mutation/selection, populational dimension must be added. With its help it becomes possible to think of small-scale changes spreading or failing to spread through a relatively stable social environment, of relatively unknown properties, as those changes lead to more or less well-adapted new practices, institutions, styles of person presentation and so on.

(a) The Material Dialectic

Any conceptual system one could develop for formulating theories of social change must prove itself against the most powerful incumbent in the field — dialectical materialism. I shall be using a simplified and to some extent caricatured version of that theory as a foil, taken from *The German Ideology*. I presume that it is widely agreed that this form of the theory does not represent Marx's mature thought. Nevertheless it is based upon some of

Marx's most fundamental principles, and its central weakness is present throughout the more sophisticated theories he developed.[11]

For the purpose of my exposition, the theory can be schematically represented as in Fig. 5.

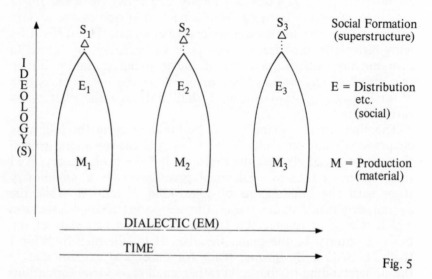

Fig. 5

The dynamic relations in the theory are confined to the base structures and evolve, according to the dialectic process, along the timeline. Social formations are not in causal relation one with another but are generated synchronically with the help of ideologies which I take in the strict sense of Marx. That is they are folk theories of the social world at least some of whose propositions, if examined from a point of view lying outside the social superstructures, can be seen to be strictly speaking false.

Difficulties

There are several difficulties with this form of dialectical theory, difficulties of which Marx himself seems sometimes to have been aware. There is a difficulty of locating a standpoint within or without the system from which ideologies will be revealed as such, since successive social formations are not perfect reflections of the EM base. This difficulty is exacerbated by the fact that social science itself must be part of the process of genesis and maintenance of social formations. I do not propose to consider this problem further, nor to comment on Marx' or other people's attempts at a solution.

For my purposes I want to point to the difficulties inherent in any such a theory that derives from its causal structure with respect to time. The mechanism of change involves two kinds of linear causal relations. There is the material dialectic which changes the social system of production and there are the processes by which transformations occurring at the material or base level throw off social formations. There are serious difficulties in this form of the theory. The explanatory structure lacks a psychology. No account is given of the mechanism by which the relevant characteristics of the system of distribution, production and exchange can generate the concepts, the attitudes, the beliefs in members, from which the superstructure as a system of public social practices and theoretically grounded institutions could derive.[12] A further difficulty concerns the nature of the objects which are thought to constitute the total entity with which we are concerned and to be in causal interaction. In this version of dialectical theory these are collective supra-individuals. So a change of social formations, which might be thought of as the real end of political activity, must be accomplished by transforming entities which have this trans-individual ontological status. Attractive though this theory might look at first sight, since it seems to identify a plausible causal mechanism and has certain satisfying emotional qualities, it will not do as a general theory of social change and political action, since it lacks a psychology. However, it provides a valuable foil against which other theories can be tested.

(b) Dialectic cum Evolutionary Processes

It may be that more than one independent and basic 'mechanism' of social change will turn out to be demonstrably at work in society. So the philosophical effort called for in designing conceptual systems with which to formulate theories explaining actual occasions of change may have to extend to devising quite massive alternatives with criteria for their differential application.

What alternatives are possible? I will develop, with examples, a case for the *a priori* presumption that either or both of two distinctive forms of historical process are possible, each with an appropriate schema, in which the components to be discovered are clearly represented. These are the dialectical and the populational; changes brought about by the need to resolve tensions, and changes brought about by the selective elimination of maladaptive types of practices, institutions and so on.

I identify the main location of dialectical tension elsewhere from where Marx thought it developed. The overall theme of this work has been the independence but interaction of the expressive and practical orders of society, and their differing relations in different historical conditions. The independence of the orders admits of the possibility of their differential development, the one lagging behind the other bringing the total social order 'out of "sync."' so to speak.

The most general form of dialectical tension, that is tension likely to lead to compensating changes, will be where people perceive their location in one of the orders as incompatible with their position in the other. An aristocratic who resents his poverty, and a rich and powerful woman who resents the ritual patronizing she receives from weaker men, will do as exemplars. When there are numbers of similar people in a society, and perhaps most of all when they are not a mere aggregate but form some simple kind of collective, then we can expect the tensions to be resolved in social change. We have already explored a small-scale and specific form of the tension in the microsocial analysis of the situations that define scenes. Let us call this the E/P dynamic.

Populational theories depend on the separation of the mutation-conditions, that is the conditions that lead to imperfect replication of the properties of successive members of a lineage, and selection-conditions, that is the conditions which favour the replication of one or another alternative form within a lineage. Populational theories of change are, of course, more clearly exemplified in the Darwinian theory of organic evolution. Let us call the general conceptual system of which particular Darwinian theories of the change of particular species are instantiations, the M/S dynamics. It is worth emphasizing that even in biological applications the M/S conceptual system is not an axiomatic super theory from which, as intermediate level deductive consequences, explanations of particular changes flow. Rather the propositions and iconic models of the Darwinian 'theory' serve to define the system of concepts and acceptable modes of explanation that will be used in different particular forms and in different concrete applications in the construction of explanations of particular changes. In biological contexts the M/S conceptual system does not have an uncontroversial, univocal application. In considering the legitimacy of borrowings from it, it will be necessary to discriminate amongst the various M/S conceptual systems to identify a model source precisely enough to examine its viability as a basis for the construction of concepts.

What reasons might one have for borrowing some suitable version of the M/S system for instantiating explanations of social change? The reasons are of rather different force.

(i) Difficulties with theories of social change, such as that of Marx, are most pressing in the formulation of an adequate account of possible processes that might generate or produce changes in social practices, customs and forms of social theorizing. Furthermore, without an adequate theory of what might be the processes linking, say, economic change with change in practices seemingly remote from the practical order, it seems insuperably difficult to explain the tendency that many changes seem to have towards social practices that are more adaptive to the conditions in which they have come to flourish than those they have displaced. The major virtue of the M/S system of concepts for me is that it allows the formulation of explanations involving the achievement of adaptiveness without any positive causation, that is without a teleology.

(ii) The impasse besetting contemporary sociology, consequent on the failure to devise an adequate empirical procedure for discovering the macro-properties of large collectives of people, would be a serious bar to the understanding of the processes of social change, if we were forced to adopt the sort of approach advocated by Durkheim. That is we would have to explain one unknown social fact in terms of its Humean concomitance to another. Observable changes in social habits, practices and institutions would be consequential on changes in the macroproperties of societies, such as are represented in the values assigned to demographic variables. But if we consider the macroproperties of a collective of people as a selection environment, it can be taken to have differential effects on different innovatory social practices effective in a Darwinian fashion, augmenting or diminishing the population of such practices in the next time-phase of that society. In short we can admit its existence and efficacy without our having to be paralyzed by our ignorance of any but its simplest properties.

16

SOCIAL CHANGE: CASES AND CAUSES

ANTICIPATORY SUMMARY

Introduction: socio-dialectic and socio-evolutionary explanatory frameworks both necessary for a social psychology of social change.

1. Examples of the use of a socio-dialectical explanatory format
   (a) Women's movements 1: changes in the practical order in tension with a stable expressive order.
   (b) Women's movements 2: changes in the expressive order in tension with a stable practical order.
   (c) The transformation of closed institutions: the decline of the practical order with the elaboration of the expressive order.
2. Socio-evolution
   (a) General theory: M/S explanatory formats. Comparison between bio-evolution and socio-evolution at the level of general M/S theory:
       (i) location of change points;
       (ii) mapping of individual/collective distinction onto mutation/selection environment distinction;
       (iii) the Darwinian-Lamarckian spectrum;
       (iv) the social consequences of studying anthropology and history.
   (b) Specific theories: R/I explanatory frameworks:
       (i) logical structure of evolutionary theories;
       (ii) metaphysical issues raised by the foregoing analysis;
       (iii) the problem of replicator identity;
       (iv) transfer of concepts: socio-evolution as parallel to gene-selection;
       (v) examination of the negative analogy.
   (c) The limits of change in mechanisms of change.
   (d) Social adaptiveness.
3. Problem: change in macrostructures and the structure of society
   (a) Law making as the registration rather than the cause of social change.
   (b) The internal properties of collectives:
       (i) conditions for continuity and change;
       (ii) the collective as its own selection environment.

INTRODUCTION

Two analytically distinct explanatory frameworks have emerged from the critical discussion of the last chapter – the socio-dialectical and the populational or evolutionary. In this chapter I shall elaborate each format, and illustrate its application. In many cases both formats would need to be applied to yield a full understanding of the appearance of a novel social phenomenon or the disappearance of an old one.

I must emphasize again that my object in this work is not to provide or to defend a sociology. I draw on what I take to be scientifically respectable and conceptually adequate sociology only to help to identify social psychological problems – how are individuals able to create social institutions as we know them?

1. EXAMPLES OF THE USE OF A
SOCIO-DIALECTICAL EXPLANATORY FORMAT

(a) Women's Movements 1

In my analysis I follow social commentators such as Shirley Ardener,[1] in distinguishing between Women's Rights Movements within the practical order, and Women's 'Lib' Movements within the expressive order. The Women's Movements of recent years represent, I will argue, various attempts to resolve a dialectical tension created by perceived incongruities between the expressive order representing the place and role of women in society in relation to men and children, and the practical order of work, professional opportunities and so on. We should notice that these orders, like everything else in social life that we separate analytically, intersect and interact. For instance, some of the pressure from women to enter certain professions is likely to be explicable in terms of the expressive advantage of being seen to be in that profession rather than any consuming interest in the practical tasks to be performed. There is no reason to suppose that women's motivation is so very different from that of men.

When the expressive and practical orders are out of synchronization anomalous occasions arise. For instance, the old expressive order would require a man to pay for both his own and his woman companion's meal, even if both were earning the same salary in identical jobs – or to run around and open the door for a woman olympic athlete or world champion tennis player so that she could descend from a car.

In the example under consideration the expressive order

represents a range of self-presentations appropriate to an older practical order and manifestly lags behind changes in that order. The processes by which these changes were brought about might have to be explained by reference to yet another explanation format, for instance Marx's material dialectic. In cases like the above there is no certainty as to how the perceived tension or incongruity will be resolved. In the case of the contemporary Women's Movements there has been a vivid attempt to promulgate a new expressive order, even in advance of the final realization of the changing practical order. At the same time there has been a complementary effort by many women to halt the practical revolution (which they take to be demeaning to their choice of lives of domestic virtue), expressively rendered in the cultivation of the traditional womanly arts, and even by a return to Victorian styles of clothing.

The power of the socio-dialectical explanatory format can be tested by using it to try to explain a very puzzling feature of the women's liberation movement, namely why it should have developed mainly in the United States. Prior to the spread of the associated rhetoric and accounting theory, American social life was marked by the influence and power of women. This was exercised both in social matters and in the control of the economy through the differential ownership of stock in most companies and banks acquired simply through alimony and longevity. The power was usually exercised indirectly through male puppets. Our general principles would lead us to expect that a change would occur to bring the expressive practices of social life into conformity with the practical order. On this view, the Women's Liberation Movement (as distinct from the movement for Women's Rights) represents a felt disparity between actual power and the dramaturgical acknowledgment and ceremonial affirmation of that power in a suitable rhetoric and recognizable symbols, for use in public.

In this case the public ceremonial, dramaturgical affirmation of felt power, at least in the form that the movement has developed, has transformed the original, indirectly exercised power and, ironically, has lessened it. In particular, in the old form of marriage, women were the dominant partners, but by demanding expressive equality, they have in fact improved the practical position of men. In sum, women like other people, prefer the shadow of power to its substance.

The Women's Liberation Movement has introduced a change in

the rhetoric within which the institution of marriage, motherhood and so on are to be expressively represented. In the 1940s Frank Sinatra could sing of marriage as the 'tender trap' — referring to that institution as a device by which women secured the man whose work in the practical and public order they could exploit. Marriage, in this rhetoric, is a sinecure. The new political rhetoric (first proposed so far as I know as long ago as the mid-nineteenth century by Frederick Engels[2]), encapsulates a rather different picture of marriage, indeed almost a perfect negative of the traditional picture. As summed up by Germaine Greer, the new picture represents marriage as 'the relegation of women to the status of supermenials enacting vicarious leisure', a reference to the role of women in producing a simulacrum of the conspicuous display identified by Veblen as the mark of the leisure class.[3]

The development of a new rhetoric and a consequential transformation of the expressive order has emerged in the experiencing of yet another tension between the actual success of the Women's Rights Movement ('So long as everyone is paid the same for the same job and women can get mortgages and checking accounts, I don't care'[4]) and the preservation of a rhetoric and the trappings of an expressive order that represents the old social relations of indirectly exercised power. In the old order, at least in the United States, women, it could be argued, enjoyed substantially greater economic and social power than men through control of the family and the home. I believe that it was this power whose direct representation was the covert aim of the first phase of the Women's Liberation Movement, as distinct from that concerned with women's rights.

In their *Too Many Women*, Secord and Guttentag suggest a demographic factor in the genesis of the original tension, so far unexplained.[5] They demonstrate that in conditions where the number of females actually available as partners for suitable males is large relative to the number of such males, changes in attitudes to marriage and sexual relations in both male and female valuations of the female are to be found. In these conditions 'women's movements' appear. Secord and Guttentag use demographic data. They base their conclusions upon correlations of the demographic conditions and the public visibility and institutional representation of women's expressive demands. The historical ubiquity of the phenomenon suggests the search for a causal mechanism. We might find it by imposing a primarily evolutionary explanatory format in two complementary phases. At the level of individual behaviour the format would produce a theory like this: men, always liable to be promiscuous, find that when there is a superabundance of females they can get away with changing partners more often than they could before. Many women experience these individual abandonments and betrayals as in conflict with the dominant expressive order, which emphasizes a protective and supportive attitude as proper for men to show to women. And so the dialectic begins to develop as a psychological phenomenon. And once set going the separation of a successful Women's Rights Movement becomes the source of a secondary dialectic tension with the revision of the old expressive order demanded by Women's Liberation.[6]

Within this combination of populational (evolutionary) and dialectic formats there is no difficulty in understanding how a demographic condition could have power to generate individual choices of behaviour and attitude, since the changing demographic condition merely favours an existing male behavioural tendency, experienceable by women.

But the evolutionary format can be reapplied at a collective level of analysis. Secord and Guttentag point out that the spread of an innovatory rhetoric to become a movement can be explained by seeing the history of these matters as the intersection of two cycles somewhat out of synchronization. There is always somewhere or other an incipient women's movement, and it rises and declines in intensity according to causal processes which are presently unknown. But it will only become a movement and lead to changes in the social world generally if it is on the rise, so to speak, at a time when the demographic cycle of changing proportions of men to women has reached a point where there are more women than men at the appropriate age. The demographic cycle serves as a changing selection environment for repeated mutations in the perception by women of their role in the social world.

The social psychological problems in this theory can be defined in terms of the three-fold questions: perception? motivation? action? Secord and Guttentag propose a theory of social perception — namely that individual women perceive the demographic conditions in the behaviour of men — men, fulfilling the reproductive strategy typical of males. Motivational resources and action templates derive from the contemporary rhetorics. People draw on what there is currently available to theorize about their situations — as they perceive it.

(b) Women's Movements 2

To explain independent change in the expressive order Shirley
Ardener has developed another aspect of the possibility of independent expressive motivations. She distinguishes between Women's
Rights Movements, that have to do with real (or practical) exploitation, and Women's 'Lib' Movements, which have to do with
expressive matters. She takes these to be traditionally publicly
represented in the conventions surrounding the treatment of masculinity and femininity. Contrary to the reciprocal character of
the traditional expressive modes, the Women's 'Lib' Movement is
concerned with the promulgation of a special nature conception.
The essential attributes of womanhood, physical, spiritual and
moral appear in a specifically female model. This model or ideal
type of womanhood in its expressive manifestations is not related
to the traditional conception of the expressive aspects of masculinity. She uses Coleridge's word 'femineity' for the model of
womanhood the new expressive order is supposed to represent.

In traditional sex-role identity there is a complementary relationship between the properties of men and the properties of
women as social beings, and these are represented in the conventions that determine the expressive order. The Women's 'Lib'
Movement looks for an expressive mode which is independent
of that complementarity. However powerful equilibrating principles have come into operation along with the rise of the rhetoric
and expressive practices that represent femineity. These have
led to the complex folding and refolding back of the traditional
practical and expressive orders that I have described in the preceding chapter.

Finally it is worth noticing that, as a programme, the Women's
'Lib' Movement is an example of image radicalism. It was an
attempt to promote a different public face, so to speak, rather
than an attempt to promulgate a different system of means/ends
practices in the social order of work. But the movement was
notable for representing its image radicalism as an instrumental or
practical radicalism, through the adopting of a Marxist rhetoric.[7]
It is only by a careful analysis that the underlying form of the
revolutionary proposal can be seen for what it is.

(c) The Transformation of Closed Institutions

In the analyses which follow we shall be concerned with institutions and societies as complexes of people-structures and action-
structures. The relations between people are illustrated and

confirmed in the performances of social practices by which social acts and practical tasks are carried out. To understand what happens we shall be depending upon the distinction between instrumental and expressive aspects of all the activities characteristic of this or that institution.

The simplest entity with which we could be concerned is the closed institution, such as a religious order, a hospital, an army and so on. In a closed institution the people-structure is transparently related to the social practices of the institution as Goffman and others have amply demonstrated. However, we have good reason to believe that a closed institution develops over time in a way which can only be understood against the background of a distinction between the practical activities represented in the official theory of the institution, and expressive activities which are concerned with moral careers, respect and contempt among inmates, and the public presentation of selves. To understand this we shall have to take the dramaturgical point of view. At this point it is worth recapitulating the principle that a closed institution tends to develop in such a way that the activities which are the realization of the official theory of that institution become formalized and empty. They are replaced, *in the attention of the members* of the institution, by expressive activities, which unless checked, tend to become the major mode of action in that institution. That is, the activities by which selves are created and sustained in public reputation become the main focus of attention, and practical activities are undertaken only in so far as they contribute to reputation. Surgeons sometimes undertake operations more to exhibit their skill than in the best interests of the patient. The continuous working of the principle which transfers interest and attention from the practical order to the expressive will finally lead an institution, if it survives long enough, into a state in which practical activities are rarely and perfunctorily performed and most act/action structures are directed towards presentation of selves. The University of Oxford in the eighteenth century, the Turkish learned hierarchy, the bureaucracy of Czarist Russia, and other such institutions, are examples of cases where the institution survived long enough for the transformation to the dominance of expressive motivations to be almost complete.

Of course, in looking at the history of closed institutions we need to bear in mind that they are embedded in a larger and more variegated society, from which reformatory influences, that is influences which tend to restore the importance of the practical activity, can be brought to bear upon the institution. However, if a whole society or nation takes on the form of a closed institution, then it will transform itself, according to this principle, in such a way that the practical activities of the production of wealth, the defence of the realm, and so on, become empty, and society falls into corruption. In particular, its bureaucracy becomes simply an institution for personal display. Such societies have not been unknown in human history.

But what is it that is responsible for the operation of this principle of change? I have already argued that the relationship between this principle and the psychology of human beings is close in that it is 'in the nature of man' to seek reputation, to look for respect and to demand its ritual affirmation. Why should this be so seems to me to be a problem to be solved only by speculative paleoanthropology since I think we are unlikely to discover an explanation in the historical record. That record, so far as I know it, seems to describe a species which has lived its life in very similar ways over seven or eight millennia.

2. SOCIO-EVOLUTION IN GENERAL

(a) General Theory: M/S Explanatory Formats

Some novel practices spread, that is are copied by lots of people and are adopted as one of their habits or customs or institutions; some do not. This is the general framework of the populational account of social change. At least two matters of philosophical interest are implicit in this simple formulation.

By what criteria do we identify and individuate practices and consequentially of what is the 'population' formed?

The fact of differential spread calls for explanation. The concept that suggests itself is the relative adaptiveness of practices to the social conditions in which they appear. What might be meant by 'social adaptiveness'? By what range of criteria would a judgement of more or less adaptiveness be made? The possibilities are broad, and we must consider social, psychological and biological aspects of the matter. I shall return to a detailed discussion of these issues below.

Before considering the details of the bio-evolution/socio-evolution parallel, relative to the borrowing of the more detailed conceptual apparatus, there are some differences to be remarked upon at the most general level of the transfer of the bare M/S scheme; particularly that the M/S scheme has univocal application to the understanding of bio-evolution, but admits of several variants in application to socio-evolution. Three important cases of this form of difference need to be remarked before we turn to examine detailed parallels.

(i) Location of change points

For the most part bio-evolution maps change and stability onto the individual/environment distinction. In consequence mutation conditions have their point of effectiveness at individuals (though individuals at which level of analysis is a point of dispute to which we shall be obliged to return). In general selection-conditions are identified with a relatively stable environment. Biologists do, however, recognize cases where more or less the same mutant appears many times, while its spread waits upon a change of environment. This is to reverse the mapping of the change/non-change distinction, *at a higher level*, since each repetition of the 'same' mutation is a departure from the form of its immediate predecessor in the lineage.

But in socio-evolution the mapping of change/stability onto the M/S conditions is as likely to require repetition of the same mutation awaiting suitable conditions to appear as to work at the lowest level of mutant individual practices in stable social (economic, geographical etc.) environments. The British coal strikes of 1926 and 1972 meet enough of certain rather weak conditions of qualitative identity to be treated as repetitions of the same mutant practice. But the socio-economic conditions aborted the spread of worker hegemony from the 1926 mutant, while the very different socio-economic conditions of 1972 favoured, or at the very least did not impede, their rapid ramification through society.

(ii) Mapping of individual/collective distinction onto mutation/ selection environment distinction

A distinction easily confused with the one just elaborated is that between evolutionary explanations in which the mutant is individual and the selection conditions collective, and those in which the selection conditions are individual and the mutant collective. This is quite simply inadmissible in biology and, I would argue, is a conceptual confusion. But it could be held that it is a possible reading of certain social phenomena. Fashion often follows the Darwinian model, an innovation appearing in whatever is individual, for example Mary Quant's miniskirt, the first Punk band

and so on, and the environment within which such an innovation must spread is formed from the expressive and practical order of some contemporary collective.

But consider attempts by African governments to introduce new economic structures requiring novel practices from farmers. The failure of these collectively promulgated innovations to spread could be put down to the individual intransigence of each farmer. With respect to a personal property like 'intransigence' or 'conservatism' farmers are a mere aggregate of individuals.

Objections to treating these cases as distinct might be raised on two points.

(a) it is not clear that the innovatory reform programme is 'ontologically' a collective property, if the conservatism of the farmers is not. At least as it comes to affect a nation's farmers it has to be promulgated in the form of lessons from individual agronomic experts, particularized notices and regulations, and personal readings and consultations.

(b) Nor is it clear that the natural kind, 'farmer', could be instantiated in individuals defined wholly in terms of external relations, that is as a mere aggregate of individuals. Lukes has argued fairly convincingly that there are no categories of persons whose members could be individuals of that sort.

It might be that cases of this kind are more aptly treated as Durkheimian conjunctions of social facts than inverted Darwinian selective elimination of variants. So treated they could be subjected to analysis into a structural network of individual interactions in the manner proposed by Bhaskar.

Neither case so far cited serves to make an uncontroversial and absolute distinction between bio- and socio-evolution.

(iii) The Darwinian-Lamarckian spectrum

In advocating an M/S type of conceptual system for formulating explanations of social change we are not confined to a purely Darwinian form of explanation. Provided mutation conditions and selection conditions are both analytically and existentially distinct a continuum of M/S explanation schemata can be defined with respect to the degree of causal coupling between the two kinds of conditions.[8] In a Darwinian schema-type M-conditions and S-conditions are absolutely causally independent. In the present state of biology I take it that all explanations of organic change are strictly Darwinian. In other fields Popper has required an exclusive use of Darwinian schemata. But in a Lamarckian schema-type M-conditions and S-conditions interact causally in such a way that they are mutually dependent. Lamarckian schemata are still populational schemata, though the mutual causal influence between M-conditions and S-conditions ensures that indeed the mutant forms will soon necessarily dominate the population provided the environment remains more or less stable.

But between the pure forms of these explanation-types there are indefinitely many M/S schemata differing in the degree of coupling between mutation and selection conditions. In application to the explanation of social change we must admit the possibility of some degree of coupling between M and S conditions.

This means that we should expect people to conceive innovations, not merely by random reshuffling of their knowledge, beliefs, rules of conduct, habits, social practices and customs, but by deliberate design in the light of the conditions that the creative and rebellious amongst the people anticipate will occur. Further, in a record-keeping society experience of the fate of previous attempts at innovation can be retained and fed into the later processes by which M-conditions and S-conditions interact. In short, change in societies with collective memories will tend to become actually more and more Lamarckian, though we have no reason to suppose that knowledge will ever accumulate to the extent that the process will become Lamarckian in fully coupled form.

In differentially drawing on different M/S schemata socio-evolution is in a quite different case from populational theory in the biological context. Here we seem to have a distinction of profound consequence between the M/S conceptual scheme as applied in different fields.

Table 2   *Summary*

Type of Theory	Relation of Conditions
Darwinian	M independent of S
Early human social conditions	M weakly coupled to S
**************	*****************
Later human social conditions	M strongly coupled to S
Lamarckian	(i) M coupled to S (ii) S coupled to M

When M is coupled to S in a commercial enterprise we have the phenomenon of market research, in which the design of a product is determined by beliefs about the state of the market. But when S is coupled to M we have advertising in which the selection conditions or market is manipulated to favour the spread of a predetermined M.

Any relatively Darwinian view is required to deal with an apparent paradox. Evolutionary theories are offered as explanations of the changes in collectives, as rivals to the Durkheimian type of theory, which supposes that a social fact can be changed by altering another social fact. *A fortiori* the organic model, as a strictly Darwinian theory, offers no account whatever about the way in which selection conditions can change mutation conditions and be changed by them. So, if a weak Darwinian theory is offered anywhere on the spectrum between the Darwinian and Lamarckian extremes, it must, it seems, have a non-Darwinian theory of how interaction between conditions might be brought about. In practice this gap reduces to the need for a theory of how large-scale phenomena are represented to individual consciousness and for a theory to understand how a myriad of interpersonal interactions form collectives. We shall return to sketch solutions to both these needs.

(iv) The social consequences of studying anthropology and history
An important consequence of the perception that an evolutionary theory need not be strictly Darwinian, is what one might call the politicizing of anthropology and history.

(a) Anthropology. The descriptive ethnographies of anthropology could be treated as accounts of alternative forms of human association. By becoming known they enter into the process by which mutant social practices and social formations are created in a contemporary society, let us say, Western Europe. To learn from an anthropologist that a certain way of organizing social life exists elsewhere, with novel ways of performing the rituals by which social life is forwarded, and that people lead apparently satisfactory lives in accordance with it, opens up for us the possi· bility of other ways of life for us. It is not trivial either to remark that science fiction may have the same effect, in that conceptions of new forms of society — in this case imaginatively created — if popular and so widely promulgated, can become effective agents in the social process. They can serve as models for the conceiving of possible social forms contemporary people might try to realize.

(b) History. Selection conditions, on the other hand, can obviously become better understood by the study of history. The effect of knowledge of history on the cognitive and imaginative resources of human beings is not only to alter the possible forms of mutation by allowing people to make use of knowledge of how mutants have been selected by specific selection conditions in the past, but by bringing about an increasing degree of interaction between mutation and selection conditions social change becomes more Lamarckian. Under these conditions any adequate theory of social change and consequential form of political action also becomes more Lamarckian. Success in the utilization of specific theories will reflect back still further upon the spectrum of possible ways of social change, continuously making successive theories more and more Lamarckian. It becomes apparent, then, that the incorporation of anthropological and historical knowledge in public shared conceptions of what is possible and what was actual, alters not only the process but demands a progressively different social theory to understand it.

(b) Specific Theories: R/I Explanatory Frameworks

Would anyone be so foolish as to argue that the mechanism of social change is literally evolutionary, that is by Darwinian selection through genes? I am afraid there are. I have already discussed and dismissed the biologism of Wilson's *Sociobiology* and *Human Nature* in Chapter 1. C. D. Darlington's *The Evolution of Man and Society*, though a good deal more scholarly than Wilson's latter work, nevertheless hovers between literal and analogical application of evolutionary theory to social change, in defiance of time-scales that must have been very well known to its author.[9] Since the line of criticism which I would take against Darlington's applications is very similar to that which I offered in Chapter 1 I shall leave the matter there.

The general idea of a populational or M/S theory of historical change encompasses a great variety of specific forms. Since they are of rather different structure it will be necessary to be fairly precise about which form of populational theory is serving as the source-model for the construction of a theory of social change. I shall try to develop and to delimit the analogy between bio-evolution and socio-evolution through the best version, so far as I can ascertain, of the gene (-complex) selection theory, popularly expounded by Dawkins[10] and extended and modified by Hull.[11]

All populational theories conceive of change as defined in terms of the replacement of a population of one type by a collection of individuals of another; under the condition that there exists a real relation between the members of the successive populations. All organic evolutionary theories of the M/S form meet these conditions whether they are Darwinian or Lamarckian.

(i) Logical structure of evolutionary theories
To identify evolutionary theories in more detail Hull has developed a set of concepts out of Dawkin's original concept of replicator.

(a) The first central concept in any populational theory is that of 'lineage', a sequence of individuals in a real relation that leads from one population to another. In the biological case the individuals are not organisms, but genes. For example an ancestral descent tree from a common family ancestor is a lineage. So is a sequence of better and better pumps, if each design arose by making improvements on the preceding one.

A lineage can be formally defined on a set of sets and a relation, that is as a sequence of populations together with a reproductive relation between members, say some form of copying.

(b) The second central concept is that of replicator, the kind· of entity through which identity and difference is actually transmitted at the reproductive stage. In general in the R/I explanatory format, lineages are populations of replicators.

(c) To define a mutation-selection or M/S theory a further concept-pair is required, interactor and environment, since it is in the real relation between interactors and environments that the differential effect on replicators occurs.[12]

Dawkin's main contribution to the clarification of the logical structure of evolutionary theories is the clear statement of the principle that replicators and interactors may be distinct existents, requiring a consideration of what real relation may obtain between them. In general interactors are generated by replicators, but their existence is a necessary condition for replicators to form a lineage. In the organic application of the theory replicators are genes or gene-complexes, and interactors are organisms. The evolving population is then a collective of gene (-complexes).

(ii) Metaphysical issues raised by the foregoing analysis
The reader may have been struck by the vagueness of the concept of gene and gene-complex, particularly with respect to the criteria

of identity and difference assumed in defining a lineage on a population of genes. The vagueness turns in the end on an inadequately clarified metaphysical distinction. The problem can be put baldly: What is a replicator? Is a replicator a gene (-complex) considered as a particular instantiation of structure in a particular molecule, or is it the structure which has many sequential instantiations? If a lineage is a set of replicators, and the issue of stable or changing lineage is to be addressed, then the way the question is to be answered will depend on the metaphysical level at which replicator identity is fixed. If replicators are identified with genes as molecular instantiations then structural similarity and difference will serve as properties criterial of change. But if structure is itself the replicator then particular molecular instantiations are an additional category of beings between replicators and interactors.

Several important issues can now be raised.

(a) a new locus for the concept of 'mutation' has been introduced. If the replicator is the structure common to several successive molecular instantiations then we may want to say the gene is imperfectly instantiated rather than that a micromutation occurred. And so far as I can see there is no *a priori* way of deciding how we should speak of this. But if we identify replicators with particular molecular entities then any difference in structure is a violation, to some degree at least of the identity conditions for sameness, and hence counts *prima facie* as a mutation.

(b) I suppose the definitive criterion for an improper replication to count as a mutation is if the interactor generated from the new replicator is actually (i.e. functionally relevantly) different from an interactor generated from the old replicator. This important test depends on our mapping replicators and interactors, at least one-many and perhaps one to one. The simplest way of achieving this match would be to ensure that the metaphysical level of both kinds of beings is the same. Indeed this is required if there is to be a real relation between particulars drawn from each category. In the case of organic evolution that would match replicators to organisms, and hence to particular molecular instantiations of gene (-complexes).

The final point concerns the relation between replicators and interactors. An uninformed reading of biogenetics would lead one to believe that there was a one-to-one relation between types of replicators and types of interactors, since there is certainly a one-to-one relation between individual strands of DNA and individual organisms. The cells of one organism are a lineage from the original fusion of gametes. But this assumption is biologically unsound. In different circumstances identical replicators can generate distinct interactors. And it may be that the fate of an interactor in the Darwinian reproductive stakes depends on its differential, non-inherited properties more than on those it derives from its replicator. In biology this possibility corresponds to the phenomenon of epigenesis.

(iii) The problem of replicator identity

To form a lineage a sequence of replicators must satisfy two conditions: there must be real causal relations between one member and the next; there must be sufficient structural similarity between successive members. For these conditions to be known to be satisfied there must be criteria by which the identity and individuation of replicators could be determined. According to Hull lineages are the proper subjects of the verb 'to evolve'. A lineage will be said to have evolved when, with respect to the relevant properties, replicators late in the succession are different from those earlier in the chain.

At least in the biological applications of this explanation-format the criteria of similarity and difference between successive replicators depend on structural isomorphisms between them. If to be a gene is for an assemblage of molecules to have a particular structure then a metaphysical problem looms. What ontological commitments does the theory have? Are the genes the structures or the particular molecular realizations of the structures? Much of the language of biology suggests the former, for example 'genepool', 'the same gene appearing in different generations' and so on.

We seem to be presented with alternative pictures.

(a) Replicators (genes) are assemblages of particular molecules, and are differentiated by structural properties. Evolution, as defined above with respect to lineages, is the replacement of old replicators by new, which are, in varying degrees, structurally similar to and structurally different from the old. No basis of continuity is required to sustain the lineage.

(b) Replicators are the material realizations of a structure. It is the structure that is the gene. Evolution is the change of the structure through time and successive realizations. The picture requires some basis for the continuity of the structure, since for us to say the structure has changed, something must be preserved unchanged as the time-independent referent. But there is no material basis for the continuity since successive replications are realizations in new molecules. We are required, it seems, to postulate some abstract entity as the bearer of continuity.

It seems that the facts, so to speak, and the explanatory format, admit of either alternative. We are then free to choose whichever accords best with our metaphysical principles. In the light of a general materialism and under the discipline of Ockham's razor, I choose to treat replicator identity and lineage change in accordance with the first picture. An immediate effect of this choice is to dissolve the rather ill-focussed notion of *a* gene into two components, particular molecular assemblages on the one hand, and the structural properties of those assemblages on the other. If genes and gene-complexes are to be identified with the structural properties of assemblages and two distinct molecular assemblages can have the same structure, two distinct molecular assemblages can be the bearers of the same gene (-complex). It follows that the replicators cannot be genes or gene-complexes.

No residual problems remain — but a careless and misleading way of speaking has been tidied up.

(iv) Transfer of concepts: socio-evolution as parallel to gene-selection
The general distinction between dialectical and evolutionary theories allows for a rather weakly framed socio-evolutionary explanatory format. At that level of generality one borrows the mutation/selection distinction, and one can speak vaguely of mutant practices, socio-economic selection environments and so on. The sharpened account of the fine structure of modern bio-evolutionary theory that I have just set out allows for a second stage of borrowing. Can we use the gene-theory as a source of concepts for developing ideas about possible generative mechanisms of social continuity and change? We could avoid a general commitment to teleology while explaining naturalistically the appearance of some measure of adaptiveness between social practices and social economic and ecological conditions.

The transfer scheme:
The replicators are cognitively rather than molecularly realized as 'memes'.[13] Replicators can be fixed as the sources of the structure of interactors. Let us take the interactors to be social practices, then the replicators should be the sources of social

practices. We may, for want of a better term, call them 'rules'.[14] We now have the following structure:

$$
\left.\begin{array}{c}
r1 \rightarrow i1 \\
\downarrow \\
r2 \rightarrow i2 \\
\downarrow \\
r3 \rightarrow i3
\end{array}\right\} \begin{array}{l}
\text{selection} \\
\text{environment}
\end{array}
\qquad
\left.\begin{array}{c}
\text{rule } 1 \rightarrow \text{practice } 1 \\
\downarrow \\
\text{rule } 2 \rightarrow \text{practice } 2 \\
\downarrow \\
\text{rule } 3 \rightarrow \text{practice } 3
\end{array}\right\} \begin{array}{l}
\text{socio-} \\
\text{geographical} \\
\text{conditions}
\end{array}
$$

Mutation is defined on the rule-sequence as a lineage, and selection on the adaptiveness of practices to the environment, relative to which practices spread or do not spread; are kept or dropped by a community. For simplicity of exposition I shall be maintaining the fiction that each practice has its distinct rule. I shall drop that fiction later, since there are some negative aspects of the transfer that require us to consider whole rule-systems.

Though the transfer schema above is more refined than the Popper-Toulmin borrowing of the M/S framework, it is still intolerably vague. Before we can examine the analogy between bio and socio-evolution carefully two further steps are required.

(a) An essential feature of the replicator/interactor theory is the principle that only replicators replicate. There is no direct real causal relation between successive interactors. To reach the next interactor the system must pass through a replicator node, where a new replicator is generated which in its turn controls the generation of the next interactor.

Under the transfer mapping proposed above the social practices of one generation are conceived not to generate the social practices of the next directly. There must be a replicator node. In socio-evolution this would be the replication of the rules held to by one generation or by the same generation at different times. New practices would be produced by the following of a new rule. In effect this condition on socio-evolution is equivalent to the condition that social change must involve a social psychological theory, involving the changing competences of the individual members of the collective. This consequence is very welcome.

(b) Lineages of rules offer the same metaphysical alternatives as did lineages of genes. Should we speak of a sequence of individual, structurally similar rules, or of the changing structure of a temporally enduring rule? In short where are we to locate a rule ontologically? Again I propose to adopt the least exciting picture. Rules are to be individuated as the cognitive resources of individual people over reasonable time-spans, so that if you and I are said to be 'following the same rule' that will be treated as a misleading way of saying that the rule I am following is structurally isomorphic, or in some other appropriate way similar, to the rule you are following.

Social practices are equally metaphysically uncertain. To formulate clear ideas about the way socio-economic and geographical environments could actually affect the way people behave I propose to treat practices in the same way as I have treated rules. Each occasion on which an act/action sequence is produced will count as a distinct instance of a practice. The expression 'the same social (or other) practice' as in 'the farmers of today are using the same practices as their forefathers' will be taken to mean that several successive concrete act/action sequences are structurally or in some other way similar. And to say that *a* practice has spread throughout the community will be taken to mean that the concrete act/action sequences produced by people on particular occasions are similar in suitable respects to some other concrete, prior and particular act/action sequences, and differ from others.

So far as I can see the issue of the metaphysics of rules and practices is no more than the choice between alternative ways of speaking, one of which involves a simpler ontology than the other. I choose the simpler.

(v) Examination of the negative analogy

(a) In drawing the positive analogy I have assumed that the rule concept is analogue to the gene concept as replicator, is, like a gene, individually and internally realized in an organism. But rules can also be social and public. And temporal sequences of social, publicly promulgated rules could be imagined. There have been successive forms of the Highway Code and the Marriage Service. Such sequences would meet the requirements for constituting a lineage, and they would produce sequences of differing sets of like social practices.

But this dissimilarity seems to me to lie within the range of possible R/I theories. The general form of the theory and its major categories and relations are preserved. This feature of the mechanisms of socio-evolution does however open the possibilities of other kinds of mutation process than the merely personal fluctuations and innovations suggested by the strict analogy with biological applications of the R/I format. There may be such mutations as errors in the transcription of the documents in which rules are written down, or other forms of misrepresentation. The merging of cultures with explicit publicly represented rule-systems, such as codes of laws, could lead to a mixing of the systems of laws, parallel to the genetic mixing of sexual reproduction. One might find an instance of this in the imposition of an alien framework of law on tribal custom in a colonial regime.

(b) In record-keeping societies the lineage of replicators is likely to be linked in more complex ways than in simpler cultures. In the biological version of the theory the n+1th replicator is produced from the nth replicator, and the influence of all those before the nth can be exerted only through whatever of their features are represented in the nth.[15] But in rule-replication in record-keeping societies there is knowledge of many past rule-systems available to influence the way the n+1th rule in a lineage of rules is formed. The records allow past features long since eliminated from the lineage to be reintroduced. Lineages of rules under such a condition are not just simply ordered structures like this

$$r1 \rightarrow r2 \rightarrow r3 \rightarrow \ldots.. \, rn \rightarrow rn+1 \rightarrow \ldots..$$

but more complex lattices like this

$$r1 \rightarrow r1 \rightarrow r3 \rightarrow r4 \ldots..$$

(c) In organic evolution, selection pressure acts directly on interactors (organisms) and only indirectly on replicators (genes). But in socio-evolution social approval and disapproval could act on either rules or practices. Indeed a proposed new rule could be eliminated from a culture before it had ever had a chance to be tested through realization in a social practice. Some legislative debates could be regarded as pre-selection processes in which proposed rules are tested by imagining their realization and its consequences, selection pressure acting directly on the replicators.

(d) In bio-evolution mutations occur through imperfect copying of the structure of the nth replicator in the formation of the n+1th. One might look upon mutation as a defect in or prevention of the normal replication process. Learning the rules from one's family, one's teacher or one's peers could be thought of as the corresponding natural process in socio-evolution. A social mutation would be an inaccurate or imperfect learning of the rules. But in human affairs it may also be possible to encourage the replication of new rules as replicators which would not 'naturally' be copied. One might think of a school as an institutional realization of such a process. Stability is deliberately ensured and mutations prevented by testing the learning to make sure that each generation has indeed accurately replicated the knowledge and principles of action of the past.

(e) The bio-evolutionary application of R/I theoretical structure requires that the successive interactors, each produced by a replicator, are not causally linked. However the possibility of direct, mimetic reproduction of practices, customs, style and so on, could occur without the intermediate fixing of the practice in individually represented rules. For instance a Maori *tohunga* might know how to perform some practical task, and be followed by an assistant who has merely copied his every move, without the assistant acquiring an individual, explicit representation of the practice. Transmission in socio-evolution could be by interactor-interactor replication without passing through the stage of replicator.

(f) Finally one should notice the possibility of interaction among the rules. In the social application the replicators may interact with each other to produce compensatory changes maintaining a stable form for an interaction. Many rules, like many genes, are required to produce a practice. We have already noticed the equilibrations that occur around important social presentational distinctions such as male/female. This could be expressed in terms of the R/I theory format as reactions of one part of a rule system to changes in another so as to yield the same social phenomenon. Some interaction between genes is now considered likely in bio-evolution.

In summary it seems that both M/S and R/I formats have something to offer social psychologists in looking for concepts in which to formulate theories of particular social changes. Again, the underlying motivation that brings bio- and socio-evolution together is the wish to explain adaptation without recourse to any stronger teleology than the nature of the beings involved (people) can sustain.

(c) The Limits of Change in the Mechanisms of Social Change

Could the processes of social change and the theories required to understand them become wholly Lamarckian? The answer, I think, must be an unqualified 'No'.

(i) Some of the selection conditions to which interactors and replicators are subject, though they can become known by historical study, could not be changed to favour a particular mutant.

Nor are these conditions the product of the spread of social practices which are the surviving mutants of past generations. I have in mind such non-social features of the environment as the weather, natural resources and so on. However, not every non-social element is stable. The growth of scientific knowledge and technical capacity may lead to some apparently non-social elements, such as the weather, succumbing to socially motivated technical intervention. It is a commonplace of economic theory that the extent of finite resources available to a society is not fixed by absolute physical quantities but by such matters as social desirability of extraction processes, capital investment and so on. It is not even clear that the laws of nature are immune from some sort of change under social influence. What we take them to be is, as we now realize, a compromise between changing forms of thought and the intransigent behaviour of the universe.

(ii) I have been assuming, though with reservations, that the selection conditions for mutant practices are, in general, to be found amongst the properties of the groups that human beings form in their various modes of association. For the interaction between mutation and selection conditions to form a closed circuit, it must be possible for these collective properties to be altered by human action. It is by no means clear to me that we have good reason for thinking this to be possible. I have reservations − one metaphysical and one epistemic. The metaphysical reservation has to do with the nature of collective properties. It may be because of the inevitability of at least some unintended consequences of human action that some main features of society will always be beyond the reach of intentional action. Every intentional action to alter something, which we have come to understand, will have, at least in principle, its own flux of unintended consequences. At least as far as human attempts to alter the collective properties of society by intended action are known, we have a record ranging from the merely dismal to the utterly disastrous. The epistemic reason is more conditional, in that in order to know what it would be rational to do, we must have some conception of the collective property which is serving as a selection condition and it is by no means clear that a methodology which reliably produced knowledge of collective properties could be worked out. It does not seem to me, however, that it is beyond human ingenuity to create such a device, but there seems to be no hint of how it might be done. Despite this pessimism, there seems to be no difficulty in principle in supposing that human collectives have distinctive properties, but it is not my purpose in this work to investigate the tension between epistemic pessimism and the metaphysical optimism that I feel on this matter.

(iii) I have already suggested that the application of an evolutionary schema must be qualified not only by limiting the degree of absolute Darwinism according to which it is constructed, but by borrowing from the organic sciences the idea that the selection environment might be subject to change. If the processes of social change are seen to be at their most effective in daily life in the selection of mutant practices by a social environment, and that environment itself is changing, a fully adequate theory of social change would have to include a way of explaining change of environment.

Could the Darwinian-Lamarckian spectrum, so plausible as a format for accounting for microsocial practices that maintain the social order of daily life be generalized to provide an evolutionary account of the change in environment by the simple device of ordering environments in such a way that each environment could be thought of as under selection pressure from a wider environment, and so subject to change? An encouraging presupposition for this approach is to be found in Marx's important observation that human collectives can be defined by the fact that they reproduce their methods of sustaining life, albeit, I would wish to add, imperfectly. This suggests there might be some level of analysis at which collectives are themselves treatable as individuals undergoing mutation. If that is the case, then it seems reasonable to look for an environment of either greater scope or of higher order which can contain the selection conditions for collectives whose properties are now the mutant element in the system. The geographical conditions of the earth might constitute such an environment. But more interestingly, there are selection conditions internal to collectives, in which the collective constitutes its own selection condition. What I have in mind here is the generalization of the biological concept of lethal mutation in that a lethal mutation eliminates an individual because it leads to the formation of organs which do not form a viable system with the other inherited organ structures of an organism of that type. Novel social practices that are suicidal in existing socio-economic conditions would be an example. Finally, and still as an effect internal to the collective, are the appearance of non-standard human beings, or non-standard practices which can serve to drastically alter the conditions

under which a mutant practice can survive. A striking example of
this internal selection property is to be found in the comparison
between the selection conditions for the mutant social practice
represented by the British miners' strikes of 1926 and 1972.
The strike itself can be treated as the public manifestation of the
mutant social practice of manual workers claiming hegemony in
society. The catastrophic failure of the 1926 strike can be explained in part by the existence of Arthur Cook, whose revolutionary rhetoric persuaded the miners to undertake a strike
which, with respect to the other selection conditions, namely
the socio-economic conditions of the time, was bound to be
disastrous. In 1972, in altered socio-economic conditions, there
was an altered governmental social psychology. But another
individual mutant social practice was of crucial importance in
bringing about the success of the 1972 strike, and the seizure of
power by manual workers. This was the introduction of the
flying picket. The decision to picket the places of the consumption of coal rather than the places of its production, enabled the
miners to seize effective power in the community, on behalf of
other manual workers.

Reflection upon these points leads us to a co-ordinated pair
of solutions to the problem of the mechanism of change raised
by the generalization of the evolutionary theory as an explanation
of change in environments. The problem turns out to be soluble
along two dimensions. In the one, the physical geographical conditions of the earth constitute an environment for all social
environments, relatively stable with respect to social change,
though not wholly immune from interaction with it. On the other
hand, as can be seen from the example of the miners' strikes, the
properties of a collective, coupled with certain individual mutations, can serve as a selection condition for that very collective.
This is possible only because the selection conditions and the
collective and its properties do not exactly coincide, nor do collectives exactly reproduce themselves in the practices of successive
generations.

The argument so far depends upon a number of assumptions
about the way in which collectives are constituted out of and yet
are independent of their individual members assumptions which
have neither been defined or defended. The next step is to show
how in a relatively straightforward and simple way, the individual/
collective relationship can be schematized for the purposes of
understanding how an evolutionary theory of a quasi Lamarckian

form can be effective.

(d) Social Adaptiveness

The concept of adaptiveness is correlative to that of function. A general criterion of adaptiveness is easily defined. A practice, institutional structure, mode of self-presentation and so on, is well adapted if it subserves the social function and personal projects of that practice and so on. But to say this is merely to display the conceptual connection between function and adaptation. Both concepts are based upon a root-idea of 'means-ends'.

Nevertheless, the display of this conceptual connection is not wholly useless. It provides a schema for formulating concrete, empirical questions about the spread or the failure to spread of innovations. The phases of an investigation might run as follows:

(i) In what means-ends relations can we say a certain practice stands? Hypotheses about the functions of practices must not be just collective-sociological (the sin of functionalism) nor just individual-psychological (the sin of individualism) but reached by a negotiation between commentators on and members of a society.

The formulation of means-ends hypotheses is made more complicated still by the necessity to separate, at least analytically, the expressive and practical orders. The 'same' practice may have to be located in two or more networks of means-ends relations. For example, a strike may be able to be seen to be functionally adaptive to the expressive end of demonstrating dignity, but functionally maladaptive to the practical end of improving economic standing.

(ii) With some means-ends hypotheses to hand, the next phase would involve the theoretical contemplation of alternative means to the given ends. But these means must be contemplated against a background of what is known about the historical conditions, and particularly the current psychology of the folk. Survival of a novel practice is, I argue, determined by an interplay between individual-psychological possibility and collective-social necessity.

In short, I presume there are no universal criteria of social adaptiveness that are specific enough to explain particular cases of the spread of a practice. But particular questions of why some innovations spread and others do not ought to be looked at in a means-end framework, with both orders in mind.

3. PROBLEM: CHANGE IN MACROSTRUCTURES
AND THE STRUCTURE OF SOCIETY

(a) Law-making as Registration and Record

If there were formal devices by which the managers of society could decide upon and promulgate explicit rules of action to which some coercive agency ensured the folk conformed, the problem of social stability and change would be solved. One could simply identify and describe the institutions and practices by which this was effected. One might be tempted to turn to the study of the law and its informal sibling, custom, as just such an institution. Could it be that the law is the source of order and stability in society and the nexus for social change? It might be argued that the political process is no more than the process of inventing new laws and devising changes in old laws in order to bring about changes in society in conformity with them. I take this view to be naive, since notoriously laws are enforceable only if they are, in a sense, already adopted. I shall not argue this point here since I am not concerned with the history or sociology of law. I shall assume that as far as the social psychological mode is concerned laws and customs are secondary phenomena. They are rhetorical representations of the perception of tendencies to social stability and change rather than any part of their causes.

From the point of view of an ethogenic study of men in society, the central matter of law is the institutions in which it is socially realized. The courts, the prisons, interview rooms, police stations and the forces that inhabit them, are matters to be investigated. The official rhetoric concerning the law should be brought in question, since we ought not to be too ready to accept it as providing an unproblematic theory of those institutions. One might be tempted to say that Parliament and other law-giving corporations are places where performative utterances are exchanged to contrive public/collective commitments to courses of action and so to determine the future. I suggest this naive theory deserves just as much scrutiny as the theory that hospitals are for curing people. Law and rhetoric that supports it becomes something to be explained. The legal institutions do not figure among the explainers of social stability and change. On this view, law is a historically generated adjunct, a way for remembering past decisions, for recording the outcomes of meetings, discussions and debates. To think of the law as an instrument of stability and change is a misunderstanding of its place in the regulation of social life. With respect to the activities of man in society, it is a memorial device, a series of reminders, and a resource for a rhetoric of blame and praise. It is not, in this view, part of the causal apparatus involved in continuous creation of the social world.[16]

(b) The Internal Properties of Collectives

(i) The conditions for continuity and of change

I shall try to show how the evolutionary theory can be applied to understanding the way in which a collective can act as its own selection environment. I shall use an exceedingly simple schema as shown in Fig. 6. I hope that the raw number of individuals which constitute a collective makes little difference to its properties, provided that the collective is sufficiently large or its individuals sufficiently myopic for it to be impossible for any one of them to achieve an overall view.

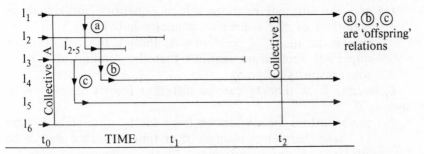

Fig. 6

I imagine the collective as consisting of six individuals, but they come into existence and perish at different times. I shall take it that the epiphenomenal properties of the collective come from its structural properties, which are based upon the interrelations of some four coexisting members. It is crucially important to this conception that the collective is thought to be continuously sustained

(a) by the existences of members overlapping one another

(b) and by the continuity of some of the collective properties which the group or set of individuals has.

The crucial relationship, then, is that a new member should be related to old members by some kind of offspring relationship. This is a generalization of Marx's idea that a social collective is constituted by the reproduction of the means of life or of Darwin's idea that a species is constituted by the population which consists of the existing members and their descendants on the one hand, and their ancestors on the other. In both social and biological collectives it is important to insist that the offspring relationship involves, in general, imperfect replication. In the social case, the typical offspring relationship might be that between teacher and pupil, master and apprectice, abbot and novice, and so on. In Fig. 6, the set of individuals, 1_1, 1_2, 1_3, 1_6 are a collective at time t_0, because of internal relations between them. They are constituted as individuals of that collective by their membership and by the structural properties of those members considered as a set.

1_1, 1_4, 1_5, 1_6, is a later stage of the same collective, if the following conditions are satisfied:

    (a) If at time t_0 some individuals of Collective A are members of Collective B,

    (b) and the structural properties of Collective B are close to those of Collective A,

    (c) and the internal relations which constitute individuals as members of the collective, generate individuals which are similar to those of collective A, though the condition of imperfect replication requires that they should also be in some respects different.

Collective B at time t_2 can be different from Collective A at time t_0 if

    (a) the members which survive from $t_0 - t_2$ — namely 1_1 and 1_6, have themselves changed over time in such a way as to alter the structural properties of the collective at time t_2,

    (b) or, neither 1_5, nor 1_4 were perfect replicas of their ancestors, 1_3 and 1_2,

    (c) and that 1_4 and 1_5 survive at time t_2.

Notice in our diagram that the mutant $1_{2.5}$ did not survive to take a place as a member in the collective at time t_2.

(ii) The collective as its own selection-environment

I have already suggested that the collective could be a selection environment for its members and their practices. The change of the nature of the collective from t_0 to t_2 now means that there is a new selection environment in existence at t_2. There is no guarantee that conditions favourable to an individual at t_0, those for example which led to the survival of 1_4 and 1_5 to be constituted as members of the collective at t_2, will be favourable at t_2. In this way it is easy to see that a fairly simple set of conditions can be laid down which ensure that the collective and its members are related in such a way that a quasi-Lamarckian theory or, if you like, a semi-Darwinian theory, can account for the change from the Collective A to the Collective B and for the difference in the natures and customs of the members whatever they might be.

Such a theory of the diachronic development of collectives resolves the problem posed by Marx's theory of change. On the one hand is his idea that human collectives reproduce the means of their existence. But on the other is his failure to provide a social psychology which could account for the dynamic relations which he supposes to hold between the elements of a social formation.[17] The resolution is simple. If we admit that there is no causal relation operating synchronically between the state of the economic system and the social formations in which it exists, we may still claim that there is a potent, and sometimes overriding influence, exerted by the economic system and the conditions appropriate to it, the production relations and so on, upon the social formations which could exist. This could be understood if the economic system and the production relations are seen as constituting a severe selection environment. Mutant practices of one sort or another will survive or fail to survive, depending upon their relation to that selection environment. This selection environment is itself constituted by the members of the collective which are being changed by mutation and selection. By adding the expressive order as another network of relations within a collective we reproduce the full ethogenic theory of social change.[18]

17

POLITICAL ACTIVITY

ANTICIPATORY SUMMARY

Introduction: the imposition of valuation on psychological possibilities.
1. Psychological dimensions of political theories
   (a) The lethal mutation as psychological impossibility of a proposed mode of association.
   (b) Varieties of psychologies in theories of political association defined by 'motivation':
   (i) linear theories, e.g. power is the sole source of political association;
   (ii) two-dimensional theories, e.g. dual interest theories with respect to personal exercise of power and willingness to form associations for specific (and/or for general) purposes;
   (iii) three-dimensional theories, e.g. an interest in the use of reason in practical decision making among those who have an interest in the exercise of power and to form associations.
   I will argue that only one cell of the psycho-political cube as defined in (iii) contains a specification of a psychologically stable form of political association with respect to the arguments of this whole work.
2. Problems in the deduction of a political programme
   (a) The general political paradox: the reconciliation of individual motivation and collective necessities for its realization.
   (b) Pragmatic paradoxes of specific political programmes:
   (i) the paradox of *laissez faire*: moral freedom opens the possibility of exploitation;
   (ii) the paradox of socialism: the institutions needed to control the possibility of exploitation become the basis of a new ruling class destroying moral freedom.
   (c) Lukes' solution examined.
   (i) the setting up of state-apparatus to see to the fair distribution of wealth and power;

385

     (ii) objections:

        (a) Wealth and power are not basic goods. Traditional wisdom warns against them since empty when attained;

        (b) Falls back into the pragmatic paradox of socialism.

  (d) Bureaucracies as a new class:

     (i) anarchism and the critique of bureaucracy;

     (ii) no programme which proposes an institutional solution to the paradoxes can succeed since all institutions evolve from the practical to the expressive as their dominant mode of action.

3. The deduction of a political psychology of social action

  (a) The psychological conditions necessary for a political programme:

     (i) it must be possible to envisage a new form of life;

     (ii) there must be criteria for assessing proposed new forms of life, prior to their realization. This introduces an element of rationality;

     (iii) there must be some conception of means to achieve a new form of life. Notice that this parallels on a macro scale the structure of action genesis on an individual scale, i.e. project, intention and belief or knowledge as to the means of its achievement;

     (iv) the means conceived must be based upon an adequate theory of social change. This introduces a second element of rationality.

  (b) The modes of political action:

     (i) the confrontation mode: must always fail to bring about social change since

     (a) leads to an increase in definition and hence in reality of the prevailing social system,

     (b) in order to overcome the prevailing system the radical organization must come to match the conservative organization point by point;

     (ii) the alternation mode: based on mutation/selection theory of social change exploiting its relatively Lamarckian form.

4. The basis of an alternationist political programme

  (a) The moral basis must be parallel multiple hierarchies.

  (b) The instrumental basis must be expressive.

  (c) Structural, e.g. economic readjustments, land tenure reforms etc. i.e. primary revolutions are ineffective unless the expressive system for generating respect/contempt hierarchies is changed in a secondary revolution.

5. Difficulties with alternation programmes

  (a) Unless mutants have some means of protection the circumambient society frequently destroys them before they have been tested.

  (b) The alternativist theory of political programmes will quickly degenerate into classical social Darwinism reproducing the 'victory of the stronger' political theory of *laissez faire* societies.

PRELIMINARY OBSERVATION

Any general psychological theory must make use of a certain conception of man. But a social psychology, as I have tried to argue, depends on assumptions about the possible forms of social life as well. While a psychology owes its readers an explicit statement of the moral position which underlies it, a social psychology is doubly bound. Its author owes his readers an explicit statement of the political consequences of his view of men in association, and the political possibilities which the adoption of his view would open up. In what follows I attempt a sketch, and it is no more than a sketch, of the politics of the ethogenic position.

INTRODUCTION

To develop a sketch of a political philosophy on the basis of our psycho-sociological conclusions a moral standpoint must be imposed upon the material. As almost all moral philosophers have argued[1] it is impossible to derive moral principles from social or other facts without introducing an ultimately arbitrary assignment of moral worth to some human attribute, social practice and so on.

Two basic personal moral principles emerge naturally from the earlier analysis of the necessary attributes of socially competent persons. I showed that we needed to attribute both autonomy and reflexivity to human beings to ground their main psycho-sociological capabilities. Autonomy was the capacity to act independently of any given influence, whether external or internal, and reflexivity was the capacity to bring lower order motivations and even causes of action under motivations and principles of higher order, in an indefinite hierarchy.

These capacities or powers vary considerably from person to person, and in any given person from time to time. They can be augmented by education, and reduced by training. Two divergent moral systems can be constructed by taking the issue of the augmentation or the dimunition of personal powers as the locus of the arbitrary choice of moral principle. I shall say, following Shotter,[2] Kant[3] and many others, that the augmentation of personal powers is an ultimate good. Diverging from this locus are the moral theories of Skinner,[4] Loyola[5] and many others, who hold that the dimunition of personal powers is an ultimate moral good.

Closely connected with the principle of the augmentation of

autonomy and reflexivity as personal powers, is a principle which leads to the limitation of the exercise of these powers in a social context. Again I try to identify a locus of arbitrary choice of moral worth. The analysis of the social interactions of human beings led from many different directions to the idea that the search for order is pervasive in human life. It is achieved in the structuring of actions, in the formation of hierarchies of respect and contempt, in the relative status that people assign to themselves. Contrary to many strands of social thought I shall be arguing for a radical theory from the very principle that social order (though it will be a social order fragmented into indefinitely many forms of association) is an ultimate moral good.

It should be evident that the elevation of the facts of personal autonomy and reflexivity and of the universal appearance of social order to moral principles leads to a system with a strong internal tension. I hope to show that each cluster of moral assignments provides the limiting conditions necessary for fruitful development in actual institutions, of the other. The need for order limits the exercise of personal autonomy by the necessity to co-operate with others in the creation and maintenance of order by dramaturgical means, and the power of autonomy and reflexivity limits the rigidity of socially maintained structure in actions, institutions and so on.

In the next stage of the argument I try to relate personal or psychological attributes to traditional political philosophies. In this way my choice of moral principles as arbitrary attributions of moral worth to certain personal and psychological properties of human beings can be related to a choice of a broad political position, as deriving its worth from the basic moral principles.

The argument however proceeds with yet another assumption of a relation between value and fact. At the heart of the analyses of social activity in Part II of this study lay speech. Speech appeared contingently as part of the action, but necessarily as the prime means of accounting, the theorizing about and criticizing of action so characteristic of human life. Theorizing opens up the possibility of the contemplation of alternatives, and as Secord and I argued in our critical study of social psychological method, accounting ultimately depends on the existence of reflexive consciousness. This line of argument would locate speaking as a necessary condition for the possibility of political activity, since it is closely related to the possibility of the private-personal conceiving and the public-social promulgating of ideas of alternative social orders to that currently being maintained by personal public activity within existing social collectives. But I want to take a further step. I want to attach worth to speaking as accounting in its own right. From this I immediately derive the principle that since, as a person, everyone has as a matter of fact the power to give an account, they must also have the right. The moral 'must' comes from the relation of that right to the conditions for being a person at all. This seems to me an independent moral principle, and I set it forth as a third locus of arbitrary association of value with fact.

1. PSYCHOLOGICAL DIMENSIONS OF POLITICAL THEORIES

(a) The Lethal Mutation as Psychological Impossibility

The rapid disintegration of most attempts at new forms of human association is not wholly to be explained by reference to the hostility or indifference of the host society within which they come into being. A survey of a wide range of such novelties, including modern communes, suggests that some forms of association for the people of a certain historical time and cultural origin are psychologically impossible. Even the most successful new societies, such as the Oneida Community, founded in the mid-nineteenth century in Upper New York State, depended for the longevity of its social forms on the personal power of one man. The survival of the community after his death was possible only because profound changes were made in its organization. The community quickly became indistinguishable from others around it. It retained its identity largely through the silver plate manufacturing for which as an industrial corporation it is still famous. It seems that a lethal mutation was incorporated within the original Oneida Community. It is easily identified. Access to the sexual favours of the women at Oneida was distributed by rank within a male hierarchy, appointment to which was in the personal gift of the founder. This proved a psychologically untenable basis for a social organization as the younger men acquired their psychological predispositions and moral opinions from the circumambient communities with which they worked.

The psychological conditions under which a particular social arrangement has to be lived act therefore as internal limiting conditions on the viability of those arrangements. Sometimes they make demands which the members can fulfil only under the control of a powerful leader. The limiting conditions lurk as latencies in the members of the society, ready to destroy it when the leader departs or is overthrown. Novel social arrangements which demand unrealizable psychological conditions are rather like lethal mutations in the biological sphere. Once special life-support arrangements are removed such an individual quickly perishes. These considerations raise the general question of the psychological conditions of reform and the psychological dimension of political thought.

(b) Varieties of Psychologies in Theories of Political Association

The argument in this section is based upon some distinctions made by J. André in a series of unpublished papers. He distinguishes political theories and their associated programmes by reference to the underlying socio-psychological assumptions upon which they are based. Essentially these assumptions amount to theories of motivation. Motivation, like intention and want, is a curiously and importantly dual concept. It has a place in the public world of planning and the attachment of a man to his project. André's classification, I believe, tacitly depends upon this important duality, but he does not explicitly identify it.

André distinguishes three different forms of psychological foundation for social life in accordance with an identifiable political theory. He differentiates them according to what he calls 'dimensions'.[6]

(i) A linear political theory proposes that the basis of political and social action is a single, fundamental, socio-psychological aspect of human beings in association. For example, the thesis that seeking and exercising power is the source of all forms of political association would be a linear theory.

(ii) A two-dimensional theory proposes that the form of a political association and its practices derives from the intersection of two axes of motivation. Political forms are differentiated as people are more or less committed to and interested in these motives and call upon them in the rhetoric of their accounts. André is able to show that analyses such as Hyeck's two-dimensional representation of political philosophies (Fig. 7): and Rockeach's two-valued theory of political ideology defined in terms of a Cartesian product of degree of freedom and degree of equality are reflections of a general two-dimensional theory of political motivation. He argues that on one dimension lies the attitude of individuals to the exercise of personal power and on the other their willingness to form associations. For example, if they have no interest in the personal exercise of power and no wish to form

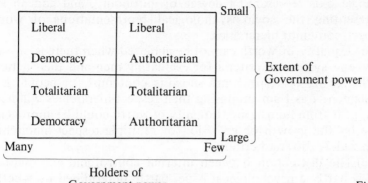

Fig. 7

highly ordered institutions, society comparable to that envisaged in the final form of Communism would arise, if those were the only motivations of the people.

(iii) André holds that two-dimensional motivation theories are inadequate to the variety of known forms of political association. He proposes a third dimension. In my terms it represents the degree to which reference to reason figures *in the rhetoric* associated with the making of day-to-day decisions in the political arena. By adding the third dimension André is able to propose a much richer classification represented in a psychopolitical cube (See Fig. 8).

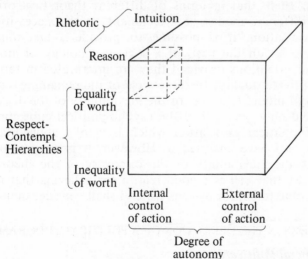

Fig. 8

(a) To take account of the central psychological importance of moral career I collapse the 'power' + 'association' dimensions into a single axis representing degree of autonomy, and add an axis representing the socio-psychological representations of worth, respect/contempt hierarchies.

(b) Equality of worth cannot be achieved when there is one and only one system of criteria for evaluating men and their actions. If the giving of respect and showing contempt for people is as fundamental as I am supposing then respect-hierarchies will never disappear from human life. Equality of worth could be approached only by the growth or provision of multiple respect hierarchies, with widely different criteria.

(c) The distinction between internal control and external control is partly a psychological issue, partly determined by whether controlling bodies are participatory or representative. There will be external control whatever the claim to be the representative, be it majority vote (Parliament), historical necessity (Communist Party) or divine right (Medieval Kings), when decisions are made for people by others. The cell which we will inhabit is theoretically identified according to the argument of this work as that located at that vertex of a psycho-political cube where equality of worth (for me the giving of multiple possibilities of achieving respect) freedom (for me the right to give an account and have one's account attended to), and reason (for me the utilization of a rhetoric of rationality for accounting for actions and decisions) are realized.

It seems, then, that in terms of different theoretical orientations and different modes of attachment to the necessities of political association, it is possible to provide a taxonomy of political theories on the basis of a socio-psychology of motives, projects and intentions provided they are interpreted in terms of the public/private duality. In the course of the remaining sections of the study I intend to argue for the inevitability of the discovery that one, and only one, cell of the psycho-political cube contains a mode of political association which is wholly appropriate to human life as I have analysed it. However, it is no part of my theory that the inevitability of the discovery of the theoretical uniqueness of that cell is a good reason for believing that it will inevitably come to be, for reasons which I shall consider in detail.

2. PROBLEMS IN THE DEDUCTION OF A POLITICAL PROGRAMME

(a) The General Political Paradox

A society consists of a network of relations among individuals. It is quite likely that the network has properties that are different from any summation of individuals. It is theoretically possible that the steps which have to be taken to realize changes in properties, the interpersonal networks that make up a society, will lead to changes in the situation of an individual that that person thinks are undesirable. This, of course, is the classical political paradox. How is it possible to reconcile the interests of individuals and society? And it is a paradox since the society consists of those individuals, one of whose interests ought to be the best interests of all. Philosophers have offered a variety of solutions, none of which, in my view, is without serious difficulty. I do not propose to rehearse the arguments of classical political philosophy in this work. General solutions to the basic political paradox fall into two main groups.[7]

There are those which emphasize collective properties of society and see individual life fulfillments in terms of them, and those which concentrate on features of individual lives in the hope that some summation of these will constitute a social advantage. Neither seems to me to locate a possible social psychological base for a theory of political association.[8] Whatever theory is advanced must take account of the possibility that the properties of collectives are distinct from the properties of their individual members, and yet must restrict intentional concepts to individual members and their projects. I hope it will be seen that the approach in this study preserves just such a structure.

(b) Pragmatic Paradoxes of Specific Political Programmes

The deduction of a political programme from any socio-psychological theory of human action is faced not just with the general political paradox but with specific difficulties which infect large classes of practical activities. There are two such paradoxes which are of central importance in the deduction I am about to undertake.

(i) The paradox of 'laissez faire'

How is it possible for freedom in the moral sphere — that is freedom to construct one's life-form and to build one's personality and character for oneself — to be achieved without leaving open freedom in the economic sphere — that is the freedom to exploit others and the environment in one's own personal interests. The paradox arises from the opportunity which the giving of absolute freedom to all opens to some, the strong and the greedy, to limit or eliminate the freedom of many. How is it possible to partition the fields of activity of human agents in a principled way? This has been the difficulty which has beset anarchistic programmes of political reform in the past. I do not propose to treat this as an issue of principle but rather as a socio-psychological problem. I shall propose a solution by paying attention to what we know and might come to know about the springs of human action.

(ii) The paradox of socialism

The perception of the paradox of *laissez faire* was, of course, one of the sources of the socialist proposal that a form of state should be devised in which the activities of all the citizens should be managed in the interests of the most exploitable group in that society. This has, of course, led to its own destructive pragmatic paradox. A necessary condition for the management of the activities of the citizens is the setting up of institutions of managers who, in principle, will act in the interests of all. But the managers form an institution, and institutions evolve in such a way that expressive activities and motivations come to dominate the instrumental ends for which the institution was founded. The managers are in danger of becoming a new exploiting class. The paradox, in short, follows from the impossibility of preventing the rise of new exploiting classes without setting up a class yet more powerful. Again, I do not propose to treat the paradox of socialism by philosophical argument. I shall examine the paradox and the possibility of its solution with respect to socio-psychological considerations having to do with the nature of human beings and their forms of association.

I take both the paradox of *laissez faire* and the paradox of Socialism to be true consequences of reflection on the actual nature of people and their modes of association. They are reflections of features of human life on which no programme of education, or moral exhortations, and no newly invented institutions, will have the slightest effect. Any attempt to alter these basic features of human life can only slow down the inevitable socio-psychological processes by which the paradoxes manifest themselves in actual public activities.

I have expressed these paradoxes in traditional political terms but in contexts which are essentially contemporary, that is in terms of political movements that have characterized the last 150 years, but of course, both paradoxes are reflections of the age-old paradox of liberty and equality. Both liberty and equality are desiderata of the moral state but the consequences of allowing ourselves liberty clash with the conditions of our equality and, on the other hand, the conditions of human equality clash with the necessary conditions for human liberty.

(c) Lukes' Solution

(i) Before I proceed to the development of an argument for a political programme based on the socio-psychology of this work, it is worth pausing to examine a well-argued and superficially attractive solution proposed by Steven Lukes in his book *Individualism*. Lukes' solution is based upon a concept which is also central to the argument of this work, namely the idea of respect for persons. In Lukes' argument this allows for a theoretical resolution of the specific pragmatic paradoxes, and the classical paradox of liberty and equality.

The paradox of *laissez faire* would disappear if economic exploitation could be made to seem a kind of contempt, and the paradox of Socialism would disappear if the transformation of the managerial *cadre* into an exploiting class in the course of a shift from instrumental to expressive motivation was seen to involve contempt for their clientèle. These suggestions are highly theoretical and contain no hint of how such reforms of fundamental human attitudes and activities are likely to be undertaken. Lukes does not make this mistake. He offers a practical solution.

Lukes supposes that the realization of respect for persons is a technical matter. It can be brought about, he thinks, by some form of a state management which is so organized as to see to distribution of both wealth and power. Lukes takes these to be the practical forms in which respect for persons is realized.

(ii) However, it seems clear that Lukes's theory falls straight back into the old difficulties.

(a) It is not clear that the realization of respect in wealth and power is a sufficiently universal feature of human societies to form the basis of an *a priori* formulation of a political programme, since both are highly problematic as goods. Traditional wisdom has it that wealth and power seem attractive only to those who have not attained them. When they are attained they are realized to be burdens. Paradoxically, the revelations of those who have attained wealth and power are never believed by those who follow after. Traditional wisdom has it that wealth and power once attained become the source of a new range of motives, which would lead one to abandon them. Only perhaps a neurotic compulsion for security compels one to hold on to them. Of course, in a social organization which provided forms of security and modes of respect other than those associated with wealth and power, the tales brought back from the summits might have some likelihood of being believed and in being believed the search for wealth and power would itself be sabotaged. The idea that power is an unqualified good whose redistribution by means of some state apparatus would resolve the pragmatic paradoxes, is again equivocal in that traditional wisdom holds that power over others entails, for most of those who attain it, the burden of responsibility; and that the burden of responsibility comes to outweigh the satisfactions of the exercise of power. Whatever may be the psychological law involved at this point, it is clear that wealth and power are not unequivocal as ultimate goods.

(b) Even if Lukes were right in identifying the key socio-psychological goods associated with respect for persons he falls into the pragmatic paradox I have associated with classical Socialism, in that he supposes that the State, or what of course amounts to the same thing in practice, a bureaucracy, can achieve the practical marks of respect for everyone in the redistribution of wealth and power without creating a new exploiting class, that is a new class who uses its instrumental activities for the purposes of expressive presentations of self. I believe this belief to be unfounded for the reasons I have argued in detail, and so I believe the political society Lukes envisages to be impossible of actual realization.

Whatever way we take which avoids the central problem, that is avoids confronting the relationship between the inevitable development of the closed societies of bureaucrats and the nature of human association, will fail. It is an irremedial feature of human association that bureaucracies will always develop towards total institutions and shift from the instrumental to the expressive mode. Human association must have a symbolic base, the symbols become detached from the instrumentality of the institution and become the sole content of action.

(d) Bureaucracies as New Classes

(i) These features of the social psychology of bureaucrats are well known and have been the subject of much critical thinking amongst anarchist social philosophers. For example, Bakunin took it as a fundamental principle that a socialist bureaucracy was bound to generate a new ruling class, irrespective of the origins of those who came to compose it, whether they were drawn from the working class or were renegade intellectuals. Machevski even went so far as to argue that Marxist Socialism was an ideological device by which the intelligentsia proposed to seize power and become a new ruling class. Sorel pointed out that revolutionary leaders could succeed only on condition that they adopted despotic practices. Any party of revolution will, of necessity, lead to a new oppressive society with the party as the new ruling class. These criticisms point to the surface phenomenon of the transformation of closed institutions without delving deeply into the socio-psychological conditions of human association from which they inevitably follow. The argument of this work has been in part designed to lay bare the empirical and theoretical foundation for these intuitive perceptions and to found anarchist criticism of Socialism on a sound footing.

(ii) It is not difficult, it seems, to locate the weak point in Lukes' programme which occurs despite the depth and power of his analysis of the moral properties that any individual in a society must preserve for that society to be counted as morally approvable. The paradox arises because his sketch of a practical programme for the realization of those moral properties involves conditions incompatible with them, given the social psychological principles of the development of human institutions. If, as I have argued throughout this work, those social psychological principles are deeply rooted, indeed are the fundamental nature of man integral to the most deep principles of human association, no programme like Lukes' could ever succeed. It follows that the occasion for the transformation of a society from a form in which every human being has a sufficient measure of respect and the means to achieve it, to one in which a new oppressive class appears, is mediated by one and only one feature, namely the coming into being of a class or institution of social managers. Our problem, then, is to consider the design of a society in which the paradoxes of *laissez faire* and Socialism can both be avoided, that is a society which contains the machinery for the elimination of exploitation without realizing that machinery in a bureaucracy.

Lastly in this romp through centuries of political theory, I want to turn briefly to Marx's solution, namely to give the management of society to the most exploitable class, the proletariat. Of course, this is an attractive solution in principle, but difficulties abound, not least the practical one of setting up an institution by means of which that management could be undertaken. And any institution which is set up must, of course, develop according to the trajectory of all managerial institutions. The necessity for some form of representative institution which manages in the interests of the most exploitable class, follows from the practical impossibility of that class exercising management for itself. The moment such an institution of management is set up the iron laws of the social psychological development of societies come into effect. Bureaucracies, I must emphasize, are total institutions in Goffman's sense, that is, they will transform themselves so that the moral careers of the functionaries become dominant over the official work of the institution unless there are other institutions which can conduct a continuous assessment of that total institution and occasionally bring it to heel. But if the institution of which we are speaking is the state apparatus itself, the central bureaucracy, there is no other institution to bring it to heel. We should expect to find formalization of the official rhetoric which describes the apparent instrumental activities of the bureaucracy. Our efforts to understand what we see to be happening in that institution demand the explicatory power of dramaturgical model and the analytical concepts associated with the idea of moral career.

3. THE DEDUCTION OF A POLITICAL
PSYCHOLOGY OF SOCIAL ACTION

(a) The Psychological Conditions Necessary for a Political Programme

The stage is now set for the deduction of a theory of political change and social action consequent upon the various theories and insights which I have proposed in earlier parts of this study. The first step in our argument will be to identify the necessary conditions for a political activity to be possible. These can be set out as follows:

(i) Psycho-social conditions

It should be possible for the members of a social collective to envisage a form of life different from that which they currently live, and they must be able to conceive of a programme by which what they take to be the most desirable form could be brought into being.

(ii) Moral conditions

They should have criteria by means of which judgements of relative desirability can be made between the forms of life which they can conceive to be possible. They must be able to compare those forms of life with the conditions under which they believe themselves to exist. I do not believe that there is any standpoint from which the conditions under which they actually exist can be clearly distinguished.

The possibility of a programme based upon a judgement as to the best form of life does not entail that it can be realized by political action. I shall be arguing that this requires that the theory that members of the collective hold as to how a desirable form of life can be brought into being is based upon an adequate conception of the nature of social change.

(b) The Modes of Political Action

If we assume that the political spectrum with which political theory confronts us, namely that between those who wish to preserve (or conserve) social formations that already exist, and those who wish to change them, is naive, we must look more deeply into the forms of possible political action. I am interested only in forms of radical politics in terms of which people might set about changing society. The basic distinction is between a political radicalism which I shall call 'the confrontation mode', and a political radicalism of the alternation mode.

(i) In a confrontation mode, the members who are intent upon a revision of society identify what they take to be the major structural properties of the existing collective and set about attempting to change them. This is a process of confrontation, of direct attack in one form or another upon the existing structure of the collective and the social practices which reproduce it.

It is not difficult to see that this is a paradoxical form of political activity. There are good historical grounds to sustain this objection.

(a) In many cases the social formation which the radicals are intent upon changing is neither well-articulated nor particularly well-defined. The effect of challenging it is to force its supporters to formulate their view of society more fully, thus making it more real. In short, the effect of confrontation radicalism is sometimes to stabilize and to make more fully realized the very social formation against which the radical programme is directed. The existing society becomes conscious of itself and thus comes to wish to defend what it now takes to be its social order in the course of such a confrontation.

(b) At the same time as this is happening to the structure

which is the subject of the programme of change, a corresponding alteration is occurring in the organization of those who are confronting it. As the existing structure becomes better and better defined, so the organization of the radical party must match it more and more closely to have a chance of successfully overthrowing it. Whatever organs come into existence on the conservative side must be matched by the radicals. This, I think, is the simple explanation of the often-remarked historical fact that in the course of a revolution the revolutionary party comes to be a mirror image of the party which is defending the status quo.

In short, we can say that with respect to the original task of altering the old social order and replacing it with something new, the confrontation programme is almost irremediably paradoxical. The conditions under which it can exist are precisely those under which it cannot succeed.

This suggests that we should look for a different form of political activity in the hope of avoiding the paradox. The programme of alternation politics offers just such a possibility, but as we shall see, though it avoids the difficulties and pitfalls of confrontation politics it has difficulties and pitfalls of its own.

(ii) It is clear that any programme which is likely to succeed must base itself on the processes of social change which we already know to occur. If the arguments of this work are correct, then some mixture of dialectical tension resolution and evolutionary selection of mutants is responsible for social change. A political programme should therefore be based upon a combination of these processes. In general, then, we should be trying to formulate a political programme which utilizes the mutation/selection conception of the way social trends fall and introduces new rhetorics to amplify tensions between the practical and expressive orders. An alternation politics will set about defining and bringing into existence mutant forms of social practice and association and novel rhetorics within the existing society. That society, its rhetorics, practices and even its ecology constitutes the selection conditions for mutants. If these spread then in the course of the social change thus deliberately brought about, the collective as selection condition will itself change, favouring some mutants rather than others. This process need not be the helpless social tinkering of the Popperean social theory, since, as I have argued earlier, the introduction of anthropological, historical and social scientific knowledge into the system ensures that the processes of social change are not pure Darwinian but go some way towards being Lamarckian in form.

Given this general picture, how might it be possible to formulate a prescription for an alternative social formation?

4. THE BASES OF THE ALTERNATION POLITICAL PROGRAMME

(a) I have argued in earlier chapters that the moral basis of society is to be found in the criteria by which human beings are accorded respect and contempt as persons. This idea derives from the micro-sociological studies of Erving Goffman which have revealed the extent to which the ritual expression of respect and contempt are the cement of day-to-day relations. The first steps in an alternation programme must be to envisage a society in which the criteria for the attribution of respect and contempt for people are radically different. The first step in freeing these criteria for imaginative reformulation is to detach them from their contemporary connection with the economic system, so that the criteria for and marks of respect or contempt for a person are separated from the accumulation of wealth or goods. But such a separation is only necessary, but not a sufficient, condition for the setting up of a quasi-Darwinian social order, since if the detached respect and contempt criteria still form a single system, the possibility of mutant forms of these criteria is still precluded. The next step, then, must be to multiply respect hierarchies indefinitely, either by looking for and amplifying existing small-scale and local respect hierarchies, or by inventing more as a deliberate act of policy. If the moral basis of a society lies in its respect and contempt criteria, then the multiplication of respect and contempt criterial hierarchies will lead automatically to multiplication of alternative micro-societies and consequently to an increase in the possibility of political change.

But the moral basis of this political psychology so far has provided only a more elaborated necessary condition for the bringing about of a new social order. The multiple alternative societies as I have so far described them exist only in the imagination of political authors and science fiction writers. There must necessarily be some revolutionary phase. As I have already argued, a confrontation revolution is certain to fail. Because of its paradoxical relation to the old structure it must lead, after a series of confrontations which could be violent and destructive, to a society which is in all respects except nomenclature and personnel, identical with the one it replaces.

(b) In order to understand the nature of an ethogenic revolution it is necessary to notice that the respect-contempt hierarchies have to do rather with the expressive devices which society can call upon than anything simply practical. Respect and contempt must be marked by conventional signs and these markers are part of the expressive order of the society. They might be clothes, manner of speech, deferential forms for address, certain kinds of possessions, or the ability to display a necklace which one has been able to persuade someone to lend one, as in the Kula ring, and so on. If all other properties of the society have changed, except the expressive devices, the continuity of the respect/contempt practices of the old society is ensured. The reproduction of the expressive hierarchies will lead to the reconstruction of a new base structure which is formally isomorphic with the old. At the heart of the imaginative anticipation of new social formations must be the conventions of an alternative expressive order by which social relations are to be actually constituted on a day-to-day basis. These, of course, will be the expressive devices by means of which persons present themselves as worthy, and the rituals by which respect and contempt are marked.

(c) I propose to call the efforts of a group of social reformers to change the major structural properties of a society, such as the means by which the legislative activities are regulated, or the relative wealth of the inhabitants is arranged, a primary revolution. The deeper changes in the moral basis of society which would be brought about by a change in the criteria for an expression of respect and contempt I will call the secondary revolution.

The distinction between a radical revision of the practical order and the attempt to create a new expressive order was foreshadowed in the French Revolution. Forms of address were altered, weights and measures were changed, and even the old names of months replaced by new. From an ethogenic point of view one of the more interesting expressive innovations was the insistence on driving and riding on the right. Traditionally the gentry had ridden on the left, to bring their sword arms into convenient relation. The peasantry walked on the right, to face the oncoming traffic so to speak. Riding on the left was aristocratic, walking on the right, proletarian. The expressive effect of keeping to the right must have been considerable. Chairman Mao's 'cultural revolution' seems to have been directed at the expressive practices through which the day-to-day order of old China was still being reproduced long after the primary revolution. But by choosing a confrontation mode he doomed the secondary revolution to failure.

It seems clear to me that primary revolutions can occur with little effect on the expressive order of society. Is the reverse true? Could there be a secondary revolution, a drastic change in the personas people project, in the moral careers open to categories of persons and so on, which had no real effect on the practical order? I think not. If, for instance, skin colour ceased to be a criterion in the respect/contempt hierarchies of certain societies would not the position of black people in the practical (more specifically in the economic) order change? I believe it would.

These theses are empirical. The arguments I have so far brought forward hinge on the central perception of this chapter that a political philosophy which lacks an adequate social psychology will be impotent to alter the moral basis of society, though it might well be highly effective in altering its gross structural properties.

If this argument is correct, then it follows that the mutants or alternative societies which I have been arguing are a necessary condition for a quasi-Darwinian, quasi-Lamarckian change in the moral quality of a social collective, must be brought into being through small-scale local, secondary revolutions. They would involve the setting up of institutions and social practices in which new criteria for the giving of respect and contempt in new expressive systems come into daily operation.

And with new expressive practices go new rhetorics, in which and through which the folk are able to theorize about themselves and their social conditions, and in so doing create their own social identities.

5. DIFFICULTIES WITH ALTERNATION PROGRAMMES

This sounds an attractive theory at first sight, since it seems to have a satisfactory moral basis and to be related to a plausible theory of social change. However, like the confrontation programme, it has problems. These problems, though, I believe are not of the fatal paradoxical kind, which infect the confrontation theory.

(a) There is no doubt that there is plenty of historical evidence that the attempt to set up mutant microsocieties within a circumambient society frequently leads to a violent attack upon that mutant. The circumambient society as a collective, acting as a selection environment, is generally hostile. If there is to be alternation politics, directed to secondary revolutions, there must be some way of protecting mutants from this hostility until they are viable and capable of being copied, that is of reproducing. It has been argued that in most societies there is a kind of sub-world composed of a variety of different kinds of individuals which is in general immune from the effects of the surrounding society and within which mutants can begin to exist. For example there is a close relation between those who pursue artistic vocations and the various strata of society that are on the borders of crime. Certain conditions would have to be fulfilled before any pocket of the under-life could serve as the nursery for nascent novel practices and the trial ground for new personas. I owe to D. Lupardo the observation that much that passes for an under-life is tightly bound, at least emotionally, to the over-life, the official orders of society. For instance an adventurer who feels anxious or guilty relative to the prospect of official discovery is leading an under-life whose motivational structure is but a vicarious mirror image of the over-life. For a new expressive social formation to be possible the alternative life (perhaps lived only part-time by a Simmelian adventurer) must be quite detached from the over-life. Its rules of action, its conventions as to the emotions it is proper to experience, its admissible styles of self-presentation and so on must be independent creations, and not just contrary reflections of the expressive order of the over-life. Perhaps we should speak of the 'under-under-life' to distinguish the practice of a genuinely alternative expressive order. But the mere existence of this sub-world is not sufficient to provide the basis for an optimistic prognosis for the existence of most mutants. Of course, I would be consistent in arguing that a society which protects its own mutants either by apathy or by deliberate policy is a morally superior society to that which destroys them, but such a pious observation is not a sufficient ground for a social-psychology of political action based upon the possibility of alternative micro-societies.

(b) It might be objected that the general outline of the theory which I have been proposing has already been the basis of a *laissez faire* political system, the result of which is far from desirable, namely nineteenth-century social Darwinism. For my version of alternation politics to take on the moral tone I have been trying to sustain, a collapse into social Darwinism must be avoided at all costs. In terms of this discussion, social Darwinism could be defined as that form of selection which favours the most ruthless and self-regarding actors. On this view existing collectives should be transformed so that they have attributes which are lethal for all radically alternative practices, whatever they might be, that represent parity of regard between persons. So that far from being a possible basis for a radical political programme, the evolutionary conception, if taken as a guide to political action, can lead only to the worst alternative.

The reply to this objection can be found in the first section of this chapter, the arbitrary attachment of value to represent one's fundamental tenets as to the nature of man. I have argued that within the constraints imposed by the historically conditioned social psychologies we already exemplify, and the intensely conservative effects of the social apprenticeship served by our children in their autonomous microsocieties, the knowledge acquired through the use of the ethogenic approach in social psychology puts us, the folk, in a position to design new forms of association. Historical and anthropological studies can show us the possibilities human beings have already explored. The task of the reconstruction of society can be begun by anyone at any time in any face to face encounter.

NOTES

CHAPTER 1: SOME BASIC PRINCIPLES OF SOCIAL LIFE

1. There will be many references to the works of Marx, Durkheim, Weber and Goffman throughout this study. Both Marx and Durkheim developed their ideas over such a long period that it is not hard to demonstrate inconsistencies in their works taken overall. I shall be criticizing the popular versions of Marxist thought that derive from his joint work with Engels, *The German Ideology*. I believe the doctrine of that work to be in contradiction to the ideas of *Capital*, Book 3, but it is very far from my purpose to engage in detailed scholarly discussions of the work of any social thinker however important.

Again it seems to me clear that the method advocated by Durkheim in his *The Rules of Sociological Method*, Free Press, Glencoe, 1965, and exemplified in *Suicide*, Routledge and Kegan Paul, London, 1952, is in conflict with the method he himself uses in *The Elementary Forms of the Religious Life*, Allen and Unwin, London, 1915. But since the unsatisfactory state of empirical sociology derives from the continuation of the methods of the former works I shall be paying attention only to them.

Most of the leading ideas of Weber's sociology appear in this work in other forms. The method of *verstehen* appears as account analysis, ideal forms appear as idiographic techniques and the intensive design. I have developed or borrowed these ideas from sources other than Weber. But his *The Theory of Social and Economic Organization*, trans. A. M. Henderson and T. Parsons, the Free Press, Glencoe, 1957, is not without influence on what I have to say.

The sociologist to whom I make the most extensive reference is Erving Goffman. This is not only by reason of the immediate recognition of one's own behaviour in the goings on of his *dramatis personae*, but because of the consistent development in his works of two interlocking source models, the dramaturgical standpoint and the analogy of social ritual to formal ceremonial. These ideas are developed in *The Presentation of Self in Everyday Life*, Allen Lane, The Penguin Press, London, 1969; *Interaction Ritual*, Allen Lane, The Penguin Press, London, 1972; *Relations in Public*, Penguin, Harmondsworth, 1972; and *Stigma*, Penguin Books, Harmondsworth, 1968. I shall also be borrowing heavily from his treatment of the life courses of people in institutions, the source of which is *Asylums*, Penguin Books, Harmondsworth, 1968.

2. The basic distinction between an actor-centred view and an observer-centred view goes back to the work of E. E. Jones and R. R. Nisbet, *The*

Actor and the Observer, General Learning Press, New York, 1971. A useful refinement of this is Tormay's distinction between expression, that is representation via a symbol or conventional sign; and display, that is the appearance of a social or psychological phenomenon as such. That the actor-spectator paradox is part of expressive order has been nicely demonstrated by Charles Antaki, who has shown that it does not exist when moral career is not at issue.

3. Neo-platonic structural images of macrocosm and microcosm were common, cf. Frances Yates, *Giordano Bruno and the Hermetic Tradition*, Routledge and Kegan Paul, London, 1964.

4. N. Machiavelli, *The Prince* (1640) trans. E. D., The Scholar Press, Menston, 1969, Chapter VI.

5. In Kepler's elaborate system of matching forms architecture, mathematics, music and astronomy reveal deep isomorphisms, cf. his *Harmonices Mundi*, Leinz, 1619.

6. I. Kant, *Critique of Pure Reason*, J. N. D. Meiklejohn, Dent, London, 1934.

7. E. O. Wilson's *Sociobiology*, Belknap-Harvard, Cambridge, Mass, 1975, and *On Human Nature*, Harvard University Press, Cambridge, Mass, 1978, have caused something of a stir, but they are very unsatisfactory works. Cf. D. Campbell's Presidential Address, *American Psychologist*, December, 1975, for a severe criticism of the former when it ventures on the explanation of human social forms, and Stephen J. Gould in *Human Nature, 1*, October 1978, 20—28, and E. Leach, *New Society, 46*, No. 836 (1978), 91—93, for a thorough and destructive examination of the latter. Unfortunately, Wilson's works have brought sociobiological ideas into disrepute. I shall be arguing here and there for some rather generalized biologically related tendencies in human social life, in particular for various kinds of bonding. It would be unsurprising to find that male-female attraction, male-male bonding in boasting hierarchies, mother-child bonding and perhaps some other relations, were grounded upon genetically based and Darwinian selected tendencies, though I shall not be assuming that they are.

8. Mary Midgeley, 'The concept of beastliness', *Philosophy, 48* (1973), 111—135.

9. R. Dawkins, *The Selfish Gene*, Oxford University Press, Oxford, 1976.

10. The story of the Ik is to be found in C. H. Turnbull, *The Mountain People*, Simon and Schuster, New York, 1973.

11. Cf. the discussion of smiles by van t'Hoff and Leach in R. A. Hinde (ed.) *Non Verbal Communication*, Cambridge University Press, Cambridge, 1975, chs. 8 and 12.

12. Some important correlations between social formations and ecologically best solutions have been proposed by M. Harris, *Cows, Pigs, Wars and Witches*, Hutchinson, London, 1974, particularly pp. 3—32, but the connection of ecology with the fine structure of social practices and folk social theories that sustain them has hardly been touched in his work.

13. This objection would not count against a virus particle theory of genetic elaboration.

14. The expressive/practical distinction runs back deep in the history of social and psychological analysis. I see it as continuous with Aristotle's three-part division of the soul into the bodily (the practical), spirit (honour,

the expressive) and reason (which we will be construing not so much as a psychological property of man but as a social demand put upon his speaking and acting). But my main source is T. Veblen, *The Theory of the Leisure Class*, The Macmillan Company, New York, 1899, particularly chs. III, IV, VII and X. Cf. *Nichomachean Ethics*, Book I, Section V, trans. J. A. Smith, Everyman, London, 1911. It is also identical to the distinction proposed by Turner as between task-directed and identity-directed principles of social action. R. H. Turner, in C. Gordon and K. J. Gergen (eds.), *The Self in Social Interaction*, Wiley, New York, 1968. Much of Habermas' apparatus of analytical concepts for communicative acts could be mapped on to their distinction, as I shall elaborate it in the chapters to come.

15. G. Ichheiser was the first writer to my knowledge to draw the distinction between practical and expressive aspects of modes of action in just the way I want to draw it; cf. *Appearances and Realities*, Jossey-Bass, San Francisco, 1970. Empirical confirmation of the viability of the distinction has come from work by Marshall Morris in Puerto Rico, where expressive matters are dealt with in Spanish, while for practical matters middle-class people tend to use English.

16. An interesting example of the priority of the expressive aspects of an activity in psychological explanation is Labov's discovery (W. Labov, personal communication) that vowel change is powered by expressive demands on women's self-presentation. Women favour vowel forms typical of high-prestige people in very local areas, whereas men align themselves against the expressive hierarchy.

17. Richard B. Lee, 'Kung Bushman subsistence; an input-output analysis', Ecological Essays: Proceedings of the Conference on Cultural Ecology, National Museum of Canada, 1966 (ed. David Damas), *National Museum of Canada Bulletin*, No. 230, Ottawa. I am grateful to P. Riviére for drawing my attention to this study.

18. J. P. Sabini and M. Silver, 'Moral reproach and moral action', *Journal for the Theory of Social Behaviour*, 8 (1978), 103–123.

19. I owe to Karin Knorr (who owes it to P. Bourdieu) the idea of summarizing one's stage in a moral career as an accumulation of expressive 'credits' which can be cashed at any time for non-expressive goods, but are usually used as the capital input into a work to obtain more expressive credits.

20. For instance, D. H. Hargreaves, *Social Relations in a Secondary School*, Routledge and Kegan Paul, London, 1967, and E. Rosser and R. Harré, 'Explicit Knowledge of Personal Style: Reply to R. H. Levine', *Journal for the Theory of Social Behaviour*, 8 (1978), 249–251.

21. K. Marx, *Capital* I, Lawrence and Wishart, London 1965, p. 81a.

22. K. Marx and F. Engels, *The German Ideology*, Lawrence and Wishart, London, 1973, p. 33.

23. Op. cit. p. 40.

24. For M. Harris's work see note 12. J. Goody has made similar claims. See his *Production and Reproduction*, Cambridge University Press, Cambridge, 1976, ch. 3 and particularly the diagram on p. 29. For an extended criticism of Harris's views see M. Sahlins, 'Culture as Protein and Profit', *New York Review of Books*, *XXV*, 23 November 1978, 45–53. I am grateful to R. Langlois for many helpful discussions on socio-materialism.

25. In his *Theory of the Leisure Class* (note 14) Thorstein Veblen describes

a society where the expressive requirements of one class dominate the practical order of all others.

26. The life of the Dinka as described by Dang. Cf. note 11, ch. 8.

27. J. Locke, *Two Treatises of Civil Government*, ii, p. 26.

28. M. M. Douglas, *Purity and Danger: An Analysis of Concepts of Pollution and Taboo*, Routledge and Kegan Paul, London, 1966. Personal and social distinctions are treated as mutual representations.

29. Marx and Engels, note 21, pp. 47–48.

30. L. Taylor, 'Strategies for Coping with a Deviant Sentence', in R. Harré (ed.), *Life Sentences*, Wiley, London, 1976, p. 000.

31. A measured argument along these lines can be found in V. Reynolds, *The Biology of Human Action*, Freeman, Reading and San Francisco, 1976. There is a particularly good treatment of the Tiger and Fox thesis of pre-programming in ch. 2.

CHAPTER 2: STRUCTURE

1. The theory of structure discussed in this chapter is not to be confused with the ideas of the French structuralists. Though there are close similarities between my uses of structure as an analytic concept, there are very considerable differences in ideas of structural explanations. Compare J. Piaget's *Structuralism*, trans. C. Maschler, London, 1971, and more particularly C. Levi-Strauss, *Structural Anthropology*, trans. C. Jacobson and B. G. Schoepf, London, 1968. For the French structuralists empirically realized structures are always projections of prior structural properties of the human mind, such as the tendency to use binary cognitive operations. For me structures are known only *a posteriori*, and though they are the product of human action their origins may be very various.

2. *The* social structure exists mostly as presently unrealized potentialities coded in each human being as shared social theory and shared practical knowledge. This cannot account even for all micro-structures since there is a large public element of precoded representations of possible structured social relations, in books of etiquette, for example.

3. A good account of this distinction can be found in B. Blanshard, *The Nature of Thought*, Allen and Unwin, London, 1939, chs. 31 and 32, though the discussion is couched in an unfamiliar rhetoric.

4. Phillip Pettit gives a comprehensive critical review of structural explanations in his *The Concept of Structuralism*, Gill and Macmillan, Dublin, 1975.

5. Marx holds a replication theory of the causation of the structural properties of social collectives, the template being the social order of the system of material production. On his theory social formations *necessarily* have structural properties. Cf. K. Marx, *Capital*, III, VA II/2. (reference 1 Chapter One) T. B. Bottomore and M. Rubel (eds.), Penguin Books, Harmondsworth, Part One/3.

Bhaskar has recently proposed a version of the assemblage view, 'On the possibility of social scientific knowledge and the limits of naturalism', *Journal for the Theory of Social Behaviour*, 8 (1978) 1–28. In his theory, though elements (institutions and episodes) are structured, the assemblage could be structureless, as for example a jigsaw could have identifiable pictures on each piece while the whole assemblage revealed no overall pattern.

CHAPTER 3: THE ANALYSIS OF EPISODES

1. Personal communication.

2. I. Helling, 'Autobiography as self-presentation', in R. Harré (ed.), *Life Sentences*, Wiley, New York and London, 1976, pp. 42–48.

3. J. Bruner, 'Communication and cognition', The Berlyne Lecture, 1978, to be published in 'Acquiring the Use of Language', in *Canadian Journal of Psychology* (forthcoming).

4. K. J. Gergen, 'Social psychology as history', *Journal of Personality and Social Psychology, 26* (1973), 309–320.

5. I refer here to the development of a line of theorizing from G. E. M. Anscombe's *Intentions*, Blackwell, Oxford, 1957, to W. P. Alston's contribution to *The Self*, ed. T. Mischel, Blackwell, Oxford, 1977. Psychological as opposed to philosophical aspects of this way of thinking can be found in D. P. Cushman and W. Barnett Pierce, 'Generality and necessity in three types of theories with special attention to rules theory', *Human Communication Research, 3* (1977), 344–353. I take this line of thought to be in sharp contrast with the mentalistic Humeanism of Davidson, Goldman, etc.

6. J. L. Austin, *How to do things with words*, J. O. Urmson (ed.), Clarendon Press, Oxford, 1965.

7. F. Saussure, *A Course of General Linguistics*, trans. W. Baskin, Fontana-Collins, London, 1974.

8. P. Pettit, *The Concept of Structuralism*, Gill and Macmillan, Dublin, 1975.

9. M. Brenner, 'The Social Structure of the Research Interview', Doctoral Dissertation, Oxford University, 1978.

10. Both Douglas and Leiber have investigated this matter. In this section I follow Leiber's unpublished transformational analysis of a number of menus, but generally understand the social significance of orderly meals along the lines proposed by M. Douglas 'Deciphering a meal', *Daedalus*, Winter, 1972.

11. North American menus tend to follow the older, Gothic cuisine, allowing both Salt and Sweet to appear in the same dish, as e.g. beef and peach jello, a combination strictly forbidden among Burgundian feeders. For details, see Brillat-Savarin, *La physiologie du goût*, 1826, trans. A. Drayton, as *The Philosopher in the Kitchen,* Penguin Books, Harmondsworth, 1970.

12. Mr Fats Waller states this principle with particular poignancy in his famous protest, 'All that meat and no potatoes!'

13. E. Goffman, *Relations in Public*, Allen Lane, The Penguin Press, London, 1971, ch. 6.

General note: Speaking and writing are not the only possible sources for a theory of structure in human action. Music has many advantages as a source model. It is ordered by rules of harmony, counterpoint and composition. Its structure is historically conditioned. Its performances range from formal and precomposed readings from scores to improvisation within conventions.

CHAPTER 4: MEANING IN SOCIAL SCIENCE

1. Mary Tiles has pointed out to me that though the primary semantic relation in the Harvard theory is indeed referential, Quine has attempted to develop a network theory of meaning, the relations within which are extensional. I think that Quine's programme for language understanding is

ultimately incoherent, and this is indicated in the problem he has himself discovered in radical translation. But it is not to my purpose to turn aside to put this right.

2. Since writing this chapter I have found an excellent formulation of the same point in A. C. MacIntyre, *Against the Self Images of the Age*, Duckworth, London, 1971, ch. 18, IV.

3. Again I owe to Mary Tiles the thought that Frege's theory of meaning as interpreted by M. A. E. Dummett, *Frege*, Duckworth, London, 1973, is as rich a structural or relational theory as that of Saussure.

She has also pointed out to me the power of the multiple relational idea to account for the properties of other things which can figure as intentional objects, for instance pieces in board games. This suggests an exploration of the likenesses and differences between social actions and moves in games, and between both of these and the locutionary forces of utterances. Tiles suggests comparing board game moves to actions, and their game effect to acts, but distinguishing games and social life through the fact that game effects are defined wholly internally to particular games, while social acts are defined externally to episodes by reference to the social orders they sustain.

4. H. P. Grice, 'Meaning', *Philosophical Review, 66* (1957), 377–388.

5. Cf. Aristotle, *Nichomachean Ethics*, Book 9, where he distinguishes three forms of friendship, depending on the kind of interest each partner has in the relation. The highest is based on each willing the good of the other.

6. G. Leech, *Semantics*, Penguin Books, Harmondsworth, 1974.

7. J. Douglas, *The Social Meanings of Suicide*, Princeton University Press, Princeton, 1967.

8. J. M. Atkinson, *Discovering Suicide*, The Macmillan Press, London, 1978, particularly chs. 6 and 7.

9. S. Lukes, *Emile Durkheim*, Allen Lane, The Penguin Press, London, 1973.

10. An excellent discussion of the distinctions required for getting these matters clear can be found in the exchange between van t'Hoof and Leach in R. A. Hinde, *Non-Verbal Communication*, Cambridge University Press, London, 1972, ch. 8 and comments, ch. 12.

11. For a careful exploration of natural meaning, cf. B. E. Rollin, *Natural and Conventional Meaning*, Mouton, The Hague and Paris, 1976. This is a penetrating criticism of Grice's use of the distinction, pp. 37–39.

CHAPTER 5: PEOPLE IN GROUPS

1. K. R. Popper's distinction between kinds of 'wholes' and the methodologies, legitimate and illegitimate, associated with them (cf. *The Poverty of Historicism*, Routledge and Kegan Paul, 1957, pp. 76–93) still seems well taken. In the controversy that followed (cf. J. O'Neill (ed.), *Modes of Individualism and Collectivism*, Heinemann, London, 1973, Parts 3 and 4) the methodological and ontological issues seem to have been seriously confused. The issue of the irreducibility of 'societal facts' has little to do with how such facts, if they existed, might be studied. That seems to turn on the possibility of their registration. (Cf. S. Lukes, *Individualism*, Blackwell,

Oxford, 1973, particularly chs. 16 and 17, for a balanced view of the consequences of admitting that the concept of a person cannot be analysed without making use of some societal concepts.) For a general survey of the metaphysical issues see W. H. Dray, 'Holism and individualism in history and social science' in P. Edwards (ed.), *The Encyclopedia of Philosophy*, Macmillan and Free Press, New York, 1927.

2. This sort of issue has become prominent in discussions of the role of psychiatry in the Soviet Union *and* in the United States.

3. One should note that the arguments marshalled against individualism are philosophical in character. They tend to show that the doctrine is incoherent rather than false. But the arguments against collectivism have a more empirical cast, and tend to show that collectivism is factually false rather than internally incoherent.

4. A careful statement of the relational theory of collectives can be found in Bhaskar, note 5, ch. 2. By looking at the relation between the metaphysics of the concept of group held by different theorists and their resulting epistemologies, he shows conclusively that only a relational theory of a group of men as a collective with a realist epistemology is viable as a general theory of a science of society.

5. L. Tolstoy, *War and Peace*, trans. C. Garnett, Heinemann, London, 1911, Epilogue, particularly Part II.

6. A. Cicourel, *Method and Measurement in Sociology*, Free Press, New York, 1967.

7. Detailed studies can be found in J. M. Atkinson, *Discovering Suicide*, note 8, ch. 4, and P. F. Secord and M. Guttentag, *Too Many Women*, forthcoming.

8. I owe to Margaret Gilbert-Kripke notice of Weberian attempts to define social groups in terms of social action. There seem to be two main difficulties with this approach:

    (i) Is it possible to give an account of the social character of a social action without assuming the concept of a social group?

    (ii) Even if this were overcome would it be any more than a necessary condition for a group to be a social group that its members performed social *actions*? Perhaps they need to have co-ordinated projects, and/or a shared myth of origin etc.

    (iii) Mrs Gilbert-Kripke proposes an intermediate concept, that of 'social group', characterized as people doing something together, which would need some further communicative requirement and something in the nature of criteria for marking boundaries and overall continuity, to become a society.

    (iv) There is the further point as to whether collectives are constituted by the network of social actions performed by members. Certainly it seems that the existence of social actions (perhaps actions which recognize the personhood of the other) seem to be a necessary condition for a network theory such as Bhaskar and Marx want, to be viable.

9. E. Goffman, *Asylums*, Penguin Books, Harmondsworth, 1968.

10. D. H. Hargreaves, *Social Relations in Secondary Schools*, Routledge and Kegan Paul, London, 1967.

11. M. Hollis, *Models of Man*, Cambridge University Press, London, 1977.

12. D. Silverman and J. Jones, *Organizational Work*, Collier Macmillan, London, 1976.

CHAPTER 6: THE FAILURE OF TRADITIONAL METHODS

1. R. B. Zajonc and B. Nieuwenhuyse, 'Relationship between word frequency and recognition', *Journal Experimental Psychology, 67* (1964), 276–285.

2. S. Milgram, *Obedience to Authority*, Tavistock, London, 1974.

3. D. Mixon, 'Behaviour analysis treating subjects as actors rather than organisms', *Journal for the Theory of Social Behaviour, 1* (1971), 19–31.

4. The distinction, though an old one, has been made in these terms by J. L. Mackie, *Truth, Probability and Paradox: Studies in Philosophical Logic,* Oxford, Clarendon Press, 1973.

5. A. Cicourel, *Cognitive Sociology*, Penguin Books, Harmondsworth, 1972, ch. 2.

6. I owe this acronym to Peter Markel.

7. And this one to Alistair MacIntyre.

8. J. Douglas, *The Social Meanings of Suicide,* Princeton University Press, Princeton N. J., 1967, cf. also J. M. Atkinson, *Discovering Suicide,* Macmillan Press, London, 1978.

9. M. Brenner, 'Interviewing: the social phenomenology of a research instrument', in M. Brenner, P. Marsh and M. Brenner (eds.), *The Social Context of Method*, Croom-Helm, London, 1978, pp. 122–139.

10. Personal communication.

11. This is really the same phenomena as that discovered by the sociologist who asked restauranteurs about their race prejudices by letter (and found it high), though few of them behaved in accordance with these principles in face-to-face encounters.

12. I owe this example to Dr Pelikan of the Institute of Advanced Studies, Vienna, and I am most grateful to him for engaging in an enlightening dispute on the matter.

13. In a lecture series at Colorado College (1977) to be published.

14. There has been a similar argument in the philosophy of history. For example see L. Goldstein, *Historical Knowing*, University of Texas, Austin and London, 1976; and his controversy with Nowell-Smith in *History and Theory, 16* (1977), 1–52.

General Note: At the back of much contemporary 'science' of human life lies an assumption that there is a universal psychology. R.Needham has demonstrated at least the possibility that there may be highly differentiated psychologies. In his *Belief, Language and Experience*, Basil Blackwell, Oxford, 1972 he argued that while certain psychological concepts such as 'intention' may be conceptually linked with the very idea of a person, and hence necessarily ubiquitous, there are other apparently universal states, such as belief, which may be only locally realized. See particularly ch. 8, sections V and VI.

CHAPTER 7: THE DEVELOPMENT OF ADEQUATE METHODS

1. A wide variety of close analyses of rather different merit are to be found in R. Turner's collection *Ethnomethodology,* Penguin, Harmondsworth, 1974.

2. The classical work in this genre is G. Ryle's *The Concept of Mind*, Hutchinson, London, 1949. There are many useful collections, such as A. R. White's *The Philosophy of Action*, Clarendon Press, Oxford, 1968, J. Perry's

Personal Identity, University of California Press, Berkeley, etc. 1975, and many others.

3. J. L. Austin, *How to do things with words*, J. O. Urmson (ed.), Clarendon Press, Oxford, 1965. The theory has been refined by J. Searle, *Speech Acts*, Cambridge University Press, Cambridge, 1969.

4. J. Cullers, *Structuralist Poetics*, Routledge and Kegan Paul, London, 1975, chs. 2, 3 and 4.

5. B. Torode, 'The revelation of a theory of the social world as grammar', in R. Harré (ed.), *Life Sentences*, Wiley, London, etc., 1976, ch. 11.

6. For the origins of the idea of using accounts as the source of social understanding cf. S. M. Lyman, and M. B. Scott, *A Sociology of the Absurd*, Appleton-Century-Crofts, New York, 1970, ch. 5. The technique of the analysis of accounts draws heavily on an essay by J. L. Austin, 'A plea for excuses', in his *Philosophical Papers*, J. O. Urmson and G. Warnock (eds.), Clarendon Press, Oxford, 1961, ch. 6.

7. M. Argyle, 'The analysis of sequences and situations', in G. P. Ginsberg (ed.), *Emerging Strategies in Social Psychology*, Wiley, London and New York, 1979.

8. E. Schegloff and H. Sacks, 'Opening up closings', reprinted in Turner, c.f. note 1 above, ch. 18.

9. A useful summary of the limitations of the competence/performance distinction as applied in linguistics can be found in J. Leiber, *Noam Chomsky; A Philosophic Overview*, St. Martins Press, New York, 1975, pp. 150 ff.

10. J-P. De Waele, *La Méthode des Cas Programmés*, Dessart, Bruxelles, 1971.

11. F. M. Du Mas, 'Science and the single case', *Psychological Reports, 1* (1955), 65–75.

12. The exploration of the idiographic domain and the use of the intensive design are to be sharply distinguished. Though in each design N=1 the individual studied occupies a very different logical niche. In the idiographic exploration he is being studied as a particular, as himself. But in the intensive design as the instantiation of a type.

13. K. L. Pike, *Language in Relation to a Unified Theory of the Structure of Human Behaviour*, Mouton, The Hague, 1967.

14. M. Harris, *The Rise of Anthropological Theory*, Routledge and Kegan Paul, London, 1968, ch. 20. Despite its air of lingering positivism this is a good secondary source for the history of social theory.

15. For a summary of the Whewell-Mill controversy see the entry 'History of the Philosophy of Science', in *The Encyclopedia of Philosophy*, P. Edwards (ed.), Macmillan and Free Press, New York, 1967, vol. 6, pp. 289–290.

16. R. Keat and J. Urry, *Social Theory as Science*, Routledge and Kegan Paul, London, 1975 give a convincing realist interpretation of Marx's social theory.

17. S. Moscovici, 'Society and theory in social psychology' in J. Israel and H. Tajfel (eds.), *The Context of Social Psychology*, Academic Press, London, 1972.

18. R. Bhaskar, cf. note 5 in Chapter 2.

19. W. Machevski, referred to in L. Kolakowski and S. Hampshire (eds.), *The Socialist Ideal*, Weidenfeld and Nicolson, London, 1973, p. 27.

20. B. F. Skinner, *Beyond Freedom and Dignity*, Knopf, New York, 1971.

21. C. Clavius, *In Sphaeram Ionnis de Sacro Bosco*, Lyons, 1602. The paradox has surfaced again and again in different forms. Recent revivals have been due to P. Duhem and W. V. Quine.

22. A good example of this is the case of the sad young man who accounted for his difficulties in life by the theory that he had inherited less than top intelligence from his parents, one a psychologist and the other a housewife, taking their professions as evidence for his belief in their intellectual limitations.

CHAPTER 8: OTHER FORMS OF LIFE

1. Munificence as a social virtue is widespread in non-industrial cultures. Anthropologists have described many customs which seem to depend upon treating it as the central virtue. Cf. the 'potlatch'. These practices suggest very different psychological relations between product and producer than is presupposed in the European idea of property.

2. B. Malinowski, *Argonauts of the Western Pacific*, G. Routledge and Sons, London, 1922. Recent work in the area by Nancy Munn, cf. her 'The spatio-temporal transformation of Gawe canoes', *Journal de la Société des Oceanistes*, (1975–6) has shown that Malinowski's descriptions were accurate and that the institution still flourishes.

3. Annette B. Weiner, *Women of Virtue, Men of Renown*, University of Texas Press, Austin and London, 1976.

4. H. Morsbach, 'The psychological importance of ritualized gift exchange in modern Japan', in S. A. Freed (ed.), 'Anthropology and the Climate of Opinion', *Annals of the New York Academy of Sciences, 293* (1977b), 98–113.

5. Weiner, op. cit., p. 218.

6. Malinowski, op. cit., p. 94.

7. Weiner, op. cit., p. 231.

8. T. Nordenstam, *Sudanese Ethics*, The Scandinavian Institute of African Studies, Uppsala, 1968.

9. Nordenstam, op. cit., pp. 99–100.

10. Elsdon Best, *Spiritual and Mental Concepts of the Maori*, Dominion Museum Monograph 2, Wellington, New Zealand, 1922.

11. J. A. Pitt-Rivers, *The People of the Sierra*, Weidenfeld and Nicholson, London, 1954. Another mixed system can be identified in the lives of the Dinka. Cf. F. D. Dang, *Tradition and Modernization*, Yale University Press, New Haven and London, 1971. For the Dinka, oratorical skill and economic standing interact in complex ways to engender social position.

12. Pitt-Rivers, op. cit., p. 160–169.

13. F. Díaz-Plaja. *The Spaniard and the Seven Deadly Sins*, trans. J. I. Palmer, Gollancz, London, 1968, pp. 11–88.

14. The supportive character of much expressive activity has been carefully analysed by Goffman, cf. 'Face-work', in E. Goffman, *Interaction Ritual*, Allen Lane, The Penguin Press, London, 1972, pp. 5–45.

15. For instance, R. Fraser, in *The Pueblo*, Allen Lane, London, 1973. This work is a collection of autobiographies representing most of the categories of persons to be found in a small Spanish town. The intersection of the relatively expressive and practical orders can be seen in almost every life described.

16. J. Soustelle, *The Daily Life of the Aztecs*, trans. P. O'Brien, The Macmillan Company, New York, 1962.

17. Soustelle, op. cit., p. 221.

18. Kinship studies were, for many years, the central focus of British social anthropology. The intimate relationship between family connection and social structure has been documented in such works as J. Goody's *Comparative Studies in Kinship*, Routledge and Kegan Paul, London, 1969. For a critical evaluation of the assumptions of classical kinship studies, see R. Needham, *Remarks and Inventions*, Tavistock, London, 1974, ch. 1.

19. C. Levi-Strauss, *Triste Tropique*, trans. J. and D. Weightman, Atheneum, New York, 1974, pp. 178–188, discusses the practices of the Moaya-Guaricuru group of Indian tribes, in particular the Caduevao. Not only is there real infanticide practiced but a kind of social destruction of children, when they are 'farmed out' to be brought up by other people than their parents, and are sometimes even painted in such a way as to make them unrecognizable by their parents. Unfortunately there is insufficient detail in Levi-Strauss's tantalizing account of these people fully to get the feel of their way of life. Detachment of lineage systems from biological parentage, however, is not uncommon. One could perhaps so regard the diachronic organization of the celibate Roman Church as just such a system, cf. the 'laying on of hands', etc.

PART II: EXPLANATORY SCHEMATA

1. A vast literature has sprung up following T. S. Kuhn's statement of a strong relativism in his *The Structure of Scientific Revolutions,* University of Chicago Press, Chicago, 1962. Criticisms can be found in I. Lakatos and A. Musgrave, *Criticism and the Growth of Knowledge,* Cambridge University Press, Cambridge, 1970. The best single paper on these matters is to my mind that by D. Shapere, 'Meaning and Scientific Change' in R. Colodny (ed.), *Mind and Cosmos*, University of Pittsburgh Press, Pittsburgh, 1966.

2. For instance, cf. H. Putnam's Presidential address to the American Philosophical Association, 1977.

3. N. R. Campbell, *Physics: The Elements*, Cambridge University Press, Cambridge, 1919; reprinted as *The Foundations of Science*, Dover, New York, 1957, ch. 6.

4. Several writers have proposed mentalistic but Humean causal theories of action. The most elaborated, and in some ways the most transparently Humean, is that developed by D. Davidson, 'Actions, reasons and causes', *Journal of Philosophy, 60* (1973), 685–700. For detailed criticisms relevant to the science of psychology see Chapters 3 and 12.

CHAPTER 9: SOCIAL ACTION AS PROBLEM SOLVING

1. M. Williams, 'Presenting oneself in talk: the disclosures of occupation' in R. Harré (ed.), *Life Sentences*, Wiley, London, etc., 1976, ch. 5.

2. I. Helling, 'Autobiography as self-presentation: the carpenters of Konsstanz', in *Life Sentences*, op. cit., ch. 6.

3. The study of alter-casting was initiated by E. A. Weinstein and P. Deutschberger in a paper, 'Tasks, bargains and identities in social interaction', *Social Forces, 42* (1964), 451–456. So far as I know the only systematic

study of 'real life' processes of this sort is B. Torode's investigation of tea-chers' speech in *Life Sentences,* op cit., ch. 11.

4. I. Kant, *Groundwork of the Metaphysics of Morals*, trans. H. J. Paton, as *The Moral Law*, Hutchinson, London, 1961, pp. 108–113.

5. Both vegetable distributions and pig feasts involve donations according to social relations, including personal (e.g. to brother-in-law) and group (e.g. bride's family). See, for instance, P. Brown, *The Chimbu*, Routledge and Kegan Paul, London, 1973, ch. 9.

6. G. A. Miller, E. Galanter and K. H. Pribram, *Plans and the Structure of Behaviour*, Henry Holt, New York, 1960, chs. 2 and 3.

7. A somewhat primitive anticipation of this distinction is due to K. G. Shaver, described in E. P. Hollander, *Principles and Methods of Social Psychology*, Oxford University Press, New York, 1976, pp. 260–271.

8. J. L. Austin, 'A plea for excuses', *Philosophical Papers*, J. O. Urmson and G. J. Warnock (eds.), Clarendon Press, Oxford 1961, ch. 6.

9. C. Backman, 'Explorations in psycho-ethics: the warranting of judge-ments', in *Life Sentences*, op. cit., ch. 12.

10. K. Gergen, 'Social psychology as history', *Journal of Personality and Social Psychology, 26* (1973), 309–320.

11. E. Rosser and R. Harré, 'Explicit knowledge of personal style', *Journal for the Theory of Social Behaviour, 7* (1977), 249–251.

12. T. Mischel, Personal communication.

13. E. Rosser and R. Harré, 'The meaning of "trouble"' in M. Hammersley and P. Woods (eds.), *The Process of Schooling*, Routledge and Kegan Paul and the Open University Press, London etc. 1976.

14. This is a very simple form of 'rep. grid' analysis – but surprisingly powerful nevertheless. More sophisticated ways of using the technique are to be found in D. Bannister and F. Fransella, *A Manual for Repertory Grid Technique*, Academic Press, London, 1971.

15. T. Mischel, 'Personal constructs, rules and the logic of clinical activity', *Psychological Review, 71* (1964), 180–192.

CHAPTER 10: SOCIAL ACTION AS DRAMA

1. E. Goffman, *The Presentation of Self in Everyday Life*, Allen Lane, The Penguin Press, London, 1969.

2. E. Burke, *A Grammar of Motives*, Prentice Hall, Englewood Cliffs, N. J. 1945.

3. An interesting study of improvised theatre and its relation to ethogenic psychology has been undertaken by F. Coppieters, cf. his doctorial disserta-tion, University of Antwerp, 1976.

4. Cf. Frances Yates' discussion in her *The Art of Memory*, Routledge and Kegan Paul, London, 1966, and *Giordano Bruno and the Hermetic Tradition*, Routledge and Kegan Paul, London 1964.

5. E. Schegloff and H. Sacks, 'Opening up closings', in R. Turner, *Ethno-methodology*, Penguin, London, 1974, pp. 233–264.

6. K. Lewin, *Principles of Topological Psychology*, trans. F. and G. M. Heinder, McGraw-Hill, New York, 1935.

7. E. Goffman, *Relations in Public*, Allen Lane, The Penguin Press, London, 1971.

8. Comparison should be made with the traces of the passage of children through this miniature social world. A graphical representation of actual transitions does not match perfectly with a projection of ideal transitions from the social topography. This point helps to make clear the psychological character of the threat/comfort representation. It is a representation of the children's meanings for and attitudes to the various elements of their *Umwelt*. This should not be surprising since the graph is constructed from their accounts. A full social psychological theory of actual movements through the space would involve complementing the graph as a shared theory of the kindergarten, with the individual and occasional contingencies that were pertinent to the following of defiant paths. Jos Jaspars has suggested to me that both plots could be compared with a more conventional 'mental map' of that world.

9. D. Joiner, 'Social ritual and architectural space', *Architectural Research and Teaching, 1* (1971), 48 ff.

10. Mary Douglas has proposed an analytical scheme upon the main dish principle with stressed/unstressed elements as the main dichotomy. For a more detailed analysis see my 'Architectonic man' in R. H. Brown and S. M. Lyman (eds.), *Structure, Consciousness and History,* Cambridge University Press, Cambridge, etc. 1978, ch. 5.

11. P. Bourdieu, 'The Berber house', reprinted in M. Douglas (ed.), *Rules and Meanings*, Penguin, Harmondsworth, 1973, ch. 18.

12. C. Levi-Strauss, *The Savage Mind*, Weidenfeld and Nicholson, London, 1966.

13. R. Ardrey, *The Territorial Imperative*, Collins, London, 1967.

14. M. Douglas, *Purity and Danger*, Routledge and Kegan Paul, London, 1966.

15. S. M. Lyman and M. B. Scott, *A Sociology of the Absurd*, Appleton-Century-Crofts, New York, 1970, ch. 4.

16. E. Goffman, op. cit.

17. E. Goffman, 'Face-work', in *Interaction Ritual*, Allen Lane, The Penguin Press, London, 1967, pp. 27–31.

18. For a more detailed account of these rituals, see E. Rosser and R. Harré, 'Trouble in school', in M. Hammersley and P. Woods (eds.), *The Process of Schooling*, Routledge and Kegan Paul, and the Open University, London, etc. 1976.

19. Cf. The wrestling match in *Women in Love*, ch. 20, and the night swim in *The Rainbow*, ch. 12.

20. E. Berne, *Games People Play*, Penguin Books, Harmondsworth, 1970. R. D. Laing seems to suggest something of the sort too, cf. *Knots*, World of Man, London, 1970.

21. Peter Collet has drawn my attention to a beautiful description of the ritual of the cut in J. Wildeblood, *The Polite World*, Oxford University Press, London, 1965.

22. See R. Harré and J-P. de Waele for a more detailed analysis; 'The ritual for incorporation of a stranger', in R. Harré (ed.), *Life Sentences*, Wiley, London, etc., 1976, pp. 76–86.

23. These rituals depend on 'joint-souls' or *ipu*. Cf. J. Pouwer, 'Signification and field work', *Journal of Symbolic Anthropology, 1* (1973).

24. The term 'monodrama' is taken from N. Evreinov's *The Theatre as Life,*

trans. A. I. Navaroff, Harrap, London, 1927. I have used the term in a slightly wider sense than does Evreinov, but I think in the same spirit.

25. B. Torode, 'The revelation of a theory of the social world as grammar', in R. Harré (ed.), *Life Sentences,* Wiley, London, etc., 1976, pp. 87–97.

26. J. Cullers, *Structuralist Poetics*, Routledge and Kegan Paul, London, 1975, particularly chs. 2 and 3.

27. For the metaphysical errors that can develop through taking the structure of scenarios as literal descriptions of psychological reality, cf. my 'The self in monodrama' in T. Mischel (ed.), *The Self*, Blackwell, Oxford, 1976.

28. Criticisms of Goffman's use of the dramaturgical source model have nearly all centred round the issue of the status of the controlling agent. Is he yet another actor playing a part? Or is he the central core of a person, the noumenal self Kant required as the foundation of his account of the possibility of human action? A useful discussion of these matters can be found in B. Wilshire, 'Role playing and identity; the limits of the theatrical metaphor', *Cultural Hermeneutics, 4* (1977), 199–207.

29. Q. Bell, *On Human Finery*, Schoken Books, New York, 2nd edition, 1976, is a quite excellent study based on Veblen's principles of social analysis.

30. One might note Tom Wolfe's comments on shoes in *The Electric Kool-Aid Acid Test*, Bantam Books, New York, 1968.

31. W. Cooper, *Hair: Sex, Society, Symbolism*, Alden, London, 1971.

APPENDICES TO PART II

1. Note the remarks by Erasmus in *In Praise of Follie*. The point is in several Shakespearean accounts of the maintenance of social order.

2. This is evident in the relatively innocent goings on in Sir Harold Wilson's 'kitchen cabinet', cf. Mr. Joe Hagen's reminiscences.

3. Here is one of the rare matters on which I am disposed to disagree with Stephen Lukes. While I cannot but agree that 'social life' is ... a web of possibilities for agents whose nature is both active and structured, to make choices and to pursue strategies within given limits, which in consequence expand and contract over time', (S. Lukes, *Essays in Social Theory*, Macmillan, London, 1977, ch. 1, p. 29), it does not follow from this that it is wise to admit the ascription of power to macro-collectives (cf. p. 9) as if it were an attribute. By so doing we tend to mislocate the point at which radical and reforming effort can best be applied. This is just what happens, I think, in the political aspects of Lukes' treatment in his monograph, *Power: A Radical View*, Macmillan, London, 1974.

4. G. Harrison, R. W. Hiorns and C. F. Kuchemann, 'Social class relatedness in some Oxfordshire parishes', *Journal of Biosocial Science, 2* (1970), 71–80.

5. See the discussion in Chapters 15 and 16, Part IV.

6. R. Bhaskar, *A Realist Theory of Science*, Harvester Press, Hassocks, Sussex, 2nd ed. 1978.

7. L. Garai, 'The uses of Marxist psychology', *Magyar Pszichologai Sezeml, 4* (1972).

8. It has been worked out in detail by some Marxist philosophers of society. The most advanced formulation might be that of G. Lukas, in his *Zur Ontologie des gesellschaftlichen Seins, due Arbeit*, Luchterland, Neuwied and

and Darmstadt, 1973.

General Note: Little systematic criticism of the dramaturgical scheme of social analysis exists. The most useful discussion is by M. A. Overington: cf. his 'Kenneth Burke and the method of dramatism', *Theory and Society, 4* (1977), 131–156.

CHAPTER 11: THEORIES OF THE SELF

1. I borrow this use of the term 'conduct' from the German, *handlung*, often translated as 'action'. It seems to me to serve nicely as a generic term, comprising both actions and acts. Schutz's use of *Akte* is not equivalent to my use of 'act'.

2. St. Thomas Aquinas, *Summa Theologica*, trans. the Fathers of the English Dominican Province, Benziger, New York, 1947, Vol. 1, Q 110, Art. 3.

3. Some of these connections have been explored by A. J. P. Kenny in his two works (a) *Action, Emotion and Will*, Routledge and Kegan Paul, London, 1969 and (b) *Will, Freedom and Power*, Blackwell, Oxford, 1976. Misguidedly, in my view, he introduces a generalized motion of 'volition' to account for the genesis of every action.

4. 'Weakness of will' greatly interested Aristotle, since he held that one could not fail to do what one had seen to be good. Cf. J. Ackrill, *Aristotle's Ethics*, Faber and Faber, London, 1973, pp. 31–33; G. Santas, 'Aristotle on practical inference; the explanation of action and akrasia', *Phronesis*, 14 (1969), 162–189.

5. I. Kant, *Groundwork of the Metaphysics of Morals*, cf. note 5, ch. 9.

6. B. F. Skinner, *About Behaviourism*, Cape, London 1974, particularly chs. 1, 4 and 12.

7. B. F. Skinner, 'The steep and thorny way to a science of behaviour', in R. Harré (ed.), *Problems of Scientific Revolution*, Clarendon Press, Oxford, 1975, p. 62.

8. D. Hume, *A Treatise of Human Nature*, London, 1739, Book II, Part III, Section III.

9. L. Festinger, *Conflict, Decision and Dissonance*, Stanford University Press, Stanford, California, 1964, and his earlier *A Theory of Cognitive Dissonance*, Row Peterson, Evanston, Ill. 1957.

A great many 'experiments' have been performed under the inspiration of this theory. Taken overall they present a very confused picture, illustrating, I believe, inadequacy in the formulation of the theory – it is unclear in its theoretical propositions and takes no account of the presentational features of action, cf. the criticism in R. Harré and P. F. Secord, *The Explanation of Social Behaviour*, Blackwell, Oxford, 1973, pp. 284–285.

10. H. Fingarette, *Self-Deception*, Routledge and Kegan Paul, London, 1969.

11. K. Marx and F. Engels, *The German Ideology*, Part I, published as *Fuerbach*, by Lawrence and Wishart, London, 1973; see particularly pp. 51–55, i.e. III, 1. 30.

CHAPTER 12: THE GENESIS OF ACTION

1. R. B. Cattell, *The Scientific Analysis of Personality*, Penguin Books,

London, 1965, ch. 3.

2. H. J. Eysenck and S. B. G. Eysenck, *Personality Structure and Measurement*, Routledge and Kegan Paul, London, 1969, ch. 7.

3. M. Argyle 'Personality and social behaviour' in R. Harré (ed), *Personality*, Blackwell, Oxford, 1976, ch. 6.

4. E. E. Jones and R. E. Nisbett, *The Actor and The Observer: Divergent Perceptions of the Causes of Behaviour*, General Learning Press, New York, 1971.

5. G. Wilson (editor and contributor), *The Psychology of Conservatism*, Academic Press, London, etc., 1973, particularly ch. 4.

6. W. Mischel, 'Towards a cognitive social learning reconceptualization of personality', *Psychological Review, 80* (1973), 252–283.

7. J. Shotter, 'Acquired powers: the transformation of natural into personal powers', *Journal for the Theory of Social Behaviour, 3* (1973), 141–156.

8. A. J. P. Kenny, *Action, Emotion and Will*, Routledge and Kegan Paul, London, 1963.

9. See particularly ch. 4 of G. Ryle, *The Concept of Mind*, Hutchinson, London, 1949.

10. W. P. Alston, 'Traits, consistency and conceptual alternatives for personality theory', *Journal for the Theory of Social Behaviour, 5* (1975), 17–48.

11. The importance of considering the structure of explanation relative to objects of explanation was first raised by Peter Achinstein in *Explanation*, S. Korner (ed.), Blackwell, Oxford, 1975, particularly pp. 1–18.

12. The very idea of there being basic actions has come under severe and instructive criticism. The idea that there are basic actions, that is actions which would be revealed as elements of human activity whatever the analytical scheme and within any human culture, goes back to A. Danto, 'Basic actions', *American Philosophical Quarterly, 2* (1965), 141–148, and has been further elaborated by A. Goldman, *A Theory of Human Action*, Prentice Hall, New Jersey, 1970. In an excellent discussion of the issue ('On the theory of action', *Journal for the Theory of Social Behaviour, 5* (1975), 145–167) B. Enç has shown how the identification of a category of basic actions is relative to a taxonomic scheme which is in turn relative to that choice of category.

Goldman (and Davidson) seem to assume that there must be a termination of regressive analysis in physical movements of the body. But this is to assume capacities for self-attention that may not actually exist. It is clear that these capacities vary widely from person to person. Further, Bruner has demonstrated that complex action routines are constructed of *complex* sub-routines. Looked at philosophically this suggests that criteria for the individuation of movements within the sub-routines in terms of which they can be recognized as complex identifies elements are below the level of the units of human performance.

13. S. Schachter, 'The cognitive and physiological determinants of emotional state', *Advances in Experimental Social Psychology*, Vol. 1, Academic Press, New York, 1964, pp. 49–80.

14. Cf. D. Davidson, 'Actions, reasons and causes', *Journal of Philosophy, 60* (1963), 685–700. In his own way Davidson falls into the trap of looking for Humean relations between psychological events and performance events. The

trouble here is partly the primitive conception of causality deployed. B. Aune, *Reason and Action,* Reidel, Dordrecht and Boston, 1978, ch. 1, Sections 2 and 5, provides a useful corrective.

15. The general theory of *ceteris paribus* conditions and the effect of the imposition of boundary conditions on the realization of natural tendencies has been well described by R. Bhaskar, *A Realist Theory of Science,* Harvester Press, Sussex, 1978, ch. 2.

16. P. Winch, *The Idea of a Social Science,* Routledge and Kegan Paul, London, 1958.

17. D. Pears, *Predicting and Deciding,* Proceedings of the British Academy, Oxford University Press, London, 1964.

18. I shall refer to what I take to be their common theme as the Taylor-Alston theory. Their individual contributions can be found respectively in T. Mischel (ed.), *The Self,* Blackwell, Oxford, 1977, chs. 3 and 4.

19. Victorian novelists, for instance Dickens, portray many of their women characters (particularly if they are upper-middle class) as presenting themselves in a public style in which inconsistency, irrationality and even practical incompetence are prominent. In *David Copperfield* Dickens represents Dora as deriving some of her charm from these attributes. In the end of course he does not hesitate to show them as destructive of her marriage to David. Trollope's heroines are made of sterner stuff, even though they are sometimes led astray through inexperience, for instance the girls entranced by the odious Crosbie.

20. Mannheim, amongst many others, has formulated such a distinction. See his *Ideology and Utopia,* reprinted Routledge and Kegan Paul, London, 1976.

21. Ryle and Wittgenstein both seem to me to offer convincing cases for treating some psychological activities as going on in public, with no private counterparts.

22. A. Blum and P. McHugh, 'The social ascription of motives', *American Sociological Review, 36* (1971), 98–109.

23. M. Silver and J. Sabini, 'The social construction of envy', *Journal for the Theory of Social Behaviour, 8* (1978), 313–332.

24. The original statement of the environment/disposition distinction goes back, like much else in social psychology, to F. Heider, *The Psychology of Interpersonal Relations,* Wiley, New York, 1958.

25. M. Fowler, 'Illusions in the Perception of Persons', Doctoral Dissertation, State University of New York, Binghamton, 1979.

26. G. Langford, 'Persons as necessarily social', *Journal for the Theory of Social Behaviour, 8* (1978), 263–283.

27. A useful summary has been made by P. White, 'The Limitations of Conscious Awareness of Mental Activity and their Relation to Verbal Reports of Mental Processes', Doctoral Dissertation, Oxford University, 1979.

28. S. M. Lyman and M. B. Scott, 'Stage fright and the problem of identity' in their *A Sociology of the Absurd,* Appleton-Century-Crofts, New York, 1970, ch. 7.

29. B. A. Williams, *Problems of the Self,* Cambridge University Press, Cambridge, 1973.

30. For details of Tajfel's conception of the cognitive machinery activated in the formation of a sense of social identity, see H. Tajfel, *Differentiation Between Social Groups: Studies in the Social Psychology of Intergroup*

Relations, Academic Press, London, 1978, particularly chs. 1–4. I would argue that Tajfelian mechanisms are activated only when social identity, for historical reasons, becomes a *personal* issue. In studies on arbitrary groups Tajfel showed that the machinery to form rival identities is content free, but this does not show that it is always active in generating a sense of social identity when there is no call for that identity to be displayed. Identity, one might say, is run up for the 'purpose at hand'. Understanding identity-illustrating occasions requires the addition of some dramaturgy. The merit of Tajfel's work is to have shown what people *can* do. It is quite another question to identify the kinds of occasions on which they do think in Tajfelian ways.

31. A. C. MacIntyre, in A. O. Rorty (ed.), *The Identities of Persons*, University of California Press, London, 1976, ch. 00.

32. S. Shoemaker, 'Personal identity as memory' in J. Perry (ed), *Personal Identity*, University of California Press, Berkeley, etc., 1975, ch. 8.

33. P. F. Strawson, *Individuals*, Methuen, London, 1959, ch. 3, sections 2–6.

General Note (i): a line of argument consonant with the considerations advanced in this chapter can be found in Liam Hudson, *Human Beings*, Anchor Books, New York, 1975, particularly Parts Two and Four.

General Note (ii): In the Vaughan Memorial Lecture, given at Balliol College, Oxford in 1979, J. Habermas has proposed a theory of action based upon an analytical scheme designed to reveal the means-end structures of motivations. These are the so-called 'rationalities'. They would be represented in the theory expounded in this work as varieties of accounts, addressed to the intelligibility and warrantability of actions.

Habermas proposed a basic dichotomy between strategic and communicative acts, corresponding roughly to the distinction Secord and I proposed between agonistic and co-operative episodes. Within communicative acts three aspects can be analytically discerned in practice, of different 'weight' on different occasions. There is the practical, the expressive and the normative corresponding to the physical, the inner (my personal/individual) and the social (my public/collective) worlds respectively.

Despite differences in rhetoric and emphasis Habermas' theory seems to involve a very similar conceptual system to that outlined in this work. But whereas I believe that in general the expressive dominates all other aspects of action and its motivations, correlative with the impressions that form the public/collective world dominated by morality and aesthetics, Habermas seems to hold that all three aspects of action are of equal social relevance. At this stage of the development of our respective theories I am uncertain how far an apparently small difference in emphasis may lead to massively distinct conclusions.

CHAPTER 13: THE EMBODIED ACTOR

1. P. F. Strawson, *Individuals*, Methuen, London, 1959, ch. 3, Section 3.

2. S. Hampshire, *Thought and Action*, Chatto and Windus, London, 1965, pp. 41–54.

3. D. Armstrong, *A Materialist Theory of the Mind*, Routledge and Kegan Paul, London, ch. 6, particularly pp. 89–92.

4. S. Schachter and J. E. Singer, 'Cognitive, social and physiological determinants of emotional state', *Psychological Review, 69* (1962), 379–399.

5. H. S. Becker, 'History, culture and subjective experience', *Journal of Health and Social Behaviour, 8* (1967), 163–176.

6. K. Wilkes, *Physicalism,* Routledge and Kegan Paul, London, 1978. Compare too the mode of argument in A. R. Luria, *The Working Brain,* trans. B. Haigh, Allen Lane, The Penguin Press, London, 1973, Part Three.

7. U. J. Jensen, 'Conceptual epiphenomeneliasm', *The Monist, 56* (1972), 250–276.

8. R. Harré, 'The constructive role of models' in L. Collins (ed.), *The Use of Models in the Social Sciences,* Tavistock, London, 1976. A systematic study of the relation between a particular psychological form of description and a physiological grounding can be found in K. J. Pribram and M. M. Gill, *Freud's 'Project' Re-assessed,* Basic Books, New York, 1976.

9. M. Boden, *Artificial Intelligence and Natural Man,* Harvester Press, Sussex, 1977, particularly Part Six.

10. J. Fodor, *The Language of Thought,* The Harvester Press, Sussex, 1976, particularly Introduction, ch. 1 and ch. 4.

11. The balance between the limbic system and the cerebellum suggests the balance between consciousness and self-consciousness, reflected in autonomy and reflexiveness as prime features of human capacities. This appears in recent phylogenetic studies of relative masses relating Man to Platyrrhines rather than to Pongidae. Cf. R. J. Douglas and D. Marellus, 'The Ascent of man: deductions based on the multivariate analysis of the brain', *Brain, Behaviour and Evolution, 11* (1975), 179–312. I owe this reference to R. Isaacson.

CHAPTER 14: INDIVIDUAL LIVES

1. E. Goffman, *Asylums,* Pengin Books, Harmondsworth, 1968.

2. E. Goffman, op. cit., p. 119f.

3. K. Kesey, *One Flew Over the Cuckoo's Nest,* Viking Compass, New York, 1976.

4. E. Goffman, *Stigma,* Penguin Books, Harmondsworth, 1968, pp. 12–13.

5. R. C. Repp, in *Scholars, Saints and Sufis,* N. R. Keddie (ed.), University of California Press, Berkeley etc., 1972, pp. 17–32.

6. I. Morris, *The Nobility of Failure,* Secker and Warburg, London, 1975, pp. 38–40.

7. E. Goffman, *Where the Action Is,* Allen Lane, The Penguin Press, London, 1969, pp. 108 ff.

8. P. Marsh, E. Rosser and R. Harré, *The Rules of Disorder,* Routledge and Kegan Paul, London, 1978.

9. It is important to distinguish idiographic designs from intensive designs. In both N=1. In an intensive design the individual studied is treated as a concrete representation of a type, while in the idiographic design the individual is the whole universe of reference.

10. A summary of this method can be found in J-P de Waele and R. Harré, 'The personality of individuals' in R. Harré (ed.), *Personality,* Blackwell, Oxford, 1977, ch. 9.

11. See the detailed discussion of personal identity in Chapter 12, section 5.

12. A. Schutz, *The Phenomenology of the Social World,* Heinemann

Educational Books, London, 1972, ch. 4.

13. I. Helling, 'Autobiography as self-presentation: the carpenters of Konstanz', in R. Harré (ed.), *Life Sentences*, Wiley, London etc. 1976, ch. 6.

14. The biological career of a human being is not an entirely clear concept. Though the biologically defined events of conception, birth, cessation of brain function and so on are sharply dateable the relations of these events to the life course of a human being are influenced by social, moral and political considerations, which often involve issues about the nature of persons. For instance the latest time at which abortion is permitted in England is related to a vaguely defined level of development at which person-like capabilities are supposed to have begun to emerge.

Again the problem of deciding when vital organs can be taken for transplant has forced a refinement in the concept of biological death, distinguishing into different categories biological events which were previously taken roughly together. In particular cessation of heart function and cessation of brain function are now taken to belong to different orders, the former being possible in someone legally defined as dead.

15. P. Bryant and S. Carey-Block have both demonstrated that pseudo-sequential staging appears because children are required to bring together for the solving of one problem intellectual skills they previously used on separate problems. For instance the capacity to order groups according to the number of their members, and intervals according to their length, are both well developed. But when a child is asked to compare (1 2 3 4) with (1   2   3   4) he is confused by the ambiguity of the problem.

16. M. P. M. Richards, *The Integration of a Child into a Social World*, Cambridge University Press, Cambridge, 1974.

17. C. Trevarthen and M. P. M. Richards, as reported in Richards, op. cit., pp. 92–93.

18. See the work of T. Kitwood, *Conversations with a Stranger,* Routledge and Kegan Paul, London, 1979.

19. E. Husserl, *Cartesian Meditations*, trans. D. Cairns, Nijhoff, The Hague, 1973, Fifth Meditation, particularly Sections 42, 47, 51, 54, and A. Schutz's *Collected Papers*, III, Nijhoff, The Hague, 1970.

20. Strawson argues for a gradual dissolution of the sense of self, in such a condition, as both content and memory of distinctive point of view fade.

21. J. McManners, *Reflections on the Deathbed of Voltaire: the Art of Dying in 18th century France*, Clarendon Press, Oxford, 1975. This short work gives a vivid picture of the ceremonial and social aspects of the management of death.

22. Among the Trobriand Islanders the symbolic representation of character at the rounding off of a moral career is transformed into the physical quantity of certain goods, whose exchange at mortuary ceremonies illustrates reputations. Annette P. Weiner (*Women of Value, Men of Renown*, University of Texas Press, Austin, 1976, p. 226) says 'At death, the full range of individual achievement is dramatically portrayed in the women's mortuary ceremony. On that day the magnitude of the worth of the deceased to other living members of the society can be traced through each individual exchange event.'

CHAPTER 15: SOCIAL CHANGE: THEORIES AND ASSUMPTIONS

1. For a summary of the 'drives' approach to explaining action, see M. Argyle, *Social Interaction*, Methuen, London, 1969, pp. 40–55. The paradox of tautology or triviality is particularly well exemplified in this passage, cf. the 'definition' of 'drive' on p. 41. Argyle has long since abandoned drives theories.

2. For a balanced view of the analogy see V. Reynolds, *The Biology of Human Action*, Freeman, Reading and San Francisco, 1900, particularly Part I.

3. The idea of an optimal reproductive strategy could be defined independently of whether it is culturally or genetically based, cf. Dawkins (note 9, Chapter 1) for the relation of strategies to energy consumption.

4. This mistake is particularly clear in D. Morris, *The Human Zoo*, Cape, London, 1969, ch. 1.

5. L. Tiger and R. Fox, *The Imperial Animal*, Secker and Warburg, London, 1971, ch. 4. S. Moscovici has proposed a similar hunter-gatherer origin for modern man, though his use of biological arguments is more subtle than that of Tiger and Fox. See his *Society Against Nature*, The Harvester Press, Hassocks, Brighton, 1976, (trans.) S. Rabinovich, particularly Part III.

6. Sociologists have been able to demonstrate that even within a fairly coherent national culture, for instance modern France, the interpretation of sickness differs radically between townspeople and countryfolk.

7. C. Levi-Strauss, *Structural Anthropology*, trans. C. Jacobson and B. G. Schoepf, Allen Lane, The Penguin Press, London, 1968.

8. For a good summary of the main features of this school see J. Leiber, *Noam Chomsky; A Philosophical Overview*, St. Martin's Press, New York, 1975.

9. This work has been summarized by M. Argyle in R. Harré (ed.), *Personality*, Blackwell, Oxford, 1977, pp. 174–180.

10. Consultation of the enormously varied literature discussing the issue can be reduced, without much loss, to W. Dray, *Laws and Explanation in History*, Oxford University Press, London, 1957, and K. R. Popper, *The Poverty of Historicism*, Beacon Books, Boston, 1957.

11. L. Kolakovsky, *Main Currents of Marxism: The Breakdown*, Vol. III, trans. P. S. Falla, Clarendon Press, Oxford, 1978.

12. For a defence of Marx's general theory of social change as conforming to the canons for a realist scientific theory, see R. Keat and J. Urry, *Social Theory and Science*, Routledge and Kegan Paul, London, 1975, ch. 5.

General Note: The broad lay-out of the argument of this and the following chapters is very similar to some considerations advanced by S. Lukes. He says (*Essays in Social Theory*, Macmillan, London, 1977, p. 13) '... *structural* constraints do not operate through an agent's reasons [in my view because he could not know what they were], and they may indeed prevent certain reasons being reasons *for him*: that is they may limit his capacity to have certain desires or to hold certain beliefs ... They may take the form either of a limit upon (internal) *ability* or upon (external) *opportunity* ...'

I differ from Lukes however in the consequences I take to flow from this observation for the possibility of action. Since I do not believe that it is in the power of human agents to have a *determinate* effect upon structural constraints, political action must be confined to the sphere of possible human action, and that is the system of expressive acts that I have been striving to design a methodology to study, and so a technology for their control.

CHAPTER 16: SOCIAL CHANGE: CASES AND CAUSES

1. S. Ardener (ed.), *Perceiving Women*, Mallaby, London, 1975, ch. 3.
2. F. Engels, *The Origin of the Family, Private Property and the State*, Lawrence and Wishart, London, 1972, p. 129.
3. G. Greer, *The Female Eunuch*, MacGibbon and Kee, London, 1970.
4. Remark attributed to a young American woman, practising as a lawyer.
5. M. Guttentag and P. F. Secord, *Too Many Women*, forthcoming.
6. This is one of the points made by S. Ardener in her contribution to note 1 above.
7. Cf. the writings of Kate Millet, *Sexual Politics*, Hart-Davis, London, 1971, ch. 2, particularly sections I, III and IV.
8. The distinction between close and loose-coupled theories is due to S. Toulmin, *Human Understanding*, The Clarendon Press, Oxford, Vol. I, p. 338 f.
9. C. D. Darlington, *The Evolution of Man and Society*, Allen and Unwin, London, 1969. As a Huguenot I was tempted by Darlington's evident admiration for the industry of my forebears.
10. R. Dawkins, *The Selfish Gene*, Clarendon Press, Oxford, 1976.
11. D. Hull, 'A Metaphysics for Evolution', address to the 75th Anniversary Symposium, Aarhus University, 1978.
12. There are some minor effects due to replicator properties alone, e.g. defective replication leading to an internally non-viable interactor being formed which does not even reach the stage of interaction with an environment.
13. This is Dawkin's term for a cognitive or culturally realized replicator.
14. For an examination and defence of the use of spectrum of rule concepts, from the literal to the metaphorical, in social psychological explanations of social regularities, see P. Collett, *Social Rules and Social Behaviour*, Blackwell, Oxford, 1977.
15. Genetic masking can occur in biological evolution, analogous to the preservation of a record of a long-abandoned social practice.
16. This is a crude and brutal way with a long and subtle controversy. For a proper exposition of the view here dogmatically proposed see H. L. A. Hart, *Law, Liberty and Morality*, O.U.P., London etc., 1963, Chapter 1.
17. One might note the strong Darwinist trend in some recent Marxist writings, where the role of innovation against a background of social necessity is explored. See, for example, J. Knita, L. Nowak and J. Topolski, 'Against the false alternatives', *Poznan Studies in the Philosophy of the Sciences and the Humanities, 1* (1975) 1–10, trans. S. Magala.
18. Throughout this study I have been assuming that the arguments of Chapters 1 and 15 are decisive against the naive socio-biology of such advocates of bio-determinism as E. O. Wilson. It is not part of my position to deny that biological factors are continuously present in social life. In general, I have argued that they present men and women with problems, but not with

solutions. But there is another form of influence, which I can best describe as 'gentle pressure'. Recent studies of the development of the social and political structure of the Kibbutsim in Israel seem to suggest that there is a continuous gentle pressure for women to return to traditional sex-roles. See L. Tiger and J. Shepher, *Women in the Kibbutz*, Harcourt Brace Jovanovich, New York and London, 1975, particularly chs. 5, 6 and 10. Just what is the mechanism by which this 'gentle pressure' is exerted, and exactly what it stems from remain to be clearly identified.

CHAPTER 17: POLITICAL ACTIVITY

1. The issue is usually framed as the question of whether 'is' implies 'ought', or of whether values can ultimately be grounded in facts. The argument for the general thesis that facts cannot serve as premises from which moral principles can be deduced is usually attributed to Hume; and the modern form of the argument to G. E. Moore. The long reign of this principle has recently been challenged by several writers. A good account of the arguments can be found in D. H. Munro, *Empiricism and Ethics*, Cambridge University Press, Cambridge, Parts I and II, particularly chs. 7, 8 and 9.

2. J. Shotter, *Images of Man in Psychological Research*, Methuen, 1975, chs. 1, 6, 10.

3. I. Kant, *Groundwork of the Metaphysics of Morals*, trans. H. J. Paton, as *The Moral Law*, Hutchinson, London, 1965.

4. B. F. Skinner, *Walden II*, Macmillan, New York, 1962, and *Beyond Freedom and Dignity*, Cape, London, 1972. The horrific vision of a nightmare society proposed by Skinner is mitigated by the rare courage he has shown in working out and publishing the political implications of his psychology.

5. I. Loyola, *The Spiritual Exercises*, trans. W. H. Longridge, Robert Scott, London, 1919, 'Rules for thinking with the Church', I, X, XVIII. I instance him as a representative of a long tradition that held that obedience to authority was the highest *social* virtue. I am well aware that in traditional Catholicism this was a derivative principle, depending on a strong person-centred morality. Cf. Aquinas, *Summa Theologica*, Q 104, Art. 5. Dominican edition, II, 1644-5.

6. J. André, 'The psychopolitical cube'. Unpublished privately circulated paper. Cf. also the more complex political social psychology in five dimensions set out in J. R. Lucas, *The Principles of Politics*, Clarendon Press, Oxford, 1966, p. 371.

7. In James Mill's 'Essay on Government', Travellers Office, 1821, the paradoxes referred to in this chapter are clearly set out. An interesting discussion can be found in J. Lively and J. Rees, *Utilitarian Logic and Politics*, Clarendon Press, Oxford, 1978, including the debate between Macaulay and J. S. Mill.

8. For a detailed discussion of Rousseau's political philosophy with respect to its social psychological assumptions, see J. Plamenatz, *Man and Society*, Longman, London, 1963, pp. 373–380. Every undergraduate student of philosophy learns that the Utilitarians fell into the trap of assuming that one can generate a collective property as the aggregate of properties distributed among a population, thus effectively denying both a social psychology and a sociology of political action.

430

SUBJECT INDEX

L. I. H. E.

THE BECK LIBRARY

WOOLTON ROAD, LIVERPOOL L16 8N